55 DAYS

The Fall of South Vietnam

Alan Dawson

55 DAYS

The Fall of South Vietnam

PRENTICE-HALL, INC., Englewood Cliffs, N.J.

55 DAYS: THE FALL OF SOUTH VIETNAM
by Alan Dawson
Copyright © 1977 by Alan Dawson
All photos reproduced by permission of
United Press International
All rights reserved. No part of this book may be
reproduced in any form or by any means, except
for the inclusion of brief quotations in a review,
without permission in writing from the publisher.
Printed in the United States of America
Prentice-Hall International, Inc., London
Prentice-Hall of Australia, Pty. Ltd., Sydney
Prentice-Hall of Canada, Ltd., Toronto
Prentice-Hall of India Private Ltd., New Delhi
Prentice-Hall of Japan, Inc., Tokyo
Prentice-Hall of Southeast Asia Pte. Ltd., Singapore
Whitehall Books Limited, Wellington, New Zealand

10 9 8 7 6 5 4 3 2 1

Library of Congress Cataloging in Publication Data

Dawson, Alan.
  55 days: the fall of South Vietnam.
  Includes index.
    1. Vietnamese Conflict, 1961–1975.   I. Title.
DS557.7.D39   959.704'3   77-22768
ISBN 0-13-314476-3

Foreword

The following story was written by Stewart Kellerman, a colleague in the UPI bureau in Saigon. It has never before been printed in its entirety, because UPI on Christmas Eve, 1971, did not have enough time to run every Christmas story as well as the regular news. When I first read the story, I knew that it would be the Foreword of a book, should I ever actually write one. Now I have and it is.

BIEN HOA, Vietnam, Dec. 24 (UPI)—Santa Claus wore combat boots and thought it prudent to omit the ho, ho, ho's. Otherwise, he might have made the major leagues at Macy's or at least a Salvation Army tryout.

He properly patted the pillow under his wash-and-wear Santa suit and smoothed out his white polyester beard, a full one so different from the wisp that used to hang from the chin of that famous Ho, the late North Vietnamese president, Ho Chi Minh.

"It's great being Santa Claus and making children happy," said Lt. Pham Kim Gioi, 31, as he handed out scores of plastic rifles, pistols, helmets, nightsticks, spaceman X-ray guns and submachine guns to the waiting kids.

The men of the U.S. 95th Military Police battalion picked Gioi to be Santa at their annual Christmas party for the children of South Vietnamese soldiers at Bien Hoa, 14 miles northeast of Saigon.

Some 250 kids, mostly the sons and daughters of South Vietnamese Quan Canh (military police), piled into a small patio Friday afternoon under the shade of an orange-and-white parachute converted into a giant umbrella.

A South Vietnamese QC, speaking over an outdoor public address system, called out a series of numbers as though he were addressing draftees at boot camp. The children timidly approached Santa to get gifts when their numbers were called.

"I love children. I've got four of my own and I love making them happy," said Gioi, handing a two-foot-long black plastic replica of an M16 rifle to 4-year-old Huong, who was dressed in cut-down South Vietnamese paratrooper fatigues.

The round-faced Gioi, chubby enough without the pillow, gave a black plastic .45-caliber revolver to Vong, 7, and a kiddie U.S. MP outfit (black helmet, white nightstick and revolver) to Nguyen, 5. He picked out a two-foot-high doll (blonde hair, blue eyes, white skin) for Mai, a 5-year-old girl.

"We're giving the kids the real idea of Christmas," Sgt. Robert Andreas, 32, of Seaside, California, an adviser to the 3rd Quan Canh battalion, said. "This is the way Christmas should be."

He said the 95th MP battalion and the U.S. advisers to the 3rd QC battalion decided to give mostly military toys to the boys and dolls to the girls. A few apparent unisex toys (plastic Boeing 707's and Ford Mustangs made in Japan) went to both boys and girls.

After the gifts were all gone, the kids battled each other to reach the refreshment table and grab orange cardboard plates loaded with vanilla cake, chocolate ice cream, and cellophane bags of cherry, lemon, and lime candy.

"This is all right, really okay," Spec. 4 John Myer, 23, of Dallas, Texas, said as dozens of kids swarmed around him, grabbing for plates and toppling over cans and dishes.

Spec. 4 Larry Wickersham, 21, of Wilmington, Delaware, spooned out a chunk of ice cream onto a plate and had it grabbed from his hands a moment later.

"I think it's fantastic," he said before the refreshment table was finally toppled over by the hordes of kids. "I think the kids love it. It makes you feel like home. This is really like Christmas."

A sagging pine, looking more like a weeping willow, was propped up on a wooden stand tripod in one corner of the patio. It was covered with silver tinsel and maroon streamers. A manger made of camouflage ponchos with chipped plaster figurines inside rested alongside the tree.

A little boy, dressed in blue Scout shorts, streaked past the manger out of the patio. He was carrying a large carton of vanilla, chocolate, and strawberry ice cream, a plastic M16 and a gold-and-red space gun.

"Goodbye, American," he said over his shoulder. "Thank you."

Author's Note

The book is factual, to the best of my ability. The interpretations for various events are mine, unless otherwise noted.

I have taken certain liberties in two instances. The first is the use of names. So many Vietnamese committed to the losing side asked me after "liberation" not to use their true names in news stories that I have not done so here. Except where noted, Communist officials and soldiers and senior Saigon officials are identified by their real names. Those remaining in Vietnam who feel they might be compromised by certain tasks they performed before the change in governments will not be exposed here by name. The second liberty is in certain cases compressing events that happened in a certain area and having them happen to a certain character. Private Duc of the Marines is an example. Every event depicted in the book happened when and where the book states, but sometimes not specifically to the person named.

I owe much to colleagues, other newsmen, and friends outside Vietnam. But the real thanks, the credit for whatever is good in this book, goes to the people who are still there. To people in both governments, on both sides of the fighting lines, I must give thanks. So far as this particular book is concerned, the people I left behind in Vietnam when I was asked to leave in September 1975 have my greatest respect. But without the hundreds who taught me about Vietnam before "liberation," I would have been helpless.

There are those, including my acquaintances of the Provisional Revolutionary Government, who will be angry at my terminology in this book. I have used the common newspaper phrases for each organization, except in specific instances when I am trying to bring out the thinking of the men and women involved. I know the terms *Viet Cong, Communists,* and *Hanoi government* bother those now in power in Vietnam. But it is the way the world knows them.

The official names of the Communist armies in Vietnam were (for the North) the Vietnam's People's Army, often abbreviated to VPA, and (for the South) the People's Liberation Armed Forces (PLAF). To the world they were simply the North Vietnamese Army (NVA) and the Viet Cong (VC). Under the Communist bureaucracy, when a soldier or a unit crossed from North Vietnam to South Vietnam he or the unit became a part of the

PLAF. I have undertaken the almost impossible task of attempting to ascertain whether a unit was made up of mostly northern soldiers or southerners. If I knew, I have identified them in the book as NVA or VC. If I did not, I have usually identified them simply as "Communists." This is not a technical term, but is standard English usage.

The term *Saigon army* was used during the war years as a derogatory term by the Communist propagandists to imply that the Republic of Vietnam Armed Forces (RVNAF) controlled only the southern capital. I have used the same term only to make certain the reader understands the difference between the anti-Communist army of South Vietnam and the Communist one.

The difference between the Republic of Vietnam and the Republic of South Vietnam is one word and an entire ideology. My purpose has been to use terms that are understood.

Major Personalities of the Book

North Vietnam and the Viet Cong

Le Duan, Communist Party Chief
Gen. Van Tien Dung, army chief of staff and chief planner of the 1975 offensive
Gen. Vo Nguyen Giap, defense minister and army commander
Pham Hung, Number 4 Politburo member and ranking Communist stationed in the south
Lt. Gen. Tran Van Tra, army commander in the Saigon region
Vo Dong Giang, chief spokesman in the Viet Cong Saigon headquarters
Maj. Nguyen Van Thang, battalion commander assigned to capture Saigon palace
Sister Nguyen Trung Kien, who reached the palace before Thang
Trinh Dinh Thao, Number 5 man in the Viet Cong and landlord to the U.S. military
Maj. Nguyen Van Sau, battalion commander at Ban Me Thuot, the start of the attacks
Ho Chi Minh, late president, in whose name victory was won
Capt. Nguyen Duc Hao
Le Duc Tho

U.S. Government

Gerald R. Ford, President
Henry Kissinger, Secretary of State
Gen. Frederick C. Weyand, Army Chief of Staff

People of South Vietnam

Private Duc, a Marine
Nguyen Cao Ky, former premier and a Thieu opponent
Tran Huu Thanh, anti-Thieu priest, who exposed Thieu's corruption
Trai Quoc Quang and Hoa, employees of USIS and the Bank of America, friends, abandoned in the evacuation
Nguyen Van Duong, a U.S. Embassy guard
Ly Long Than, a businessman and friend of the Thieus, in-law to Mrs. Thieu
Nguyen Hoat, part-time newsman and rider of the Convoy of Tears
Nguyen Van Hao, economic czar, who saved some gold for the Communists
Phan Quang Dan, minister
Archbishop Nguyen Van Binh

Saigon Government

Nguyen Van Thieu, president
Tran Van Huong, vice-president and Thieu successor
Duong Van (Big) Minh, successor to Huong, who surrendered Saigon
Lt. Gen. Dang Van Quang, accused drug dealer and aide to Thieu
Tran Thien Khiem, prime minister
Nguyen Ba Can, successor to Khiem as prime minister
Tran Van Lam, ex-foreign minister, senator, and presidential aspirant

U.S. Embassy in Saigon

Graham Martin, ambassador
Wolfgang Lehmann, deputy ambassador
Thomas Polgar, CIA chief
Maj. Gen. Homer Smith, military chief
George "Jake" Jacobsen, special assistant to the ambassador
Alan Carter, chief of the U.S. Information Service (USIS)
Albert Francis, consul-general at Da Nang
Moncrieff Spear, consul-general at Nha Trang
Paul Struharik, provincial representative at Ban Me Thuot, a POW

American Citizens in Vietnam

Ed Daly, flamboyant owner of World Airways
Fred Gulden, architect, who stayed to help his employees leave
Y. L. Ching, who returned to help his family, and was abandoned
Bill Smith, left behind in the evacuation
Mike Mielke, volunteer POW worker
Jay Scarborough, scholar and POW from Ban Me Thuot battle
Paul Vogle
Dr. Patricia Smith
Leonard Dow Judson
Lyndsey Davis

Saigon Military

Cao Van Vien, Chairman of the Joint General Staff
Maj. Gen. Pham Van Phu, Commander of II Corps, the Central Highlands
Lt. Gen. Ngo Quang Truong, Commander of I Corps in northern South Vietnam
Brig. Gen. Nguyen Huu Hanh, Commander of ARVN for the last day, Viet Cong
    member
Sgt. Le Er Tang, Vietnamese CIA analyst, Viet Cong infiltrator
Lt. Gen. Nguyen Vinh Nghi, commander of task force at Phan Rang
Lt. Nguyen Thanh Trung, Viet Cong sympathizer, bomber of Thieu palace
Brig. Gen. Le Minh Dao, Commander of 18th Division and Xuan Loc battle
Maj. Gen. Tran Van Hai, 7th Division Commander, ex-police chief, abandoned and
    a suicide in the evacuation

Lt. Col. Le Trung Hien, command spokesman
Lt. Gen. Nguyen Khoa Nam, IV Corps Commander in the Mekong Delta
Capt. Tran Ba Phuoc
Nguyen Van Muoi

Others

Jean Marie Merillon, French Ambassador
Rhee Dai Yong, South Korean Chargé d'Affaires, abandoned in evacuation
Peter Whitlock, Australian visitor to Ban Me Thuot, a POW

The 55 Days

MARCH

9

10 Communists attack Ban Me Thuot.

11 Saigon attempts to organize counterattack.

12 North Vietnamese victorious at Ban Me Thuot; counterattacks fail.

13 Scattered fighting continues at Ban

14 Me Thuot; foreigners captured by North Vietnamese.

15 Thieu orders Central Highlands abandoned.

16 "Convoy of Tears" begins. Gen. Giap orders 2 more military drives from north and west-central Vietnam.

17 "Convoy of Tears" clears Pleiku; Communist forces "liberate" city.

18 Communists attack "Convoy of Tears"; convoy decimated by March 24.

19 Tank-led Communist soldiers overrun Quang Tri. Private Duc flees to Hue. Hue shelled.

20 Thieu, in speech to nation, says his troops are winning; vows to defend South Vietnam. Hue filled by refugees.

21 Saigon mayor orders civil defense drills. Hue mayor advises civilians to leave.

22 250,000 flee Hue. Saigon command denies city abandonment. U.S. planners prepare new, better weapons for Saigon. In Hanoi, Le Duan hints Saigon may fall.

23 Communists attack north, south defenses of Hue; refugees flee to Da Nang. Thieu accepts cabinet resignations, names "fighting administration."

24 Quang Ngai, Tam Ky overrun in surprise Communist attack, cutting South Vietnam in two. Private Duc retreats to Hue.

25 Saigon orders Hue abandoned. Communists capture it within hours. Troops flee to Da Nang.

26 Communist flag raised on Hue Citadel; U.S. orders "nonessential" staff from Da Nang, promises refugee evacuation aid. More than 300,000 refugees are in Da Nang.

27 First World Airways refugee flight from Da Nang; panic builds in Da Nang; panic cancels further refugee planes. Ambassador Martin returns to Saigon with Gen. Frederick Weyand. Nguyen Cao Ky calls for Thieu ouster.

28 Americans and Vietnamese hierarchy flee Da Nang; Da Nang troops, civilians riot in general panic. American briefers in Saigon— military and civilian— optimistic South Vietnamese troops will hold. In Da Nang, Americans abandon Consulate employees.

29 Final evacuation of Da Nang; last flight from city by World Airways and UPI's Paul Vogle. Men and women guerrillas capture Da Nang. Private Duc heads south by boat again.

30 Gen. Weyand "heartened" by
ARVN performance. "Nonessential"
Americans ordered from Nha
Trang.
31 Marines seize ship, fire on White
House photographer. Ten U.S.
families leave Saigon. Buddhists in
Saigon demand Thieu ouster.

APRIL

1 Americans evacuate Nha Trang;
city falls to guerrillas. Duc arrives,
leaves Cam Ranh Bay. Americans
in Saigon begin mailing, shipping
valuables out. Giap tells Hanoi
meeting victory possible at Saigon.
Americans desert Nha Trang
employees. Lon Nol leaves
Cambodia.
2 Saigon premier Khiem resigns,
calls on soldiers to fight. World
Airways orphan plane declared
unsafe. First refugees reach
Saigon; government bars entrance
to city.
3 Dalat abandoned by Saigon army
before Communist attack. Saigon
archbishop calls for Thieu ouster.
Polish ambassador says North
Vietnam still favors negotiating
end to war.
4 Thieu arrests 2nd group of alleged
civilian coup plotters. Air Force
orphan plane crashes. Thieu forms
new cabinet, blames U.S. foreign
press for setbacks; political hack
Nguyen Ba Can named Prime
Minister.
5 Orphans and U.S. officials leave in
airlift, beginning U.S. pull-out
from Vietnam; U.S. bankers leave
Saigon.
6 Gen. Ngo Quang Truong, Da Nang
commander, goes on hunger strike
in Saigon. U.S. evacuation speeds
up—officials used as orphan

"escorts"; U.S. Fleet beefs up off
Vietnam.
7 Saigon neutralists call for Thieu
resignation; Communists shell
Saigon suburbs.
8 Nguyen Thanh Trung, in F5 jet,
bombs Thieu's palace, defects to
Communist side. Evacuation lines
form at U.S. Embassy.
9 2 Communist divisions probe
Saigon outer defenses. Orphan
airlift steps up tempo. Battle for
Phan Rang begins with North
Vietnamese attack.
10 Battle for Xuan Loc opens with
massive shelling of provincial
capital. U.S. jet carries first load of
increased military aid to Saigon.
Communist troops at Xuan Loc
fight within 25 miles of Saigon.
Ford asks Congress for more aid
for Saigon.
11 Paratroopers helicoptered to Xuan
Loc battle; road to Mekong Delta
cut most of day by Communist
attacks; pro-Thieu forces
optimistic at Ford support.
12 Paratroopers walk into massive
ambush at Xuan Loc; regiment
effectively wiped out; defenders
beat back third North Vietnamese
assault on town.
13 Communists blow up ammunition
and arms meant to rearm Saigon
troops. Newsmen fly to Xuan Loc,
where Saigon forces claim victory.
14 Communists attack Xuan Loc
again, are beaten back again. New
Thieu cabinet sworn in. Thieu vows
he never will surrender.
15 Saigon shakes as Communists blow
up main ammo dump at Bien Hao.
Radio Hanoi guarantees safe
evacuation of Americans.
Communist artillery grounds
planes at Bien Hoa, main air base in
Vietnam.

16 Congress forces Ford to order U.S. evacuation speeded up. Phan Rang falls; James Lewis and Gen. Nguyen Vinh Nghi captured. Private Duc bulldozes Thieu family graves. U.S. Gen. Homer Smith promises free transportation, end to red tape for those leaving Saigon.

17 U.S. evacuation speeded up, Americans bypass Martin to evacuate "nonessential personnel"; Communist commandos attack communications center on Saigon edge. American Embassy begins burning papers. Communist victory in Cambodia.

18 Thieu urged by Martin to remain in office, by French to resign. Advance North Vietnamese troops probe northern Saigon. Saigon command orders Mekong Delta troops north of Saigon, opening delta to Communist attack.

19 Communist main force within 100 miles of Saigon as Phan Thiet provincial capital falls. Viet Cong call for Thieu ouster and negotiations. Moderate Catholics, congressmen call for Thieu ouster. Viet Cong order attack on Saigon, if necessary. Bien Hoa air base closed. Air Force moves to Saigon. U.S. spokesman Alan Carter denies U.S. evacuation under way. Five Saigon generals arrested for failure to fight.

20 Thieu ponders fate in palace bomb shelter. Communists pound Bien Hoa with artillery. Main North Vietnamese force attacks Ham Tan, 75 miles northeast of Saigon.

21 Thieu resigns in bitter anti-American speech. Ham Tan falls. Xuan Loc falls. Saigon front line now 26 miles from downtown. Ailing Tran Van Huong sworn in

as President. Communists and neutralists attack him as member of "Thieu clique."

22 U.S. evacuation slows as Embassy claims shortage of aircraft; Huong receives conflicting advice from Martin, French to stay or resign; says he will form new government. Hanoi Radio says no negotiations with Huong.

23 Record 26 planeloads of evacuees leaves. Suspected army deserters show up for evacuation. Huong administration pledges adherence to Paris agreement, including sharing power with Viet Cong.

24 General lull in fighting in South Vietnam settles over battlefields lasting five days, as Communists apparently wait to see developments in Saigon politics. Huong pledges cabinet to seek negotiations with Communists. Twenty-eight loads of evacuees leave for U.S. British Embassy in Saigon closes. U.S. abandons Bien Hoa Consulate, leaves U.S. flag flying.

25 Saigon politicians approve selection of Big Minh to replace Huong, insist on Senate-House session to make it legal. Huong again fails to form cabinet as he attempts to keep power, with Martin's backing. Nguyen Cao Ky calls for fighting stand in Saigon, calls evacuees cowards.

26 Huong agrees to hand power to Minh if legalities are followed. Near-panic builds at Tan Son Nhut. Saigon tense and prices rise. U.S. flies Thieu to Taiwan exile. Vietnam Congress approves Big Minh to take power Monday.

27 Three rockets hit Saigon, first in 3½ years. Big Minh meets Martin, orders American military out by

Tuesday. Communist offensive continues at low point. Vietnam Congress, in formal meeting, votes 134-0 to hand power to Big Minh.

28 Four Communist rockets hit Saigon just after midnight. Communists attack northern Saigon at Newport. Martin attempts to help Vietnamese general remove antiques. Minh is sworn in as President. Communists bomb Tan Son Nhut, shell air base in signal for final attack on Saigon; 2 U.S. Marines are killed.

29 Martin, after personal tour of Tan Son Nhut, orders final U.S. evacuation. Helicopters begin ferrying out Americans and Vietnamese; Martin promises all at Embassy they will be able to leave; evacuation completed at midnight.

30 Martin leaves shortly after midnight, abandoning 600 persons in Embassy grounds. Communist forces enter Saigon fighting. Minh surrenders South Vietnam. Communists run up flag at Presidential Palace.

MAY

1 Communist forces secure Saigon.

2 The capital has its first Communist

3 May Day celebrations. Viet Cong flags are raised all over city. In Mekong Delta, some fighting continues as Communists move to take full control of the nation. Communications with outside world cut in Saigon. Offensive ends after 55 days; Communists in full control of Vietnam.

4 New authorities in Saigon announce May 7 victory rally.

Contents

Foreword   v

Author's Note   vii

Major Personalities   ix

The 55 Days   xiii

FLASH / Saigon Government Surrenders   1

PRELUDE TO THE BATTLE   17

THE BATTLE BEGINS   33

"FATAL MISTAKE"   57

THE ROUT BEGINS   83

END OF THE BEGINNING / The Battle for Hue   117

BEGINNING OF THE END / Flight From Da Nang   151

"A VERY FINE PERFORMANCE"   189

PLANES AND BOATS AND THINGS   211

DIGGING A LAST DITCH   233

GOODBYE, AMERICAN   259

"YOU AMERICANS"   281

PRELUDE TO SURRENDER   299

. . . THANK YOU   325

Afterword   349

Acknowledgments   357

Index   359

FLASH...

Saigon Government Surrenders

At 8 A.M., the last helicopters came. Marines on the roof of the U.S. Embassy threw canisters of tear gas at the crowds in the yard seven stories below them before they boarded the choppers. Most of the crowd fell back, after an initial press forward, as they realized that they had been suckered.

Y. L. Ching was too busy looking after his children to press forward. One, with a heart defect, had collapsed in the gas. For a moment, he stopped breathing. He began again, and Ching told his woman and children to pack up. They headed for a doctor.

Bill Smith, the Greyhound mechanic who had returned to Vietnam to try to find his former girl friend, was one of those who pressed forward, then reeled back. Smith was with the thousand or so people who swarmed over and through the gates of the Embassy. Smith pushed up the stairs and mounted the helicopter pad, where he could breathe again. He stood there for a while, not really believing he had been left behind.

Most of the South Koreans were thunderstruck, and not a little terrified. General Rhee Dai Yong, who could not believe he had been abandoned by his American friends at first, believed it by 9 A.M. He gathered up those of his countrymen who wanted to go with him and returned to his residence to await what he believed would be capture, internment as a POW, and, probably, death.

General Tran Van Hai, with 75 other high-ranking South Vietnamese officers, most of them police, and their families, tried telephoning the U.S. Embassy. Then he tried his radio. There was no answer. At 9 A.M. he, too, realized that no helicopters were on the way to pick him up. He went into a deserted building in the compound in which the now panicky Vietnamese were waiting, drew his gun, and killed himself.

At the luxurious villa of Alan Carter, on a quiet street in the rich people's section of Saigon, about 30 senior employees of the United States Information Service and their families were still awaiting the promised telephone call for instructions from their boss and USIS head on just how they would be evacuated. They realized at 6 A.M. that they were going nowhere. They split up and went home. One stopped at a pharmacy to buy poison. He believed the Viet Cong would kill him if they found him. He waited for capture, and luckily it never came. He survived.

A Vietnamese CIA agent, close to many Americans, waited for his evacuation instructions, which of course never came. He headed for the Saigon port and got aboard the last barge known to have left the city. Down the Saigon River the barge floated, for about 15 miles, struggling to reach Vung Tau and the South China Sea. Viet Cong in sampans came from the mangrove banks of the river and stopped the barge. There was some shooting, but no casualties. His friends never saw him again.

Quang and Hoa, the USIS and Bank of America employees, were certain they would die this day, April 30, when the Communists took over. They wept quietly for some moments. They were not bitter at having been left behind. They wished their employers had leveled with them from the first and told them they would not be evacuated, because they then could have tried another escape route. Now they were trapped.

In the sixth floor UPI office at the Peninsula Hotel, above the popular Viet-My American restaurant, it was still busy. The power had gone off several times during the night in the midtown building just off Tu Do Street, but a newly installed generator had kept the teletype machines working. About half of the press corps were sending stories through UPI, and the three teletype operators had plenty to do. At 66 words per minute, word of the scene in Saigon sped around the world on UPI machines.

There was a last-minute attempt to get a helicopter to land on the roof of the Peninsula to pull out a few more UPI employees and several Vietnamese. But the White House said no, and that was that. Several persons who had been waiting for final word on the helicopter now fled.

Paul Vogle sat glued to Radio Saigon. He was listening to a lot of music and little else. The others were more active.

The Communists were inside Tan Son Nhut now. They were armed with SA7 surface-to-air missiles, one of the sweetest antiaircraft weapons ever made. Recently improved so they could bring down aircraft from 9,000 feet, the shoulder-fired weapons were showing how it was done.

From the roof of the Peninsula, a photographer could see a South Vietnamese Air Force C119 Flying Boxcar go down in a cloud of smoke over Tan Son Nhut. A small, single-engine Saigon-based 01 Bird-dog observation plane crashed in Cholon. An American-supplied helicopter was hit and burned.

Most newsmen now thought a battle for Saigon was inevitable. And there was no doubt as to the winner.

At 6:30 A.M., Communist troops overran the 8th Precinct police head-quarters. Just across the river, North Vietnamese troops tore through the Phu Lam signal center without a fight and pushed the airborne back. The paratroopers stopped every so often to fight, but more often they were running. Through the Phu Tho living quarters the Communists came, fully alert and not stopping to talk to residents, who now were "liberated."

At Ba Queo to the west of Tan Son Nhut and at Go Vap to the northwest, the Rangers were retreating, but fighting as they pulled back. Rockets were hitting in Gia Dinh City on the northern edge of Saigon.

Mike Mielke was awakened by his wife, who was frightened by the rockets. The Special Forces veteran listened for a few minutes and agreed that for the sake of the family, it might be best to pull back. Wrapping daughter Linny in a pillow in case of a rocket hit, Mielke and Misty piled into a station wagon and headed for downtown Saigon. Where their residential side street intersected with the main Gia Dinh Street, the driver had to run over the legs of one of five bodies of dead rocket victims. Mielke carried an American flag, neatly folded and wrapped in plastic. He did not remove the picture of President Gerald Ford from his outhouse, where he had placed it after the President gave partial amnesty to draft evaders in 1974.

The Mielkes drove to the Ministry of Foreign Affairs, where they had a couple of friends. Amazingly, the ministry was manned, if with but a skeleton staff. Mielke tried to give one of the employees a Republic of Vietnam flag. He swept it off the table onto the floor. Mielke watched the traffic to and from the next-door Presidential Palace and reported to a newsman by telephone on activity there. Misty listened to Radio Saigon and heard President Minh speak at 10:20.

Marine Private Duc had made it to Saigon. It had been a long trip from Phan Rang. In the Phu Quoc Island refugee camps he was almost killed by Saigon Military Police, who were summarily punishing raping and looting Marines. He had changed from his uniform and forced his way aboard an airplane to Saigon.

There, he had found a friend and slept on the floor for three nights, staying in the house during the day to avoid the possibility of being picked up and sent back to fight. Had Duc been an American, he would have said he wanted to take a week off to get his head together again.

Duc also was following events by Radio Saigon.

Big Minh was trying to save the situation. On Tuesday night, April 29, his aide and Information Minister-designate, Congressman Ly Qui Chung, volunteered and was accepted as a middleman between Minh and the Communists. On the telephone to Camp Davis, a former American base inside the airport and occupied legally by a Communist delegation after the 1973 Paris agreements, he had received little encouragement for a negotiated settlement. Now, the next morning, he was shuttling between Big Minh at the Presidential Palace and the North Vietnamese at Tan Son Nhut airport.

At 7 A.M. he brought Minh what he felt—correctly—was a final offer from Camp Davis. He spoke privately to the new President for about 15 minutes. Then other aides were called in—Nguyen Van Huyen, who would be Vice-President if there was a swearing-in; former Thieu economic czar Nguyen Van Hao, who had prevented the Thieus and Ly Long Thang from raiding the National Bank for its last 15 tons of gold; former Foreign Minister, Senate opposition leader, and now Prime Minister-designate Vu Van Mau, and others.

Minh, obviously fatigued from a virtual lack of sleep for 60 hours, listened as Chung gave the bad news. Communist insistence on instant dissolution of the Saigon armed forces remained unchanged. Although neither the North Vietnamese nor the Viet Cong called directly for a surrender, Chung was convinced this was the demand. There was to be no guarantee of negotiations and no guarantee of a government position for any man in the room. The safety of everyone, however, was guaranteed. If demands were not met, no cease-fire could be called. In other words, there would be a battle for Saigon.

Minh asked whether the Communists wanted him to address Saigon residents and others in zones not yet overrun by the North Vietnamese. He wanted to know whether Hanoi or the Viet Cong wished to write the text of the address. Chung left for Camp Davis again.

He was back at 9 A.M. with the answer. Minh should call for the military to lay down their arms. He could write the speech and say what he wanted. If he called for this military surrender, there would be no battle for Saigon. Chung returned to Tan Son Nhut again with Minh's decision. Minh would speak on Radio Saigon within the hour.

It took him a little longer than that to write his speech. Just before 10 A.M., he got in his car—not the presidential limousine—and drove to the radio station half a mile away. There, as at the Foreign Ministry, there was only a skeleton staff. It was enough.

Chung brought several Communists back to the palace with him at 9 A.M. They were in civilian clothes. Their safe passage was assured by the President himself. They listened without comment to the Chung briefing. It was a serious moment.

One of the North Vietnamese asked a lanky, crew-cut sometime-journalist and full-time spy for the Big Minh organization named Ky Danh what he did for the Minh group. Ky Danh told him he wrote stories, took pictures, fed news to the local and international press. The North Vietnamese asked Ky Danh if he had any broadcasting experience, and the Minh supporter said he had some, although he was primarily a photographer and reporter. Ky Danh then was given the job of announcing "liberation" to the nation over Saigon Radio. The North Vietnamese took him into a room and roughed out a script. Ky Danh arrived at Radio Saigon just after Minh left and stood by.

It was the only story in the world, and for the four Americans, one Dutchman, and half a dozen Vietnamese in the UPI office it is unlikely that there will be a more exciting and remarkable moment in their lives. It was the same for the handful of other newsmen who had instant access to the outside world by leased teletype lines.

Paul Vogle, who learned to speak Vietnamese in the army and perfected it in 18 years in Vietnam, and who was the best simultaneous interpreter to be found anywhere, warned the UPI staff that Minh was about to speak. Tape recorders flicked on; three radios were going, two of them battery-powered just in case the lights failed.

Big Minh's speech was short and to the point:

> . . . All soldiers, be calm and remain where you are now.
>
> I call on soldiers not to open fire, so that together we can discuss ways to hand over the reins of government without bloodshed.
>
> In the interests of peace, national conciliation, and concord of the people, to save the lives of the people, I believe deeply in conciliation among the Vietnamese people.
>
> Therefore, I call on all the soldiers of the Republic of Vietnam to stay where you are.
>
> I also call on the soldiers of the Provisional Revolutionary Government not to open fire, because we are here waiting to meet with the government of the PRG to discuss the turnover of the administration, both civilian and military, without causing senseless bloodshed to the people.

In the news business, a flash is a call to action. It cuts off whatever story is running on a teletype. The machines' bells ring 10 times, a signal that galvanizes newsrooms in any country of the world. A flash is not a story. It is a headline, of a few words only, signaling a great event. The assassination of a U.S. President rates a flash. And so does the end of the Vietnam War.

While Minh was still speaking, Leon Daniel of UPI typed out a flash and handed it to a teletype operator. The operator in Saigon calmly but quickly began typing, and within 20 seconds the flash was on its way to UPI regional headquarters and computers in Hong Kong, Brussels, and, of course, New York. Within 40 seconds, and while Minh was still wrapping up his short speech, bells on 7,500 teletype machines around the world rang 10 times. Crowds gathered at almost every one of them, and this is what they read (the apostrophes ring the bells):

```
ZCZC VHA025 NXI
BB HUP HTD HSB
ZCZ NNN

FLASH ' ' ' ' ' ' ' ' ' '

    SAIGON—SAIGON GOVERNMENT SURRENDERS

                                        NTL 1021AM


ZCZ NNNN
```

```
ZCZC VHA025 NXI
BB HUP HTD HSB
ZCZ NNN

FLASH ' ' ' ' ' ' ' ' ' '

    SAIGON—SAIGON GOVERNMENT SURRENDERS

                                        NTL 1021AM


ZCZ NNNN
```

A flash is always repeated, to avoid chances of a mistake or a hoax. It also is always followed by a bulletin, as this one was within 60 seconds.

```
ZCZC VHA026 NXI
BB HUP HTD HSB
ZCZ NNN

    BULLETIN ' ' ' ' ' '
    PEACE 4-30
    BY ALAN DAWSON

SAIGON, APRIL 30 (UPI)—PRESIDENT DUONG VAN (BIG) MINH
```

TODAY ANNOUNCED THE SURRENDER OF SOUTH VIETNAM AND
TOLD GOVERNMENT SOLDIERS TO STOP FIGHTING.

(MORE)LD/PDV

NTL 1022AM
ZCZ NNNN

Controlled panic in the most exciting story of the decade. And so it was in
the other news offices around Saigon. At the Associated Press, Bureau
Manager George Esper was getting an excruciatingly (it seemed) slow
translation of Minh's speech. He, too, got halfway through and realized it
was a surrender. He typed a bulletin. Peter Arnett ran the story to the
teletype operator, who took one look at the paragraph, turned pale, and
began to rise from his chair to flee this American office. Arnett shoved him
back in the chair and said he could leave after he finished typing the story.
Shaking, the operator typed that paragraph and several more, then took
off out the door. AFP, the French news agency, was only slightly behind the
Americans. Reuters, the British agency, was slower because the volunteer
who manned the office—a bilingual French citizen—had moved to a hotel.
The Reuters office, he felt, was too close to the Presidential Palace, a
potential war target.

I had a staffer call an employee of the Post, Telegraph, and Telephone
system, where the PTT man cut off a telephone conversation to the United
States and punched through a call to UPI Audio, the wire service's radio
branch, in New York City.

Walter Cronkite, the television correspondent who himself had turned
against the war after the 1968 Tet offensive, was narrating an hour-long
special on the U.S. evacuation and the war on CBS as the flash and bulletins
came into his news room. Calmly, Cronkite waited for a spot, then told his
viewers of the end of the war. Within minutes, CBS had asked for and
obtained the UPI Audio report from Saigon on the surrender—the only
one that got out this last day of the war. It was played on the television
sound, with a slide of Saigon as the picture.

Most of the reactions in Saigon were different, of course, as the population got ready to meet the end. Within 30 minutes, the sporadic street
shooting died. Most of it in the downtown area was into the air and either
enabled looters to intimidate the looted or chased off would-be looters. The
looters themselves grabbed up a final armful and headed home.

A police lieutenant colonel who wore a name tag identifying him only as
Lieutenant Colonel Long stepped up to the military statue in the main
downtown square, saluted, and shot himself in the head. Amazingly, the
huge .45-caliber bullet passed through his skull and did not kill him

instantly. Matt Franjola of the Associated Press bundled him into a car and took him to the French-run Grall Hospital. He died shortly after arrival.

Doors and shutters were drawn to the locked position. Even the French shop and restaurant owners of Saigon who felt they could survive almost anything took their stools indoors. A hush fell over the city.

In Can Tho, three-star General Nguyen Khoa Nam, commander of IV Corps and the Mekong Delta, finally admitted it was all over when he heard the Minh broadcast. One of a tiny handful of combat generals who stayed on, Nam had fought to the end.

There had been little hard battling in the delta throughout the offensive. The North Vietnamese preferred the blitzkrieg west-to-east and then north-to-south approach to Saigon. Nam, an unlikely hero with a history of mainly corruption and staff positions behind him, was personally affronted by the surrender of the Saigon armed forces. With little combat in his area, he had a hard time even understanding the retreats.

He forbade anyone under his command to leave his post. He himself left only to go further toward "the front," ordering officers to remain where they were. He shot a province chief at Sa Dec, just west of Can Tho, because the man insisted he was going to leave in the American evacuation.

And when the colonel who was chief of Kien Giang province on the Gulf of Siam disobeyed the stand-and-hold orders from his commander and left Rach Gia city by boat to the south, Nam had three helicopters pursue the boat and sink it with rocket and machine-gun fire.

Lieutenant General Nguyen Khoa Nam had little to be ashamed of during his last days as a fighting man. He had—literally—dedicated his life to the last battle. Within 30 minutes of Big Minh's speech and order to surrender, Nam put his .45-caliber pistol into his mouth and pulled the trigger. Unlike Long, he died instantly.

In the cities and villages of what was left of the Republic of Vietnam, and particularly in Saigon, there was a silence.

At the Tham Thuy Ha ammunition dump six miles east of Saigon, soldiers threw down their weapons and fled. The commander of the dump, a lieutenant colonel, was not in that big a hurry. With material assembled and earmarked for just such an occurrence, he began rigging booby traps. In three sections of the dump, he set clock-activated explosive switches. The first he set for 7:30 P.M. Satisfied with his hour's work, he took off his uniform, put on civilian clothes, and left the dump.

On his way out the gate, he set up three separate trip wires so that if the gate were opened, the time charges would go off immediately. Then he walked to the Saigon River, appropriated an unused sampan to cross the river, and headed for Saigon and his home. He watched the entrance of Communist troops to Saigon from a noodle shop in the suburbs. He was never discovered by the administration as the commander of Tham Thuy Ha. He reported as a soldier, underwent reeducation, and was released.

His final work would be seen by about 4 million people that night.

From the north and the west they came, the defeated and bitter paratroopers and Rangers who had fought the last battles in defense of Saigon. They were angry as they came into the center of the city, although they were not panicking. They were ready to loot, and in many cases were ready to kill foreigners.

With Minh's radio speech, the attitude changed. Now, for the most part, they wanted to shed all signs of their military involvement. On the main street of Saigon, Tu Do, where for years American soldiers packed the bars and restaurants, the soldiers stripped and became instant civilians.

In front of the government information office, half a dozen paratroopers took off their camouflaged fatigues, threw down their guns and ammunition, fled to no one knows where. Most had civilian clothes in their packs, ready for this moment. The North Vietnamese army, when it arrived, found few uniformed soldiers ready to surrender.

The police, as always, were ahead of the soldiers in abandoning their posts. At some police stations, officers ran up white flags. In most (for example, in a subprecinct station just off the main square), police officers emerged from the building, siphoned the gasoline from police Jeeps, poured it into their motorcycles, and left for home. Policemen always had civilian clothes to change into.

Mike Mielke did not argue with the two soldiers who told him to throw his rifle and pistol over a wall at the Foreign Ministry. He, his wife, and his uncomprehending daughter stood motionless and silent as the soldiers began to strip them of their belongings. The men thought they had better pickings, however, in a warehouse behind the ministry, where emergency rice was stored. A Vietnamese sailor with an M16 killed them, apologized to Mielke for the inconvenience, and commented he could not stand looters. He melted off.

The capital waited, mostly in silence, for the new rulers of Vietnam.

For Major Nguyen Van Thang of the People's Army of Vietnam, this cloudless day of April 30, 1975, was especially bright.

Thang had fought his way to Saigon from North Vietnam. The career officer had been in South Vietnam for more than five years. He had a chestful of battle ribbons and was officially a Hero of the Revolution. On the slightest provocation, he would dig his medals from the mirror-lined box in which he kept them and pin them to his baggy green fatigue uniform.

Major Thang was a prima donna only occasionally, however. His superiors recognized him as an excellent officer in the field, cool under fire, and a fine leader of the highly disciplined troops of the unit code named the 316th Brigade.

During the offensive that now officially is called the Ho Chi Minh campaign, Thang's unit was a spearhead aimed at the southern capital. Thang and his soldiers considered their shock force duty an honor.

And the major himself, three days before the final attack on Saigon, was given a singular honor. He was to lead a small detachment of his troops, along with a tank force and Saigon guerrilla guides, to the downtown Saigon Presidential Palace. There he would hoist the red, blue, and gold-starred flag of the Provisional Revolutionary Government of the Republic of South Vietnam, otherwise known as the Viet Cong.

The symbolism was that Doc Lap—Independence—Palace had housed the pro-American generals-turned-Presidents who had tried to lead the people of South Vietnam in the anti-Communist war. When the palace fell, the war would be considered over. A Communist flag flying over Doc Lap would mean that the Hanoi-led forces of the Vietnam war had become the victors.

On April 27, when he received the assignment of securing Doc Lap Palace, Thang made preparations. Although his unit was involved in some tough fighting between Bien Hoa air base and Saigon city at the time, he took a couple of hours off. He commandeered a captured Jeep and drove to the rear to the quartermaster unit. There, he bullied a supply clerk into issuing him a brand-new uniform. The light green fatigues were not given up easily by the quartermasters. They demanded proof that Thang would be entering Saigon, where the eyes of the world would be upon him. Thang wanted to look his best during the high point of his career, and he got the new uniform by pulling rank.

That night, Thang carefully folded the uniform. He polished a fresh pair of boots, captured from a warehouse and therefore brand-new. He polished the gold-colored star on his pith helmet and scrubbed his medals with charcoal and a piece of leaf plucked from a nipa palm. He did all this himself, although he could just as easily have ordered one of his privates to do so.

On April 28, in the late afternoon, Thang listened to the bombing attack on Tan Son Nhut air base, the first air raid by the Communist side during the Vietnam war. He tuned his field radio to the correct frequency and heard the code words confirming what the attack signaled—the final assault on Saigon.

The main Saigon army blocking point to Major Thang's advance was at Go Vap, just outside the district town about seven miles northwest of downtown Saigon. On April 29, American-made tanks of the Saigon forces battled the Russian-manufactured tanks of the North Vietnamese. Infantrymen fought on the ground.

The tank battle went on throughout the night, but by dawn it was over. The 316th Brigade and its attached tank and guerrilla forces were on the move again. Thang now was very busy. He detached one segment of his 2,000-man force to occupy the headquarters of the South Vietnamese Joint General Staff on the edge of Tan Son Nhut air base. He himself headed into the city.

There was resistance from small, disorganized Saigon army units in Gia Dinh, the northern suburb of the capital. They were overcome in minutes each, but Thang's advance was slowed somewhat.

By 10:20 A.M., Thang, at the head of his forces, was in Saigon proper, although still about two miles from the palace. On a street near the old American commissary, abandoned and looted 24 hours before, he heard on a radio the surrender order by the newest and last Saigon President, General Duong Van (Big) Minh.

There was no one on the Saigon army tank at the Thi Nghe Bridge near the main radio and telecommunications stations in north-central Saigon, but the vehicle and half a dozen sand-filled barrels blocked the road. Thang's tanks smashed aside the roadblock within a few minutes.

Thang now sent smaller units out to the sides of his own spearhead. A force captured the radio stations. Another went straight ahead down Hong Thap Tu Street, which is on one side of Doc Lap Palace. Thang himself swung to the left with his third force, over a block to Thong Nhut, a major boulevard although only half a dozen blocks long. The wide street ran from the Prime Minister's office and the zoo at the north to the palace at the south. The American Embassy was halfway between.

And at 11:30, Thang and his troops ran into the first resistance in more than an hour. This was from Saigon troops holed up in and around the Prime Minister's office and the Saigon zoo.

Clutching a pistol in one hand and lightly holding the shoulder bag containing his new uniform, boots, and medals in the other, Thang watched the battle. There was no doubt of the outcome. It took, however, 45 minutes for his forces to get into the Prime Minister's office. Thang went immediately into a room in the building and changed his clothes.

On his right flank, meanwhile, a tough woman guerrilla who had seen much combat in the war was making faster progress. Sister Nguyen Trung Kien, 20 years old, orphaned by the war, peasant-soldier, and Saigon guerrilla, was actually supposed to be only a guide to the forces entering Saigon. Now dressed in floppy black pajamas and a camouflaged hat, her hair pulled tightly back from her face, she was a survivor of the 1968 Tet offensive fighting in the capital. She knew Saigon well. In late 1975, she became the subject of a Saigon television series, marking the first time her name became known.

Sister Kien watched infantry and tanks secure the radio and communications sites without a battle. In fact, only two persons were in the telecommunications building—a technician and a photographer from United Press International, sending a radiophoto to Tokyo for distribution around the world.

With the radio facilities secured, Sister Kien and a small force, now riding on tanks, headed down Hong Thap Tu Street. They heard the fighting at the Prime Minister's office to their left, but did not participate. Instead, the unit slipped one street to the left, to Thong Nhut, past the U.S. Embassy, stripped by looters and now silent.

Sister Kien was on the first tank that crashed the metal gates to Doc Lap Palace without waiting for a soldier to open them. The tanks wheeled up, ignoring the semicircular driveway, onto the lawn in front of the palace. Infantrymen took the palace guard at gunpoint and ordered the troops to empty their weapons by firing them into the air.

At the Prime Minister's office less than a mile away, Major Thang's unit was still involved in fighting remnants of the Saigon army now holed up in the zoo and botanical gardens nearby. There was not a significant force fighting, but it had to be put down, and Thang had to command the operation.

Sister Kien, a rifle in her hands, raced into the Palace along with other infantrymen. There was no resistance. Big Minh and several advisers awaited the "Liberation Forces." Nervous soldiers fanned out to make sure there would be no fighting. A private entered with a huge Viet Cong flag. Neither Kien nor Minh knew how to get to the flagpole, because a bombing attack on the palace three weeks before had knocked out the main front stairwell. Servants in the palace refused to tell how to get to the upstairs balcony.

Sister Kien and ex-President Minh went themselves, with soldiers covering them, and found the back stairs. A soldier hauled down the yellow flag with the red stripes of the Republic of Vietnam. He attached the flag of the Viet Cong.

At 12:45 P.M. April 30, Sister Kien, black pajamas ruffling slightly in the breeze, pulled the lanyard that raised the Communist flag, symbolizing the end of the Vietnam War.

An hour later, Major Thang, looking sharp in his new uniform, his shined boots, his medals attached to the chest of his fatigues, walked up the steps of Doc Lap Palace.

And that is how Major Nguyen Van Thang, hero of the Revolution, was late to the most important event of his life.*

At 10:30 A.M. April 30, the man in charge of the Vietnamese military was a one-star general, Nguyen Huu Hanh. Hanh, it turned out, was a long-time Viet Cong sympathizer working within the Joint General Staff and feeding information to the Communists. He, of course, did not wish to leave Vietnam with most of the other generals, and found himself the com- mander of the Saigon army for the last few hours of its existence. He issued only one order during his short spell as commanding general, and that by Saigon Radio. He ordered his troops to lay down their arms and to surren- der themselves at the first opportunity to troops of the Provisional Revolu- tionary Government. It was one of hundreds of ironies that the actual cease-fire order was issued by a Viet Cong infiltrator.

Ky Danh, the "spy" for Big Minh, took two North Vietnamese army soldiers in plain clothes to the office of the Associated Press, where two Americans and New Zealander Peter Arnett were waiting for "liberation." The part-time journalist told the startled foreigners there was nothing to fear. The North Vietnamese had orders to treat newsmen and in fact all foreigners, including Americans, well.

Major Nguyen Van Thang's highly disciplined and well-briefed troops were under orders to fire only if fired upon. These were the same orders issued to the first American "advisers" in South Vietnam, almost 15 years before.

UPI's Hu Van Es finished sifting through the negatives from other photog- raphers. He picked four of the preliberation scene, including one of a plane being shot down over Tan Son Nhut and another of looters at the U.S. Embassy. He then dispatched Nguyen Van Tam to the radiophoto point at a post office building to send the pictures to Tokyo. From there, it was hoped, they would be distributed all over the world. Tam got to the post office just after the surrender order, found a single technician on duty, and got down to work sending the pictures.

Out on Cong Ly Street, Saigon soldiers retreating from Tan Son Nhut approached the building always known only as 192 Cong Ly. A huge building, it was another irony of the war. It was owned by Trinh Dinh Thao, a Viet Cong since 1968 and about the Number 5 man in the PRG. It

*Rather abashedly, the major told me this story in August 1975, when I met him during a security check he was personally conducting on another American. By that time, he had been appointed a precinct chief of the southern capital. With rather less urging than necessary, I convinced him to pose for pictures with all his medals, which he still kept in the same box with the mirror in the top. He said the photographs were the first he ever had of himself in color.

was leased by the U.S. government for members of its military in Saigon. Thao collected the rent through a middleman. Right now, guarding the empty building was Nguyen Van Duong, who had held an American guard officer hostage the previous day for his salary. He was still on duty, although he had not received any of his salary or termination pay. When the Saigon troops fired at the building, a frustrated firing that showed their disgust of the American pull-out, Duong left his post. Defending an empty building with his life for no pay was not to his liking.

Several South Koreans, terrified at the prospect of staying behind with the Viet Cong, sought refuge at the French-run Grall Hospital. This is not far from the U.S. Embassy building, where they had waited 18 hours for evacuation. The French took them in and promised whatever protection they were able to provide.

A 16-year-old girl named Dao cried. Her entire family had got out of Vietnam by boat the day before, leaving Dao trapped in a huge mob. Until the surrender order, she had tried to get on another boat and had failed. She headed for a church, where she knew the priest would let her sleep on the floor. She did not stop sobbing for two days.

Fred Gulden, who had given up his chance for evacuation while he tried to help his Vietnamese employees out, went to the roof of the U.S. Embassy and stood on the helicopter pad. When he heard the surrender order, he headed downtown and found some other Americans, who gave him moral support. He was "not too worried" about staying with the Communists. He was bitter at what he considered the evacuation debacle.

Ky Danh went to Radio Saigon and waited.

It was a strange two hours. After Minh and Hanh had ordered the surrender, looters and most of those trying to get out of Vietnam headed home or to the shelter and friendship of family or acquaintances. The streets quieted as if there were a curfew. There was no law and order at all, but few if any took advantage of this. Soldiers, those still in uniform, appeared dazed on the downtown streets. Some continued to clutch their weapons, although most had discarded them.

Others were better organized. They were the gangs of Vietnamese tongs or triads. These were composed of groups of thugs patterned loosely after the old Chinese gangs that controlled vice in the cities of China before the Communists took over, then emigrated to America, Hong Kong, and Europe. The gangs knew the Viet Cong were coming. The best disciplined ones sent out their scouts and agents, forged Communist identity cards, and armed themselves with guerrilla-type weapons. They were mostly old, castoff rifles and pistols originally brought to Vietnam by the Americans.

American Cliff Randolph, who hadn't made the evacuation because he had realized too late that it was under way, was in his villa near Tan Son Nhut when one of the gangs came in. Brandishing their loaded weapons but not firing them, they indicated to Randolph—who owned Randy's Bar on the GI strip—that they were "liberation soldiers." He believed them. In short order, they stripped him of cash, clothes, and furniture. Anything that could be lifted by four men or fewer was taken and loaded into trucks, and the "soldiers" sped off. Randolph was convinced for several months that he had been ripped off by the vanguard of the Communist force entering Saigon. There were other, similar victims, mostly Vietnamese. The gangs worked quickly, methodically, and according to carefully laid plans. When the Communist troops actually entered the capital, the tongs broke up and went to ground, content to wait and see what happened.

A calm descended. There was sporadic shooting, but very little. In the distance, there were some booms, but no more than on an ordinary night of the war, except that they were closer. Perhaps 99 percent of the Saigonese praised Minh's decision to surrender. "It was the only thing he could do," said an ex-soldier, ex-CIA employee. "He saved thousands of lives." There was to be no battle for Saigon. A war that had taken 30 years and three million lives, by conservative estimate, was ending with a whimper.

At the palace, waiting to surrender, Big Minh told a foreign newsman he had decided to hand over power to those better qualified to run the country. He was drawn, somber, haggard. So were his aides. The tanks came and smashed down the palace gates.

That was when Minh and Sister Kien found the stairs to the balcony, stripped off the red-and-gold flag of the Republic of Vietnam and hoisted in its place the red, blue, and gold of the Republic of South Vietnam.

When it was clear that there was to be no resistance, three North Vietnamese soldiers found the office used by Thieu in former days. They rifled his cigarette box and lit up. They sat down in chairs in the office. One of them put his feet on the former president's desk—the ultimate sign of disrespect—and posed for a photographer.

General Hanh surrendered the Joint General Staff headquarters and embraced the Viet Cong captain who "liberated" the building. The tanks and trucks of Major Thang headed down Tu Do street, where U.S. GI's had once frolicked on their time off from the war. At the post office transmitting site, power was cut and Nguyen Van Tam had sent the last UPI radiophoto from Saigon.

At Radio Saigon, Ky Danh was unfamiliar with the equipment. The first words spoken on the radio after the capture of the seat of power at the palace were in English: "Is this the way?" Then there was a throat clearing and Ky Danh spoke. "You know me, I am Ky Danh. Liberation troops have entered Saigon and the city has been liberated. Remain calm. . . ."

The three dozen or so remaining guards at the palace were lined up inside the North Vietnamese tank formation. They were told to bring their M16 rifles. Gathered on the lawn, they were instructed to point the weapons into the air, take off the safety catches, place the selector switches on automatic fire, and pull the triggers.

Symbolically, these were the last shots of the Vietnam War.

PRELUDE TO THE BATTLE

Headquarters for South Vietnam's Central Intelligence Agency was situated on the banks of the Saigon River alongside the naval headquarters. From its windows, a large square was visible, dominated by a towering statue of Tran Hung Dao, patron "saint" of the Vietnamese navy.

For five years, Army Sergeant Le Er Tang* had worked in some of the most secret rooms in the CIA headquarters. They were closely guarded by totally trustworthy men of the military police.

One of Sergeant Tang's jobs was to sort intelligence reports from field agents and troops. He and a few other intelligence specialists culled the reports, trying to separate wheat from chaff, identifying Viet Cong and North Vietnamese troop movements across South Vietnam's 44 provinces. More than almost any other intelligence available to Saigon officials, news of troop movements gave hints of just where—and sometimes when —Communist attacks would come.

Sergeant Tang's specialty was the Saigon area, but by late January of 1975 he also had taken over a desk that plotted the movements of North Vietnamese soldiers in the Central Highlands more than 200 miles from the capital.

He and other analysts received their reports from a variety of sources, most of them supposedly unknown to Tang and his assistants or even their

*His real name.

superiors. Like the American CIA, its spiritual and structural counterpart, the South Vietnamese CIA distributed information only on a need-to-know basis. Tang had the reports, but he had no need to know the sources. But over the years, Tang had figured out where the reports came from. He learned to recognize certain call signs, signals, and phrases that gave clues as to the reporting agents or troop commanders.

A peculiar thing began to happen in Tang's section at CIA headquarters in early February, although he said later no one else seemed to notice. On his desk began appearing intelligence reports that had not gone through the normal communications channels. In turn, the contents of these reports were used to create battle maps within the CIA and later at the Joint General Staff, the Presidential Palace, various corps headquarters, the U.S. Embassy and military headquarters and, it is said, the Pentagon and the White House.

The maps, which we can call Tang's maps because they were exclusively his products, showed a huge Communist buildup around Pleiku and Kontum, two towns 20 miles apart and 250 miles north of Saigon in the highlands.

No one questioned Tang's maps. He was a highly qualified technician and analyst. He simply made maps, after all, from the reams of documents on his desk and in his classified files, which in turn came from field reports.

In his way, Sergeant Tang was just another Vietnamese soldier, mildly anti-Communist, but a man who did not stand out particularly except for the job he held and his brighter-than-average mentality. Because of his intelligence, he had been selected for the CIA job many years earlier.

There was no major military activity around Pleiku and Kontum early in 1975. It was centered well to the south, around the town of Ban Me Thuot. Sergeant Tang's reports, and the maps he drew from them, were fakes.

On April 28, Sergeant Le Er Tang did not show up for work at the CIA headquarters. His superiors, caught up in the panic of Saigon's final hours, did not seem to notice his absence. Indeed, many of them were not at their desks that morning. Some already were safely in American hands outside South Vietnam—in Guam or the Philippines.

Tang reappeared in Saigon on the morning of April 30, "Liberation Day." During the next 72 hours he guided North Vietnamese military units. In and around the fallen capital he pointed out key offices and residences that needed searching and/or securing.

On May 3, Captain Le Er Tang of the People's Liberation Armed Forces of the Republic of South Vietnam assumed command of the military police intelligence battalion he had been secretly working with for more than three years.

Three months later, when he attended my going-away party with one of my acquaintances, Tang told me his story. He also gave me a souvenir of "liberation"—his military pith helmet. Autographed by him, it now hangs in my home.

The Army of the Republic of Vietnam (ARVN) had been falling apart for years. There were those who said it had never been well put together. Internal squabbling among Americans was as much to blame for the poor shape of the ARVN as the more publicized and more reviled political infighting among the powerful in Vietnam.

The core of the ARVN in 1954 was the pro-French Vietnamese force that had naturally ended up in South Vietnam when Ho Chi Minh's forces took over, finally and officially, in Hanoi. There were those Americans then, most prominent among them Colonel Edward Lansdale—the consummate spook—who thought all along the ARVN should be small and mobile. These men argued that the South Vietnamese army should be highly trained in antiguerrilla, counterinsurgency tactics, because armed opposition to the Saigon government, at least into the 1960's, was small in numbers. It consisted mostly of Viet Minh guerrillas and political cadre left behind in South Vietnam.

But for understandable, if faulty, reasons ARVN was destined to become a large, immobile, poorly trained army. It was outfitted with the very best arms in Southeast Asia, especially following the U.S. withdrawal, which began July 10, 1969. But its officers often could not use the weapons. Its men were unable to maintain them.

When United States officers took over the war effort in Vietnam and began to "advise" the ARVN directly, the potential enemy was China. It was 1954, and the human wave attacks of the Chinese and the large-scale battles of Korea were the most recent lessons learned by U.S. military men. Guerrilla warfare was something new to most of them, to *all* of them who held the purse strings.

Mao Tse-tung was not required reading for Americans, let alone Vo Nguyen Giap or Ho Chi Minh.

Advocates of a small army, highly trained in the art of fighting guerrillas, went unheeded and largely unheard. What was needed, according to popular opinion, was a large army fully equipped to deal with a massive, across-the-DMZ invasion like that staged in South Korea in 1950.

So the ARVN became larger and larger, on paper more than one million men by 1975. It had proved totally incapable of dealing with guerrillas 10 and 15 years before. But what none of its members or supporters wished to admit—because no one wants to admit failure—was that it also was incapable of dealing with main force attacks. The same American officers who readily admitted that only U.S. air power had saved South Vietnam from defeat in 1972 were putting out the often-heard word that the ARVN had magically, mystically transformed itself into an effective fighting force three years later.

Like Frankenstein, the sellers of the ARVN were reluctant to admit that the monster built in their image was incapable of doing well. It became much a belief in the "good guys"—the ARVN—prevailing over the "bad guy" Communists. The belief was necessary because there was no alternative save North Vietnamese victory.

Saigon's army was predictably enough the main part of the South Vietnamese hierarchy. Only Ngo Dinh Diem, President from 1955 to 1963, was a strong leader and not a general at the same time. Diem was beholden to the army, and other civilian posts quickly fell to the military. When Nguyen Van Thieu took over as chief of state in 1965 (he became President after the elections of September 1967) he was a three-star general. He technically dropped his rank, but his power, the power structure, and the support that kept him in power came directly from the military.

The faults of the Vietnamese system have been pointed out often. They include the nepotism of the generals, the dependence of civilians on full military support in their programs, the jealousies and rages and feelings of omnipotence that give rise to coups, and the desire to seek power—in an Orwellian manner—for power itself.

Thieu, of course, showed no protracted desire to be President of all the people. Had he done so, he would have been in trouble. His power depended on generals, who depended on other generals, who depended on colonels, and so on down the line. At only one point was anyone dependent on a civilian. That was as the bill payer, the person who paid for the corruption, which sometimes masqueraded as taxes.

What few Americans, and surprisingly few Vietnamese, realized by March 1975, was that the morale of the army was disintegrating. The South Vietnamese military had better weapons than any Asian nation, more warplanes than any client government in the world, more ammunition and gasoline and uniforms and office machines and vehicles and food than most armies in the world. It lacked only one thing.

An American who remained in Vietnam for reasons that had nothing to do with his political sympathies put it this way in a conversation with a former soldier bemoaning his fate under the new government: "We gave you everything you needed but guts. You just didn't have those." Cruel, and technically untrue. But the idea is correct. By the time the Communists decided to try for an offensive, the South Vietnamese army was in no position to fight them. Not because they lacked the means but because the soldiers lacked the desire.

American military men call it motivation. It is considered very important that an American fighting man have it. He must know for what he is fighting, or he will not fight. It is not enough, as later events proved well in Vietnam, that a soldier know *against* what he is fighting. Most of the South Vietnamese by 1975 could be said to be anti-Communist, and it was more than a simple knee-jerk belief with many. Most believed in capitalism, and all knew that a Communist victory would finish capitalism.

But, the average South Vietnamese soldier asked himself unconsciously, for what am I fighting? The answer was: a continuation of the present system—growing corruption and growing differences between rich and poor, with the middle class growing ever poorer in the squeeze between the richer rich and inflation. A relative few were fighting for a better life. Those who had a better life to look forward to were not fighting. Thieu's son, daughter, and son-in-law all were abroad studying. If any South Vietnamese general had a son in the armed forces, it never became publicly known. Generals actually involved in combat were a pathetic percentage of those wearing stars.

The Communist soldiers, on the other hand, knew what they were fighting for: to "liberate" their oppressed countrymen in the south and to build the revolution. ("Are you happy the war is over now so that you can go home?" I naively asked a North Vietnamese soldier the day after the war ended. "I'm happy the war is over," he replied, "but that is only one phase of the revolution. We have much work ahead of us before we can go home.") That much of what they "knew" to be truth was actually nonsense mattered not at all. The typical North Vietnamese citizen, soldier or civilian, believed the people in the south to be desperately poor. The first visitors to relatives in the south brought, for example, thick, rough rice bowls and cheap bamboo chopsticks as presents, and were amazed to find Saigon residents were not eating with their hands from banana leaves. The point is that the Communist soldiers were motivated to fight for a better life for their southern countrypeople.

This "knowledge" was imparted and instilled by the political officers attached to each Communist army unit in Vietnam (and most Communist countries), who proved their points frequently by using selected examples of Saigon corruption, the history of "western imperialism," and stories of American atrocities. It was made to stick largely by the isolation of North Vietnam's people from other points of view. Compared to their North Vietnamese counterparts, the South Vietnamese soldiers or civilians were sophisticates and had, if they so desired, direct access to cultures, ideas, and philosophies not their own. The North Vietnamese were much more likely to be shaped by the all-consuming, intertwined goals of their government—to "liberate" the south, chase out the Americans, and build Vietnam into a united, Communist country.

There is another morale factor, a valid one, often put forward by military men, and particularly American officers. At no time was it the policy of the American side to "win" the war. So long as North Vietnam continued its attacks (near the height of fighting in the late 1960's, the CIA estimated that Hanoi could sustain its manpower losses indefinitely, given the country's high birth rate), the best that Saigon could hope for was not to lose. American troops, who came no closer to defeating the Communists than did the Saigon forces, had the same problem: how to avoid losing, while the enemy kept attacking. Total victory was banned.

One development which was not well publicized abroad but which spread mouth-to-ear throughout the middle and lower ranks of the South Vietnamese Army at the time, was one of the final nails in the ARVN coffin.

It occurred at Phuoc Binh province capital, chief town of Phuoc Long province and 66 miles north of Saigon, in an area peopled mostly by mountain tribes and soldiers. Phuoc Long was chosen by the Communists as the testing ground for their 1975 offensive. So it was that on December 6, 1974, Phuoc Long province began to fall to the North Vietnamese army. It took one month to capture Phuoc Binh, a fact that is a key to the final fall of South Vietnam less than four months later.

Hanoi is just far enough north to get chilly in the autumn, brisk enough to put a little more energy in the steps of the men and women who live there. The North Vietnamese army chief of staff, General Van Tien Dung,* remembers that the briskness of the fall season gave him and others more energy as they laid plans in 1974 for the final battles of the Vietnam War.

Between October of 1974 and January 1975, the North Vietnamese hierarchy laid its plans for victory. In their curious bureaucracy, officials made contingency plans and passed them to meetings of the senior bodies—the politburo and the standing military committee of the Communist Party. The plans were amended and approved at large, almost unwieldy meetings that functioned well only because of strict discipline. They then were sent back to the lower committees for refinement and implementation.

During the summer of 1974, the Party approved plans for a test. This consisted of what came to be called the mini-offensive, beginning December 6, 1974. The mini-offensive was concentrated mainly in the Mekong Delta and the region just north of Saigon. It saw some heavy fighting, and

---

*General Dung later compiled his notes, diaries, and after-action reports into a book-length report on his leadership of the final Communist offensive. It was broadcast in installments by Radio Hanoi between April 1 and May 22, 1976, and is unique in the Vietnamese Communist history because of its personal anecdotes. It is, as of two years after the Communist victory, the single best source both of the thinking of the officials in North Vietnam who controlled the offensive and of the tactics used by the North Vietnamese in their final, winning attack on the south.

victories by both the Saigon and North Vietnamese troops. Who won this offensive was neither here nor there to the leaders in Hanoi. The attacks were meant to test reactions.

After three months of mid-level meetings, General Dung's military committee was optimistic in October 1974. Although the mini-offensive would give definitive answers to several vexing problems, Dung believed he already had the answers. He approved a four-point resolution to be passed up the bureaucratic line, stating that the war in the south could be won in a relatively short period, say two years.

The resolution to the Politburo, maker of all important decisions, said basically this: North Vietnamese forces were stronger than the Saigon army in South Vietnam; U.S. aid would continue to drop off, while North Vietnamese forces were getting more and more aid; and demands for Thieu's political head in the cities of the south were a great help to the Communists.

Through some clever political balancing, North Vietnam set up a system of incoming aid that was not completely dependent on any of its allies. Hanoi feared a cutoff of direct Soviet aid, as the Russians indicated they wanted closer relations with Washington. In fact, in 1972 the Soviets did halt much of their military aid to North Vietnam when Henry Kissinger indicated to Moscow the Americans were holding back Saigon military forces. Military supplies to Hanoi from the Soviet Union slowed to such an extent that when the United States stopped its all-out bombing just before 1973, North Vietnam had only enough surface-to-air missiles to combat the U.S. planes for one more day. Sources who were in Hanoi then said later that North Vietnam would have been forced to surrender had the bombing continued, although that view appears on reflection too extreme.

China was just as unreliable a supplier as the Soviet Union, although Peking continued its shipments of small arms and mortars to Hanoi. What Hanoi did in late 1972 was to use Cuba as a middleman. The willing Cubans—still two years away from direct involvement in Angola but beginning to think outward movement—shipped much of their Soviet-donated aid to Hanoi. It is believed that the Soviet Union was unaware of the Havana Connection for many months. And when Moscow tuned in to the unorthodox Soviet-to-Cuba-to-Vietnam military aid route, there is no evidence that Soviet authorities tried to halt it.

The Soviet Union could claim with a straight face that it had lessened its military aid to Hanoi, just as Washington was providing less aid to Saigon. But the weapons and ammunition continued to flow into North Vietnam just the same. North Vietnam thus remained independent both of détente and the Sino-Soviet split.

U.S. aid had fallen from more than 2.1 billion dollars to 700 million dollars in two years. North Vietnam reasoned from its political reports, correctly as it turned out, that it was likely to continue to fall. According to agent reports to Dung's office, 170,000 Saigon troops had deserted in 1973 and 1974, and total manpower in the Saigon army had dropped by 15,000. In short, Dung wrote in his diary in the fall of 1974, "Nguyen Van Thieu (is) forced to fight a poor man's war."

In October, the full Politburo and the Central Military Committee of the Communist Party met in joint session to approve a combat plan for the future. The guidelines of this important conference were loose. Nothing was predetermined. It was a tough session, with much arguing and more than a little bickering.

Le Duan, first among equals in North Vietnam because of his position as Communist Party boss, focused on a single question: what would the Americans do if the North Vietnamese armed forced launched an all-out offensive? He listened to reports and off-the-cuff statements of the men at the meeting, then answered his own question. Le Duan said that since the United States had already withdrawn its troops from the south, there was little chance that they would come back. If they came back, their presence would have little effect on the outcome of battle, because their infrastructure was gone. With no support bases in South Vietnam, the Americans would be unable to put up more than a token fight against the North Vietnamese army.

It was at this October meeting, which lasted several days, that the General Staff of the armed forced proposed making the Central Highlands of South Vietnam the main 1975 battlefield, a decision that was to become crucial.

In early December 1974, senior commanders in the south were summoned to the north. This was the pattern throughout the war. It showed how subservient to Hanoi the Southern Communists were. What was commonly called the Viet Cong was a creature of Hanoi. The important men in the south came directly within the North Vietnamese chain of command, reducing the so-called Viet Cong to a sort of side show, a necessary front and a subordinate body that implemented the policies of Ho Chi Minh and his followers.

Chief among those called to Hanoi in early December were Pham Hung, the Number 4 man on the Politburo and the effective leader of the Communists in the south, and three-star General Tran Van Tra, commander of the Saigon military region. Also summoned were senior members of the shadowy People's Revolutionary Party, the Communist party of the south. Conspicuous by their absence were the leaders of the Provisional Revolutionary Government and the National Liberation Front, the two official bodies of South Vietnamese Communists.

The meetings until now had been prologue to the actual decision-making. On December 18, a 20-day session of the North Vietnamese

Politburo met to set the policy. As it met through Christmas and the new year, the fighting raged in the south. North Vietnamese soldiers zeroed in on Phuoc Long province, where the die would be cast for South Vietnam.

Phuoc Binh, and indeed the entire province, had no regular army troops. It was defended by a couple of thousand so-called border rangers—some of them good soldiers and former mercenaries for the U.S. Green Berets, but most of them by 1975 draftees from minority groups. The Special Forces had their own private army of 35,000 during the 1960's, and as the Green Berets pulled out, the mercenaries were absorbed into the South Vietnamese army, mostly into the ranger corps. Phuoc Long also had the normal complements of militiamen and other irregulars. Ninety percent of the soldiers in these units could be counted on to run from any battle and hardly figured into the planning of either side for all-out war.

District after district of Phuoc Long province fell. Even the most unschooled military tactician on the streets of Saigon could see that the provincial capital was going to come under attack.

It became clear that Vo Nguyen Giap and General Dung—the North Vietnamese defense minister and armed forces commander—were trying out their new tactics in Phuoc Long. They cut the province into little pieces with offensive thrusts, then overwhelmed the cut-off defenders of each piece with mass attacks backed by intense shelling and tank assaults. It was in fact the closest that Giap and the North Vietnamese guerrillas—as they still liked to think of themselves—had come to taking instructions from a West Point or St. Cyr handbook. Remarkably few military men in South Vietnam, American or Vietnamese, recognized the tactic, or at least few suggested countertactics. First, roads to the target area were cut. Outposts at the edge of the ARVN artillery support ring were overwhelmed in human wave attacks that sometimes lasted only minutes. Then the main target, by now surrounded, was put under heavy siege by long-range guns. Finally, North Vietnamese troops piled from trucks and tanks and simply overran the final target. Defenders, often powerless because their artillery had been wiped out by super-accurate 130-millimeter guns provided to Hanoi by Moscow, either retreated or surrendered. That is, those who were not killed fled or gave themselves up.

The battle for Phuoc Binh shaped up around Christmas. The generals in Saigon waited, together with Thieu, who always insisted on the final word on any important military engagement. Nothing was done. And that was the incredible fact which, more than any other event, undermined the morale of the entire South Vietnamese Army. Thieu's outer ring of advisers told him Phuoc Binh definitely could not hold if attacked. (The inner ring said nothing unless asked, and then gave Thieu the advice he indicated he wanted to hear.)

The final siege of Phuoc Binh city began on January 2. Within hours, the North Vietnamese occupied all the high ground around the provincial capital. They used mainly the 130-millimeter guns, which fire farther and more accurately than any gun the South Vietnamese possessed in the area. The North Vietnamese proceeded to blast apart every military installation and every important civilian installation in the town, which in good times had a population of 35,000. The Communists worked into the middle of town by encircling each military position, annihilating or accepting the surrender of those inside, then moving on to the next one.

By January 3, Thieu realized he was about to lose Phuoc Binh. Never before in the South Vietnamese war had the Communists captured an entire province. What also was clear was that if Phuoc Binh should fall, there would be no question of regaining it. There simply were not enough troops available for a counterattack.

When he did decide to move, Thieu did not opt to send regular army forces. Nor did he decide to send large numbers of troops. He picked out the 300-man 82nd Special Forces Airborne Battalion, his military's most elite special unit, and sent it off with orders to hold Phuoc Binh "at any cost"—Thieu's favorite words.

The 82nd was composed of some of the toughest troops in South Vietnam. It was used mainly for reconnaissance and ambushes in the Saigon area, most notably in the area of Bien Hoa air base. When rocket attacks on Bien Hoa began to get heavy in late 1974, the 82nd was ordered in and the attacks dropped off noticeably.

There was no indication, however, as to how 300 soldiers, no matter what their credentials, could possibly hold a large town against an attacking force that was estimated by Saigon intelligence officers at two divisions—possibly 20,000 men.

In waiting until the situation was hopeless, and then sending in his best intelligence troops, Thieu had made two horrendous mistakes. This became clear on January 3.

The 82nd Special Forces Airborne Battalion had three companies. One of the companies "saddled up" on helicopters to get into Phuoc Binh. When it arrived in the general area, the North Vietnamese and Viet Cong already had their antiaircraft guns set up. Helicopters cannot fly into or through antiaircraft guns. The company was dropped about five miles from Phuoc Binh, told to do its best, and was abandoned. Stragglers came into Saigon after the city fell four months later, but none ever got into the battle. The other two companies never even got onto the helicopters.

Most of the company that did get in managed to survive, because the unit broke up as soon as it hit the ground. It lived off the jungle. Many of the men managed to avoid the Communist soldiers because of their intense training in intelligence-gathering, in which stealth is vital.

Three intertwining stories of Phuoc Binh spread through the Saigon army: Thieu's indecisiveness, the lack of support to the people and troops at the provincial capital, and the abandonment of the company of 82nd Battalion soldiers. No soldiers outside Saigon now could be sure in their own minds that fellow soldiers would come to their aid if their position were under attack. Consciously or subconsciously, the ARVN decided at that time that survival was the important thing in case of attack.

Surrender, defection to the Communist side, and flight all became viable alternatives to fighting when South Vietnamese soldiers were attacked.

In Hanoi, different decisions were being made. Generals Giap and Dung were joyous when the last resistance in Phuoc Binh ended on January 7. (The town was in Communist hands by January 4, but there was scattered fighting for another three days.)

For the generals, there were three big questions they wanted answered before beginning any large-scale military adventure. What could their newly developed tactics do? What would be the military reactions of the Saigon government and generals to an offensive? What would the United States do in case of a large-scale attack?

The answers were basically and respectively: win the war, very little, and nothing.

The Western-style military tactics of encirclement and siege, it was clear, could win the Communists a lot of territory, although at this point none of the Hanoi hierarchy was seriously considering the sort of victory at Saigon that came to be. What even they failed to realize fully was the state of terror and desire for self-preservation building in the minds of South Vietnamese soldiers because of the artillery sieges, the human-wave assaults, and the apparent lack of concern for their troops by the Saigon high command and President. Atrocious air support in many battles added to the lack of morale in the Saigon armed forces.

Even without knowing this, Generals Giap and Dung were happy men after the fall of the mountain province north of Saigon. Their military tactics were working and had been, so to speak, successfully field tested.

So far as Saigon and its generals and civilians were concerned, they had been virtually frozen—petrified—during the month-long battle for Phuoc Binh. Giap and Dung did not underestimate the possible Saigon reactions to future attacks, when more important targets would come under their guns. But the lack of response to the Phuoc Long victories was heartening to the two generals in the Defense Ministry in Hanoi.

The American reaction was different, but it heartened Giap and Dung even more. In effect, the Americans did nothing as Phuoc Long went to the Communists. Within a day of the capture of the chief town (the last stronghold of the Saigon army in the province) 7th Fleet ships sailed from

Subic Bay in the Philippines. Headed by the nuclear carrier Enterprise, the warships sailed toward Vietnam. There was much excitement, both inside Vietnam and out, when UPI carried my dispatch that the Big E was heading for waters off Vietnam. The report came from highly reliable American officials in Saigon, but was erroneous. The closest the Enterprise and its task force got to Vietnam was about 350 miles. It sailed almost directly into the Indian Ocean.

The American government was forced to say publicly, however, that under no circumstances would Americans on the ground, on the sea, or in the air reenter the Vietnam war.

And that was exciting news to Giap and Dung. Conditioned by years of unpredictable but highly military responses from President Richard Nixon, the Communist military leaders were overjoyed by the fact that every indication pointed to President Gerald Ford's keeping America out of Vietnam.

(So concerned were the North Vietnamese about American air raids that there was some evacuation of North Vietnamese cities when the full offensive got under way in March. No nonessential repairs were made to facilities damaged or destroyed in the 1972 air raids. Hanoi officials never were sure whether the B52's and other bombers might be back again with a message from Washington.)

When it became clear that the United States was going to content itself with fighting the Vietnam war of 1975 with words instead of bombs, there was joy in Hanoi.

The news of the capture of Phuoc Binh reached Hanoi two days before the end of the Politburo conference, which was setting policy for final victory. For a day, January 7, little work was done, as the hierarchy waited for the U.S. reaction. When it came, General Dung noted in his diary, "Having withdrawn from Vietnam, the United States can hardly return." He wrote this only after the Washington statements that GI's would not be back.

On January 8, the final session of the 20-day meeting of the Political Bureau of North Vietnam was held. General decisions had been made, and Le Duan, Communist party First Secretary, summed them up.

A senior Communist source (who asked not to be named) told me during an interview in Saigon in August 1975, that Le Duan said the situation now was clear to all. The struggle in South Vietnam had become national in scope, with the North Vietnamese army backing up the Communist political infrastructure in South Vietnam. Military, political, and diplomatic conditions were ripe. U.S. forces had pulled out of the south and were not returning. Meanwhile, North Vietnamese forces were in South Vietnam in strength.

Le Duan stated that in the southern countryside the military situation was under control. In the cities, the Communists had secured a stepping stone, where "mass movements" were flourishing. The world supported Hanoi.

The military task, he said, was clear. In the far south, the northern Mekong Delta, and Saigon areas, it was necessary to create interlocking zones of Communist control, so that easy movement of troops could be accomplished. The main force army of North Vietnam would have to bring military pressure closer to Saigon than at present, a task made easier with the capture of Phuoc Long. In the Mekong Delta, the pressure point should be My Tho, a provincial capital only 35 miles south of Saigon. The southern delta was unimportant.

As for the immediate future, the Communist source quoted Le Duan as saying, "We have agreed that this year the attack on the Central Highlands will begin." He gestured behind him to a huge wall map of Vietnam. Attacks must be launched at Ban Me Thuot (pointing to the town on the map) and Tuy Hoa (gesturing from the west to the coastal province capital 250 miles north of Saigon to indicate the direction of attack). Forces from the central area would have to form a "liberated" zone in and north of Binh Dinh province above Tuy Hoa. Further north, there must be another "liberated" zone between Hue and Da Nang to provide freedom of movement for a future attack on those two important cities. If this much could be accomplished successfully, he said, an important change in the balance of forces would occur.

Victory, declared the North Vietnamese leader, would take two years. In the first year, 1975, the battles would be in the countryside. The North Vietnamese Army would establish bases close to the cities. Large surprise attacks would be launched in 1975, creating conditions for the general offensive and uprising—total victory—in 1976. By then, the Saigon troops would be so weak and demoralized that the Communists could easily win the war.

He added a proviso. Le Duan said the Politburo had drafted in the 1975 plan a contingency, an extremely important guideline of action, as he called it. If opportunities presented themselves early or late in 1975 (in midyear, the rains halted major warfare), South Vietnam would be liberated in that year.

The next day, the Communist military committee went back into session, with General Dung as chairman and senior commanders from the north and south on hand. Just after the meeting began, Le Duc Tho walked in the door unannounced. The Number 6 man in the Politburo and Henry Kissinger's antagonist at the Paris peace talks was carrying a message from

Le Duan and others. They were unsatisfied with the planning for the Ban Me Thuot attack.

Tho claimed the planning was inadequate. It would be absurd, he said, if with almost five full divisions in the Central Highlands near Ban Me Thuot, an attack should fail. Better written plans were desired. Tho then walked out.

General Giap took charge. With the political wind at the moment blowing away from the military, Giap gave a blistering lecture to the generals and colonels, speaking now as Defense Minister and politician. The planning *was* inadequate, he said. The legendary general, called the white-topped volcano because of his periodic outbursts of vitriol at incompetent staff members, laid out the principles of battle for those present. They were force, secrecy, and surprise.

Giap said it was necessary to deceive the enemy into thinking the attack would come to the north of Ban Me Thuot. Penetration agents (such as Sergeant Le Er Tang) could help fool Saigon forces, he said. For the first time, then, the spring offensive in the highlands was given a code name: Campaign 275. Staffers updated, combined, and rewrote the plans for the Ban Me Thuot attack until Giap and the political bureau members were satisfied.

The commanders of the southern fronts drifted back to South Vietnam to prepare for the 1975 battles. They carried with them detailed plans and objectives, and in their heads had the warning of Le Duan firmly in mind: just maybe, 1975 could be the year of victory.

General Dung went to southern North Vietnam for talks and pep talks with troops bivouacked there and preparing now to move south. At the First Army Corps headquarters at Ninh Binh he spoke with the troops, comparing them to musicians ready to play when the conductor—the Central Military Party Committee and the high command—raised the baton. "We can do it. We can do it. Determined to win. Determined to win," the troops shouted back at him in unison.

He talked to the troops of the 316th Division at Tan Ky, near Ho Chi Minh's birthplace in southern North Vietnam. After serious talks with the commander, Dung read a poem to the troops. He had forgotten the author, he said, but the poem was this:

> *In our country after 30 years of bearing arms,*
> *Beckoning are battlefields, opportunities, and duty.*
> *Now is the time for us to set out together with the people of the entire country*
> *To restore our moon to its full glory.*

The cynical figured Dung himself probably had written the poem, but no matter. It was unsubtle enough to encourage another round of "Determined to win. Determined to win."

Dung told the division in his pep talk that a tougher, more stubborn, cunning, and experienced enemy would face the 316th than ever before. But the ARVN, he said, was an enemy without a just cause, suffering from defeatism, beset by many difficulties. Dung got tough, too. He would accept no justification for defeat of the 316th.

And a final, important decision. Dung was ordered by the Party to head a committee of Communist Party and Central Highlands generals of the military. Hanoi was taking full control of the 1975–76 offensive. There were to be no slip-ups. More important, there was to be no loss of control by North Vietnam.

THE BATTLE BEGINS

General Van Tien Dung, who was close enough to hear the sounds of the battle, alertly listened to every report flowing to his jungle headquarters on March 10. Spread on his wooden table top were the written reports that made Dung both happy and concerned. There was no hint of either emotion on his face.

His plan was in motion. He had issued the orders and committed his men, and there was little he could do now but monitor the reports. Once these reports had been neatly stacked according to source, but now they were spread across his desk as the general went through them again. They came from near—around and inside Ban Me Thuot—and far—Hanoi—and included little-delayed news written by the foreign news agencies in Saigon and illegally monitored in Hanoi. Reports from his own staffers were perhaps a shade more optimistic than those from the foreigners, but that was to be expected, since the news agencies were based in Saigon and mostly dependent on the word of officials in the Saigon administration and the American Embassy.

This battle obviously was to be Dung's stepping stone, and the favor seekers on his staff showed more deference than usual toward the general, knowing that his success could also be theirs. His failure, if such it was to be, could later be explained away in their favor.

As General Giap was at Dien Bien Phu, so Dung now was at Ban Me Thuot. The normally secretive North Vietnamese had been more secretive than usual in arranging Dung's trip to South Vietnam. Among steps taken to guard knowledge of his absence from Hanoi was a double left behind to drive to and from the Defense Ministry daily in Dung's car and in Dung's uniform. From southern North Vietnam, Dung had driven south along the new Ho Chi Minh trail, reaching the Ban Me Thuot area in mid-February to plan the attack.

Two events had bothered Dung much during the three weeks he had been at his jungle headquarters, although in retrospect one was amusing and the other insignificant. At the time, they had both been highly unsettling.

First, a herd of wild elephants had stampeded near the headquarters, killing and injuring a number of soldiers—an unimportant detail—but more to the point, knocking down almost all of his communications wire. The network of wires was his link to Hanoi and to his major commands. Only what Dung considered a magnificent job by his Communications Corps—although he had only grunted approval of the job—had restored the telephone network in time to avoid disaster.

Then, on March 8, an officer-messenger with full knowledge of Communist troop dispositions around Ban Me Thuot and plans for the attack had been captured by Saigon troops in a stroke of bad luck.

Dung's original idea had been to attack in the latter half of March. But the capture of the man dictated his decision to launch the battle as soon as possible—less than 48 hours after the man had been captured. Dung trusted the officer to hold his knowledge as long as possible, but he also knew that with drugs and torture and help from the American CIA there was no doubt the ARVN would soon have the officer's secrets.

So Dung ordered the battle joined immediately, and now on March 10 he was without sleep for 24 hours, and watching the incoming reports closely.

Foreign news agencies and agent reports were remarkably similar as to facts: Dung's forces had driven into Ban Me Thuot early that morning. They had seized much of the city and about half its military defense posts, including both airports. ARVN was fighting back. And the Saigon command indicated that it was organizing a counterattack, drawing reinforcements as quickly as possible from other highland areas.

Agents and messengers brought similar reports from Dung's lines. Dung had stressed honesty in reporting, to avoid the overoptimistic and face-losing statements of the past. As a result, the reports on Dung's desk in the jungle tonight said primary objectives within Ban Me Thuot had been achieved, and the battle was proceeding as closely to the original plan as possible. But they also stated that resistance from the South Vietnamese soldiers remained heavy. Much fighting would be necessary before the town could be claimed.

The general was satisfied. He had not expected to overrun the important highlands city 150 miles north of Saigon in a matter of hours, even with the careful planning, the tricks, and numerical superiority. His beloved 320th Division, which he himself had formed in the Red River Delta of North Vietnam in 1950, was the main attacking force. Dung's reputation, if not exactly at stake, would be greatly enhanced by victory at Ban Me Thuot.

He himself had planned, and over the objections of some of the North Vietnamese leaders had pushed through, the idea of an offensive for the spring of 1975. He had told a meeting of senior military and political leaders three months before:

> The Saigon administration and American imperialists are trying to sweep us away from the liberated areas of the South with nibbling attacks. We are going to have to take the offensive if we are going to keep from losing large amounts of our territory over the next year.

It had been a tough battle, that meeting and others in succeeding days. But Dung, with heavy backing from most of the military and a substantial part of the civilian leadership, had pushed through his plan for offensives in areas where the Saigon army was considered vulnerable. After the December–January test of new tactics and simultaneous probing of the Saigon-Washington political fiber, the first major attack was to be at Ban Me Thuot. Others would follow. If the attack on Ban Me Thuot failed, Dung's idea of heavy military attacks would be criticized by his contemporaries at future meetings of the military and political councils of North Vietnam. So Dung had planned well. The course of battle proved it.

President Nguyen Van Thieu followed the progress of the battle for Ban Me Thuot from his office in Independence Palace, a cracker box on massive grounds two blocks from the U.S. Embassy in Saigon. The palace was built in the early 1960's with U.S. money by former President Ngo Dinh Diem, who did not live to see it finished.

Near the top of Thieu's "Hold" basket was a plan that had been submitted in January by contingency planners in his Joint General Staff. In essence, it called for retreats over much of the nation so that the million-man army of South Vietnam would be able to protect the populated areas.

The plan called for a full retreat from most of the Central Highlands, which run from Ban Me Thuot north through the western part of Vietnam. The colonels who wrote the plan and the generals who approved it said the rugged terrain could not be defended against any massive Communist troop build-ups. And such build-ups were obviously under way in early 1975.

Therefore, the planners said, it might well be necessary to retreat from the lightly populated areas. If the retreat were handled well and kept a secret for the few days necessary to move the troops and city-dwelling Vietnamese civilians, forces could be moved to block Communist advances into the more important coastal lowlands.

When the plan was first presented in January, Thieu considered it seriously. He shelved it because it was his unswerving stand that he could not retreat from an inch of territory held by his forces. But it made so much sense that he did not reject the plan outright. He kept it at hand for what it was—a contingency plan. The problem was that when the contingency finally arose, Thieu was no longer able to institute the plan as written.

Thieu was able to "observe" the Ban Me Thuot events, thanks to the relatively sophisticated communications that had been installed in Independence Palace. Colonel Edward Lansdale, the Defense Department-Air Force-CIA-State Department man who got along so well with former President Diem, had the gear installed following an abortive anti-Diem coup in 1955. It paralleled, but was not dependent upon, the military Vietnamese communications system. Diem, during the coup, had been temporarily unable to call for help from friendly officers because the coup leader had cut off his telephones. Over the years, the communications system was refined, improved and when necessary rebuilt after coups.

(Lansdale, an advocate of unorthodox and unremitting tactics against the Asian Communists, came to Vietnam in 1955 after a term as adviser to Philippines President Ramon Magsaysay. According to the Pentagon Papers, he and his team gleefully launched black propaganda attacks against the Communist Vietnamese in Hanoi during the post-Geneva one-year period when soldiers and civilians were moving to the zones of their choice. He put sugar in the tanks of the Hanoi buses, for example, to cut down available public transport.

(His unorthodox style amused most, impressed many, and infuriated the American regular military and bureaucrats. Lansdale was an advocate of constant special warfare and "dirty tricks." According to friends and supporters, the American "establishment" forced him out of Saigon in the late 1950's. He had another tour of Vietnam under President Kennedy, himself impressed by Green Berets and other special warfare tactics to counter guerrillas, and reported to the President that in effect the war was being lost by the Big Army concept of fighting the Communists. After the death of Kennedy and as the U.S. military took control of the conduct of the Vietnam war, Lansdale again was moved out of Vietnam. He had become, by then, a general, and retired with two stars.

(During the mid-1950's, he had singular—although not complete —influence over Diem. His contacts were such that he could impress the

Vietnamese President with "gifts" such as the special communications setup.)

Until Ban Me Thuot fell, Thieu was able to talk directly to his field officers. and while his propagandists were putting out the word that the Communists were being beaten back by fierce counterattacks, Thieu knew differently.

The President was in a difficult position. He looked over the battle maps in his office in the right wing of his palace, and didn't like what he saw. And he didn't even know the maps lied. They lied because his intelligence forces were uninformed and misinformed, and had been infiltrated by Sergeant Tang and other Viet Cong. In addition to the array of Communist soldiers around doomed Ban Me Thuot, Thieu's maps and others like them in Saigon showed between two and three divisions—an estimated 20,000 to 25,000 men—poised around Pleiku and Kontum, 100 miles north of Ban Me Thuot.

What Thieu didn't know, and what would therefore make his next move perhaps the single most crucial in the loss of his nation, was that those Communist troops were not really where the maps showed them to be. The soldiers thought to be around Pleiku were actually fighting, or poised to attack, to the south at Ban Me Thuot.

Giap and Dung had lured the bulk of the pro-Saigon highlands defenders into Pleiku and Kontum with a feint at those two towns, while moving most of their combat troops south to Ban Me Thuot. The ARVN, Thieu, and the Americans all fell for the ruse. The maps produced by Sergeant Tang aided the ploy. South Vietnam and the United States underestimated Communist strength around Ban Me Thuot, failing not only to reinforce that town but actually moving troops out of it to the north. They overestimated Communist strength around Pleiku and Kontum and moved their troops into those two towns. But, Thieu thought now, even those Saigon troops to the north were outnumbered.

A main reason for the breakdown in the intelligence system was that the Saigon army had all but abandoned intelligence-gathering missions. The centuries-old tactic of scouting the enemy had largely gone by the boards. Dependence on helicopters, for one thing, had doomed many behind-the-lines missions when fuel prices grounded the choppers. And the Vietnamese army had never had enough long-range patrols anyway. With the American scouts gone in the early 1970's, the Saigon army failed to fill this vital gap.

At about the time the red-and-blue, gold-starred Viet Cong flags were being raised over important sections of Ban Me Thuot on March 12, Thieu was making his fateful decision. So far as is known, he did not discuss it with anyone. He certainly did not talk it over with any Americans.

U.S. Ambassador Graham Martin was not in Saigon. He was on the tail end of a long, long vacation, his second in six months, and was at home in North Carolina when Thieu might have wanted to talk to him. The Vietnamese President trusted no other American in Vietnam (he did not trust Martin much, either, aides said later, but he did let him in on most—if not all—of his future planning). So when Thieu needed an American shoulder to lean on, Washington's representative was not around.

To the north, the battle for Ban Me Thuot was going well, in the opinion of General Van Tien Dung. That was obvious, even from the most pessimistic reports on his desk. And he had all available information. His field officers might not know that United Press International was reporting the formation of a large task force to go to the rescue of the embattled defenders of Ban Me Thuot, but Dung did. He did not wish to be shielded from any news, good or bad. And he was not.

Paul Struharik awakened at 3 A.M. on March 10 in Ban Me Thuot, to the sounds of a rather intense barrage of incoming artillery. It tapered off within a couple of hours and he went back to bed at five. At six, he was up again. He was not to sleep in a bed again for almost eight months.

Struharik held a number of job titles at Ban Me Thuot. He was the only "official" American in town. A Foreign Service Officer of the U.S. government, the 34-year-old Ohio native officially was "Area Development Officer" in Darlac province. In the telephone book he was simply the American provincial representative.

He worked under Colonel George Jacobsen, one of the shrewdest observers and analysts of the Vietnam war. Jacobsen became known as the "Lansdale of the 60's and 70's."

Other than the French plantation managers outside town, there were 12 foreigners in Ban Me Thuot as the attack began. All were to become prisoners of war. They gathered at Struharik's midtown house—with the exception of Canadian missionaries Norm and Joan Johnston, who were trapped in a village on the outskirts and taken prisoner only hours after the fighting began and the Communists advanced into Ban Me Thuot.

The foreigners also included American missionaries John and Carolyn Miller and their blonde 5-year-old daughter, LuAnne. The Millers had been in Vietnam for about 15 years, were married there and raised their children in the war zone. Three other Miller children were at school in Nha Trang, and did not see their parents again until their release as POW's from Hanoi October 30, eight months after the battle for Ban Me Thuot. The Millers were translating the Bible into Montagnard dialects. Their manuscripts were not returned to them when they were freed and allowed to return to their parent organization, the Summer Institute of Linguistics.

Richard and Lillian Phillips and Betty Mitchell also were missionaries and American. Like the Johnstons, they worked for the Christian and Missionary Alliance, a basically fundamentalist and nondenominational Protestant group based at Nyack, New York. Mrs. Mitchell, the most strictly religious of all the missionaries, had lost her husband Archie to the Viet Cong in 1962. She had watched, helpless, as he was led away during an attack on Ban Me Thuot. U.S. officials still listed Archie Mitchell as a prisoner of war, although there appears little doubt that he died or was killed. Betty Mitchell had remained at Ban Me Thuot to do God's work, until this new attack.

Enrique Tolentino, Ike to his friends, also was there. A Filipino who once had fairly clear ties to the CIA, he had been recruited to Vietnam by Operation Brotherhood, Colonel Lansdale's front of the mid-50's. A slight man who wore wire-rimmed glasses and spoke good Vietnamese, Tolentino had worked in rural development programs for years. He taught villagers to dig wells and shoot guns so that regular troops—in theory —would be freed to quit the villages and meet the enemy at the battlefront.

Two "tourists" had also made it to Struharik's home, American Jay Scarborough and Australian Peter Whitlock.

Jay Scarborough was a 29-year-old Ford Foundation scholar whom many of his friends called a professional student. He had an extensive background in Vietnam and a full command of the nation's difficult language. Scarborough was in Vietnam for the spring term, photographing Cham manuscripts in and around the coastal city of Phan Rang. He said it was something he owed the Cham people, whom he knew from the time he had worked for the International Voluntary Services organization for four years. He "knew something was going to happen in Vietnam soon," and wanted part of the Cham culture preserved. He had lost his bulk film holder, and rather than wait around Saigon until a new one was air freighted in, he decided to visit some friends at Ban Me Thuot. He arrived by bus at dusk on Sunday, March 9, eight hours before the first shots of the battle.

Scarborough did not want to be with the American adviser to the province, but rather with the International Commission for Control and Supervision (ICCS), the so-called peacekeeping outfit. An Indonesian and an Iranian were stationed in Ban Me Thuot, were later captured, and were released just before the end of the war. The Communist delegations from Hungary and Poland had long since cleared out, having no wish to observe a war that killed innocent peacekeepers from time to time. Scarborough's guide had no idea where the ICCS compound was, so he wound up with Struharik and the others.

Peter Whitlock was the other "tourist" member of the "Ban Me Thuot 12." He was government adviser to a radio station at Chiang Mai, Thailand, which broadcast to hills tribesmen. For several months, he had been seeking permission from authorities at the Australian Broadcasting Corporation to visit the Aussie-built station at Ban Me Thuot, which did similar work. He arrived six days before the battle, with Struharik's name from an American acquaintance in Chiang Mai. He and Struharik teamed up, drinking, eating, and even doing some work together.

Struharik's concrete home was near the center of the city of 70,000. Historically, Ban Me Thuot was largely a memory, with little to recommend it now except that it was the strategic key to the southern highlands. In the past, American President Theodore Roosevelt had hunted tiger from the hunting lodge here. Bao Dai had used the same lodge as Vietnam's last Emperor. The lodge survived the war, but not natural hazards. While U.S. forces were using it as a regional headquarters in 1969, the fine old wooden building burned to the ground.

The fighting was close to Struharik's home, very close. There was no question of the foreigners' resisting any Communist attempt to break into the home. What they hoped for now was that the battle would end quickly, so they could emerge and present themselves to the Vietnamese. Struharik and Whitlock, with some support from Scarborough, considered and rejected an escape on foot. The missionaries made it clear that they would put themselves in the hands of God and, eventually, the North Vietnamese.

A one-year-old Vietnamese child presented the immediate threat, because silence was the thing most valued. Noise would attract nervous and combat-ready Communist soldiers. Little LuAnne Miller was behaving beautifully, as was another Vietnamese child, four years old. The pith helmets of the North Vietnamese soldiers bobbed by the windows of Struharik's home at intervals, and silence was mandatory. The one-year-old was taken into an inner bedroom, and the door was locked.

Toilets were flushed only when South Vietnamese planes swooped low over the town to bomb, to hide that giveaway sound. It was a rough 52 hours for the inhabitants of the house. They could hear too well the sounds of rifles, machine guns, and other instruments of war in the street outside their living room window.

Struharik had a single PRC25 military radio for communication. He thought Communist forces would be closely monitoring American frequencies and basically did not want to talk at all on the radio. But it was necessary to report. Every 60 minutes, Struharik came on the air for 30 seconds, giving snatches of information to an orbiting U.S. aircraft of Air America. He reported who was with him and what the situation was. He had nether the time nor the inclination to be an adviser, to tell of troop dispositions, or to give other information that might aid in the battle for the town.

Wolfgang Lehmann worked late at his Saigon desk the night of March 10. His obvious big problem was Struharik. Lehmann, filling in during the lengthy absence of vacationing Ambassador Martin, was well aware of the problem a captured American official could create for the United States. America was supposedly out of the Vietnam war and Hanoi could make tremendous political hay out of another American POW. Frantic messages from the State Department and the White House informed Lehmann, as if he did not know, that no effort was to be spared in extricating Struharik from Ban Me Thuot. On the other hand, Lehmann was told, no other American lives were to be put on the line to get him out. It was a touchy problem, obviously insoluble, but Lehmann wrestled with it.

Lehmann wished that Martin were in Saigon to make the decision himself. He knew if Struharik were left in Ban Me Thuot—and it was clear he probably would be—Martin would be upset over his actions no matter what he did. Lehmann had no idea when Martin might return to Vietnam. Martin had stayed out of touch with the Embassy, as he had done the previous summer during another lengthy absence from his post in Saigon. No one was even sure where Martin went on his sojourns from South Vietnam, except that he made visits to his farm in Italy, purchased when he was Ambassador there, and to his home in North Carolina.

Lehmann looked over the reports and notes he himself had made at an Embassy staff meeting earlier that day. With almost no combat troops in Vietnam save for the U.S. Embassy guards, the hope of getting Struharik out of Ban Me Thuot by military means depended on the South Vietnamese. There would be no chance of Saigon's diverting a single soldier from the battle to help the Americans out of the provincial capital.

The only legitimate hope, his staff had told him, was for a helicopter of Air America—the CIA airline "chartered" in Vietnam by the U.S. Embassy—to drop into Struharik's area and snatch him and other foreigners. One helicopter had tried exactly that during the afternoon, but heavy antiaircraft fire and reports of shoulder-fired surface-to-air missiles had turned the UH1 chopper back to Nha Trang headquarters.

So Lehmann was helpless. He was confronted with the inevitability of losing an American prisoner of war. In the face of the heavy attack and the fact that his staff told him Ban Me Thuot would fall to the Communists, at least temporarily, Lehmann just stared at his desk.

News media based in Saigon knew immediately that there were Americans in Ban Me Thuot. Embassy Press Officer John Hogan had received conflicting reports on how many there were and had at one point identified the Johnstons as Americans rather than Canadians. Paul Struharik, the provincial representative, was trapped in the town. Hogan told newsmen that Struharik was in radio contact with Nha Trang headquarters. He did not say, but newsmen quickly learned, that the radio contact was maintained through a circling Air America Porter aircraft. Newsmen also learned of the abortive helicopter attempt to pick up Struharik during the first afternoon of the Ban Me Thuot battle. But on request from Hogan, they did not publish this piece of news.

The reason for the request, a valid one, was that Struharik's immediate freedom, and perhaps his life, depended on a helicopter rescue. Printing information about the failure would perhaps endanger the man more, because it is possible the Communists would commit forces to ambush the helicopter, Struharik, or both. So newsmen, while reporting the possibility of another POW in Vietnam, withheld for a while the details of the planned rescue mission.

It is not known whether the station chief of the Central Intelligence Agency in Saigon was having self-doubts that evening. Vietnam was known commonly as an "open station," in that anyone really wishing to know the name of the CIA representative, and able to crack the exceedingly simple code of the telephone book could know his name was Thomas Polgar.

Polgar, a European Communist specialist who became Mexico City station chief after the Vietnam War ended, had in his desk and safe in the U.S. Embassy numerous reports predicting stiuations exactly like the one that was taking place in Ban Me Thuot, and worse. One said the highlands must be written off quickly in case of any determined Communist drive.

The reports had come from Agency representatives and agents in the field during the preceding two months. They were uniformly pessimistic and uniformly ignored. When the reports on the serious situation first began coming in, the station chief had tried to transmit them to Washington. Going through Embassy channels, the reports had been stopped by Martin. It was the Ambassador's belief that negative reports should be played down, balanced by positive ones, or simply and preferably not sent. Most of the CIA field reports were not sent out of Saigon.

Among the station chief's subordinates in the field in Vietnam there was deep resentment. A month later, these men would begin taking their case directly to the American public through newsmen in Saigon. But for now they avoided any contact with the American public for whom they worked. They sat and fumed, wondering what, if anything, Polgar would do to get their reports to Washington.

In his own way, Embassy aides said, the station chief was a happy man in Saigon and had no desire to go to the wall with Martin. He felt he performed well, served his country effectively, and probably was in line to rise in the Agency. He had a good social life, his wife being a regular art exhibitor at the miniculture Saigon served up.

And he was not all that positive, Embassy officials said, that his young agents, however dedicated, really knew what was happening. Their reports often contradicted rosy position papers from other U.S. agencies, and there was legitimate room for doubt. Of all people, Polgar should have known better. As a former field agent himself, he well knew that the CIA—more covert than the other agencies and therefore less interested in showing progress than in telling the truth—was consistently the most reliable source of Vietnam information.

The station chief had other things to occupy him, as well. He directed some energy against the Communist members of the International Commission of Control and Supervision. Since the four-nation peacekeeping force had come into being with the January 27, 1973, Paris peace accords, he had been deeply involved in arranging for defections of three members of the Polish and Hungarian delegations.

Polgar played his cold war games with the Poles and Hungarians assigned to Saigon. He was himself a native Hungarian, and delighted in speaking Hungarian when briefing the Communists. "If any of you do not understand my English, I will translate my words into Hungarian," an aide quoted him as saying at several such briefings. And he imported at least one banned Hungarian pre-1956 movie to show the delegation from Budapest.

He arranged for the defections to the West of two Hungarians and one Pole who resettled, at least temporarily, in Australia and New Zealand, and it is possible this was his main assignment to Vietnam. If it was, the station chief performed well. But U.S. intelligence on the Vietnam situation, criticized for years by many Americans, suffered as a result of the attentions this CIA man in Saigon gave to what essentially were side matters to the war.

At least three field agents and one CIA man from the Embassy felt strongly enough about what they felt was Polgar's inattention to the matter at hand that they took the unusual step of seeking out newsmen in April 1975, and criticizing their boss.

One of these men showed a reporter a copy of a report he said he had cabled to Polgar before the assault on Ban Me Thuot. The cable not only predicted the attack, but said there appeared to be no alternative to total Communist victory in the Central Highlands. It warned of a huge Communist build-up and said South Vietnamese government forces would be unable to deal with the build-up because they were spread too thin in the area. The informant claimed that neither his report nor even a summary of it was allowed to be sent to officials above the Saigon Embassy, except for the section dealing with the build-up. This was leaked to most Saigon-based newsmen as proof of the lack of good will on the part of the Communists in the American search for peace in Vietnam.

Major Nguyen Van Sau* of the People's Army of Vietnam—the North Vietnamese army—was elated on the evening of March 10. Sau's battalion was the spearhead of the main attack by the North Vietnamese army into Ban Me Thuot and so far as Sau was concerned, he had done his job perfectly. The 420 men who took their orders from him had fought their way into town and were almost all in place around the airfield known as L-19 inside the northern part of Ban Me Thuot, and in other key positions around this provincial capital.

Sau was interested, for now, only in what his men were doing. He looked at the notebook in his hand, crammed with figures, maps, and notations. The latest report indicated he had three men killed and five wounded too badly to fight. The medical corpsman had removed three of the wounded and the other two probably would be carried out on stretchers shortly.

Sau called over the commander of the elite combat engineer platoon which had been attached to his battalion for this attack. The man was a senior sergeant and respectful of Sau's rank and position. But the sapper still managed to swagger slightly as he reported to the battalion commanders. Sau remembered stories about the expertise and bravery, sometimes suicidal, of the sappers, and allowed the tiny bit of disrespect the swagger indicated.

Fighting was tapering off slightly, although heavy fire was still coming from a company or so of Saigon soldiers on the southwest side of the airfield perimeter. Just before dark Sau had dispatched one of his companies to that area and a fire fight was now building as his forces attacked. But elsewhere around the airfield, things were quieting. The crump of mortars still could be heard. From his command position not far from the center of the airfield, Sau knew that the planes would come soon, more than likely the Magic Dragons that spat 6,000 bullets per minute on his forces. Sau was not particularly afraid of them, but he had to make preparations. First, he wanted the ammunition dump blown up. That was his immediate objective, and he snapped out an order to the sergeant to head down to the south side of the airfield and dispose of the 75 tons of mortar, machinegun, and rifle ammunition as soon as possible. After that, Sau's job was simply to hold his ground as long as possible. There was talk of staying in Ban Me Thuot for a long time, but no one seemed to know exactly what was being planned for this battle.

What was happening was just about what the North Vietnamese leadership had expected. The battle for Ban Me Thuot was going well, thanks to good

---

*This name was given to me during an interview in Saigon with a soldier who said he was in the battalion and spent most of the battle with the major. The facts are consistent with other, official reports from both Communist and non-Communist sources.

planning, good agent penetration, and overwhelming superiority of forces. The Saigon forces were being weakened by the campaign here, just as they had been weakened earlier in the dry season by the Mekong Delta and Phuoc Long attacks.

And Generals Giap and Dung found that with the chips down in the battles before Ban Me Thuot, both Saigon and the United States were to be found lacking in direct retaliation. They wrote later that North Vietnamese tactics "had pushed the enemy into a weak position on all fields, unable to fight back, and had forced them to be on a strategic defensive on all battlegrounds."

Still, no one in Hanoi, in Saigon, or in Washington felt that Communist victory at Ban Me Thuot would be the beginning of the end for the Republic of Vietnam. North Vietnam had overestimated its enemy as much as Saigon and Washington had overestimated their own abilities. Hanoi did not feel that victory was at hand.

For propaganda purposes, Saigon high command spokesman Lieutenant Colonel Le Trung Hien told newsmen on March 11 that the Ban Me Thuot attack was part of a nationwide offensive. But actions and reactions by Saigon forces showed that Hien was only mouthing a slogan.

Within the U.S. Embassy, there was some concern over the events at Ban Me Thuot, but certainly no panic. The most astute observer in that big white building was probably retired Army Colonel George Jacobsen. This most realistic—and therefore pessimistic—of seasoned observers certainly was not moved to a tremendous amount of concern. Even nine days *after* Ban Me Thuot had fallen, Jacobsen was able to assess the situation calmly as he saw it.

He said the attacks were the biggest since 1972, but had yet to approach the ferocity of the seriousness of the Easter offensive of that year. He felt the Communist drive was aimed merely at creating political and military hardships, with the aim of forcing the collapse of the Thieu government. There was no way, he said, that the Saigon government could be defeated until the last soldier was killed. The flight of refugees, in a way, backed him up, Jacobsen insisted. The movement toward Saigon and away from the Communists was a form of voting—with the feet—which would bring about a massive fight for survival by the anti-Communists, should the North Vietnamese threaten victory.

In fact, there were very few people who really thought the Communists had a chance to win a military victory in the Vietnam war. A few of the war correspondents thought so, a much derided minority that seldom went to any lengths to defend their theories. Certainly the only pro-Communist diplomats in South Vietnam, the representatives of the Polish and Hungarian international peacekeeping teams, all of them intelligence officers, did not feel Hanoi had the military punch for a victory. Polish reports to

Warsaw said Saigon troops had enough strength to win the war, but lacked
the high command leadership necessary, and were restricted by political
inhibitions against an attack into North Vietnam. The Hungarians felt the
two military forces were evenly matched and saw little hope of a military
breakthrough.

Among the best-informed military intelligence reports being filed out of
Vietnam in late 1974, later events indicated, were those coming from the
two-man military attaché office of the Australian embassy. From their
seventh-floor cubbyholes in the Caravelle Hotel, Army Lieutenant Colonel
Ray Bernard and Air Force Group Captain Bill Connaughton were sending back to Canberra perhaps the most perceptive cables coming from
Vietnam. Their pessimism was matched only by that of the young field
operatives of the American intelligence community, whose reports might
as well have been filed to the moon, since Washington officials seldom saw
them.

The two Aussies were reporting in late 1974 that it was almost certain
that South Vietnam would lose all of the Central Highlands and all of the
northern quarter, known as I Corps, or first military region. At lunch one
day, after several drinks, they told a newsman it was unlikely even the city of
Da Nang could hold against any determined North Vietnamese military
push. It was the first time the reporter had heard anyone predict such a
thing, and it shook him. There were few heretics among the establishment
in Saigon in late 1974. The line was that the Saigon army could hold any
major strongpoint indefinitely. The two Australians were the first to believe they could not hold even the country's second city.

General Dung did most of the planning for the offensive, partly because
Giap continued to be unwell (reportedly with blood cancer) and partly
because the Ban Me Thuot attack involved Dung's 320th Division, which he
had formed in the Red River Delta during the war against the French.

In handing his subordinate the leadership in planning, Giap had stressed
secrecy. Part of this directive, Dung knew, meant that he was to employ
ruses when possible. The generals ordered large numbers of troops west of
Pleiku City, about 240 miles north of Saigon and nearly 100 miles above
Ban Me Thuot. But most of these forces were not combat troops. They
were rear area soldiers, many of them pulled across the border into
Vietnam from the Laotian frontier area, where they maintained the Ho Chi
Minh Trail supply highway. If nothing else, Giap knew, overflights by U.S.
spy planes would pick up the troop movements around the Northern
Highlands city.

During daylight hours, truck convoys, sometimes with a tank or two
thrown in, moved out of the border regions into the Pleiku-Kontum area.

They were duly spotted and bombed. Naturally enough, there was an intense fear of an attack on Pleiku and Kontum, cities only 30 miles apart. In fact, the troops and supply movements were part of the feint by the North Vietnamese.

In Saigon, Sergeant Tang and men like him did their work with fake maps, fake intelligence, false information.

The ruse worked. As North Vietnam's combat forces moved stealthily toward Ban Me Thuot in force, the Saigon command moved its troops out of Ban Me Thuot to defend against the apparent threat to Pleiku. An entire regiment of the 23rd Infantry Division and many Ranger battalions rushed to the north from Ban Me Thuot. By the time the real target of the offensive became known, it was too late to do anything about it. The Communists had cut the highways into and out of Pleiku and Ban Me Thuot and with much of the Saigon air force grounded by ill-considered gasoline rationing, there was no way to defend Ban Me Thuot when the attack came from the 320th division and other units of the North Vietnamese army.

In early 1974, following the October Middle East war, an oil boycott by the Arabs, and the subsequent rise in fuel costs, Saigon planners and American advisers had to make a hard decision. The result was that about half the South Vietnamese air force was grounded. Jet fighters and bombers were kept in the air, along with other attack planes, but virtually all of the troop-carrying aircraft, including helicopters, were mothballed, along with propeller-driven bombers. The plan was to save fuel by moving troops and supplies by ship and truck. Unfortunately, Ban Me Thuot was not on the seacoast and the North Vietnamese had cut all roads to the town.

There was a limited troop-carrying capability by the Saigon air force in early 1975, by pressing attack helicopters and small cargo planes into service to ferry soldiers. But the aircraft were widely dispersed, and it took bureaucratic measures to have their missions changed. Thus, Saigon had jet bombers on call to support a battle, but a hugely reduced capacity from 1973 to carry reinforcements quickly to a threatened area.

The day before the attack began, March 9, the Saigon forces finally realized what was going on. On that Sunday afternoon, troops and police in and around Ban Me Thuot were placed on full alert. Police and internal security forces took up positions on the tops of buildings and were told to prepare for street fighting. The warning was in time, but there was still nothing anyone could do to stop what had become inevitable victory by the Communists at Ban Me Thuot.

A valid question is why the Americans failed to evacuate Struharik and others from Ban Me Thuot when the city was placed on red alert Sunday. No one would answer that question in Saigon, but apparently there were several reasons. First and foremost, it *was* Sunday, a holiday for Americans in the war zone. The old theory of seven-day work weeks and 12-hour days of General William Westmoreland had gone by the boards. There was no one to handle the immediate decision that needed to be taken, to pull out the potential POW's.

There also was overriding confidence of the Americans in the South Vietnamese Army, thought to be fully capable of defending any large town such as Ban Me Thuot. The warning reports of possible imminent battlefield disasters filed by American field operatives had not, after all, been read by many American officials.

Later, there would be overcompensation in evacuation plans, resulting in panicked Americans fleeing Da Nang, Nha Trang, and finally Saigon. But during this first attack of the offensive, few people were worried. The few duty officers on hand felt no compelling reason for bothering superiors on a Sunday simply because of an alert at Ban Me Thuot.

Nguyen Van Muoi* was not a happy soldier. He had been drafted into the Saigon army from his Mekong Delta home at 19, just over four years earlier. Muoi's name meant "Ten" in Vietnamese, and in addition to not liking the army, Muoi hated the constant punning on his name by fellow troops. His nickname was "Number 10," American GI pidgin for "very bad, the worst."

Muoi did not appreciate the humor after a while, much as an elevator operator gets tired of hearing people comment on life's ups and downs. Muoi had deserted once, and was picked up by military police and reassigned to the 23rd division at Ban Me Thuot as punishment. The 23rd was the resting place for many dissatisfied South Vietnamese G.I.'s, and, as a result, was one of the weakest of the 13 Saigon combat divisions.

Muoi found himself this morning in a foxhole at the outer wall of the office and home of the Province Chief and the most powerful man in Ban Me Thuot. He had heard the fighting drawing closer for 31 hours as he watched from his hole at 10 A.M. on March 11. He kept his head down, but from the sounds and the flames and smoke in the sky, it was obvious the Communists were getting close.

In addition to his M16 rifle, Muoi had a few M72 LAW's (Light Antitank Weapons), hand-held bazooka-type weapons which are fired once and then thrown away. Most South Vietnamese units now had the weapons because of the large number of tanks being used by the North Vietnamese forces since 1972.

*The story of Nguyen Van Muoi was given to me by a member of his family in Saigon, just before he himself was sent to a reeducation center following the end of the war. He said another member of Muoi's platoon had told the story to him. The details are corroborated by both Vietnamese and foreigners who were in Ban Me Thuot during and after the battle.

Muoi did not know, nor did the approximately 12 other soldiers in and around the Province Chief's home, that the man had already fled. He had sought safety in the 23rd Division headquarters about a quarter of a mile west of where Muoi sat in his foxhole. It did not really matter, but Muoi did not know he was protecting an empty building.

A T54 Russian-made tank clanked up the street toward the Province Chief's house. Muoi was surprised by the lack of firing at the tank as it moved up, its top buttoned down, and looking fierce. It was the first enemy tank Muoi had ever seen.

The tank turned at the archway which led to the Province Chief's home. Muoi froze. The tank started to approach the home of the Province Chief. The 100-millimeter gun on its front began to fall from its upraised firing position. And Muoi suddenly realized that it was going to blast the Province Chief's office with point-blank fire. He stood up out of his hole and pulled the string on one of his M72 weapons. The projectile flew out of the tube and hit the tank on the left front tread. The vehicle stopped, as if stunned. Muoi rose again with another LAW. He fired again just as the tank gun belched at the house.

All 12 defenders of the Province Chief's home and all five North Vietnamese in the tank died. The tank itself was still parked in front of the house, its gun aimed at where the front door used to be, when Communist cadre began to direct the residents of Ban Me Thuot in cleanup work two weeks later.

Paul Struharik and the other foreigners in his home heard the tank shot and realized their grimmest moment might be at hand. If they were discovered now, it was possible they would be killed accidentally, in the heat of battle, by tense troops mopping up resistance. But as they waited in Struharik's home, speaking soothingly to one another and particularly to little LuAnne Miller, seconds and then minutes and then hours passed with no other sound of war nearby. The second tensest moments of their lives went by, and they began to breathe more easily again. The tensest moment was approaching.

Struharik reported the developments as well as he could to the orbiting Air America Porter, and thus to the American headquarters at the coastal town of Nha Trang. He did not know exactly what happened, but he was able to report that the war had at least temporarily bypassed him and the other potential POW's. The group did not know until the next day that Communist cadre moving cautiously behind the combat forces had run up the Viet Cong flag.

With the red-and-blue, gold-starred flag flying over the provincial headquarters, the Communists were able to claim victory at Ban Me Thuot.

Meanwhile, the town was being destroyed by fighting and even more by bombing from the South Vietnamese Air Force. Residents estimated later that up to 4,000 civilians of Ban Me Thuot died, most by the intense minigun and rocket fire of the AC47 and AC119 gunships, by the A37 and F5 jets, and by the artillery of both sides. As usual, there was no way to check the claims of civilian casualties.

In an analysis of the offensive written shortly after the capture of Saigon, Generals Giap and Dung summed up the first stage of the battle for Ban Me Thuot this way:

"Our army employed daring and surprise tactics of swiftly moving the forces to get through the defensive line of the outer perimeter of Ban Me Thuot, to launch direct attacks on important targets right in the chief town. We occupied two airfields, destroyed the base area of the armor and artillery units, the provincial military headquarters, the base of the 23rd Division. After nearly two days, we totally occupied Ban Me Thuot."

The battle for the city actually was far from over, and it would take until March 14 before the tide of battle would swing directly to the forces of the People's Army of Vietnam and away from the Saigon troops. The massive strength, superior tactics, and ultimate victory of the North Vietnamese army would take place in the following three days. Fast, proper and well-directed counterattacks against the occupying North Vietnamese forces at Ban Me Thuot might have saved South Vietnam for the Saigon government and army, although the lack of troop-carrying aircraft probably made this impossible, as events would show. In the all-important factor of morale, such action would have been a shot in the arm for both the military and civilians.

Instead, a combination of inept leadership and inferior intelligence gathering by Saigon and excellent generalship by the North Vietnamese army swung the victory to the forces of Hanoi, hastening the shattering of the morale of the Saigon army and the panic of President Nguyen Van Thieu and the American establishment in Vietnam.

Nguyen Van Sau, his battalion, and other spearhead units mopped up the last resistance in the Ban Me Thuot town center. They then attacked to the west and took under siege the headquarters of the 23rd Division, the last major stronghold in the town. Troops inside the headquarters tried twice to break out, but Sau and the other North Vietnamese soldiers held them in siege with heavy shelling and some of the greatest North Vietnamese firepower that the Saigon troops had ever seen. The troops from the headquarters were trying to flee either to the jungles to the northwest or to the northeast, from where the counterattack was to be launched.

In the end, most of them surrendered. But there were heavy casualties on both sides. Nguyen Van Sau left to fight other battles.

The Saigon counterattack consisted of a force that was hastily formed. It was made up mostly of Rangers, but included another regiment of the 23rd Division pulled down from Pleiku in a desperate gamble to save Ban Me Thuot and the situation in general. They were to launch the attack from Phuoc An district town (equivalent to a county seat or English township), 18 miles east of Ban Me Thuot. The North Vietnamese themselves had decided there were only two possible bases for a counterattack—Phuoc An or another county capital at Buon Ho township, about 20 miles northeast of Ban Me Thuot. By March 12, Buon Ho had fallen to the Communists almost without a shot.

The counterattacking troops from both sides met at Phuoc An, and heavy fighting broke out. From the beginning, the North Vietnamese had the Saigon forces outflanked and—as in most of the battles along the Phuoc An perimeter—outnumbered. Saigon warplanes heavily attacked the North Vietnamese, but the soldiers were dug in and the bombs did little effective damage. There were heavy casualties again at Phuoc An, as there were at the 23rd Division base in Ban Me Thuot, but the North Vietnamese contained the attempts at breakout with relative ease.

The cutback in the Saigon press corps had paralleled the withdrawal of American forces. ("Gooks killing gooks doesn't get it as a story," one editor said in 1969.) Like the U.S. military, the foreign press corps had diminished to a relative few by the time North Vietnam's leaders decided it was time to win the war. The majority of newsmen in Vietnam had been Americans. U.S. interest in the war by 1975 was almost nil on a day-to-day basis, and the major newspapers, news agencies, and television networks, stung by inflation and recession, were trying to save money.

Compounding the budget problems and the fact that few people cared about the Vietnam situation was the conflict in Cambodia. Phnom Penh was being staffed mainly out of Saigon by early 1975. When the Khmer Rouge launched their ultimately successful offensive New Year's Eve, three months before the Vietnam offensive, the eyes of the Saigon newsmen inevitably focused on Cambodia.

The Associated Press frequently dispatched one or two of its three American staffers to Phnom Penh. United Press International's two foreign correspondents often traveled to the Cambodian capital to cover events there. The Reuters and Agence France Presse bureaus in Saigon covered only Vietnam, but with only one and two men respectively. Each of the four wire services had only one Vietnamese staff member capable of writing literate and factual dispatches.

There were other newsmen covering Vietnam, but again they tended to focus on Cambodia in early 1975. *The New York Times* was caught unprepared. Its Saigon bureau had fallen from two men to one, and he was busy packing up for an imminent transfer to Moscow. The Washington *Post* and Chicago *Daily News* had pulled their men out. The Los Angeles *Times* man spent much time on other stories. The American Broadcasting Company closed its Saigon bureau in mid-1974 and was trying with varying success to cover Indochina with rotating staffers from its Asian headquarters in Hong Kong. The Columbia Broadcasting System had replaced one correspondent with another, and the replacement was an experienced Vietnam reporter; the National Broadcasting Company's man in Saigon was a part-timer, hired on short contract and not a member of the regular NBC staff.

Of the salaried American correspondents based in Saigon and working for major organizations, only those of the AP and UPI had been in Vietnam long enough to nurture the kind of contacts necessary to push away the smoke screens of bureaucracy, the half-truths, and the lies that frequently made up the official briefings. Some part-time newsmen also had good working relationships with officials.

As it became clear that another major offensive was under way, newsmen based elsewhere began to flow in. The admittedly cynical and self-protective residents put them in two categories, "old hands" and "virgins." The old hands had been in and out of Vietnam for a long time. Denis Warner, who in 1975 worked for both Australian and British newspapers, went back to the Dien Bien Phu days when he launched on his personal Vietnam reminiscences. Many had lived in Vietnam for years, mostly during the days of the American fighting war.

The virgins were involved in a new story. Many worked for major publications, yet came to the suddenly climaxing Vietnam War with no more knowledge than what they remembered from reading newspapers over the previous 10 years. The Australian and British media, in particular, often sent ill-prepared newsmen to cover Vietnam. Seemingly to balance the scales, some of the best and most knowledgeable newsmen also were from these two countries.

The old hands had some sources, but many had not been in Vietnam for years. Charles R. Smith of UPI last saw Vietnam in 1966, and had been writing for many years exclusively of China. He returned to Saigon after the fall of Ban Me Thuot. Malcolm Browne of *The New York Times* won a Pulitzer Prize for his skilled coverage of Vietnam—in 1963. While they still maintained some sources, the war to a large extent was behind these men. They had left Vietnam for other stories. As for the virgins, they had no sources save the information officers of their own embassies.

Lieutenant Colonel Le Trung Hien was a main source for many of these men, particularly those outside the main news agencies. For many, he was the only source.

The affable Hien could and did sit down with old acquaintances, like Paul Vogle of UPI, and admit freely that he knowingly lied on the podium.

But he did not, of course, say this to, for example, the man from the *Times* of London. For *Times* readers, Hien was a main Saigon news source. Hien was fully capable of telling a newsman whom he trusted to keep his name out of the story that a town had fallen, then officially telling the entire press corps three hours later that defenders were valiantly holding out against Communist attacks.

At the fall of Phuoc Long, the first province captured by the Communists, Hien did precisely this. The result was that after most resident newsmen had written the province off, some correspondents informed readers that 3,000 brave defenders of the provincial capital were holding back the advancing North Vietnamese tide. Hien, probably on orders of his boss, three-star General Nguyen Tran Truong, had no compunction about stating such falsehoods.

The news agencies like UPI and AP also had the advantage of manpower. Although highly restricted by some standards, they still were able to field reporters and photographers to many of the hot spots. With efficient staffs of Vietnamese, they were able to use non-English-speaking field reporters. And with contacts gained during the quieter days of the war, they had ready access to many of the decisions once the fighting heated up.

The more harried out-of-town correspondents, who arrived when the story was in full swing and were expected in most instances to match every story the wire services put out, had a tougher lot. The luckier ones were allowed by their editors to write feature stories and analyses, while the wire services supplied the actual news. But those from newspapers whose editors wanted the entire big picture presented by their own correspondents had an impossible task.

Lieutenant Colonel Hien's untruths did not make their job easier. Often, in fact, there were wildly differing versions of the same story abroad, depending on the reporter's sources, background in Vietnam, and gullibility quotient.

And so it was that on March 12 Hien told newsmen at the daily Saigon briefing that the counterattack against the Communists at Ban Me Thuot was going well. That small part of the town in North Vietnamese hands should be recovered by Saigon forces within a day, two at most, said Hien.

The telephone and military lines from Ban Me Thuot to Saigon told another story, for those correspondents who had access to what was humming along them. The battle was going badly, Ban Me Thuot had been lost, and the counterattack was a probable failure. Correspondents, in what became a pattern during the 55-day offensive, were scolded by Hien for inaccurate reporting this day. "No comment" came next for a day or two. Finally, after the world knew the town had fallen, the fact was confirmed by the spokesman.

Newsmen who continued to report the stunning reverses of the Saigon army found themselves worrying about whether their continued pessimistic view—always a day or two ahead of the Saigon command confirmation—would lead to high level criticism and thus expulsion from Vietnam. But none of them held back on the stories and their decision in the end was proved right. No journalist was expelled during the offensive and there was little inaccurate reporting, as compared with the announcements of the high command and the American embassy.

When newsmen learned of the fall of Phuoc An, the would-be counterattacking base, they declared Ban Me Thuot lost and wrote it off as the second provincial capital—the first being Phuoc Long—to fall to the North Vietnamese Army in just over two months. But even now there was little panic in Saigon. While it was becoming obvious to the correspondents and to those responsible for running the war that the Saigon army had lost some of its punch, there was no general feeling of despair. Rather, officials believed the loss of Ban Me Thuot, like the loss of Phuoc Binh, was more an isolated incident that only proved that North Vietnam could win a battle when it outnumbered defenders of a small town. There were few persons stating what in fact was the truth: that the South Vietnamese army was about to fall apart.

Phuoc Long was the test. Ban Me Thuot was the plan. The town fell, to all intents and purposes, on March 12, little more than two days after the first shot. It was the most important stronghold in more than 100 miles in any direction, yet its defenders crumbled under the massive Communist assaults and surrendered, ran, or fought and died. There was little time even for the usual heroics of the Vietnam War.

The South Vietnamese air support, although better than it was to be throughout the rest of the offensive, was ineffective. One of the very first airstrikes knocked out the main communications site in the town, making it almost impossible for would-be defenders to talk to the outside. Coordination of defense and reaction forces thereafter was nonexistent.

The defeat of the reinforcements at Phuoc An and Buon Ho sealed Ban Me Thuot's fate and made its fall only a matter of time. The time was about 52 hours.

North Vietnamese forces controlled Ban Me Thuot by the morning of March 12. There was scattered shooting and a little fighting in the town for the next two days, but it was strictly a mopping-up action. The first battle of the 55-day Ho Chi Minh campaign ended with the surrender of most of its survivors.

The mopping-up involved a house-to-house search, and Paul Struharik and the others in the home of the American adviser saw troops headed for their house. After a quick conference, Struharik and Vietnamese-speaking Jay Scarborough, the Ford Foundation scholar from Harrisburg, Pennsylvania, edged out the front door under a white flag.

North Vietnamese rifles, a half dozen and then a dozen, were trained on the Americans. Scarborough spoke loudly enough to be heard but did not shout. He told the soldiers there were a number of unarmed foreigners in the home, that they had been unable to leave because of the fighting. Scarborough, choosing his words carefully, told the edgy Communist troops that no one inside posed any threat, that all guns had been disposed of.

A Communist officer, probably a captain or a major, appeared quickly and ordered everyone out of the house and up against a nearby wall. Peter Whitlock, the Australian radio station adviser, recalled that the first 30 seconds were the tensest. The group was searched, the women getting no preferential treatment as the North Vietnamese thrust their hands into all possible places in which a weapon could be hidden. The women did not complain, at least partially because the search was impersonal and with none of the smirking and giggling that other, less disciplined soldiers might indulge in.

As minutes passed, the breathing in the group became more regular. Struharik began to realize he would be kept with the missionaries and others, and not singled out for special treatment, at least for now. This is what he had hoped. The others began to feel slightly more confident that they would survive. Experience had proved that if one got past the first few minutes of capture, the chances of survival and release were good.

The foreigners were herded into a camp for POW's of the South Vietnamese army, where they were to spend almost a week in what their captors described as "initial processing." They were kept separate from the Vietnamese (the two Vietnamese children were taken from them) but received equal treatment, including food and water, such as it was.

The food was filling, and kept body and mind alive. The missionaries were now joined by the Canadian couple the Johnstons, who were captured on March 10 just after the battle began. They prayed often. Struharik, Scarborough, and Whitlock occasionally joined them.

Communist forces operating under their new 1975 instructions, gave the foreigners decent treatment for the most part. Struharik and James Lewis, captured a month later at Phan Rang, were eventually singled out and received thorough grillings. They also spent time in solitary confinement. But even for the two American officials, there was no physical torture.

(Lewis was officially a consular officer at Nha Trang, on the central coast. The Communists accused him of being an intelligence agent of the CIA or DIA, but Lewis denies this. The young officer was dispatched to Phan Rang,

165 miles northeast of Saigon on the coast, about the time Nha Trang itself fell, April 1. He was to monitor the building battle for Phan Rang, which was defended by a special task force under a three-star South Vietnamese general. Phan Rang fell in heavy fighting two weeks before the Communists captured Saigon. That battle is detailed in Chapter 11, "Goodbye, American." Lewis and the Saigon general were taken almost immediately to North Vietnam, where they were incarcerated at the Son Tay camp, alongside the Ban Me Thuot captives, although the two groups were kept separate.)

The 1975 rules on treatment of captives and enemies of the Communists grew out of experience and an evolving situation on the war. The massacres of 3,000 persons or more at Hue in 1968 had created stunning propaganda setbacks, and never were explained convincingly to the population of Vietnam. Furthermore, the Viet Cong in mid-1969 had become the Provisional Revolutionary Government, with a Prime Minister and cabinet. Bargaining sessions in Paris began early in 1969, with Viet Cong participation. And the regular army of North Vietnam took over most of the fighting at about the same time, replacing the guerrilla-oriented Viet Cong.

So for reasons of diplomacy and propaganda, terrorism faded in importance and slaughters were virtually halted. Regular soldiers were not authorized to arrest and maltreat foreigners, although they had permission to "detain" foreigners until the cases were settled by higher authorities. The random terrorism of the Viet Cong ended in the late 1960's. This was most noticeable in Saigon, where by 1971 rocket attacks had virtually ended. Even selective terrorism was reported infrequently after 1970, and when it was reported the reason for its use (for example to kill a corrupt policeman in a village) was always obvious.

In short, North Vietnam and its Viet Cong by 1975 wanted to show that they were civilized and able to take over the governing of a nation of the world community. They never cared, in the main, whether any of the captured foreigners *liked* them. But they demanded—and occasionally commanded—respect from the Americans and others. In trying to be representative of something more than a terrorist group, the North Vietnamese and Viet Cong now had become basically fair to their captives.

"FATAL MISTAKE"

There is no indication that Martin, the absent Ambassador, would have or could have dissuaded President Thieu from taking the disastrous step he was contemplating on March 12. The day Thieu took the move, Americans praised the strategy ("It's the only possible option," said one military man), thus showing an abysmal lack of knowledge of the thinking of the Vietnamese soldiers they were advising. Another reason for the President's decision was offered by Thieu's senior military aide, Lieutenant General Dang Van Quang. Quang, according to an NBC correspondent's charge in 1971, was the nation's largest drug dealer and a front man for Thieu in other matters of corruption. Quang claimed the Viet Cong had got word to the Presidential Palace to clear out of the Central Highlands or see the cities there leveled, with resulting appalling loss of civilian life. The story was entirely self-serving.

By March 15, Thieu's decision to abandon the highlands had been made. On that Saturday morning, the President boarded his personal DC6 and told the pilot to head for Cam Ranh Bay. He chose Cam Ranh for his showdown with military commanders because the generals would be unable to gang up on him there. The base was little used, and was home base for none of the Saigon military commanders. There would be no "home court advantage" for the generals in the argumentative session Thieu was sure would come.

Thieu was not wrong. The generals met him near the twin airstrips that undulate across two miles of Cam Ranh's sand. Within minutes of his arrival, Thieu had given the order to evacuate Pleiku and Kontum and the surrounding area.

Major General Pham Van Phu was near apoplexy. One of the army's best generals, the II Corps (and thus, highlands) Commander was morally unable to accept a retreat before battle had been joined. He was not overly surprised by Thieu's order to pull out; he had heard rumors of such an order even before Thieu called the meeting. But he acted surprised.

Reports from participants in the meeting said Phu appeared shocked at Thieu's instructions to abandon the mountains and retrench along the central coastline around Nha Trang. He asked Thieu if perhaps he wasn't joking. How could they retreat before an attack? Phu said he wasn't even sure of the Communist strength around Pleiku, because it appeared now that they had siphoned off many of their troops for the Ban Me Thuot battle. For what it was worth, Phu thus became the first general to suspect the feint at Pleiku and Kontum had been the move that had won Ban Me Thuot for the North Vietnamese.

Phu next became angry, when Thieu insisted he meant what he said about retreating. The President listened because Phu was a combat commander with one of the few genuine battle records among Vietnamese generals. It was Thieu who had promoted Phu from deputy division commander to lead the 1st Infantry Division and then to take charge of II Corps. Phu, in his anger, told Thieu the morale of every Vietnamese soldier, most notably those in the central area of the country under his command, would plummet if retreat were ordered. It was the second time in an hour that he was right.

But Thieu stood fast. He maintained that standing and fighting would only waste the men who would die in the highlands. Those men, the president said, could be better employed defending the more strategic —and more densely populated—coastal strip.

After 90 minutes, Thieu repeated his order to pull out of the highlands. He faced Phu directly and told the tuberculosis-weakened general he had two choices: carry out the order, or be replaced and jailed, and have the order carried out by someone else. Phu accepted the order. Thieu turned on his heel, boarded his DC6 and flew back to Saigon. Phu took a helicopter 25 miles north to his rear headquarters at Nha Trang. Late Saturday afternoon, he flew to Pleiku and told stunned officers there to get packed up and moving.

What then happened, in the heat of the moment, is shrouded in mystery and self-serving statements. Someone, if not Phu then an officer with considerable influence and rank, countermanded the retreat order. Soldiers were again ordered to prepare to stand and fight. The civilian population, already in their first signs of panic as soldiers spread the word, calmed slightly.

Sunday afternoon, final word came to retreat. Prodded by their officers, the soldiers began getting ready to pull out. The civilians, told nothing but aware of the retreat, started packing what they could. The Central Highlands were getting ready for history's greatest exodus since the Moslems fled India for Pakistan in 1950.

Captain Nguyen Duc Hao* of the North Vietnamese army was excited Sunday evening, as he always was before he went into battle. Hao was a member of the Lao Dong Party, the Communist party of Vietnam, which is officially called the Workers' Party. He sensed that tonight's combat might be different from other battles. He was nervous. For the first time, he was taking relatively green troops into battle at the edge of Pleiku, the "enemy's lair."

Green troops would have to fight this battle, because Hao's more experienced combat forces had gone south. The captain had learned two days before that they had been sent to Ban Me Thuot for the battle there, stripping most of the Communist combat strength from the Pleiku-Kontum area.

Hao's troops then, would be mostly South Vietnamese recruits. Not that they were untested in battle, for most of them had proved themselves in guerrilla actions. One tough sergeant had survived more than 10 years as a part-time combat soldier in the Pleiku-Kontum area. But they had been organized into a regular army unit only a couple of weeks before, on direct orders to Hao from the headquarters unit in the area, the B3 Front. The Front was essentially a corps headquarters, covering all of northwestern South Vietnam except for the four top provinces. In terms of area, the B3 Front was the largest corps in all of Vietnam, and the three-star general who ran it was known both as a taskmaster and a perfectionist. Hao, well-indoctrinated fighter and Communist that he was, desired to please the general.

He gathered his platoon leaders for a final briefing about 9 P.M. Sunday, March 16. None of the men had an inkling that Pleiku was busy packing up, that panic had already struck the Pleiku airport, and that troops were fighting women and children for places aboard cargo planes to Saigon and Nha Trang. After the meeting, the platoon leaders would give their men final instructions. Then there would be the customary final political lecture, a pep talk of sorts.

---

*A Communist officer who said this was his name gave me this story when I met him with my interpreter in a Saigon restaurant in July 1975. His story matches known facts from Saigon military reports involving the Pleiku province base concerned.

A large number of men would die tonight, Hao told the platoon leaders candidly. They were attacking a force of roughly the same size, a Ranger company of the Saigon army, five miles west of Pleiku city and not far from Camp Hollaway. Hollaway was an old U.S. base still used by the South Vietnamese army, mainly for artillery units. Hao's company was to have the support of a rocket platoon, several mortar crews from a sister company, and little else. The guerrillas-turned-regulars were expected to overrun the Rangers, occupy their position as long as possible, then pull out to predesignated linkup points back in the jungles.

As usual, Hao told his deputies, the rockets and mortars would open the attack with what they hoped would be a coordinated and concentrated barrage on the camp. Volunteer sappers would try to crawl under the barrage up to the barbed wire surrounding the position and cut holes with wire cutters, bangalore torpedoes, grenades, or whatever they could find. The main ground assault would come 10 minutes after the first mortar was fired to signal the attack. A few men were given specific positions to attack inside the camp, but most of Hao's men were ordered simply to breech the wire, kill or capture as many of the Rangers inside as possible, find a fighting position, and hold on for further orders.

A young volunteer private whose brother had been killed two months before by a South Vietnamese Air Force bomb was given a 4-foot by 6-foot Viet Cong flag. His job was to follow the first attackers and hoist the standard on the makeshift flagpole where now flew the flag of the Saigon governent, gold with three narrow red horizontal bars.

Hao spent most of the next three hours listening to his tiny transistor radio, stolen from the battlefield carnage of a fight almost forgotten. It had been two years before, just before the signing of the Paris peace accords. From his mood, my informant said, Hao appeared to be thinking of the time he had hoped the killing would end in 1973. There was no question, of course, of the revolution's ending, and Hao's seniors had pointed out in 1973 that killing was only part of the revolution. The revolution was going to be never-ending during Hao's lifetime, they said. If the killing stopped tomorrow, the revolution would continue. There was much to be done raising the standard of living in the south, where he knew people starved and were tortured and lived under an inhumane government in Saigon and that part of the nation which was not liberated.

The captain was little given to introspection or philosophy. Political officers told him and other soldiers he had been put in this position at this time so that he could help his fellow Vietnamese throw off their shackles and become truly free under a democratic socialist regime. Enmity would be wiped out when the people became triumphant. If it was necessary to kill to gain freedom, so be it. If it became necessary to die to give freedom to others, that was a privilege. Hao did not want to die. He wanted a long life, in peace, building the revolution in the north and in the south. But he did not fear death.

At 11 P.M., Hao got to his feet and issued the orders to send the attackers on their way, seven miles to the east, where a dull glow from Pleiku lit the sky. The time of attack was to be as close as possible to 3 A.M. Given the inevitable delays often caused by patrols, guards, and unnoticed defensive measures around a city as large as Pleiku, attacks normally started somewhat late. Hao wanted to be in the wire and holding the Ranger post by the time dawn started to streak the sky around 6 A.M.

Hao made a last tour of his own guard positions. Some of his 140 troops would remain behind to guard their food, equipment, and base position. Most appeared sorry they could not accompany the attack. Tonight Hao would carry an AK47 rifle as well as the K54 pistol that marked him as an officer.

Seven miles away, a Saigon Ranger captain was giving orders to his own men. The 120 South Vietnamese Rangers targeted by Hao were getting first news that Pleiku was being given up. The word had come indirectly. A Ranger had gone to town to see his family early that Sunday. Being a good soldier, he had helped his family pack and board a plane to Saigon. He had used the muzzle of his gun to ensure them a place, although the panic was only just beginning on Sunday afternoon. After watching the plane take off, he had returned to camp, where he had informed the other soldiers of what was happening in town.

The Ranger captain had at first not believed that Pleiku and all of them were being abandoned. He had sent his lieutenant into town to discover what was going on. The lieutenant had returned and clambered from his jeep at about 10:30 P.M. to confirm that the city was packing up and panic was beginning to become general. Entrance to the airport was impossible. Senior officers were unavailable to a lieutenant, but it was obvious that they, too, were packing to go.

The captain thought things over for about five minutes, then gave the order to get moving. Within three hours, every working vehicle had been packed with arms, ammunition, and whatever else would fit. The captain figured he would be able to shove off into Pleiku in good order by 3 A.M.

Captain Hao had his men deployed in combat positions by 2:30 A.M. They met no resistance to within 800 meters of the barbed wire perimeter of the Ranger camp, and were waiting just outside the forward listening post perimeter for the mortar and rocket barrage.

Hao dispatched two scouts up to the barbed wire for a last look at the target, just in case of last-minute alerts or other preparations by the defenders. One of the men scurried back to him within minutes to report something very strange—trucks were loading with men, trucks already loaded with boxes of what obviously was ammunition. Not an outpost was manned, and there was only a token guard on the perimeter on this side, obviously the most vulnerable to attack.

Captain Hao, military man and Communist, at that moment became the first North Vietnamese soldier to show decisiveness in battle in the Ho Chi Minh campaign of 1975. He ordered an immediate attack, literally kicking the mortar man beside him in the deep grass into action. The first mortar shell was to be the signal to the other soldiers in Hao's command to begin the battle.

Using the communications he had, mostly runners but including one radio link to a platoon on the far side of the camp, Hao shortened the rocket and mortar barrage to about three minutes from the planned 10 to 15 minutes. He decided that for some reason the Rangers were retreating. He did not know why, but he knew that catching the Rangers in this position would give him a greater victory than he had anticipated.

The attack went perfectly so far as Hao was concerned. In his after-action report, he noted: "The enemy was caught completely unaware by the fast movement of our troops into their position." It was indeed. About 50 of the Rangers were killed outright; an estimated 50 others were captured. (Communist reports often tend to gloss over specific numbers. Even when numbers are mentioned, they are highly suspect. Reliable statistics are simply not produced by North Vietnam or the Viet Cong.) About 20 men fled, many of them with no weapons of any kind. A few made it to Pleiku, to the central coast, to Saigon, and eventually into the reeducation centers after the fall of Saigon. Among them was the Ranger captain.

Hao's swift attack and his last-minute change in battle orders marked the first time the new military training of the North Vietnamese Army had been put into practice. The old tactics had consisted of very careful planning, full attention to detail, and rote following of the battle plan.

Senior officers and a large number of bright young men like Hao had been taught for a couple of years, however, that changing the battle plan in mid-fight to take advantage of a different situation was a good thing. Hao was among the first to employ it. But the tactic was to be a hallmark of the entire offensive and in fact make possible the fast movement of the North Vietnamese army, and the collapse of the Saigon armed forces.

Until 1975, Communist units had been tradition-trapped and planning-bound. It had cost them many victories. It had probably cost them final victory in 1965, when the power vacuum in Saigon demanded to be filled and the Viet Cong could not fill it. And it was a decisive factor again in 1968, when Saigon was on the verge of defeat during the Tet fighting but Communist generals were unable to move their troops around quickly enough to win and avoid the military setback that American mobility managed to inflict on them.

The most obvious example of Communist inability to capitalize on an advantageous situation quickly was in 1972. Communist troops led by General Dung swept down from the north and routed the weak defenders of northernmost Quang Tri provincial capital. Twenty-five miles to the south, soldiers and civilians in Hue rocked with panic. An attack probably would have captured Hue, left Da Nang open, and created the sort of morale letdown that finally hit the Saigon army in 1975. But the North Vietnamese forces were told to halt after the Quang Tri victory and did. The attack on Hue was never seriously mounted, and Saigon forces recaptured Quang Tri city in bloody fighting.

Hao's conduct in the battle for the Pleiku Ranger camp, although few on either side recognized it at the time, proved the North Vietnamese army could be made a mobile force capable of the battlefield adjustments necessary to turn a fairly good army into a winning one.

The Convoy of Tears began that Sunday night, March 16, but did not really get rolling until late Monday. With the inefficiency they were to show throughout the offensive, South Vietnamese officers ordered soldiers to bulldoze the town and put to the torch as much as possible. Meanwhile, military bases were merely abandoned. At Pleiku and Kontum, 62 aircraft capable of flying with only the most minor repairs were left behind. A multimillion-dollar radar, capable of tracking movement on the ground and in the air, and also of following rockets in flight, was left intact for the new forces to capture and use against the pro-American forces.

Airplanes that flew, of course, were taken out on Sunday. That in itself was a tearful event, as thousands flocked into the airport, trying to get aboard the few planes that flew. Shots were fired and people fell, dead or wounded. The panic grew and authorities did nothing to alleviate it, so intent were they on getting out themselves.

A panicky soldier-father threw a tiny child onto the back of a C130 cargo plane as the plane taxied away from the tarmac, its rear clamshell door just beginning to raise into a sealed position. The baby did not make it into the plane. No one knows whether passengers or crew inside the plane saw the child, caught between the door and the aircraft fuselage as the door thudded closed. Presumably, the infant died instantly.

Crowds ran after the airplanes. So great was the crush that people were badly injured. Unconfirmed reports said some people were crushed to death by the mobs or trampled when they stumbled and fell. Pilots, accustomed to taking passengers only if they could pay bribes for a flight from Pleiku to Saigon, considered themselves lucky to get away from the highlands city at all. They complained later to friends. Only other cargo pilots gave them sympathy.

Helicopter pilots did better. They could land at prearranged, more secret places. Though some of them later would be hailed as the heroes of the Convoy of Tears, these American-trained pilots made a considerable amount of money from the fears of their fellow men and women. The going price was a hundred dollars for a flight from Pleiku to the coast, about 80 or 100 miles away. It quickly went up to a tael of gold (1.2 ounces, worth almost $200) per seat, and later in the evacuation rose even higher. The moneymaking in Pleiku lasted only a little over 24 hours and spanned two days. But many helicopter pilots got enough cash to enable them to begin new lives when they arrived in the United States aboard Uncle Sam's (free) airlift a month later.

Three-wheeled Lambretta taxis commandeered by government authorities for use as sound trucks went through the streets of Pleiku that Sunday, spreading the word that it would be best to get out of town. Not far behind came the torch squads. In Saigon, the usual "sources" said explosives experts had blown up the airport. They did nothing of the sort, except that after the last plane took off Monday, one hole was blown halfway down the runway.

"It is recommended that you get out of your homes and prepare to move to another area of our country," said the men in the sound trucks. The people were not told directly that a general, and probably dangerous, evacuation was about to get underway. They found that out soon enough anyway.

As the lack of planning and the contradictory orders received by the military men soon showed, this was no retreat; it was a rout. Retreats, as military men pointed out later, are done with careful planning and in a leapfrog style, with full military protection. Civilians, if any, are not mixed with troops. Tremendous discipline is necessary to pull off a successful retreat.

But the rout from the Pleiku-Kontum area was not like this. Highway 7B, long unused and winding through tough jungle, over unbridged rivers and streams, was designated as the route out. Depending on who told the story—Viet Cong or Saigon soldier—troops either mingled with the civilians or were horrified to see the civilians mixing with them.

General Dung watched all this from nearby, aided by agent reports and the radio traffic from military commanders. Dung remembered how he had led the 1972 offensive, traveling from Hanoi to the south of North Vietnam to direct the attack on Quang Tri. It was at least partly the failure to exploit the massive ARVN defeat at Quang Tri that led to his formulating new battle tactics in 1975.

Now, with the hindsight of the 1972 experience, Dung sat in the highlands and wondered what Thieu was up to. He recognized the retreat order by the Saigon President as potentially the most important of the war. After learning of the order from agent reports and foreign radio braodcasts, he quickly commanded all highland forces to attack, as quickly and as strongly as they could.

The order, stripped of the rhetoric, noted that in the past the North Vietnamese Army had often lost battles because of overcaution. American warplanes, he noted, were no longer flying in South Vietnam. The Saigon air force was undependable and smaller, and posed much less threat than U.S. planes. Troops were to abandon their overcaution and fear of airstrikes, and move swiftly, even during daylight, to attack the retreat.

"One of our units was assigned with a combat mission, was ordered to move urgently to Highway 14 and 7B [intersection] to stop the retreating enemy's troops, which they did at Cheo Reo [a provincial capital southeast of Pleiku on the route of the Convoy of Tears]." So wrote Dung and Giap in their lengthy analysis of the Ho Chi Minh campaign. When the Communists attacked the convoy, its fate was sealed. In rout from the beginning, the large majority of the forces had no possible way to resist the determined Communists. With not enough food, water, gasoline, or ammunition even for survival, the disheartened troops had no hope of taking on the attackers as well.

A North Vietnamese scout force was dispatched quickly from coastal Binh Dinh province to the southwest. At Son Hoa district town, this force blew up the Highway 7B bridge, almost within smelling distance of the South China Sea. The convoy was blocked at the wide river, and the Viet Cong and North Vietnamese proceeded to attack at will between March 18 and 20. In the words of Giap and Dung, "Our troops encircled, isolated, attacked, and destroyed the enemy's troops and at the same time liberated Cheo Reo . . . By March 24, most of the troops who had retreated from Pleiku and Kontum were destroyed." Communist generals are given to hyperbole when describing their success. This time, Giap and Dung were accurate.

Dung is one of the new leaders of North Vietnam. The men originally gathered by Ho Chi Minh are aging and will soon die. Dung in 1975 was the Number 11 man in the 11-man Politburo, the only general other than Giap in the top leadership, and a rising star. Giap was content to rest on his laurels and deal with politics and general theory, while Dung was ready for his biggest test—the "liberation" of the south.

Born a worker in North Vietnam, Dung was just 58 years old in 1975, not old by Asian Communist leadership standards. The French jailed him for five years during the 1939 crackdown on the Communists, but he escaped and worked in the OSS-sponsored resistance to the Japanese during the Second World War. When the Viet Minh took over Vietnam briefly between the Japanese occupation and the return of the French, the decidedly unmilitary Dung was assigned to head the political department of the army, and a year later became a two-star general.

By 1951 he was an alternate member of the Communist Party General Committee and was responsible for indoctrinating the entire Viet Minh army. He had already formed the first army division, the 320 Delta. Chief of Staff of the army in 1953, he played a large part in planning and executing the victory at Dien Bien Phu. Giap got the credit, of course, but Dung was a major planner. He reverted to politics after the French war, and served as an armistice negotiator and later as head of the Viet Minh liaison office to the International Control Commission in Saigon. He instructed Viet Minh stay-behinds in the south to build up arms caches and prepare for guerrilla war, and then returned to the north in 1956.

Ho Chi Minh liked Dung because of his worker background (most of the party chiefs, including Ho himself, came from middle-class backgrounds) and promotions came quickly. In 1959, he was promoted to three-star rank and in 1960 he was appointed to the National Defense Council, a senior planning board. His troops also liked the man, and the general played volleyball with them at his Hanoi home.

Dung traveled to the south for the 1971 defense of the Ho Chi Minh trail when the Saigon army invaded Laos, and again to lead the 1972 offensive—a startlingly poorly planned, uncoordinated, and unsuccessful operation by any military standard. The Paris talks followed the U.S. bombing of Hanoi, however, and the United States removed itself from the battlefield war, a stunning political victory that was to make all the difference in the 1975 offensive.

For this trip to South Vietnam to lead the battle, Dung made extensive preparations to foil pro-American agents known to be operating in Hanoi. He signed national day greetings to several countries. These were broadcast after he left, as though he had just signed them. A look-alike traveled to and from Dung's office and home each day in the general's official car. The volleyball games continued, and the fact that the general did not participate did not leak out to the agents.

Dung meanwhile traveled in secret to the airport in the middle of the night to fly to the southernmost airport of Dong Hoi. His personal secretary faked an illness. An ambulance picked him up and drove from Dung's home toward the hospital. The vehicle then delivered him to the airport, where he flew off with Dung.

From Dong Hoi, Dung and his small party traveled by car down the new Ho Chi Minh trail. Even the general, who had supervised the work on the new road from Hanoi, was stunned at the achievements. More than 30,000 soldiers and other youths from the north had built a road from the western demilitarized zone to within 75 miles of Saigon in a year. It was a two-lane road, mostly gravel. Alongside ran a fuel pipeline and pumping stations. The road eliminated the need to use Laotian territory to ship troops and war materiel south.

Dung was close to Ban Me Thuot and ready to make the decision for battle two weeks before the attack began. He entered into little debate, and his orders were firm and simple throughout the offensive. He specifically did not consult with members of the so-called Viet Cong, the National Liberation Front, who supposedly ran the war in South Vietnam. His military orders went either to North Vietnamese division commanders or to Lieutenant General Tran Van Tra, a senior North Vietnamese general in charge of the war in South Vietnam proper, from the Saigon area south. His political orders were to Pham Hung, the number 4 man in the Hanoi Politburo and head of the Communist Party's southern branch.

After the Ban Me Thuot victory, Dung moved close to the scenes of the important battles. Now he was at the forward headquarters of the B3 front, the central Vietnam military region, west of Pleiku city in the jungles.

Why, he wondered, had Thieu decided to abandon the highlands. It was, he noted in his diary, probably a "fatal mistake." In previous offensives, he might have spent weeks or months pondering, discussing, waiting for orders. But this was the difference in 1975. Dung was flexible, and he had the authority. He was able to issue the orders to take advantage of the Saigon retreat and move his troops in fast pursuit.

Nguyen Hoat was a resident of Saigon who had visited his father and mother at Pleiku for the Tet, or Lunar New Year, in February, and then had stayed on for a while. He made money in Saigon doing odd jobs here and there, had just enough to survive for a month or two, and really was in no hurry to return to the capital. There was little or no work available in Pleiku, but the pleasure of visiting his family in the cool highlands air made him reluctant to return to crowded Saigon for the moment.

On March 16, he was sitting on the family stoop sipping a beer and reading a two-day-old newspaper from Saigon when the sound trucks came around. At first he paid no attention, for there are many ways of spreading government propaganda and Sunday was a good day for doing so. More people were at home on Sunday.

Hoat worked sometimes as a part-time writer and photographer for the Saigon newspaper circuit and one or two foreign press agencies. His English was poor, but foreigners always had a few English-speaking Vietnamese around and his pictures and their money both spoke an international language.

Nguyen Hoat was not old, but he remembered the trek from North

Vietnam 21 years before with his family. As Catholics, they and the rest of their village had decided they would rather move south than live under a Communist regime. Their priest had told them the Virgin Mary was going south, had urged them to move and they had done so. They had come south on an American navy ship and wound up here in the Central Highlands, at Pleiku. From time to time the family talked about the danger to themselves of a Communist takeover in the south, but the subject was never broached very seriously.

Now Hoat listened a little more closely to the sound trucks. He straightened up and put down his paper, then his beer. He listened to the short announcement as the Lambretta came up the street toward his parents' home, and listened again as it retreated toward the next street. Hoat rose quickly and entered the house.

"Did you hear that?" he asked his mother, who was lying on the polished, raised board that served as the bed in most Vietnamese homes. "We're supposed to leave. The government says we have to leave."

"What do you mean, leave?" his mother demanded. She had no intention of leaving. She had left her home 21 years before and even now did not feel at home in this city of Pleiku. But it was the closest thing to home that she could have, and it would take more than a sound truck to remove her from it.

Hoat briefly explained what the sound truck operator had said. He told his parents to wait at the house while he attempted to learn what was happening. He had a government press card in his pocket. Nguyen Hoat picked up the camera he had not used for more than a month and wandered off up the still-quiet street at the edge of Pleiku.

A brisk half hour of alternate jogging and walking along a highway whose traffic was noticeably heavier than on a normal Sunday brought him to the gates of the Pleiku airfield. In front of the runway stood the old villa-style headquarters of II Corps, a headquarters built and used by the French forces during their losing war and now about to be lost by another armed force.

The guards at the gate of the air base would not let him through the II Corps gate, but Nguyen Hoat had other ways of entering. He retreated 200 yards back along the road and stepped in front of a military Jeep with two soldiers inside. He flashed a smile, his camera, and his press card at the Jeep's occupants in that order, talking all the while and asking for a ride into the headquarters, where he was supposed to see a Colonel so-and-so, a good friend of his, and so on and so on. The soldiers wearily motioned him into the vehicle.

Hoat dropped back off the jeep at the front door of the Corps headquarters, approached it and asked a man what was happening. The major, in two minutes, filled Hoat in on everything he wanted to know.

Then over to the nearby airport, where he saw panic building. Planes were flying in and out. Soldiers' families at this point were receiving priority for the jam-packed flights to coastal Nha Trang, where II Corps was retrenching. It was still early, and there was not much pushing and shoving. Late in the afternoon, Hoat watched and photographed as military police rifle-butted several dozen panicky civilians away from a loading C130 cargo-passenger plane. Nguyen Hoat became frightened and headed back to his parents' home.

"Mother, pack a suitcase for each of us. We've got to get out of here," he said as he came back in the door of his home. His mother was cooking rice. His father had taken up the newspaper abandoned early in the afternoon by his son on the front porch. At first they argued. There was no reason to run, they said. Certainly there would be citizens who chose to flee, but the vast majority of the residents and protectors of Pleiku would stay. After all, it was a major city wasn't it? What would Saigon do, just abandon them, just give up Pleiku overnight?

Yes, said their son, that was exactly what the government was going to do, in fact *was* doing. He described to them what he had heard and seen during the afternoon. They began to feel the same panic as others around Pleiku. Hoat stifled the charcoal fire over which his mother was cooking, while she ran to fill her market basket and Hoat's cheap Air Vietnam suitcase with whatever she could lay her hands on. A couple of loaves of bread went in, a change of clothes, some cold cooked rice. They did not carry water, since they had nothing in which to carry it.

There is a three-cornered traffic circle in downtown Pleiku marking the effective end of Highway 19 from the coast and a crossroads for Highway 14, the Hue-to-Saigon highway through the western highlands of South Vietnam. It was to the three corners that Nguyen Hoat, his mother, and his father plodded on the first short leg of their trip away from the second home they had known in their long lives. At the end, Hoat assumed, lay Saigon, for it was the only safe haven that Vietnamese knew any more. Most had forgotten the Tet attacks of 1968 on the capital, but even so knew that Saigon was the closest thing to an immune city in all of Vietnam. For now, the point was to get out of Pleiku. Hoat had seen panicked cities before, most noticeably Hue in 1972. He did not want his parents exposed to that.

The three joined a crowd of thousands at the three-cornered traffic circle. It took four hours of waiting to find a truck and boost themselves up on it, along with perhaps 50 others. About a dozen were near hysteria. Few paid any attention to them.

No one has described the start of the Convoy of Tears as movingly as Nguyen Tu, an employee of the Saigon newspaper *Chinh Luan*. Tu, like Hoat, a North Vietnamese refugee. He rode the Convoy of Tears from start to finish, and filed reports by helicopter courier each day. *Chinh Luan* became a best seller during that time, and tens of thousands shed tears at his reports:

> "By Sunday evening, officially or unofficially, Pleiku was abandoned. I can see fire, at least 14 bright spots of fire in the city. The people smashed windows and set fire to the houses. There was no explanation to the civilian population, no organization, and no help to the poor. As I look back to Pleiku now, I can see smoke billowing from the city from the fires."

As the convoy moved out of Pleiku early Monday, as the Ranger position fell to Captain Nguyen Duc Hao, the Saigon government was forced to lie.

By Monday, western press agencies were sending out bulletins on the abandonment of the Central Highlands, and while no one was yet sure where the orders had come from, it was evident that an exodus of troops and civilians was under way.

The press agencies got their first stories from American friends, and friends of friends, who had themselves been ordered out of the highlands by the Saigon and American governments. Missionaries had been summarily cleared out, apparently to avoid a repetition of the capture of the men, women, and child at Ban Me Thuot. Dr. Patricia Smith, who hid under a bed during the 1968 Tet offensive at her hospital at Kontum, was out of the highlands, probably for good. A couple of doctors had stayed at her hospital, but there was no indication of their fate. (They survived the offensive but were expelled from Vietnam after Saigon fell.) The American Embassy had quietly ordered all foreigners out of the area. Or in the peculiar think-speak of the bureaucrat, it had "urgently recommended immediate relocation" of foreigners in the area, and had provided transportation.

Reporters, of course, ran the story as soon as it could be confirmed from various sources. UPI had the first bulletin on the voluntary loss of Pleiku. The Associated Press soon had expanded the story, quite correctly, into the abandonment of almost all of the Central Highlands area. The dispatches came back quickly on news wires in Saigon government offices and officials hastily consulted.

Lieutenant Colonel Le Trung Hien, as usual, received the assignment of lying for the government. On Sunday afternoon, March 16, the chubby Hien took the podium in the stifling upstairs briefing room on Tu Do Street and told still-confused reporters who had heard rumors of the abandonment of Pleiku: "II Corps headquarters is still in Pleiku. It is just a tactical command post that is moving to Nha Trang. There is no order to evacuate the civilian or military personnel from Pleiku." This was while Nguyen Hoat and his family were standing at the Pleiku three-corner traffic circle waiting desperately for a ride out of Pleiku. And it was hours after sound trucks had spread word of the order to flee.

On Monday afternoon, Hien continued the fiction. Why he was doing it—or rather, why his superiors ordered him to do it—is hard to say. With Pleiku and Kontum in flames, with the abandonment of the cities completed, with the Convoy of Tears already under some fire from Communist and pro-Communist troops, Hien straightened his face, took his tongue from his cheek, and told newsmen: "No decision has been taken to abandon these two provinces. Some of our units were moved to and from these areas, but only for tactical reasons."

But then suddenly, at the end of the Monday briefing, there was a hint that maybe, just maybe, an evacuation might be under way after all. But if there were to be an evacuation, it was the fault of the newsmen. "Reports carried by you which are either imaginary or unconfirmed will cause confusion and panic to the population in the Central Highlands," Hien declared to reporters. The confusion and panic, of course, would cause an exodus. This made journalists in Saigon careful in checking their facts, but no newsman suffered from the government smear campaigns.

This was because the government and the military were themselves beginning to panic and no one slowed the panic enough to take reprisals against newsmen. There is no doubt that if the offensive had lasted longer and moved more slowly, some would have been expelled. That they were not is not to the credit of the Saigon government.

With the Convoy of Tears under attack and hundreds dying of thirst and hunger, and the refugees performing acts of cruelty to one another, Hien was briefing again Tuesday afternoon. But with pictures of the evacuation already in the newspapers, he relented a little. "We have moved out some of our troops (from Pleiku and Kontum) in what you would call a tactical movement," Hien said. Not many called it that, although the kindest observers around Saigon did use the word *retreat*, which is much softer than *rout*.

On Wednesday, March 19, Hien came to the podium again. "All we know is that there are between one and 1500 vehicles of all kinds on the road. . . . The army has received orders to assist the refugees wherever they can." Hien presented the evacuation now as "the biggest in the history of the Vietnamese people," but stuck to his story that troops had remained behind to defend the town. Who gave the evacuation order, he said, no one knew.

That was the view from Saigon. Luckily, the world did not have to take that view, although newsmen reported it alongside the story of what really was happening. Again, *Chinh Luan*'s Nguyen Tu described it best in a story that appeared the next day:

> "The evacuees jammed on trucks along the blooded way included soldiers, children, very old people. They were spilled all over by the impacting Communist shells.
> "Refugees moving on foot were hit by Communist machine guns, falling down on the road. The blood flowed on the road like a tiny stream. The sound of roaring artillery and small arms, the screams of seriously wounded people at death's door, and children, created a voice out of hell."

Nguyen Hoat meanwhile realized, too late, that it was not good to run from Pleiku. People had told him before that those who stayed put during a war action had more chance of survival than those who tried to run. Now he knew what that meant. Hoat's mother was near death from thirst by Monday afternoon. His father had gotten onto another truck and Hoat had no idea where he was.

There was no feeling of togetherness among the 100,000 persons in the Convoy of Tears. No one shared. Scores had died already, by Hoat's count. Most were old people and children, who simply dropped at the roadside from hunger and thirst. There was not enough water on the convoy for everyone, and those who had water guarded it jealously. Rumors said at least three persons had been shot dead by soldiers when they tried to take water from the armed men. Hoat and his mother were riding on a 2½-ton truck, which lurched itself and about 50 persons down rutted and broken Highway 7B, Nguyen Tu's "blooded way." They used less energy on the truck than those walking, but riders who had no water and food were dying all the same, if more slowly.

The convoy was proceeding at perhaps two or three miles an hour. It was going slowly because there were too many vehicles, the road was too bad, walking civilians got in front of the trucks, and every vehicle was overloaded.

The only organized military units were a small engineer detachment leading the convoy under the direction of their commander, One-Star General Pham Duy Tat, and a unit of Rangers, which was due to be cut to ribbons by attacking Viet Cong forces. The engineers managed to get makeshift bridges across about a dozen streams and rivers along the road. The Rangers did their best to beat back the Communist assaults on the convoy. But it was not good enough.

With the rear of the convoy just leaving Pleiku, the Viet Cong hit the front. The attacks were light, consisting mostly of sniper fire and a few shots from ambush, short and only occasionally deadly.

Now it was Tuesday afternoon, however, and the unit sent by the orders of Generals Giap and Dung (probably part of the 320B Division from the Western Highlands) was closing in on the convoy. Nguyen Hoat had been under fire before. He was always afraid, but never immobilized. He knew what to do. A major problem for him as he heard the first sounds of artillery, mortar and machine-gun fire, however, was his mother. The old lady was very sick, sometimes incoherent. Hoat managed from time to time to get her water from the roadside. Sometimes he had to fight his way back onto the truck after dismounting, but he had made it so far. On most occasions, the people on the truck grudgingly returned to their cramped positions to let him back on to take care of the sick woman.

Now the firing got close and Hoat's heart seemed to move a little closer to his mouth. Then a mortar shell—Hoat remembered later that it had the distinctive whoomp of an 82-millimeter shell—hit the truck he was on. Passengers went flying in all directions and the truck began to burn immediately. Hoat landed against a tree with a fantastic headache, whether from the close explosion or because he hit his head he never learned. The truck had been pushed out of the way by the time he regained his senses, as other vehicles tried to speed through the ambush. Hoat's truck had turned upside down. He never found the body of his mother. He presumes it was trapped under the truck. Without the vehicle, he said later, she had no chance of survival in any case.

Nguyen Hoat, now freed by the death of his mother from obligations to anyone but himself, headed to his right and into the relative safety of the jungle. His idea was to get away from the mass of soldiers and civilians that was the main target of the Viet Cong.

Viet Cong, rather than North Vietnamese, were the first troops and cadre into Pleiku. This became a pattern throughout South Vietnam, except at Ban Me Thuot, where there was one of the two fiercest battles of the offensive (the other being a month later at Xuan Loc, near Saigon). It was not always planned, but where it could be planned it was done. In a few cases it was accidental. The Viet Cong were first into Pleiku, for example, because they were the closest combat troops to the city when it was abandoned.

The Convoy of Tears had cleared Pleiku city Monday afternoon, March 17. Viet Cong units were right behind it. In most cases, North Vietnamese-trained leaders and cadre were with them as they moved into the smoldering town. Combat troops moved quickly into the air base, or as quickly as they could, because they feared booby traps. Guns at the ready, they secured the sprawling perimeter of the air base.

No one touched the multimillion-dollar radar or any other equipment.

Specialists would come in due time to take a look at their new American equipment, which had been abandoned by the South Vietnamese. But for now the Viet Cong merely guarded them. In fact, at Pleiku and elsewhere, the first troops into the cities touched nothing. They put down resistance if necessary, moving everywhere with weapons at the ready. But there was no looting reported from anywhere in the country during the 55 days. Even the spoils of war—say a watch on the wrist of a dead soldier, or a weapon beside a body—went untouched by the soldiers who first entered towns, villages, and cities across South Vietnam.

The few thousand souls who had chosen to remain at Pleiku rather than flee on the Convoy of Tears came warily out of their homes and shops, what was left of them. There was no great greeting of the "Liberation Soldiers" in Pleiku or elsewhere. Soldiers and civilians watched one another carefully, looking for hostility or friendliness. In most cases, there was neither, but a respect for the civilians by the soldiers, who had seen little of South Vietnamese city living.

Flags, in Pleiku and elsewhere, broke the apprehension between triumphant soldier and apprehensive civilian. Viet Cong flags appeared everywhere. On "request" from the soldiers, Pleiku residents took flags and hung them wherever it seemed appropriate—the fronts of homes and shops, poles, even trees. Hanging flags, often a national obsession by both sides in Vietnam because it supposedly showed control of an area, became almost a sport in the first hours of "liberation" of most towns in March and April. Hanging them gave both newcomer and resident something in common, and both were relieved at the ice-breaking opportunity of putting up flags together.

Propaganda cadre followed the troops, sometimes only by minutes, as they spread out and secured Pleiku. There was little to secure. Later reports indicated that not a shot was fired by pro-Saigon residents or soldiers in defense of Pleiku.

The "information" specialists of the propaganda squads walked or rode through the town. Many had specific places to go. Some of them had had these assigned spots to proselytize since 1968, when they failed to gain effective control of Pleiku during the Tet offensive.

Wherever they went, the Communists spread the word:

> There is nothing to be afraid of; Liberation troops will not harm you. We protect your right to own your own property. Any instances of looting or "requisitions" should be treated as theft and reported to the authorities. You are now under the protection of the People's Liberation Armed Forces of the Provisional Revolutionary Government of the Republic of South Vietnam. You no longer have anything to fear from the harsh and repressive puppet

government in Saigon. No longer will you work for foreigners, but for Vietnam. All of Vietnam will be soon in the hands of Vietnamese. Pleiku is in the hands of the people.

It was a message spread wherever the North Vietnamese army traveled through March and April. And they never took a step backward during the last 55 days of the war. Of course, the troops followed their instructions to the letter. They were good soldiers, perfect at following orders, never questioning why a superior wanted this or that. One of the reasons for this was that virtually every order was explained as it was given. While their counterparts in the South Vietnamese armed forces or the American Army were off getting drunk or watching a movie or whatever, the men of the People's Liberation Armed Forces were as often as not tuned in to a political session. It could take the form of a lecture, a seminar, a question-and-answer session, or a self-criticism period.

The underlying intent of these sessions was to make the individual soldier understand not only what he was doing but why. The political sessions—indoctrination to nonunderstanding minds—produced motivation. If there was anything the American generals admired about "Charlie," it was the motivation of his soldiers.

So troops who took Pleiku and other cities in South Vietnam not only knew that they were not to loot or take reprisals on the population—at least until they received orders from above—but knew why. In a sense, the rule was an extension of the Chinese guerrilla warfare rule of Mao Tse-Tung that soldiers must not touch so much as a needle or thread that belonged to the people.

They were guerrillas no longer, either in China or in North Vietnam, but the rules remained the same. What belonged to the people was theirs. All else belonged to the people too—because the state was the people. It sounds like gobbledygook to those brought up in a Western capitalist society. But as a cornerstone and cliché of the Marxism-Leninism, it was understood, believed, and carried out by Viet Cong and North Vietnamese from the Delta to the DMZ throughout 1975.

By April 1, the policy was formally written into the so-called 10-point Policy of Treatment for the People. In about 500 words, the Viet Cong proved they could not improve upon what Mao had said.

There were so few complaints of looting or theft that even Communist officers were surprised after the liberation of each locality. It apparently was one of the reasons that no uniformed military police units were brought into the Saigon area. (A company or two of covert intelligence agents worked under an MP cover.) The troops disciplined themselves so well, on the whole, that MP's could be better used in the field in a combat or combat support role.

Superb discipline of the soldiers bearing the standard of Ho Chi Minh caused a major problem in the cities—that is to say, the more westernized, sophisticated areas of South Vietnam. The problem was that once an order had been given a soldier, it was never going to be flexed or interpreted, let alone changed.

Item: A soldier was told by his nominal superior to instruct the people of his district to hang their flags with the blue on the top. In fact, the blue should be on the bottom, a fact known to the soldier. Nevertheless, the soldier did not argue, but went from door-to-door passing on a message that he himself knew to be wrong.

Item: Soldiers who occupied Da Nang were given money to eat at one particular restaurant. Rice was provided to the restaurant for cooking. The soldiers were not told to take off their military web gear which included tubes of cold cooked rice. They wore the rice for weeks before an officer thought to tell his men that they did not need to wear the cold rice tubes any more.

Item: A thrifty officer told his men one noon to turn off the light in the hotel in which they were billeted. The soldiers used candles for four nights until the officer told them he meant that they were to turn off the lights only during daytime.

This kind of conduct laid the troops of the Communist side in the war open to charges of being robots, and to a large extent they were. From the time of their entry into the army until they got out—and the teaching stuck with them until death—they learned that every order had a reason. If the reason was not explained at first, that meant it would become clear later, perhaps years later. Few, if any, questioned the orders.

In Pleiku, in short, the conduct of the troops was reportedly exemplary. It apparently was good elsewhere, too. The individual soldier might think Americans were dogs who should be shot down on sight for what they had done to his family, his friends, his country. But his orders at this time were to treat them with respect, and he did so. There was no question of mistreating an American, or any other member of "the people." Not even the most insignificant item was to be taken from them. In most instances this rule apparently was followed, unless there was an order to take something "in the interest of the revolution." In such a case, appropriation of the item would be explained, although not necessarily to the satisfaction of the owner of the item. This, at least, was what residents of provincial cities later reported in the days immediately after victory.

Such orders, however, covered only those who were passive. Because they were on the move fleeing Communist advances, and because they were intermingled helter-skelter with soldiers, the civilian men, women, and children of the Convoy of Tears were discovering that they were not entitled to the treatment reserved for those who remained at Pleiku and did not resist when "liberated."

Nguyen Hoat found himself scrambling up Chu Del Hill. He did not know the name of the jungled slope and had only the foggiest idea that he was about four miles west of Cheo Reo, province town of Phu Bon province. All he knew was that he and about 200 other persons had the same idea—to get away from the main body of the Convoy of Tears. The artillery, mortar, and rifle fire were murderous.

In Hanoi, the propagandists were churning out stories of the People's Liberation Armed Forces destroying the Saigon military in the Central Highlands. In Saigon, the propagandists were publicizing the attacks as atrocities on defenseless civilians. At the base of Chu Del, Communist gunners had spotted Nguyen Hoat's group clambering up the hill, fired a few mortar rounds desultorily at the men and women, but gave no chase.

Hoat and the 200 spent a day and a night and another day on Chu Del, before a Ranger with a radio managed to tune to the frequency of the helicopter squadron assigned to fly support for the convoy.

High above the hill, UPI photographer Lim Thanh Van and helicopter pilot Captain Huynh My Phuong listened to the appeals for help from the radio. Below them spread a scene of horror that had the captain crying. Van said later that he had seen a lot of sad things during 10 years as a soldier and photographer, but nothing like what he saw that day.

It was Sunday again, March 23. The Convoy of Tears was partially engulfed by the Communists, who struck from the rear time and again, capturing the soldiers and civilians who lagged behind. At the front, Communist gunners and sappers tried to slow down the convoy. The engineers worked frantically at the head of the column to get the convoy through.

As Van and Phuong watched from the chopper in horror, artillery opened up on the main body of the convoy. They could see the death throes of dozens of men, women and children. Phuong now was weeping openly. He was trying to figure out what he could do. Whatever it was, it would be too little, but he could not just fly off.

Phuong, leader of a two-helicopter reconaissance team, had been ordered not to land under any circumstances. Officers feared, with good reason, that civilians and soldiers would mob the choppers, causing them to crash. It had often happened before in tight situations.

The captain paid no attention to that order. He only wondered where to begin. At that moment, Van said later, the call came from the Ranger officer on Chu Del Hill, crouched not too far from Nguyen Hoat and frantically calling for assistance from the helicopters he could see overhead. Finally, the Ranger got the right frequency. He and Captain Phuong talked for a moment and the helicopter pilot picked out the Ranger's position on the ground, near the peak of Chu Del Hill.

Chu Del was made for a helicopter rescue, unless there was ground fire. It had a sharp peak on it, meaning that only a few people at a time could rush the choppers that might choose to hover just above the red dirt-covered top of the hill.

Phuong swept down, passing first over the suspected positions of the Viet Cong mortars, the most worrisome weapon to him. He and his wing man blasted rockets and machine-gun fire into the Viet Cong, then swept onto Chu Del as the Communist firing stopped.

The door gunners and UPI's Van leaped out and headed for the children in a group that was going toward Phuong's helicopter. Thirty persons rushed the helicopter, more than anyone had believed could be on the peak at the same time. The gunners and Van tried to hold the children up so that they would not be crushed, and everybody tried to pile onto the helicopter. A load of about 20 people in one UH1 Iroquois helicopter, better known as a Huey, landed at Tuy Hoa provincial capital later. Fifteen normally is a near-dangerous number on a Huey.

Phuong headed out again. He flew low over the convoy, and found himself unable to resist the pleading looks, the men and women on their knees below him beseeching him to land. He put down anywhere where it was flat. Hundreds rushed his helicopter. Van was snowed under by the rush of people, pinned to the floor. Seconds after he had landed, Phuong began to lift off again. An old man and an old woman, presumably husband and wife, clung to the skids of the chopper for a moment, then let go and tumbled into the dust. A child screamed. His mother was aboard the helicopter; the child was not.

Phuong swung around, intending to land again and pick up the abandoned child. His helicopter would barely turn. He was dangerously overloaded and could stand no more strain on his craft. Gingerly, he turned for Tuy Hoa. Another family was split by the tragedy called the Vietnam War.

Nguyen Hoat did not get aboard the first helicopter to land on Chu Del. But he gathered his strength, what little he had after two days and a night without water. He rushed for the second, shoving people out of his way. He said he thought he was careful to push only men aside, while helping women and children aboard. But he was not sure, and has nightmares sometimes that he might have pushed off a child or an old lady.

Nguyen Hoat made it aboard that second helicopter, and flew to Tuy Hoa and safety. From there, he used his press card as a reference and made Saigon two days later with the first on-the-ground photographs of the Convoy of Tears. By that time, the government was claiming a tactical victory for the "retreat" from the Central Highlands.

Saigon officials also were using the attacks on the Convoy of Tears for their own propaganda. They ignored the fact that soldiers were in the convoy. The Communists, for their part, ignored the fact that civilians were in the convoy, and played up the success of their attacks as a resounding military victory.

An officer of the Polish delegation to the International Commission of Control and Supervision—self-styled peacekeepers—summed it up for me later. We were discussing the refugees, this Communist and I, over lunch in an American-owned restaurant.

"You must remember," he explained to me as we agreed upon the sad plight of the dead refugees, "that revolutionaries do not care about people."

On March 16, there was a top-level government meeting in Hanoi. Giap was happy. The first five days of the offensive had gone well, ahead of schedule. The abandonment of Pleiku, Kontum, and even southern neighbor Darlac provinces, was a plus for the generals. It meant that much less fighting would have to be done. That the offensive would succeed in crippling the Saigon army Giap and Dung doubted not at all. South Vietnam would feel the further blows of an offensive in the near future.

The North Vietnamese hierarchy was gathered for the meeting that day, as usual. Workers' (Communist) Party Chief Le Duan, National Assembly Chairman and guerrilla warfare proponent Truong Chinh, and Prime Minister Pham Van Dong were the luminaries. Another dozen of the shadowy men who run the Communist part of Vietnam were there as well. Giap was a star, of course. Even Truong Chinh, who favored prolonged warfare over the all-out offensive, supported the current drive.

The Spring Offensive, as it was still called, had been planned, of course, not to capture South Vietnam, but to weaken it. The aim of the drive, according to the original plans drawn up in 1974, called for localized offensives in three or four selected—and weakened—regions of South Vietnam. The local offensives, if successful, could be expanded.

But the idea was to expand current Communist areas of control. Using the main force North Vietnamese army, the Communists hoped to win guerrilla-type goals. It was a compromise plan, forced by the powerful Truong Chinh, who was not that keen on huge regular armies in any case and dead set against the type of nationwide battles that had virtually destroyed the guerrilla infrastructure and nearly wiped out the Viet Cong Army during Tet, 1968. By 1972, the aims had been changed, as the leaders in Hanoi looked for a winning formula. The North Vietnamese Army was the instrument, but the goals were limited.

Giap outlined the plans for the next stage of the battle. It had all been gone over before, but the general wanted to be sure everyone understood.

Beginning almost immediately, as soon as the final go-ahead was flashed from Hanoi, two more local drives would be started. The first would sweep south from northernmost Quang Tri province in South Vietnam, the second east from "liberated" Ban Me Thuot, Pleiku, and Kontum.

The southbound push would first test, and if possible overrun, the defenses around Hue. The former imperial capital had long been a major target of North Vietnamese soldiers. Their success in capturing most of the city in 1968 had heartened most officers. But the political failure, the execution of thousands of Hue residents, had forced new planning. Orders had gone to every soldier and political cadre that random executions would not be tolerated.

Before aiming directly at Hue, however, the southeastern part of Quang Tri province would have to be captured. A corner of the province and what was left of the provincial capital—leveled by bitter fighting in 1972 and never resettled—were in the hands of South Vietnamese Marines.

Dung (reporting from the front in the south), Giap and virtually every North Vietnamese officer agreed that some tough fighting lay ahead with Saigon's Marines. They were hardened, volunteer troops, and had been involved in almost daily propaganda battles with the North Vietnamese soldiers camped across the Thach Han River from Quang Tri city. On occasion, tiny fire fights broke out in the Quang Tri area. But the disciplined main force troops on both sides had pretty well obeyed the two-year-old cease-fire orders. Quang Tri, the most heavily fortified area in all of South Vietnam, also was the most peaceful.

The Saigon Marine division was probably the best single division in South Vietnam. It was kept close to its 10,000-man authorized strength, and was the subject of tough training exercises. There was only one problem: the Marines had not fought for so long that they actually were forgetting how.

Brigadier General Bui The Lan led the Marines. Lan was a fair but tough, lean combat leader. He was respected by virtually all his men. He was unusual in that he spent a lot of time with his division and his men knew him by sight. This, in the South Vietnamese armed forces, was unusual. Lan also was believed to be generally noncorrupt and nonpolitical. All in all, an unusual man indeed for the Saigon military.

Giap told the political leaders at the conference that the military intended simply to drive down on the Marines on a night in the near future. There would be little finesse to the attack, they said. Their forces could overrun the Marines by sheer numbers, surprise, and superior fire power.

To the south, meanwhile, the main attacking force at Ban Me Thuot would be pulled away from the town, leaving it in the hands of regional and local forces. This onward motion of the main force army was to become a pattern throughout the winning offensive. The largest body of the North Vietnamese army in the area would follow the retreating Saigon troops from the Ban Me Thuot area.

At the same time, forces west of Pleiku would head east down Highway 19 toward the coast, roughly speaking. Some had already been ordered to press closely behind the Convoy of Tears, and in fact were already beginning to take over villages and towns after the convoy passed through.

Still another attacking force from the highlands area—the 3rd, or Gold Star Division—was ordered into action in coastal Binh Dinh province. For a couple of years, the Gold Star Division had been largely inactive. Now, hopefully not undertrained by the long period of inaction, the division was to begin from the southwest corner of Binh Dinh and work to the northeast, liberating the small district capitals in the province.

Binh Dinh was one of the keys to victory. A huge province with a population that was largely sympathetic to the Viet Cong, Binh Dinh lies just below the dividing line of I Corps in the north and II Corps in the center of south Vietnam. The American 173rd Airborne Brigade and the 1st Cavalry Division both had started their Vietnam tours in Binh Dinh and had failed to do more than dent the Communist infrastructure. On the American computer printouts, it had ranked 44th among the 44 provinces in terms of "security" for as long as there had been computers helping direct the war.

The country's fourth largest city, Qui Nhon, was in Binh Dinh province, at the extreme southeast corner. This, Giap explained to the civilians who heard the briefing, would be the last target of the Binh Dinh stage of the offensive. Their troops, after trekking northeast, would do a 150-degree turn to the south and follow Highway 1 into Qui Nhon.

Giap told the leaders that with the victory at Ban Me Thuot and the rout from the Pleiku-Kontum corridor, the Saigon army was on the run. It appeared, he said, that a great victory was in the making, because what would be "liberated" in this offensive probably could never be recaptured by Saigon forces.

For the first time, he touched lightly on the question of complete victory. He noted the contingency plans for an all-out offensive. Giap reiterated what the others wanted to hear, that military victories now in the process of being won would give the Communist side tremendous bargaining power. They were gaining control of huge parts of South Vietnam, including important towns and whole provinces, for the first time ever. He did not broach the idea of a total victory in the foreseeable future.

Special orders were going out to the Communist soldiers at the battlefronts and the rear areas in South Vietnam. They were inspired by lessons learned and by the probability of taking over huge areas and large populations of the south in the current fighting. The orders came directly from Giap, Dung, or their closest aides, and were to be obeyed without question by the troops.

The most important, later to be issued as a communiqué by the Provisional Revolutionary Government—the Viet Cong—as a government command, dealt with the treatment of the "liberated" population, civilian and military. All military equipment, especially vehicles, belonged to the conquering Communist forces. They were to be well taken care of for use by the People's Army, either immediately or later, as circumstances warranted.

Captured soldiers were to be well treated. When possible, all were to be given an initial interrogation session. This was for the purpose of finding those willing to work for the People's Forces, in whatever capacity necessary. It was, in effect, an order to look for reliable guides and intelligence of a local nature. Communist troops coming into an area for the first time found it necessary to know how many troops guarded a given bridge, how many tanks were in a specific camp, how much below strength a given unit was.

As soon as possible, local administration was to be turned over to nominal PRG representatives to allow regular soldiers to move up and get on with the business of fighting the war.

All foreigners were to be detained, preferably at the point at which they were captured. (As for Struharik and the missionaries from Ban Me Thuot city, they already were walking north to a camp behind Communist lines. The North Vietnamese officers honestly felt, and feel, that the move was for the safety of the Americans and other foreigners captured in the city.)

The orders were aimed at avoiding all forms of retaliation by the conquering forces. Lao Dong Party officials, including Giap and others, had decided that the "liberated" southerners must now be treated benignly. For the first time since 1954, there was an excellent chance that hundreds of thousands of civilians were about to fall under PRG rule. To avoid ill feelings as much as possible, the Communists decided, in effect, to "be nice" to their new subjects.

THE ROUT BEGINS

The attack began at 11 o'clock at night, March 19. The North Vietnam offensive was nine days old, and four provinces were in Communist hands. Marine Private Duc had never seen so many tanks in his life, and he was scared.

All around Duc men were firing or staring, transfixed, at the tanks. Lines of them, ranks of them, clanking slowly across the field. It was 1 A.M. and defenders of the nearest flattened village had pulled out after about 10 minutes of fighting tanks, which came from three directions.

The platoon sergeant, disobeying orders but egged on by his men, had switched frequencies on the field radio and was listening to the sounds of frightened men. The Marines up front of the platoon were trying to avoid death. Some were fighting, and they were looking for help on the radio band. Others were running. They were not interested in their radios at all.

Marines had seen tanks before, most notably and recently in 1972 when they fought to keep part of Quang Tri province and then retake the chief town. But they had never seen ranks of tanks before. Not even in Saigon, where U.S. tanks once could be seen on just about any street corner.

The assault on the Marines was massive. Later, it seemed that at least three infantry divisions and at least a regiment of tanks had taken part in the push that recaptured the province of Quang Tri and then some for the Communists.

Duc peeked again over the edge of his bit of trench line. Like most of the Marines in the area, he had made himself a roof of branches, palm fronds, cardboard boxes, whatever he could find. It kept the sun and most of the rain off him. It would not withstand artillery shells or mortars or tank fire. And that was the immediate worry. The shelling had begun in earnest.

And now, five minutes after Duc had heard the tanks, two minutes after he had seen them, the Marine company in front of Duc rose out of its trenches. For a second, Duc thought they were going to assault. But they turned around, toward Duc's platoon but angled off to the right a bit. They crouched and ran, away from the battle. Against the flare and shell-brightened sky, Duc now could see hundreds of crouching figures, most of them carrying M16 rifles, heading away from the tanks.

Incredibly, there was little shooting, aside from the shelling. Communist soldiers were on and following the tanks, and a few brave ones were just in front of the steel war machines. But they were firing only occasionally. The Marines were running from the threat, not from the fire power.

Private Duc had never been in a battle before. He had almost never seen a shot fired in anger. Though trained better than most of the South Vietnamese government armed forces, Duc just had no idea what a big battle was like.

Duc was from Saigon, was born and raised in the capital city. At 17, with authorities requesting his presence in the armed forces, for the privilege of fighting for freedom, Duc had talked over his future with friends and relatives.

Duc had been taken out of school at 14 to go to work to help feed his family of nine. He was the fifth child and third son. An older brother had been in an army unit stationed close to Saigon, but able to get home only on the very occasional weekend pass.

Duc had the usual options open to a South Vietnamese youth who had reached draft age. He could attempt to dodge the draft, staying in alleys and off the streets. This meant, in the long run, the probable payment of large bribes to police agents and no job. He could become a monk, but by now—1973—novice monks were as likely as not to be drafted right out of the pagoda. He could join a ragtag militia group, but that led more surely to death, Duc and his counsellors felt. So he joined what friends told him was the best damned fighting unit in Vietnam, on the theory the best fighters had the best chance of surviving the battle. Duc went to a Marine recruiter and signed up for the duration.

Training was tough for the city boy, but he gritted his teeth and made it. Within three weeks, and after a two-day leave to say goodbye to his family, Duc got on an LST and sailed to Huong Dien, the Marine Corps forward headquarters, fifteen miles south of Quang Tri city itself.

There was little fighting, other than the occasional patrol south into Thua Thien province when the airborne became hard-pressed to cover the whole area north of Hue. The make-believe mortars of the training range, the machine-gun fire above him as he crawled through the infiltration course, and the Saigon battles of the Tet offensive had come closer to harming Duc than the tiny encounters after he became a full-fledged Marine.

Time, not danger, marked the duty of a South Vietnamese Marine in the two years between Henry Kissinger's peace of 1973 and the Communist offensive of 1975. Duc talked, read, slept, cleaned his rifle often. He sent almost all $20 of his pay home every month, witholding only enough for an occasional beer.

Duc had not heard the first shots fired at Quang Tri city. The sergeant woke him up just after 11 P.M. as he put the unit on full alert. An attack was expected. How large it was going to be became evident as they listened to the Marine rout on the radio.

The tanks were within 400 yards of Duc's platoon now, just rumbling along. There was no signal given, not a word spoken, that Duc could remember later. But everyone in the platoon rose and clambered backwards over the foxholes and trenches. Automatically, they crouched, cutting down their silhouettes in case of hostile fire. No one fired at them as they ran, sometimes stumbling, to the rear.

After about half a mile, Duc stopped to rest, throwing himself on the ground. It was the longest run he had experienced since basic training two years before, and he was winded. He was not particularly frightened. But he saw no use in standing and fighting an obviously impregnable force bearing down on him and his companions.

For a battlefield, southern Quang Tri province was in its way silent, Duc remembers. The loudest sound was the steady rumbling, the clanking of the tanks. Occasional shots, impacting artillery from time to time, and the pop of flares lighting up the general area also could be heard. But no steady shooting from any sector of the "battlefield." Not like the movies, he thought.

The tanks were rolling now a little faster than Duc could run, catching up to him. They were about 200 yards away. Duc was falling behind most of his platoon. He was close to bringing up the rear of a column he thought had about 1,000 Marines in it. Actually, "column" is not the right word. It was not organized. It was another rout for the Saigon armed forces, and if there was no panic, neither was there organization.

Tired Marines, Duc among them, now began stumbling. They had almost reached Highway 1, the main north-south road, and were heading in the general direction of Hue. Down Highway 1 now came more tanks, seemingly just chasing the Marines, not in any hurry to run them over or down, not trying to kill them. And now, as the Marines and tanks reached the highway, the tanks turned on their lights.

Duc turned, flabbergasted, and looked a headlight square in the eye. The tanks stopped briefly, about a dozen of them in a sort of semicircle behind Private Duc and his group of fleeing marines. The Marines continued fleeing, and the tanks kept their lights on. The tanks, Duc suddenly realized, were showing the Marines the way, aiding the retreating troops in picking a safe route.

Duc had no interest in finding out how long this humanitarianism would last. He turned back down Highway 1 and began jogging. He did not stop until first light, when he staggered into an already abandoned militia camp about 12 miles north of Hue and got in line with his friends for a long, long drink of water.

It took 11 days for the loss of South Vietnam. Between a speech by President Nguyen Van Thieu on March 20 and the fall of Da Nang on March 31, the Republic of Vietnam was finally, irretrievably handed to the Viet Cong and North Vietnamese armies and officials. After the end of March, the fighting continued, the propaganda and official anguish and calls for aid of Americans and their friends were heard. But South Vietnam was lost.

The fatal 11 days began with that great pilot of South Vietnam, President Thieu, taking to the airwaves again for his version of a fighting speech. From the well-guarded ivory tower of Independence Palace, Thieu spoke platitudes while his country collapsed. Never had a speech by the President seemed so out of touch with reality.

To all intents and purposes, he ignored the stunning losses his nation had taken, at his order, during the preceding five days, Thieu could not resist his usual dig at the United States for reducing aid to Saigon. But he had passed the point of reality to the extent that he was able to tell his people: "In the past two weeks . . . our armed forces and people have valiantly destroyed the enemy and succeeded in halting their advance at heavily populated battlefields."

It was brave talk, but unfortunately it fooled no one. The Vietnamese people knew well that divisions and whole provinces had been lost for the first time in the war. The mildly censored press of Saigon was carrying breathless accounts of the tragedy of the Convoy of Tears, complete with gruesome pictures that caused tears in more than one Saigon home.

For Thieu to claim that his army might be able to hold the lines would have been virtually unbelievable at the time. For the President to say the enemy was defeated was more than any citizen or resident of South Vietnam could accept.

Except, of course, for the official American community. As Thieu wrote his fanciful March 20 speech, the Americans were considering a brainstorm of a so-far-anonymous employee. It is not known whether the idea came out of the Embassy itself or from the Defense Attaché's Office.

DAO (the Vietnamese giggled at the acronym, which as pronounced in their language means "sick") was separate, autonomous, and—many believed—parent to the Embassy itself in the American hierarchy in Saigon. It replaced in Vietnam the Military Assistance Command Vietnam (MACV), the U.S. command of the American war in Indochina. The 1973 Paris agreements ordered the withdrawal of U.S. troops, so MACV was disbanded. Whether MACV really left Vietnam, or merely changed its name to a euphemistic DAO (virtually every embassy of every country has a defense attaché) was a subject of debate in the two years between Paris and final Communist victory.

But in March 1975, the DAO was housed in the former MACV headquarters at Tan Son Nhut air base, six miles from the Embassy, in the steel prefabricated buildings erected in 1967 under the orders of Gen. William Westmoreland. The complex was nicknamed Pentagon East (Disneyland East by the most cynical officers who worked there in the late 1960's) and was a tribute to the logistic genius of Westmoreland. At one time, more than three dozen generals walked its halls. Now, officially, about 90 percent of its staff were "civilians," many of whom were on loan from the U.S. armed forces. This staff was composed of 5,000 Americans, including about 2,800 contractors directly employed by DAO, whose functions will be examined in more detail later.

The idea of the brainstormer, in any case, was to calm the gradually growing fears that South Vietnam was on the edge of disaster, from the American point of view. U.S. residents were becoming noticeably edgy, and it was proposed that a couple of briefings could get out the word that all was well in Vietnam.

Acting Ambassador Wolfgang Lehmann particularly liked the idea. So did the powers at the U.S. military headquarters. As Thieu performed his parody of the fighting President on Vietnamese radio and television, Lehmann and the DAO briefing officers were getting their own platitudes in order. A little pep talk from the leading Americans to the followers, they felt, would do a world of good.

This was to be another case of the United States establishment in Vietnam accepting information spoon-fed it by the South Vietnamese government, believing it, and spreading it. Reports from the field operatives still went unheeded, unbelieved, or both.

The U.S. establishment in Vietnam in 1975—diplomatic, military, and intelligence—seldom questioned the Vietnamese reports, and so far as an outsider could determine rarely attempted independently to confirm them, as one example will illustrate shortly. An exception to the general rule was retired Army Colonel George Jacobsen. Jake, as he was known, had a certain claim to hero status in Vietnam, and was Graham Martin's "Special Assistant for Field Operations," which could mean a lot or a little.

For a long time, it meant a lot. Jake sat in on the highest councils and had the ear of Martin. Somewhere along the line during the last days of the war, he lost it. Sadly for the United States, Jake himself ceased to have significant influence on the Embassy. He spent a day in his office literally weeping at the abandonment of pro-American Vietnamese later in the war. His advice was largely neither asked for nor received.

Instead, Martin and the military chose to accept the words of generals, many of whom in other circumstances or other nations would be criticized as combat know-nothings. Shown factual reporting against the word of a Saigon-based general, Martin and the American military establishment, and even the CIA, seemed unerringly to believe the word of the Saigon general.

Martin rightfully shouldered the full blame for the blocking of field reports by U.S. agents and similar acts. But only part of the blame was his. There were ways around the Ambassador, but rather than risk battle with him over field reports that did not tally with the official U.S. estimate of how things were going, the political, diplomatic, and intelligence chiefs in Saigon apparently chose to "get with the program."

This concept of officials withholding or doctoring field reports to prove that everything was well in Vietnam has become an overworked, simplistic, clichéd tool of reporters of the war. Yet that does not make it less true. Whole books have been written by newsmen, retired U.S. officials, and at least one former U.S. Marine colonel in an effort to explain the concept. It is still not entirely clear how the American establishment permitted it to happen. It is my supersimplistic belief that human beings need self-justification, and that the American in Vietnam who was able to "prove" that progress had been made in his field during his 12- or 18-month tour achieved that self-justification. Those who were not able to record progress considered themselves failures. I contend, while admitting the facile nature of the argument, that the entirely human need of Americans in Vietnam always to succeed caused an unconscious, almost unanimous decision to —as the old song says—accentuate the positive. (The only simplistic solution to this problem, I think, is to have a devil's advocate at virtually every stage of the reporting and decision-making process. This solution is almost certainly unworkable, however, both because of the heavy logistic requirements and the fact that the devil's advocates probably would not be permitted to survive in the civil service and military jungles. One cannot really imagine this conversation: "What does your daddy do?" "Oh, he's the House Radical in the Latin American section of the political-military section at the State Department.")

But "getting with the program" had caused huge security lapses in the U.S. community in Vietnam many times in the years before 1975.

Because the policy was that the war was going well, the Tet offensive had killed thousands more than necessary, when most Vietnamese soldiers were given three days off. Building the myth that the ARVN was the best army in Southeast Asia cost untold suffering when it became necessary to save South Vietnam in 1972 by partially destroying the north with U.S. warplanes.

There are many stories about how Graham Martin refused to allow and to heed reports that made points in which the Ambassador did not believe. Martin preferred the word of an interested, involved Vietnamese politician over the truth. This single tale is offered in partial illustration.

In late 1974, the forces of right-wing Roman Catholic priest Father Tran Huu Thanh were in full cry against Thieu and his government. Several demonstrations had gotten a little out of hand and combat police and demonstrators alike were wounded in hand-to-hand battles. (In fairness to the Saigon government, it must be noted that guns were never used against the demonstrators and tear gas only seldom. The police and combat police fought like the demonstrators, with rocks and sticks.)

The Catholics were tired of being penned up in their Church compounds in suburban Saigon this day and had announced to reporters —from whom it inevitably leaked—that a march downtown would be staged the next day.

The mayor of Saigon, Brigadier General Do Kien Nhieu, issued a communiqué over his own name announcing that about 75 blocks of downtown Saigon would be blocked off in order to prevent the march. A map was given to Saigon newsmen showing the area involved. Included was the Saigon market, which had not been closed through warfare or internal strife since the 24-hour curfews of the Tet offensive six years before. The story was dutifully filed about midday.

I was watching the 8 P.M. Saigon Television newscast when the call came from Martin's representative. (The Ambassador often called himself to complain about stories or to try to wheedle the source of articles from American newsmen, but this time used another Embassy official.) I won't name the man involved because he is a friend, a capable government employee, and under different circumstances would be a worthy representative of the American people.

The man told me the Ambassador was highly displeased by my story because it was not factual, and "is giving the wrong impression to the people back home." Stunned, I asked why he thought it was not factual. The Ambassador protested, said the Embassy man, because there would not be the massive blocking of streets I had written of. In fact, only four buildings—the Presidential Palace, two courts, and the National Assembly—would be sealed off.

As if on cue, a map of Saigon appeared on the television station, showing the downtown area to be blocked off the next morning. Slightly bolstered but still confused, I told this to the late-working Embassy man. He was slightly taken aback but pressed on. "Very good sources have told the Ambassador that downtown in general will not be blocked off," he said. "In particular, the Saigon market will not be blocked off." To make it short, I asked for his sources. He made vague references to someone "very high" in the Saigon administration. I told him I would have to go with the mayor of Saigon, who said the downtown area would be barricaded, rather than with unnamed sources, who said it would not.

There was a slight stiffness in his voice as he reminded me—quoting Martin—of my responsibility toward the American people. Then he hung up.

That night after curfew, the barricades went up in the precise locations announced by the mayor. The Saigon market was closed. Unable to resist and because the man was a friend, I called him back and asked him if he had seen the barricades.

He said no, he had not, and asked me if the Saigon market was closed. He would never tell me later whether he was kidding when he said he did not know whether the central market was closed.

The point was that Martin, on a matter that could easily have been checked by having one person listen to the radio, watch the television, or get into a car to make a tour of the barricades, refused to do that. His "very high sources" were to be believed and that was that. The fact that the Vietnamese might want to hide information or even lie about facts never seemed to register with the American Ambassador.

A report of the U.S. Senate foreign relations committee, written by Richard Moose and Charles Meissner and released August 5, 1974, charged that Martin held back or altered reports to Washington that made the Saigon army or government look bad. The report was based on earlier testimony, which included a sometimes heated exchange between Moose and Martin over the issue. During the hearings and the debate on July 23, 1974, Martin denied holding back reports.

Rather, he said, he deleted sections of some reports (and, presumably, had other officials in the Embassy similarly delete sections of reports he did not personally see) because there was no need to send all parts of all reports to his superiors. He did not feel it necessary, he said, to report actions more than once. In addition, military information was reaching Washington through military communications channels, he told Moose.

The Moose-Meissner report said that U.S. Embassy reports to Washington from Saigon distorted or deleted information in three different areas: deliberate cease-fire violations by the Saigon military, deteriorating security and poor performance by Saigon troops, and the actual course of battles. It is reasonable to assume, on the basis of what was happening in Vietnam at that time, that Moose had in mind alleged withholding or altering of information on battles in which it later was determined that the Saigon forces, rather than the Communists, broke the cease-fire. Another example might have been failing to report the eventual loss of a battle by the Saigon army after an initial gain. (This would fall under Martin's example of not reporting the same action more than once.)

To at least one of his staff members, who told me of the incident in late 1974, Martin wanted reports written mainly on the "big picture," leaving Saigon to deal with the local matters. All were "considered seriously," even if they were not transmitted verbatim to Washington.

Presumably, those local problems involved things like the Marines blowing up a bridge on Highway 1 in a desperate effort to halt the Communist advance.

Private Duc and his buddies had been organized after their flight from Quang Tri province. Duc himself had been picked up on the road to Hue. A little bit of leadership was all that was needed to get a couple of thousand Marines back to the northern border of Thua Thien province, where it meets Quang Tri at the My Chanh River. The Marines had retreated from Quang Tri in relatively good order, at least those on Duc's sector had, and a minimum of resupply of food and ammunition had them reorganized into an effective fighting force within a day.

The order to blow the My Chanh bridge, in fact, had been passed down to Duc's company while the Marines were listening to Thieu's address the evening of March 20. It was less than 24 hours after the massive tank attack had overrun Quang Tri city and province. Duc and the rest of the Marines, as they made ready to blow the bridge and officially cut off Quang Tri from the rest of South Vietnam, heard Thieu on transistor radios:

> North Vietnamese infantry tanks massively crossed the front line
> at the Thach Han River to launch a large-scale attack against the ancient
> citadel and the Quang Tri provincial capital. At the same time, they heavily
> shelled the city of Hue. . . . From Quang Tri and Hue along the coast down to
> Military Regions 3 and 4 (the Saigon area and the Mekong Delta), we are
> determined to preserve our territory to the last. Rumors about abandonment
> of Hue or a few other places are merely rumors aimed at creating confusion
> among the people, and are entirely groundless.

There was some grumbling about Thieu's use of the word *we* while he talked about who was going to defend Hue and the rest of the country. The one-third of the Marines still fighting, alongside Private Duc, knew well who "we" stood for. Nevertheless, as Thieu spoke and as the Marines began making ready to blow up the My Chanh bridge, there were 2,500 Marines prepared to fight.

To the south, in fact, still another 2,000 or 2,500 Marines were being rounded up from the rout at Quang Tri. Officers, including division commander Brigadier General Bui The Lan, were making the rounds of Hue and other likely spots around the former imperial capital looking for their men. The Marines were beginning their last week as an effective fighting force, but they were beginning it well. That Lan and his officers could salvage anything from the Quang Tri debacle was to their credit and that of their Marines.

If the Marines were getting ready for a defense, more sanguine residents of Hue had decided it wasn't worth it. The province chief of Thua Thien, of which Hue was the capital, had gone on local television and advised noncombatants to get out, and they were getting out. The flight of 100,000 persons right in front of the Marines from Quang Tri took away their last hope of being able to stay at home. To the Hue resident, who had been through it before, it seemed the war was coming back.

In 1968, the people of Hue had not fled the Tet offensive, mainly because the fighting began from the inside of the city and there was little opportunity to leave. They had suffered from both sides—from the guns of the Viet Cong and the artillery of the ARVN. The Communists committed one of their major political mistakes and their worst moral decision of the war. They assassinated, often by brutal means including burial alive, certainly well over 3,000 persons, and probably more than twice that number.

There was no denying this atrocity, which was carried out as a matter of policy by the provincial authorities of the Viet Cong after they thought they had secured the city. It was the big argument the Americans had used in the propaganda about a blood bath by the Communists after a victory. And it had frightened the people of Hue badly. Enough, at least, so that at the first hints of Viet Cong infiltration in 1972 and 1975, citizens of Hue took off south as fast as they could.

Now, as the Marines were blowing up the My Chanh bridge and the Communists were merely outflanking them and crossing waterways in their amphibious tanks or on underwater bridges, the people of Hue were hightailing it to Da Nang. By road and ship they flowed south in a seemingly unending mass of humanity. All military men, except those from the Marines and most of the 1st Infantry Division units, were given permission to take off if they so chose. The reason for this order was to prevent soldiers from going AWOL to take care of their families. Authorities hoped troops would take their families south, then return to Hue to do battle.

The arrival of the refugees from Quang Tri spread panic in Hue and also led to some heartrending scenes. After an exhausting walk of 25 or so miles down sandy Highway 1 from Quang Tri, the refugees found there was no safety in Hue either. Many were penniless and had neither food nor water for another trek. But having fled one place, they feared the North Vietnamese soldiers and were forced to try to draw on a nonexistent stock of energy to resume the walk south.

Duc, not knowing much of this at the Marine front lines at My Chanh, watched the Marine engineers set charges on the bridge over the river. The bridge had been blown up in 1972 during the fighting for Quang Tri, and rebuilding it had been meant as a morale booster for the Vietnamese under Saigon government control.

The refugees who had fled Quang Tri during the past day or two, in fact, were only newly resettled in the province. All of Quang Tri had been put off limits to civilians for more than two years because it was so close to the Communist lines. Then, under U.S. aid masquerading as a United Nations project, Quang Tri had been reopened. The first big project in the province, an irrigation system, was just getting under way.

Engineers pulled back off the bridge now, and troops within 400 meters were ordered back and under cover temporarily. As a Marine captain set off the charge of plastic explosive and dropped the My Chanh bridge into the river, jaws tightened up and down the lines. This was fresh proof, only 24 hours after Duc had seen the tanks, that the front line was here. The Marines, at one-third strength, were about to take the brunt of battle again. The question was when.

To the south, and while Thieu told his nation the Communists were being defeated on all fronts, there was a partial answer. Duc and his buddies were looking behind them temporarily when they saw some flashes in the sky. Soon, on the radio, they discovered what the flashes were. Hue, and particularly the Phu Bai airport just below the provincial capital, was taking Communist shells, about 50 of them that night. The imperial capital was nearing the end of Saigon control.

Another blown-up bridge brought misery to an even larger number of people that night. Viet Cong soldiers, volunteers for the dangerous combat engineer corps—sappers as they become known in the Vietnam War

—dropped the bridge at Son Hoa. They trapped the tail third of the Convoy of Tears behind the river at that district town 25 miles from the coastal target of the Convoy. Flight was over for most of the 30,000 persons behind the bridge.

Nguyen Thi Phuong, 32, the mother of eight, was trying to get to the coast from Pleiku. Her husband was a major in the ARVN. He was one of the most popular officers with the western press, whom he served notably well as a public information officer. The major had more information, lied less, and was more helpful in arranging for reporters to cover the war than any other Vietnamese officer.

The major had left Pleiku three months before to attend a six-month school in propaganda and intelligence at the Dalat Military Academy. When he had been sent to Dalat, he could not afford to take his family along. His wife was a native of Pleiku and her mother and father would help look after her and the children during the course.

When the major heard about the evacuation of Pleiku ordered by Thieu, it was too late to help his wife. He abandoned the school and went to Nha Trang, the coastal enclave that now served as the headquarters of II Corps. He made trips to Tuy Hoa, about an hour's drive to the north, searching for his wife and children.

Three of his children he never would see again. They and his father-in-law died of dehydration on the Convoy of Tears, although the major did not know this. They had perished during the dusty trip down Highway 7B, a road unfamiliar to all those who obeyed the laws of the Saigon government, because it was deep in Viet Cong territory.

The blown bridge at Son Hoa district town split the family for another two months. On one side was the major. On the other were his wife, his mother-in-law, and the surviving five of his eight children. They were seven among 30,000 and who now would know what suffering really was.

They were on the edge of dehydration, virtually all of them, although with the river so close the thirsty days of Highway 7B were gone. Food was virtually nonexistent. Son Hoa itself and the neighboring villages, all of them small, were stripped of food within a day by the rapaciously hungry of the Convoy of Tears.

And coming up on their heels were the Viet Cong and the North Vietnamese armies. The Communists were on all sides of the Convoy of Tears now, and there was no way to avoid them. Most of them in the convoy feared the Communists. But with the blown bridge blocking them from the safety that lay a day or two away at the most, they could do little but wait.

The strongest swam the river, but the Viet Cong took the small groups that managed the ford and herded them back to Son Hoa. There was no escape. The major sat in Nha Trang and cried for two days, unashamedly. His wife cried for weeks. She mourned her dead and she mourned the living.

President Gerald Ford was making another move now. Calling for reason rather than irrationality in February 1975, Ford and the White House staff had managed to convince a disparate group of Congressmen to visit Indochina before they voted on the aid bills. The group had come and their reactions on Vietnam had been predictable, in the main. Those who had previously supported aid continued to support it; those who had opposed it continued their opposition.

Only a flying trip to Cambodia March 1 had changed any minds. Those who visited Phnom Penh were clearly shocked at the situation in that tragic country. Representative Bella Abzug, outspoken critic of administration aid to Vietnam, told me she intended to vote for more aid to Cambodian refugees.

A chief architect of the Congressional trip was U.S. Ambassador to Saigon Graham Martin. He had long felt that personal visits to Vietnam by Congressmen was the best way to get votes for aid. George Romney called 1967 U.S. Embassy briefings and tours brainwashing and lost a bid to become President. Martin called them fact-finding.

No more Congressmen were in a mood to visit Vietnam. But Ford decided to send a senior military man for a first-hand look. The choice was General Frederick C. Weyand, last commander of U.S. combat forces in Vietnam in 1973. Martin, who had flown to and from Vietnam with the Congressional delegation, was to accompany Weyand on the tour, this time remaining in Vietnam.

Now, as Thieu spoke to the nation of drawing lines and fighting, Martin, Weyand, and their party were flying into the sunset through a long night, in their White House jet. In the next few days, Weyand was going to get all the facts on Vietnam that Martin could give him. It was 11 days after the start of the North Vietnamese offensive. Martin, Ford, and Weyand never suspected that the end of the U.S. role in Vietnam was 39 days away, that the offensive already was 20 percent on its way to completion. In 40 days, Graham Martin and Gerald Ford would be allied in a fight to bar all U.S. aid to "liberated" Vietnam, despite the fact that now it often was cited as "humanitarian" aid.

There were those who said stridently that the United States had not really pulled out of Vietnam following the signing of the 1973 Paris agreement that won the Nobel Peace Prize.* Chief among them were the Communist Vietnamese, who claimed that in 1975 the United States maintained some 25,000 military advisers in civilian clothing.

The Communists were wrong in the numbers. The 5,000 Americans who worked directly for the United States in Vietnam in 1975 were committed by U.S. government policy to work for the survival and victory of the South Vietnamese government. That Washington used covert and semicovert means to attain this goal was indisputable.

In 1975, according to official records and the spokesmen of the U.S. Embassy in Vietnam, there were 854 Americans assigned to the Defense Attaché's Office (DAO) of the Embassy. A total of 12, including secretaries, worked inside the Embassy building attending to usual DAO functions. Another 35 were assigned to various units supposedly implementing the Paris agreements. But all except the 12 worked at the Pentagon East headquarters, built when the American military establishment in Vietnam was known as the Military Assistance Command, Vietnam (MACV).

But not only did the DAO have a larger staff than any other complete U.S. Embassy in the world, it also had more than half of the 4,000 or so "civilian technician contractors" working for the United States in Vietnam. Again, according to official records, there were 18 contracting firms with 46 different offices employed by the DAO. The "offices" were located as far north as Hue and as far south as notorious Con Son Island. At these two places, Americans operated the U.S.-installed radar navigational aids used by Saigon warplanes. At all major air bases, Americans maintained the planes and helicopters themselves, and during the offensive they worked furiously to keep the aircraft flying to make airstrikes.

Official records do not show exactly how many, but a large number of the "contract personnel" were either on loan from or recently discharged from

---

*The relevant sections of the Paris agreement are part of Chapter II, entitled "Cessation of Hostilities—Withdrawal of Troops," and read:

    Article 4. The United States will not continue its military involvement or intervene in the internal affairs of South Vietnam.

    Article 5. Within sixty days of the signing of this Agreement, there will be a total withdrawal from South Vietnam of troops, military advisers, and military personnel, including technical military personnel and military personnel associated with the pacification program, armaments, munitions, and war material of the United States and those of the other foreign countries [allied with the United States]. Advisers from the above-mentioned countries to all paramilitary organizations and the police force will also be withdrawn within the same period of time. . . .

    Article 7. . . . The two South Vietnamese parties [Saigon and the Viet Cong] shall not accept the introduction of troops, military advisers, and military personnel including technical military personnel, armaments, munitions, and war material into South Vietnam.

As can be seen even from these excerpts, North Vietnam was under no restrictions for the resupply of its forces and was not even mentioned in the section on troop withdrawals.

the U.S. military, and openly admitted this even in the most casual of conversations.

The U.S. Agency for International Development (USAID) outnumbered DAO, both in number of assigned personnel and contractor firms. USAID's 977 direct employees were supplemented by about 1,500 to 2,000 contractors employed by 72 separate companies, according to official records printed in October 1974, and made available by the U.S. Embassy spokesman in early 1975.

USAID, particularly in Indochina, often had been listed in Congressional hearings and press reports as a major "cover" for the Central Intelligence Agency. How many CIA agents worked for USAID in 1975 is not known. But virtually all remote posts in Vietnam—such as the Provincial Representative positions—were staffed by USAID, and it is reasonable to assume that some of these men were gathering intelligence for the CIA. USAID's furthest north representative was based in Hue. To the south, USAID was represented permanently in An Xuyen, the province on the tip of the Vietnamese peninsula.

Just by way of comparison, U.S. Embassy records that listed the 2,270 American officials in Vietnam as of October 1974 by assignment showed that only 195 were assigned to the Embassy proper. A breakdown by section showed 62 in the administration section, 33 in the consular section (many of them assigned to points outside Saigon), 26 identified in the code that indicated they worked directly for the CIA, 28 in the political and political-military departments, with the rest spread among sections dealing with drug enforcement, communications, the Ambassador's office, the commercial section, and the like. Another 134 were identified separately as employees of the Special Assistant to the Ambassador for Field Operations, under former Army Colonel George Jacobsen. The United States Information Service also had a fairly large contingent in Vietnam.

Several other Americans were the only foreign staff at the United Nations Development Program (UNDP) office in Saigon, and although there was no proof, most newsmen in Saigon believed UNDP was a form of covert aid to South Vietnam. Its main project was resettling Vietnamese in northernmost Quang Tri province. These South Vietnamese had been driven from their homes by heavy fighting in 1972, and any success in resettling them near the Communist lines would be a major propaganda victory for the Saigon government.

In addition to the massive American presence in Saigon, the United States was represented regionally by four so-called Consulates-General, which just happened to be located in the same cities—and same buildings—as former American corps headquarters. They were at Da

Nang, Nha Trang, Bien Hoa, and Can Tho. The idea that a normal U.S. Embassy would also need a Consulate at Bien Hoa, just 15 miles northeast of the capital, is ludicrous. But the Vietnam Consulates were, of course, much more than the normal information and visa offices that nations maintain as part of the diplomatic process. Within their Marine-guarded and secure confines, intelligence was gathered, "contractors" were directed in advising the Saigon military, and decisions directly affecting the course of the war were made or passed to Saigon or Washington for action.

The Da Nang Consulate was perhaps typical. It had about 40 persons directly assigned from U.S. government service, employed either in the Consulate building or in outlying provinces but reporting to Consul-General Albert Francis. Francis himself was a political-military specialist from the Embassy in Saigon, and had a background of long service in Vietnam. In the official listing of job titles, no one at Da Nang had anything to do with the Saigon military forces. But when the heat of publicity made Francis' actions known as Da Nang fell, he was with the Vietnamese corps commander, and in fact saved this general's life during the evacuation. For this reason, when referring to the U.S. establishments at Da Nang, Nha Trang, Bien Hoa and Can Tho, it was common to refer to the "U.S. command" or "U.S. headquarters" of the corps area concerned.

In addition to those U.S. government employees assigned to the Consulate, an unknown number of "contract personnel" were stationed in the I Corps area that surrounded the northern South Vietnamese city. Among the purely military jobs performed by these Americans were the following:

• Supervising unloading of military aid equipment at the Da Nang port;

• Maintaining a LORAN (radar navigation) station at Tan My, the Hue port;

• Maintaining, expanding, and reorganizing the communications of the Saigon military;

• Keeping Saigon air force planes and helicopters flying, supervising correct loading of munitions, and assembling replacement aircraft for those that were judged out of date or that had crashed;

• Assisting the Vietnamese Navy on technical matters.

No American actually fought the war in Vietnam, for reasons more of politics at home than the choice of many of those involved. But one American, Eugene Kosh, who was assigned as an Embassy representative in Da Nang, was along when the Vietnamese Navy fought the Chinese over the Paracel Islands in January 1974. He was taken prisoner by the Chinese, and spent some time in that Communist nation as a POW before he and all the Vietnamese sailors taken in the losing battle were released in Hong Kong. U.S. officials maintained that Kosh was merely present on the

Vietnamese ship as an observer on a regular exercise when the fighting broke out and he was unable to return to shore. The story was credible, although it was slightly less so when U.S. officials refused to allow newsmen to interview Kosh after the incident.

It is argued by some that the Paris agreements got America out of the war so that it could retire to the sidelines and see a Communist victory after what Secretary of State Henry Kissinger once told newsmen was "a decent interval." But that view is simplistic. The United States was violating the Paris Accords, even in its most scrupulous sections. America was allowed 15 military personnel in Saigon to oversee the implementation of the agreement, but there were 35 Americans in that office. And even the 5,000 American officials and contractors were supplemented by several thousand Vietnamese and citizens of other countries, notably the Philippines and Taiwan. The exact number has never been publicly released.

The North Vietnamese violations of the Paris Accords were massive, and ended with huge military buildups that simply overwhelmed the defenses of the Saigon military. There is some evidence, however, that the Communists attempted during the first months of the accord to abide by the military cease-fire provision. The first documented cases of cease-fire violations were almost exclusively by the Saigon military, as President Thieu ordered his troops to retake territory lost to the Communists during the last few days before the armistice came into effect. The U.S. establishment in Vietnam contended the opposite, with spokesmen claiming that only North Vietnam was in serious violation of the accords, and that Saigon was forced to answer military attack by the Communists with military action of its own.

This argument probably will never be settled, and it is probably enough to note that North Vietnam, South Vietnam, and the United States all were in flagrant violation of the Paris agreement.

Communist Vietnamese had been burned twice in the past, in their view. First, they had failed to gain independence after World War II and had to build up an army. Then, in 1954, they were promised at Geneva there would be elections in two years, and they prepared for the eventuality of no elections by leaving some Communists and some weapons in the south when they went north. In 1973, when they signed the Paris agreements, they left their whole army in the south, then moved even more men and more modern weapons and support equipment to South Vietnam.

They were ready for the fight if, in their view, the Americans and Saigon failed to live up to the peace agreement. It now was their view that the Americans and Saigon had so failed. And one of the main reasons was the 5,000 Americans still pursuing an active pro-Saigon and anti-Hanoi policy in Vietnam.

The man who would preside over and shape the writing of most of the rest of the last chapter of America in Vietnam was 63 years old. But Graham Martin, Ambassador to Saigon since July 20, 1973, was not his robust self. Friends insisted later that he should have been in a hospital, that he was physically unfit to resume his hectic duties in Saigon. He had suffered from pneumonia in the United States, had been on medication, and had almost literally risen from his sickbed to return to Saigon, first with the Congressmen, and finally with General Weyand on March 27. From the end of March to the end of April, he worked punishing hours before he was forced to leave.

America's senior representative in Vietnam always provoked controversy. He had risen and fallen and risen again during the administration of Lyndon B. Johnson. In Martin's own words, according to a story he told almost every visitor to his third floor office in the U.S. Embassy in Vietnam, he was no hawk on the war. He had, he said, argued too loudly and too well against the use of U.S. forces in Vietnam, while he was Ambassador to Thailand. As a result, since heretics were not welcome in the Johnson administration, he had been moved out of his area of expertise, Southeast Asia. He was appointed U.S. Ambassador to Italy. Or, as Martin liked to put it, while others were losing their heads over Vietnam, he was already carrying his around under his arm.

Martin made do in Italy. He ended up with a farm, which critics liked to call a sharecropper farm. Italian workers kept it going for him when he was not in the country.

Born in North Carolina the son of a Protestant minister, Martin first became a reporter, working for newspapers in his native state and then moving to the Memphis *Tennessean,* often referred to as a "farm team" of *The New York Times.* Martin's clashes with *Times*men in Saigon in 1973 and 1974 would lead the Ambassador to comment often, loudly, and publicly, that the quality of the *Times* had declined more rapidly and more deeply than he could ever have imagined.

He was no man to shirk controversy, was Graham Martin. Most of his enemies hated him so much they could not even bring themselves to respect his stands for what he believed to be right. Certainly, for a diplomat, Martin often lacked diplomacy and taste.

In 1974, he implicitly blamed a prominent American church official, Dr. George Weber, of the New York Theological Seminary, for a Viet Cong mortar attack that killed more than score of children in the Mekong Delta. The churchman, it seemed, had failed to take Martin's advice that he telephone the Viet Cong delegation camped in Saigon, to make an appeal for peace.

And Martin certainly did not shy from fights with Congress. Bluntly, he told Congressmen and Senators his own feelings on the war. He recommended that Secretary of State Henry Kissinger—Martin's boss—slough off a request by Senator Edward M. Kennedy for a statement of America's intentions in Vietnam and Southeast Asia. He saw Kennedy, accurately, as an enemy.

But America's representative did not ignore his enemies. He took his case to them privately, in their offices, in the corridors of Congress. He buttonholed them away from the public eye of the floor of Congress and the committees and forced on them his plans for Vietnam.

Yes, Graham Martin had plans. He spent most of the first year in his ambassadorship formulating them. Martin, initially, listened to many dissenters in Vietnam. When his plan was ready, early in 1974, he shut off the dissenters and went to work on the details. When the details were ready, he began his campaign with Congress.

Martin's plan was sifted from others in Vietnam but it was essentially his and his alone. So much did he work on it and push it and lobby for its passage, against resistance of Congress and the administration, that his first words after the evacuation of Saigon were: "If they had done what I had recommended . . ."

Martin's plan was simple and typically American. The United States representative to South Vietnam recommended the granting of vast amounts of economic aid to Saigon. He argued this would make the Republic of Vietnam self-sufficient and self-reliant.

Specifically, Martin and Kissinger—who spent much time on Capitol Hill pushing the plan—wanted about five billion dollars poured into South Vietnam over a five-year or three-year period. They pleaded with Congressmen to earmark the entire sum in 1974, so that Saigon officials would not have their yearly doubts, hanging by their thumbs waiting to see whether Congress would vote enough aid for the next year.

Martin honestly felt that the large amount of economic aid, starting with a huge expenditure the first year and tapering off eventually to nothing, would turn Vietnam into another Asian economic miracle. He cited the success of South Korea in rising from the ashes of its war after 1953. He cited Taiwan, which had succeeded in resettling two million refugees from the China mainland and building a state that now was buying its own military equipment.

Those who opposed Martin on nonemotional grounds had severe doubts and pointed out what they believed to be fallacies in the Martin plan. The most important point, glossed over by the Ambassador and the Secretary of State, was the war. No one thought the Vietnam War was going to end in five years. No one predicted victory for Saigon. A stalemate, an erosion of the North Vietnamese side, yes. But even Martin was forced to admit that there would be, into the foreseeable future, a war in South Vietnam.

Martin's plan was a dream, unfettered by certain realities. The U.S. government, fighting on one hand for Martin's plan, refused on the other to institute government insurance for the investors who, the Ambassador felt, would flock to Saigon. Substantial investment in a war zone without insurance, of course, was virtually unthinkable to American businessmen and other foreigners.

Americans wrote the world's best foreign investment law for South Vietnam. Its tax breaks, its promises of cheap labor, its incentives, its industrial areas were a dream. On paper. The truth of the matter was that the bureaucracy and corruption of the Saigon government chased away investors by the dozens.

And there was Martin's very challengeable statement that all U.S. aid to Saigon could end in three or five years if his plan was accepted. He never explained, and his supporters were unable to explain, how military aid was to be ended. Only once in public, before the House Foreign Affairs Sub-committee on Asian and Pacific Affairs on August 1, 1974, did Martin even approach this particular problem. Economic self-sufficiency, he said, would so enrich South Vietnam that the nation would be able to buy all its military aid.

Actually, the only chance for fast money for the Saigon government was oil. Oil companies had moved to Saigon in 1973, and had begun drilling operations in 1974. By 1975, they had yet to find a well capable of pumping any oil or gas. Since it takes—by oil executive estimates—five years to get a well into production after discovery, there was no chance of making money within three years from this industry.

So in reality, Martin's critics charged, there was little chance of the Ambassador's plan working. Therefore, there was no hope that Congress would pass it into law, despite Martin's constant lobbying efforts.

What Martin wanted was a show of faith in South Vietnam by the American nation. His cruelest critics charged that the death of his son during the 1968 siege of U.S. Marines at Khe Sanh had closed his mind to argument and dissent. He was unable to consider, these men said, a softening in the U.S. line. Martin, it was charged, was so autocratic that he would not consider, would not even read, a field report that showed weakness or fallibility in the Saigon forces or government.

But he missed the greatest single chance to buck up the Vietnamese nation.

Mike McTighe, young and aggressive manager of the First National City Bank branch, hit the nail on the head in a 1974 report to his superiors which he showed me and expanded upon in private conversation. He said there would be no development of Vietnam until the Vietnamese themselves were willing to invest in their own nation. McTighe foresaw conditions early in 1975 that might bring this about. Hundreds of the most powerful men in Vietnam were alleged to have their money tucked away in foreign bank accounts and investments. Lieutenant General Dang Van Quang, the alleged drug dealer* who officially was President Thieu's security adviser, owned land and companies in Singapore and Malaysia. Pham Kim Ngoc, a former Economy Minister and a darling of many Americans, was another example of this thinking. According to reliable banking officials, Ngoc had money totaling eight million U.S. dollars in accounts under his own name in the Chase Manhattan's Taiwan branch.†

McTighe felt in 1974 that the rising exchange rate of the Vietnamese piaster as compared to the American dollar, would make it attractive for Vietnamese investors to begin repatriating their money soon. Only after a year or two of Vietnamese investment, McTighe told his bosses in New York, would Vietnam even be approaching the day of foreign investment of any magnitude.

Martin chose to ignore advice and predictions like these. His confidence in the corrupt leadership of Vietnam and the Saigon army remained intact, unshaken by disclosures of incompetence or warnings of disaster.

He became, then, a stifler of criticism, a critic of critics, seemingly ignorant of the malfeasance around him.

Graham Martin also was imperious. He ran his Embassy more secretly than any predecessor, and had little to do with the Saigon press corps,

---

*On July 15, 1971, NBC Saigon correspondent Phil Brady told a national audience via the *NBC Nightly News* that Quang was "the biggest pusher" in South Vietnam. He further alleged that President Thieu and Vice-President Ky were using money from narcotics sales for their presidential campaigning that summer. A presidential spokesman denied that Thieu was receiving or using such money, but neither Quang nor any South Vietnamese spokesman ever addressed the charges of drug dealing or other corruption leveled against Quang. Brady was expelled from Vietnam "for providing help and comfort to the Communist enemy."

†The U.S. banking official who told me this during a party in Hong Kong in 1974 later implored me not to use the information so long as Ngoc remained an influential official in Saigon, and to refrain from identifying the source of the information. Such information on private accounts is generally not open to the public, and bankers are expected by their employers to keep such information confidential. Since Ngoc is no longer an influential official in Vietnam, however, the stipulation impressed upon me to withhold it from publication has been met.

particularly the resident Americans, except in his personal, critical telephone calls to some of them. He was Ambassador only because he had got a
promise from Richard Nixon that he could run the Embassy his own way.
He represented himself in Saigon, as he had a decade before as envoy to
Thailand.

Hubert Humphrey, when he was vice-president, had a story about
Graham Martin. Visiting Southeast Asia, Humphrey was in the anteroom
of the palace of the King of Thailand. He bore a gift from President
Johnson to the King.

Martin, as Ambassador, told Humphrey just before the audience with
His Majesty that the Vice-President should allow him—Martin—to make
the presentation. Martin said he was, after all, more aware of court protocol
and it was most important that no gaffes be made in the presence of the
King.

At which, Humphrey told newsmen later, "I told that son of a bitch, 'Mr.
Ambassador, whose ambassador are you?' "

The Washington *Post* in April 1975, carried an editorial criticizing Mar-
tin for representing Saigon views to Washington more than he represented
American views to the Saigon government. The title of the editorial was
"Whose Ambassador Is He?"

Yet Graham Martin was his own ambassador. Like an honest advertising
man, he refused to attempt to sell any product in which he did not believe.
Martin believed implicitly in the Thieu government, in a harsh anti-
Communist policy in Vietnam, in the idea of American help to a needy
ally—Saigon.

The problem was that few Vietnamese had the faith that Martin himself
had. When Vietnamese fled Saigon, Martin wanted to stay. While Vietnamese stashed their money abroad, Martin asked for the money of his
own people to replace it. When President Thieu became an inept leader,
hated by his entire people, Martin still believed in him.

Brigadier General Do Kien Nhieu, the mayor of Saigon since 1969, felt
he had to do something after Thieu's speech to the nation. A military man
with no noted accomplishments or medals and a low-key master of corruption as mayor, Nhieu had coasted for six years. He had the support of U.S.
officials, since keeping the city of Saigon on an even keel was a major task of
the United States in Vietnam. And he had forced support from the Chinese
community in Saigon, who were paying tribute to him both in money and in
words because of the power he wielded.*

*Nhieu was the brother-in-law of long-time Thieu Prime Minister Tran Thien Khiem.
Through my wife, a Chinese, I was introduced in Saigon to many Cholon businessmen who
openly admitted that Nhieu both demanded and received gratuities for general influence-

Nhieu decided it was about time he did something, so he issued a statement ordering regular alert drills by the boys and old men of the People's Self-Defense Force (part of the "million-man army of South Vietnam"). Nhieu also ordered the PSDF, the only troops under his command, on a "state of alarm and readiness."

The government had its own idea of what should be done in an emergency, which on March 21 someone finally decided it was facing. Ministers were ordered by Prime Minister Tran Thien Khiem—who was on the edge of a battle royal with Thieu—to put aside all routine work. The cabinet was to discuss only business related directly to the offensive and the threat it posed to South Vietnam.

This order brought some drama to the situation for the first time, so far as the government was concerned, but meant little. What the Minister of Agriculture, say, or the Minister of Veterans' Affairs was supposed to consider as emergency business never was clear. And the ministers intimately involved—refugees, information, defense—were already working long hours on the emergency.

Once more, various strata of government at the top of the South Vietnamese hierarchy had dealt in their own unique decisive manner with an emergency—first, by denying one existed (as Thieu did), and second, by issuing statements showing how well they were dealing with the situation.

Another morale-raising victory was won by the Communists on the battlefield just about the time Thieu spoke to the nation to say his army was winning on all fronts. North Vietnamese troops had been battling with the ARVN for more than a year for a tiny but fairly strategic district capital called Kien Duc. Located 110 miles north of Saigon, the tiny town —little more than a village by American standards—had changed hands twice and was battered by war. Both sides wanted it.

Defenders of Kien Duc did not hear Thieu's words of victory because they were too busy fighting. The town fell in an ARVN rout, following the pattern of the day. As the Saigon soldiers fled to the nearby jungles, trying to get to safety, it was obvious that they would not be back. The Communists

---

peddling. "When he says jump, I ask how high," an English-speaking Chinese told me on one occasion. In return for the payments, Nhieu let it be known publicly that he was the personal friend of the businessman concerned, usually by attending a social function or ostentatiously giving a large gift of money at a wedding or funeral. Saigon's active Chinese-language press carried numerous pictures of Nhieu bestowing personal attention on selected businessmen throughout the early 1970's, almost to the end of the war. Because of his military rank, his title, and his Prime Minister brother-in-law, Nhieu was an influential position in Vietnam three times over. He could, and allegedly did, approve or block virtually any business in Saigon. In 1972, when the Chinese business community and the Taiwanese Embassy cooperated to stage a benefit for refugees, more time was spent by speakers (by actual count) praising Nhieu's presence at the theater than on the plight of those who had suffered during the heavy fighting.

had won the year-long battle for Kien Duc. The heroes of that little town would not be remembered.

The trickle from Hue meanwhile turned into a flood. Thousands, tens of thousands, and finally hundreds of thousands of Hue and Quang Tri residents took to their heels and headed south.

Captain Tran Ba Phuoc* of the First Regiment of the First Division of the Army of the Republic of Vietnam watched from his headquarters as the tide surged past him on Highway 1 and wondered whether he would have the guts to resist flight. Phuoc was a battalion commander in the 1st Infantry Division.

He lived with the knowledge that the division was the best regular army unit in South Vietnam. And with the knowledge that he was at heart a coward. At least he thought he was. He didn't want to die in battle, so he must be a coward. In the 1st Division, officers and men alike were expected to stand and die where duty took them.

Captain Phuoc had no desire to be a battalion commander. He was an officer because he came from a moderately rich family with enough pull to get him his commission with a minimum of problems. Officers lived better than enlisted men in the Vietnamese Army and usually less died . But the family did not have the pull to keep Phuoc from the 1st Division, a combat unit if ever there was one. The former commander of the division was Major General Pham Van Phu, the general with the guts to argue with Thieu about the pull-out from Pleiku and Kontum.

The captain was a battalion commander by default. The appointed battalion commander had been seriously wounded two weeks before in a shelling attack. Another major would come in to take over the battalion later, but for now, Phuoc was in charge. He hadn't minded being executive officer. That job, except for the terrifying moments under fire, had been good because it took little decision making. The major made the decisions and Captain Phuoc made sure they were carried out.

Phuoc knew how to command the battalion, having watched the major for three years. He could follow the book and make the right decisions at the right time. He just didn't want the responsibility of sending men— possibly including himself—to their deaths.

*His real name. From the time I first saw a Radio Hanoi report that he had surrendered, I wanted to get at the story of Captain Phuoc, whose crossing of the lines was then the only one of an officer of the division he served. I never met him, but did talk to three men who said they were part of his headquarters section, and another source who served nearby and who was able to confirm the military actions that took place. The paraphrased dialogue in the sections on Phuoc is reconstructed from statements of the three men who were with him at various times during the period.

There were hundreds, thousands of soldiers in the tide of people fleeing Hue to Da Nang. Phuoc saw shoulder patches in particular from the militia and dozens of the unique uniforms of the Marines. But he saw few soldiers of the 1st Division. Discipline was being maintained, despite the shelling of the Hue headquarters, which now was growing so heavy that he could hear it.

In fact, action was picking up all around Hue. In Phuoc's own sector here, just off Highway 1 at the district town of Phu Loc, 15 miles south of Hue, his battalion was under fire and in rifle fights with tiny advance Communist units. The fighting had been going on almost all day. Casualties were very light. But Phuoc and his men knew the fights were merely probes, with the North Vietnamese and Viet Cong advance volunteers picking up information about where Phuoc had placed his listening posts and outer defenses.

Supposedly, Phuoc's battalion was screened to the west by 1,000 Rangers, two battalions of troops Phuoc would not have given you one piaster for. There was a time when Rangers were elite troops, proud of their traditions, a small, crack force. Now they consisted all too often of draft dodgers and the scum of the ARVN—men picked up from the jails of Saigon. They couldn't follow orders and the only mayhem they were capable of was on the streets of Saigon or in the bars and brothels of Hue or Da Nang.

When the North Vietnamese decided they wanted to break through from the mountains to the coast in Phuoc's sector, the captain knew there was no chance of the Rangers' so much as slowing their drive. And the shelling was getting heavier now. Eight hundred yards away on Highway 1, Phuoc could see the occasional rocket (notoriously inaccurate) slam into the never-ending southbound convoy. When it killed or maimed, or damaged a vehicle, there was a barely perceptible pause in the traffic. Then the refugees moved on, sometimes bearing the dead and wounded and sometimes not.

The river of refugees was not moving cheaply, either of human life and suffering or of cash. Because the traffic on the highway was one way only, because it was slow on account of its hugeness, and because the Vietnam War bred war profiteers naturally, it cost a lot to get to Da Nang any way but on foot. Taxis, 20- and 30-year-old Peugeots that looked like something out of a 1940's French gangster movie, jacked their fares from about $5 to $150 for the trip from Hue to Da Nang. Nine persons normally could jam into the cars; now there were more.

Boat owners were doing the same thing. To go from Hue's "port" at Tan My to Da Nang now cost the same $150 as a car, although more could get into the boats. Normally it cost something under $10 for the trip.

Phuoc at least did not have to worry about that. His family was in Saigon, his home. If the time came when he felt he had to run, well, he had his own Jeeplike Toyota gassed up. That, after all, was one prerogative of being battalion commander—your own vehicle and driver. Phuoc kept the keys and distributor cap in his pocket to make sure the car didn't go without him.

Those who did have to run to Da Nang, or felt they had to, had their own worries. They included the little bit of war that reached Highway 1, but it was the least of their problems.

At the end of their journey over the Hai Van pass and as they came into Da Nang, they were greeted by a 60-foot white Buddha statue. On the base of the statue, in huge letters, were the Vietnamese words "Welcome Travelers." The Buddha had been built by the refugees from Hue caused by the Tet offensive. It represented a heart-felt thanks from the survivors of that bit of the war and the massacre of February, 1968.

But now, March 22, 1975, was another story. And before the Da Nang Buddha was able to welcome these travelers, the refugees had their own private wars to fight along the two-lane blacktop.

First was the fight of finding transportation, of course, and as usual the poor took last place. Most walked, although a few managed to find a corner in the back of an American-supplied Army truck manned by a relative or family member.

Then there was the traffic. It was claustrophobic and fantastic, the biggest single exodus in Vietnamese history. At 250,000 persons at the least, it dwarfed the Convoy of Tears, in size if not in sheer human tragedy.

Not that the Hue-Da Nang convoy lacked tragedy. The Hai Van Pass, steepest pass on any road in Vietnam, became a deadly traffic jam. Cars stalled and their brakes failed. Vehicles went over the steep sides of the pass and those behind just kept going. You had to imagine that only death lay at the bottom of the drop, but no one stopped to make sure.

The convoy just kept rolling—military trucks and Jeeps, buses, motorcycles, and three-wheeled Lambrettas used as taxis and trucks by Vietnamese civilians. In the main, it was a one-lane convoy, but at any halt in the traffic, drivers piled into the left-hand lane, trying to pass the bottlenecks. The effect was to make it impossible for anyone to travel from Da Nang to Hue. The traffic was one way.

For the approximately three days and nights that the flight from Hue lasted, it took about a day and a night to travel the 50 miles to Da Nang. The trip normally took a couple of hours.

Lieutenant Colonel Le Trung Hien had a denial to make as he took the podium March 22. He wished to say categorically that Hue was not being abandoned. Correspondents writing about any flight from Hue would have to bear the consequences. This was generally taken as a threat to take away the press card of an offending reporter, a step that usually led to deportation.

Hien's denial of a retreat was partially true. Hue city had been ordered evacuated of civilians and "nonessential" military and police personnel. About 20,000 combat forces, including the Marines, were at the same time ordered to remain in the city. America's favorite combat commander, Lieutenant General Ngo Quang Truong, visited Hue around the time Hien was speaking to newsmen in Saigon. He flew up from his Da Nang headquarters by helicopter to look at the situation.

The "diplomatic sources" at the U.S. Embassy also wished it known that Hue was not being evacuated. Of course the Americans assigned there were commuting from Da Nang, and those "nonessential" Americans were being taken out of Da Nang as quickly as possible. But all information available at the Embassy was that the ARVN was going to put up a battle for Hue.

The consensus of diplomats, newsmen and Vietnamese military officers in Saigon was that Saigon would *have* to fight for Hue. Loss of that city, even if it did not come on the heels of the Thieu's Central Highlands debacle, would be a severe morale blow to the rest of the Vietnamese who supported American principles, if not policies, in South Vietnam. The Communists, according to Gen. Dung's memoirs, also expected a stand by the ARVN.

Hien and the U.S. Embassy sources, usually Press Officer John Hogan but occasionally others, were making their statements on logic. Apparently few in Saigon had any idea of the magnitude of what was going on in Hue.

This was at least partially because as of now there were few in Saigon who believed the Communists could follow up one battlefield success with another quick attack. But in fact, this is exactly what they were doing as they moved from Quang Tri to Hue from the north, and into Hue from the southwest of the former imperial capital. Hien, Hogan, and all others would become believers later, but they were not now.

In fact, the move from Quang Tri to Hue was easy for the North Vietnamese troops involved. The most crucial factor in the ability to consolidate and move on was the flight of the civilians. As refugees poured south to Hue and beyond from Quang Tri, and as the Marines were allowed to retreat, the North Vietnamese had little to consolidate. Their already relatively mobile supply lines merely moved up a few miles, following the troops. With almost no prisoners, civilian or military, to look after, the North Vietnamese could keep on going.

While most Vietnamese were leaving Hue, newsmen were struggling against the tide to visit the city. They were given no help in reaching the former imperial capital, and most made it by boat from Da Nang. Those who did make it talked to Truong this day.

It was March 17, a week before the first uniformed Communist soldier walked into Hue. A handful of newsmen had made it to the city they usually insisted on calling the ancient imperial capital. Actually, Hue was not ancient. But it was so rundown by 1975 that it seemed older than its 200 or so years. Imperial capital it once was. Ornate tombs of emperors around the city prove it. The mother of the last emperor, Bao Dai, still lives there.

Use of the word *ancient* by the English press apparently comes from the French *ancien,* which merely means "former."

The newsmen who made it to Hue against the grain of the fleeing population, civilian and military, made it there by a variety of means. A few went by military helicopter, others by navy ship, and a couple rented their own sampans in Da Nang for the 22-hour water trip. Experience in covering the war in that area got them there. None of the "tourist" newsmen —assigned briefly to Vietnam for the offensive—made it to Hue on their own, and only a couple of foreigners made it at all. AP's Peter Arnett, probably the most respected newsman ever stationed in Vietnam, a combat veteran and an expert at getting around, did not make it to Hue. He spent a day bucking the traffic and finally was swept back to Da Nang with the human flood.

It was easy getting to Da Nang. Air Vietnam, one of Asia's most underrated airlines, flew to the port city until the end. An Air Vietnam DC4, in fact, was one of the last planes to land at Hue's Phu Bai airport a few weeks before. Mortar shrapnel struck that plane as it landed at the almost-besieged airfield, ending all commercial flights and most military flights to Hue even before the Communist offensive officially began.

Ngo Quang Truong, the pro-American general par excellence, made it to Hue this day. Tall for a Vietnamese, braver than any other general, Truong was the inevitable example when Americans talked about what South Vietnamese soldiers should become. He stood tall and wore his stars well, all three of them. Lieutenant General Truong also was so apolitical that most Vietnamese could not believe it and, believers in Machiavelli, suspected he actually was on the verge of launching his own coup. This was, however, something that apparently never entered Truong's head.

His bravery, his dedication, and his instincts as a soldier were proved the previous summer, when crack Communist troops were pushing at Da Nang from the west. They had already taken Thuong Duc township, and were about to take a second, Duc Duc. Truong, at midnight, sent his helicopter pilots home, asked for a volunteer gunner, and headed for the second town, already under shelling attack. Truong, a fully qualified pilot, flew his own chopper.

He landed the helicopter and worked his way to the front lines. He walked from trench to foxhole to trench, talking to his men, praising them, bucking them up, convincing them they could win. When the attack came 24 hours later, the Saigon troops beat it off and held Duc Duc. There was no press release on this trip. Truong wasn't looking for glory, but for results. He was that kind of man.

But now he, like many of the supposedly good Saigon officers, would disappoint those who believed in him. Posturing, speaking openly to newsmen, bragging, doing everything he had refused to do in the past, Truong made an ass of himself.

He would hold, he told the scribbling reporters. He, personally, General Truong, would fight in the streets to save Hue. If the town fell, so would he. Truong was prepared to die to defend Hue. The cowards might run away, but he would fight and die.

Then Truong boarded his personal American-supplied helicopter and, first-hand look completed, flew back to Da Nang. It would be his last sight of Hue, which still had a week to prepare its last stand.

The scene moved a newsman in Saigon to comment that generals always seemed to talk about last-ditch defenses. "Just once," he said, "I'd like to see a general digging one of those last ditches, and then staying in it."

Eventually, there would be one. It would occur on the last day of the war, long after good examples meant anything in stopping the Communist offensive.

What the visitors to Hue saw this day and for the next week, before they too fled, appalled and frightened them. The city was deserted of civilians, with the exception of a few thousand stragglers. These people wanted to leave, but were too poor and in most cases too exhausted to go to Da Nang. The poor souls, for the most part, had already trekked from Quang Tri, to the north. They did not have the spirit to continue south.

An exception to the exodus was the aforementioned "queen mother," Bao Dai's mother. Doan Thuy told her servants she was too old to leave. Weak with age and given to periods of mental instability, or possibly senility, the old lady lived in comfort but not splendor in a villa in Hue. She no longer feared death. Most of her servants, given the choice to leave or stay, chose to stay with their mistress.

Food in Hue was jealously guarded by the few who had it. With no idea how long it might be until the next shipment of food, Hue, a food importer, had closed its markets. Those who stayed kept their own food in their own pantries. Restaurants were closed; the portable noodle shops disappeared.

A reporter who spent two days in Hue looking for his own family was unable to get so much as a bowl of rice.

But those who stayed had done so on their own. There was no sign of panic in the city. Rather, even among the 10,000 or so troops ordered to dig the last ditch, there was an air of resignation. Most of the troops, sensing they had little other choice, told newsmen they would stand and fight. If they had to die, well, it was better to die in battle than against a wall. Most believed they would be executed if captured.

On March 20, as the exodus from Hue slowed and Thieu spoke about a halt to retreats and a solid stand against the enemy and even of victory, the peacekeepers in Hue decided enough was enough. With shelling of the city and bases around its perimeter, with no peace to keep, the International Commission for Control and Supervision packed up and left.

The Poles, Hungarians, Indonesians, and Iranians of the ICCS said, in effect, that the time to leave had come, perhaps even had gone. With the concurrence of their chiefs in Saigon, the peacekeepers left Hue.

It was as if a signal had been given, although it is highly unlikely that the Communists knew or cared what the ICCS was doing. But the shelling immediately became heavier, notably at the Phu Bai airport, at the Phu Loc battalion base manned by Captain Tran Ba Phuoc and his 1st Infantry division soldiers, and in Hue itself. The shelling of the city was centered on the Citadel, where a headquarters of the 1st Division and supply headquarters for the Marines were situated.

The Hue Citadel had become famous during the 1968 Tet offensive. It was in and around the high, thick stone walls of the "inner city" of Hue that the worst combat had taken place. It was on the flagpole atop the wall that the Viet Cong flag flew for a month in 1968; and there, it seemed, it would soon fly again.

Phu Bai was described by newsmen as a mini-Khe Sanh for months, because Communist guns had closed the landing strip even to the mobile choppers. Artillery, rockets, and mortars hit Phu Bai regularly. The two-mile runway was deserted.

Refugees seeking a flight out of Hue were inexplicably lured to Phu Bai. On March 21, an artillery barrage hit one group. Ten persons were killed. The wounded were not counted.

The shelling of the highway near Phu Loc, near Captain Phuoc, had made up the minds of all but the very desperate that road evacuation was also impossible. The build-up began at the Hue "port," a polite name for a beach by the city by the sea. Some estimated that 40,000 persons awaited evacuation at Tan My port, also known as Thuan An. There might have been 20,000 or 70,000. In any case a lot of people were still trying to get out of the Hue area. A brilliant strategist decided that maybe ships would be needed, and plans were drawn up to get LST's to Hue. But most of the people on the beach would not get out of the way of the Communist advance. Many would die waiting for ships.

Most things during the offensive took just a little longer than necessary.

The evacuation of the ICCS gave the first good hint at what lay in the future for Vietnam. Angry mobs and looters broke into the compound minutes after the peacekeepers were pulled out. Those who were angry wanted to demonstrate that they felt the ICCS had let them down by failing to keep the peace.

The looters simply felt, with the political indifference of most Vietnamese, that it was a good chance to make a dollar or add a little something to their homes. The ICCS buildings were cleaned out in hours. Only their shells remained. This would be the pattern everywhere—including Saigon—where pull-outs occurred before the Communist troops came in.

As the Communists advanced, counter measures were, of course, ordered up, both in Saigon and in Washington. Most of them, as always, were secret. It had become an axiom in both capitals that their own people and the people of the world should not know steps that were being taken. The rationale for not making public political decisions escapes many of us who thought that the given reason for the war—and particularly American involvement—was ideological. Secrecy, except for strategic military decisions, could never be defended. To say that the Communists also do it appears to be the most odious explanation of all.

In any case, decisions were being made. Washington, presumably with President Gerald Ford's knowledge and permission, was moving to introduce more and "better" weapons to the Vietnamese military.

In Saigon, the major decision was also secret. President Thieu signed orders drawn up by his various staffs for an even more complete mobilization than he already had. Novice monks—criticized by many as draft dodgers—were to be picked up and inducted. Street checks were to be intensified to find real draft dodgers. Draft ages were extended both ways, to pick up younger and older men. The effect of this was to draft into the regular army many of the irregulars in the "million man army," particularly the armed but largely untrained Popular Self-Defense Forces, who patrolled city streets during curfew hours. They had a kill ratio of approximately 100 of their own men (because of carelessness and murders in anger) to one Communist. They were not exactly the tigers of the Saigon military, and they were untried in battle.

The crackdown and extended draft were kept largely a secret, particularly from the press, because of the political implications. More families were to be split up, more untrained soldiers pressed into service. Wide publicity would only work against Thieu.

It is not only a defense of Thieu but a fact to say that the President had little choice. His army was admitting to losing a battalion of combat troops a day to the offensive—and this did not include what he was losing as areas were overrun. The killed, wounded, and captured on the battlefield were running at 500 a day, and there was no sign that losses would soon stop.

South Vietnam was able to churn out replacements from the training centers and draft stations, although the recruits would not be the equals of the men killed, wounded, or captured. The men had to come from somewhere, and Thieu's secret press ganging order was his only hope of surviving what was quickly becoming a blitzkrieg.

The American military decision—supposedly made in the Pentagon with overseers from the White House—was less defensible, especially from the historical viewpoint.

America, through its leaders, had announced to the world in 1969 that it intended to arm and train the Vietnamese military to make it the equal of U.S. forces. The new decisions to add new equipment, in a panic move, was an admission that the arming and training of the previous six years had not worked. Asia's second largest (next to China) and best-equipped armed force, the Pentagon was tacitly admitting, couldn't make it.

Not only new weaponry but more began to flow into Vietnam. New tactics were drafted, planned, and acted upon.

American B52's were gone. When they left, Americans and Vietnamese alike bragged that they were no longer needed. But now, it was realized, they were needed, if not for tactical then for psychological reasons. There's nothing like believing that those 30 tons of bombs are being dropped on your enemy to boost battlefield morale a bit.

The answer to the loss of the B52's was "mini-B52's." Still-cased racks of bombs were loaded on C130 cargo planes and pushed out the open back door of the lumbering turboprops. They went off in a string, like the B52 strikes, although they did only a fraction of the damage.

Daisy cutters, 15,000-pound World War II surplus bombs used by the Americans only to cut "instant landing zones," were placed aboard Vietnam-bound ships. These huge packages of explosive had tentacles, like World War II antishipping mines. The tentacles exploded the bomb just before it hit the ground, keeping the force of the explosion out and around, instead of down—thus the name. Now the daisy cutters were used in areas where Communist troops were based.

Also aboard the ships were CBU55 bombs, truly a terror weapon and never used by anyone in warfare before 1975. The CBU55 has been called, technically incorrectly but colorfully, the implosion bomb. The effect of its explosion is to suck all air from a large surrounding area. This in turn crushed chests and other cavities of people and other animals in its range, 100 yards or more, depending on the exact terrain. Also dropped from a cargo plane, the bomb was used only once by the South Vietnamese. This had nothing to do with politics or humanity. The ships bearing the CBU55's were late in arriving and the battle for Saigon had begun before one could be loaded into the C130's. It killed hundreds of North Vietnamese troops.

For the record, Washington also made a few decisions, almost all of which went out over the name of President Ford. It was clear that the United States was not going to return to the Indochina battlefields in any guise. But Ford himself spoke of the tragedy, of allies going down the drain, of American commitment. The United States, he said, would give its noncombat best. The President diverted cargo and military ships for use as carriers of refugees. The decision that the Communists wanted to hear was the one saying the United States would not fight, on the ground, in the sky, or on the sea.

While North Vietnam and the Viet Cong managed to get in a few propaganda licks about American interference in their nation, there were sighs of relief in Hanoi in March when Ford again made it clear that U.S. forces would not stand in the way of Communist victory.

One of Ford's major decisions was to fight Congress for more aid to Vietnam. Castigating the Senate and the House for refusing to help an ally, he mounted his forces and went to the barricades with a Congress that was not interested in giving much more of America's money to Saigon or Phnom Penh. Indications were that the final cut-off in military aid could well come in spring votes on Indochina aid.

Now he announced he wanted the facts on Vietnam. Reports from his own people on the scene and from the press were not enough. So Ford put together the last official "dog and pony show" America would send to the Vietnam war zone. Army Chief of Staff General Frederick C. Weyand—the last American combat commander in Vietnam—would head the show. An impressive staff of experts would attempt to find out just what was going wrong out there.

Graham Martin, the American Ambassador to Vietnam, would direct the briefings and set up the schedule for the general.

In Vietnam, Social Welfare Minister Phan Quang Dan, a medical doctor, made a statement concerning U.S. aid. It was little noted outside his nation, because of other events, like the crumbling of Vietnam. Dan said there were already 300,000 refugees in Da Nang, and another 300,000 on the central coast from the Convoy of Tears.

"American aid to Vietnam should be increased, not cut," he said.

Dr. Dan, like most people who took the same line in Vietnam and in the United States, lumped all aid into one package. They ignored the reality that aid came in two packages from Congress—military and "economic," the latter meaning all programs not directly related to fighting the main force war, and including refugee aid and the like.

In fact, according to Congressmen before and after the change of government in Saigon, Vietnam had had a good chance of receiving increased aid to help its refugees. It was military aid that the bulk of the Congress opposed. Twin feelings combined to make a cut—or halt—in military aid almost inevitable in 1975.

First was the continuing recession in America, and the feeling it produced that feeding the Vietnam War was taking food from the mouths of American citizens. And second was a war weariness, particularly with the Vietnam conflict.

END OF THE BEGINNING

The Battle for Hue

The UPI reporter in Hue, Paul Vogle, telephoned Saigon and said 800 artillery, rocket, and mortar rounds hit the northern city and its surrounding territory on March 22. It was the heaviest shelling in several years. The end was coming, although some optimists in Saigon preferred to call it the showdown.

Captain Tran Ba Phuoc was still frightened that evening. At his battalion base south of Hue at Phu Loc, just off Highway 1, Phuoc was thinking of running. What stopped him was an article he had read in an American magazine, he didn't remember which one now, probably *Time* or *Newsweek*. Phuoc said the article was "several years old" and was more or less an interview with an American GI.

The GI said he was always scared in combat—a startling admission to Phuoc, who thought infantrymen were not supposed to be afraid. But the experienced, bemedalled American sergeant said that fear was natural. It was necessary to use the fear, to harness it. Stop; gulp once or twice, he said. Listen to orders and then use your head. A soldier who isn't scared, the sergeant said, is stupid or insane. A soldier who does not admit to being afraid in combat is either lying or a candidate for the funny farm.

Phuoc remembered the article now, but still he could not accept being frightened. He could not admit he was afraid, even to himself. He was doing a lot of gulping, however.

Artillery flares lit up the perimeters of Phuoc's battalion and the unde-

117

pendable Rangers to the west. There was constant shooting now, as troops
fired at targets, imagined or real. Shadows moved, and this night they
frequently were the enemy.

Often, Phuoc could hear the sounds of shells impacting at Phu Bai, Hue,
the port area where refugees waited for boats—digging holes in the sand
and in the bush up from the beach, praying to their gods to get them out so
they would have long lives and be especially pious.

As a battalion commander, Phuoc had several radios in his "headquarters," a tent and small trench. One was tuned to the "command net," the
Hue-based headquarters of I Corps Forward. The network gave General
Truong, still comfortable but working hard in Da Nang, up-to-date information on his crumbling northern flank.

It was on the command net that Phuoc heard the Marines running. Radio
monitoring can give an exciting, full picture of what is happening, as any
police reporter knows.

The Communists took about half an hour to overrun the Marines along
the My Chanh River. The elite and still combat-ready Marines simply
folded, and headed south. This time, they did not stop to blow up bridges.

The My Chanh River was calm and flat early in the evening of March 22.
Private Duc of the Marines, volunteer, runner from Quang Tri, was not
even thinking of fear. The shooting around him and the sounds of shells
hitting Hue, 20 miles to the south, did not particularly bother him. His
sector was quiet. Many Marines were sleeping as best they could in their
holes and trenches.

The pilings of the My Chanh bridge were now familiar. The first couple
of nights after the engineer captain blew up the bridge, the pilings were like
stalking enemies. Now Duc and his buddies were used to them.

Duc was in the middle of the line and not particularly worried, even when
he thought about an attack. A guerrilla raid by sappers was unlikely. It
would be hard for them to get across the river undetected. A shelling attack
was the most likely thing, but no sense worrying about that—there was no
defense save huddling in a hole and praying. Any large attack would hit
other Marines before Duc. He would have lots of time to get ready—or to
run. Yes, he thought, he might have to run. Strange, a week ago, running
was the last thing on his mind. Now it was right up there first.

So now, on guard duty, he watched the river, the bank opposite, about
100 yards away. Nothing moved. Wait, did that bush move? Better make
sure. Half a clip of M16 ammunition, the rifle on automatic, would give an
answer. Duc fired. Nothing moved, there was no groaning, no screaming of
a wounded man. He guessed it wasn't anything.

The Marines in Duc's platoon were still gung ho. They talked about fighting and last-ditch stands. But they also talked about running, and had talked about it since that night at Quang Tri.

The thought of running from battle, when he had been taught to stand and fight, and to attack, was not particularly attractive. But the more Duc and his friends talked about it, the more acceptable it became. There were times, after all, when you were outnumbered and outgunned. Fighting and dying was stupid, if the attack overran your position anyway. An English-speaking Marine, a former interpreter with the U.S. Marines, remembered and translated the American expression *advance to the rear*.

Retreating, for the first time ever in Duc's unit, had become an accept-able alternative to advancing. The men knew of the retreat from the high-lands; they knew their own President had ordered it. If the highlands meant nothing, what could My Chanh mean?

Psychologically, this was a tremendous seed to have planted in the Saigon armed forces. The Communists had failed in 20 years of propaganda to win mass retreats or defections from the Saigon army. Now, particularly with the highlands order to retreat given by President Thieu, South Viet-namese leaders were implanting the idea of retreat—if not surrender—in their own men.

As Duc sat in his trench that night, his feet raised slightly from the damp, chilly ground and leaning on his stolen poncho, he thought of fighting. But right up there in his conscious mind was the idea of running. Most of the survivors of the million-man army had similar thoughts that night.

As confused thoughts of fighting, retreating, and defecting ran through the minds of Captain Tran Ba Phuoc and Private Duc of the Marines, there was no such indecision in Hanoi. This evening, March 22, the elite of the North Vietnamese government and military would make their most impor-tant decision ever.

The obsessively security-minded Communists still will give few details about the meeting, but it apparently was held in a large conference room of the Hall at Ba Dinh, the major square in Hanoi. It began early in the evening and broke up around midnight.

The main speakers were military men, but Le Duan was the guiding force. Le Duan had grown to the status of being first among equals in the triumvirate that ran North Vietnam and the war effort following the 1969 death of Ho Chi Minh. As in many Communist nations, he held the major share of power, despite the fact that he was not so well known outside the councils of government as the other two men in the triumvirate—Prime Minister Pham Van Dong and National Assembly Chairman Truong Chinh. He was neither an elected representative of the people nor a member of the government.

Vietnamese Communism, like all of the major Communist movements in Asia, had a firm nationalist base. Many of its leaders were educated abroad—not in the Soviet Union, but in France, England, Germany, and even the United States. In 1975, many of its leaders could illustrate an old, glib definition of a Communist as "a socialist in a hurry."

Ho Chi Minh, like Mao, had driven himself to the top of the Communist leadership in his country by sheer force of will, hard work, and ruthless purges of personal and political enemies inside the movement. Working for most of its history against French colonialism, Vietnamese Communism had developed almost unbelievable security systems to escape the long arm of the French-run secret police. From its founding in 1933, Ho's Communist Party of Indochina (which would carry a number of different names until 1976, when it became the Communist Party of Vietnam) had developed both overt and covert groups to work towards the eventual goals: control of Vietnam and influences over all Indochina.

By doing two things at the same time, Ho and the Party could, on the one hand, establish and participate in a political front that grouped all parties from far left to far right, while at the same time his secret Party Central Committee could slowly and ruthlessly take over all positions in the front and emerge as the only participant. This was the exact history of the Viet Minh, a coalition that once included even the pro-Nationalist China Kuomintang party, but which emerged as a synonym for Vietnamese Communists.

Two years after the Communist victory in Vietnam, an American who accompanied a negotiating team to Hanoi to discuss U.S. relations with Vietnam described the Vietnamese bargaining as "one step forward, then two steps forward." There was little give and take when one dealt with members of Ho's Party.

This incredible will always to move forward and to persevere until victory marked all the leaders—survivors, really—who led the Party in 1975.

Le Duan, like all the other Hanoi elite, had grown up a revolutionary. His official biographies prove his revolutionary credentials. The man's power officially came from his position as Communist Party boss, or, officially, as First Secretary of the Vietnam Workers' Party. He also was a leading member of the National Defense Council. Political and military decisions never, never were separated by the North Vietnamese. Military leaders were part of the political establishment and men like Le Duan were part of the military elite, although they held no rank.

Le Duan rose from a poor village of Quang Tri province, a part of South Vietnam in 1975 but considered by all Vietnamese to be part of the central section of the nation. By 1930 he was a member of Ho Chi Minh's Indochina Communist Party, and by 1931 he was a political prisoner of the

French on Poulo Condore (later Con Son Island). Released in a 1936 general amnesty, he went directly back to work as a professional revolutionary with Ho.

Four years later and now a member of the Party Central Committee and the Politburo, Le Duan went back to jail. He remained there through the war and was released by Viet Minh when they took over Vietnam for a brief period just after the Japanese surrender in 1945.

Le Duan made his name in South Vietnam as one of the major leaders of the anti-French war in the region. Arriving in the south in 1946 after a year's refresher training in Hanoi, the seat of the Viet Minh government, Le Duan became secretary of both the Viet Minh and the Communist Party in South Vietnam proper, the area from Saigon south.

In 1951, Le Duan formed an organization called the Central Office of South Vietnam—COSVN. This group was the southern branch of the Communist party. It never was publicly spoken of by the Communists. Some of the most important men in the Hanoi Politburo have been its chairmen. In 1975, Number 4 Politburo man Pham Hung headed it. Command of COSVN automatically meant a major voice in the running of the war and other matters in all of Vietnam.

It was COSVN that was the major target of the American troop invasion in 1970 into Cambodia. That it was never found by the U.S. forces probably says less of American troop capability than of the ignorance of American leaders in understanding just what COSVN was and how it was run. President Nixon described COSVN to his citizens in effect as a huge, sprawling, underground Pentagon type of operation.

In fact, it was nothing of the kind. COSVN was what its name said it was—an office, little more, and a dispersed one at that. Unless there were very important decisions to be made, its leading members seldom met. American intelligence officers, after the fact (and their statements were backed up by Cambodian security police) said COSVN officers communicated with one another and with Hanoi through the Viet Cong Embassy in Phnom Penh until the coup against Prince Sihanouk in March 1970. By then, communications were much better throughout Communist areas in South Vietnam and in the Cambodian and Laotian sanctuaries, and there was little trouble despite the loss of the diplomatic mission.

COSVN was one of the ultrasecret, covert groups set up by the Communist Party to control events in South Vietnam. It was the secret complement to the public, southern-controlled groups that comprised the Viet Cong—the National Liberation Front, the Alliance of National, Democratic, and Peace Forces, and the Provisional Revolutionary Government of the Republic of South Vietnam.

COSVN's exact membership, and therefore its actual size, remains a state secret today, although the emergence of some of its figures after the Communist victory give a good indication that it had perhaps a dozen persons with any power. In any case, it had changed little between Nixon's speech and final victory, and the outlines of the group can be seen by the student of Vietnam.

There were three major figures: COSVN director Pham Hung, Number 4 man in the Hanoi Party Politburo; Vo Chi Cong, head of the Party's southern branch, known as the People's Revolutionary Party; and Nguyen Van Linh, a man about whom little is known but who was the second or third most powerful Communist in South Vietnam. In matters of vital policy, these three men *were* COSVN. On momentous decisions, they issued orders only after agreement had been reached in discussions with Hanoi. On lesser decisions, a selected few other COSVN personalities would be consulted, or even given authority to act in a limited manner.

COSVN was highly mobile, well protected, and kept from all fields of battle. Its guards were so rigorously chosen that—according to several senior defectors in separate interviews during the war—they were never allowed to leave their place of duty, had no vacations except in camp, and could expect to go home only in one of two ways: when the war ended or if they were killed. COSVN members for the most part stayed in the sanctuary areas inside Cambodia, and orders they issued passed through at least two cutouts along the way to field commanders to lessen the chances of the Americans' or others' discovering their hideouts by capturing and interrogating couriers.

Members of COSVN, however, dealt only with the highest policy matters. The group perhaps most closely resembled the U.S. National Security Council. It did not participate in the day-to-day running of the war in South Vietnam. Rather it gathered, sifted, and planned only the most important of decisions. One example is the 1968 Tet offensive, which COSVN ordered with the expectation of winning the war. COSVN officials ordered the 1968 attacks after careful consideration of both the political and military sides of the equation. The orders simply said that field commanders should launch coordinated attacks at Tet, occupy the cities, and win the war.

COSVN members did not, however, issue orders more specific than that. How the attacks were to proceed, which troops were to participate at which battles—these were decisions always left to field commanders. (General George Patton wrote in his memoirs that a commander should concern himself only with the unit directly under him—a division commander with regiments, for example—a rule apparently adhered to by the Communists.) Tactics were left to tacticians.

Most COSVN decisions, even the military ones like the 1968 Tet attacks, were taken on the basis of political realities as COSVN members perceived them. Vietnamese leaders never truly doubted that the United States could defeat Vietnam in a no-holds-barred war.* But they dealt with the political realities, and made virtually all of their military decisions based on politics. American planners and the Saigon officers they trained too often paid only lip service to the cliché that politics and warfare are inseparable, perhaps because it was a cliché.

Le Duan set up COSVN. In 1951, when he did so, he specifically took for the director of COSVN—himself at the time—only political control of the war in Nam Bo, or South Vietnam proper. Military decisions were given to the military. The Party in Hanoi controlled northern and central South Vietnam directly.

Le Duan's deputy when he formed COSVN was an up-and-coming revolutionary named Le Duc Tho. Tho later gained more publicity than any other North Vietnamese except Ho Chi Minh by conducting peace talks with Henry Kissinger. Unlike Kissinger, he turned down the Nobel Peace Prize that the two somehow were voted.

Le Duan went north in 1953, as victory over France became inevitable. His job for the next three years was setting up and implementing the regroupee program. Under terms of the 1954 Geneva agreements with France, the Viet Minh were to regroup all their soldiers in the north. In practice, some went north for further training and later infiltration back south. Others stayed behind to look after everything from important political matters to the secreted arms caches the Viet Cong would pick up and use later.

The program was, of course, a success in the eyes of the North Vietnamese, since pro-Communists had a decent revolution going against President Ngo Dinh Diem within three years of the 1954 armistice. Le Duan's star continued to rise.

---

*An apparently true story, widely told by Eastern European Communists stationed in Hanoi at the time and later confirmed reluctantly by several Vietnamese officials following the 1975 victory, is that the United States came close to defeating North Vietnam in 1972. News reports from Hanoi in early 1973, and others from Europe at the same time, quoted officers in Hanoi as saying that if the United States had kept up its bombardments and port blockades, it could have demanded the surrender of North Vietnam. The intense attacks by B52's on Hanoi and Haiphong were hurting the morale of the government and people badly. One story said that after the last B52 strike on Hanoi on December 28, 1972, there were only five more SA2 surface-to-air missiles in place at the capital, and no more SAM's to speak of were making it through the port blockades. That the United States could have destroyed North Vietnam by military means at any time during the war was never disputed, and it is a matter of public record that many senior U.S. officers often complained of restrictions placed upon their military actions by "the civilians" in the government. It is equally true that at no time was it official U.S. policy to destroy North Vietnam.

Truong Chinh botched the communization of farms in North Vietnam in 1956, and Le Duan was elevated to top Politburo rank. It was to him that Ho turned in an effort to regain the ground lost by the antigovernment feelings of the farmers and the slaughter of tens of thousands by the North Vietnamese army. Le Duan succeeded brilliantly, even achieving much voluntary cooperation among peasants for land communization. Le Duan used tactful persuasion rather than naked force, and his method became a model after the "liberation" of Saigon in 1975. His success along this line probably would save thousands of lives in a blood bath in South Vietnam.

By 1958, the Communist Party was losing ground in South Vietnam. Le Duan trekked south for a first-hand look. The results of his trip, which carried over into mid-1959, were formation of the National Liberation Front—a South Vietnamese party, in effect—and the beginning of the infiltration south of the "regroupee" Viet Minh living in North Vietnam.

Le Duan later favored, and helped prepare North Vietnam for, the use of North Vietnamese troops in the south. He helped plan and prepare the Tet offensive, which was to run the Viet Cong political and military structure and make the southern Communists even more dependent than ever on the northerners. There is no evidence of any Machiavellian scheme in all this, however. By 1968 the northern and southern branches of the party were intertwined, with the leading lights actually hailing from the central part of the nation and often holding office both in the Workers' Party in the north and the Peoples' Revolutionary Party in the south.

It was this man who announced the big decision this evening of March 22 in Ba Dinh Hall in Hanoi.*

As with most of the meetings throughout the offensive, relatively junior military officers—two- and three-star generals—briefed the assembled officials on just what was happening in the south.

The briefing was factual, if optimistic. The officers felt, and there was no argument, that all planned targets of the offensive and others as well would be in Communist hands in days. That Hue would fall there appeared little doubt. Advances had been more spectacular than planned, or even than hoped for. The easy victory in the highlands, the officers pointed out, left

---

*The basic source material, and most of the paraphrased speeches, for this and other top-level meetings in Hanoi before and throughout the offensive, is a lengthy report issued under the names of Generals Giap and Dung and printed in four installments in Hanoi newspapers in June 1975. Although it contained no anecdotes of the kind that made Dung's later effort so fascinating, it went much deeper into the decision-making process as the offensive developed. The color and details of procedure at the Hanoi meetings were provided by a senior Viet Cong government official. This man, who has some Western education and a good understanding of the workings of the press, asked that his information be kept "on background," meaning that his name not be used in connection with the material provided.

their units virtually intact. South Vietnamese resistance on the battlefield had been, thus far, woeful.

The briefing officers were frankly surprised at the lack of a stand by the Saigon army. A few had predicted a mass retreat from highlands outlying areas, but all were surprised at the abandonment of Pleiku city and at the rout it had turned into: An entire South Vietnamese division, the 23rd, had been rendered "combat ineffective," that is, it had been wiped out.

General Giap took over after this general briefing. His report, which obviously was leading up to something, was more particular. He listed the following points:

• The Saigon army was in its worst state of demoralization ever.

• Saigon troops were being wiped out at the rate of more than a battalion a day. Their replacements would be untested.

• North Vietnamese agents within the Saigon administration reported that Saigon had no real idea of the Communist troop disposition. Almost any attack by the North Vietnamese army would come as a surprise, in strength if not in location.

• It appeared obvious, that America would not re-enter the war, although it was always possible. Comrade Le Duan's prediction, made last December, that the Americans would not interfere on the battlefield, appeared certain. Antiaircraft guns and missiles in the north were on full alert, just in case. Introduction of U.S. ground troops, while highly unlikely, was possible. But it would take a month or more before they could begin fighting.

• Saigon and Washington were not yet ready to concede defeat by any stretch of the imagination. But it was entirely possible, with more and greater victories, to push them into a position where they would be forced to sue for peace.

• The Saigon army of two years before, armed and trained by the Americans and still remembering American troop participation, could hold the North Vietnamese army. But the North Vietnamese army had gotten better and Saigon forces were deteriorating. [Giap's actual words, reported later, were: "Because of their extremely reactionary acts against the people, the puppet government and army has many basic weak points, in every field. Because of their extreme dependence on the United States, these weak points have deepened more and more since the U.S. troop withdrawal (of 1972 and 1973), and the puppet regime has weakened in a very clear manner. It cannot cope with the ever stronger forces of the Vietnam revolution, militarily or politically."]

• Within a week, Communist forces should control at least 12 of 44 provinces in South Vietnam. The capture of Da Nang, the 13th, was likely, although it was possible that the more elite units of the Saigon army might gather there for a major battle.

General Giap was a warm-up man at this Ba Dinh meeting. Now the star, Le Duan, began to speak. There were tremendous cheers throughout his address, which lasted about 30 minutes. According to one participant: "We all were very jubilant." Le Duan clapped while the others applauded, the typical Communist gesture signifying that the speaker is merely one of the people and speaking for them.

Presumably there is a written record of Le Duan's exact words, but it has not been published. The following is reconstructed from interviews and other documents.

Le Duan took the gathering through the revolution, a common method of beginning a speech for a Vietnamese Communist. The seeds of Vietnamese revolution were sown by the great Ho Chi Minh, nurtured in his mind and body in jails, in jungle hideouts, and in the seat of government at Hanoi. The Party, led by Uncle Ho and even now following his teachings and his last will and testament to the letter, had made all the great decisions of the Vietnamese people.

The Vietnamese people were on the verge of throwing off the last vestiges of foreign regimes. For 2,000 years, the valiant people of Vietnam had fought foreigners and while sometimes Vietnam had been subjugated, never had it been enslaved.

Uncle Ho had once lived in Saigon, and had died (1969) without seeing the southern city again. But under him, the Vietnamese revolution had flowered and matured and Uncle Ho had put victory within reach of the Party and the people.

For scores of years, the Vietnamese people had battled French colonialists, Japanese fascists, and American imperialists and neocolonialists. The new colonialism of the American imperialists was the most odious of all foreign controls over the Vietnamese people. But the Vietnamese people were fighting under the glorious Party banner, and as with French colonialism and Japanese fascism, neocolonialism also was doomed to failure in Vietnam.

The reason for the imminent failure, Le Duan went on, was the correct assessment of the situation by the Party. Not only did the Party correctly assess the overall failure of U.S. neocolonialism, but it also had correctly assessed the failures on a day-to-day basis.

Because of the correct assessments and decisions of the Party, the American imperialists had become more and more abashed by their setbacks in Vietnam. At home and abroad, U.S. imperialism was encountering more and greater difficulties in the political, economic, and military domains.

(Le Duan did not give examples, but the North Vietnamese press, naturally enough, printed a wide selection of Western news articles about the

American recession, problems with allies, and the like. North Vietnam exaggerated many of these stories. Students of North Vietnamese propaganda were amused to notice that the Watergate problems and resignation of President Nixon were—so far as Hanoi was concerned—directly attributable to the Vietnam war. The failure of American policy in Vietnam, went the official line, was directly responsible for Nixon's ouster. This deep-seated belief of North Vietnamese officials that for Americans Hanoi lay at the center of the planet continued through 1975. When President Ford fired part of his cabinet and reduced Henry Kissinger's role—if not his status—in the November Sunday Night Massacre, Hanoi again interpreted this as a necessary move because of the U.S. failure in Vietnam.)

Le Duan continued that America had been forced, as a result of correct Party policy, to take a giant step backward in Vietnam and the Indochinese peninsula and even to revise its world strategy. Because of the resistance of the Vietnamese people and their support by the people of the world, U.S. capabilities in Vietnam were becoming more restricted day by day. *Even if American forces were committed they could not save the situation in Vietnam.*

But while the forces of the U.S. and their puppets in Saigon had become progressively weaker, the revolution had grown progressively stronger, Le Duan told his excited audience. Never before today had the balance of forces between North Vietnam and the U.S. puppet armies been so favorable to the revolution.

Le Duan was ready for the climax of his speech. In his almost-raspy, distinctive voice, accustomed to hours-long speeches, Le Duan would tell assembled friends and officials what they wanted to hear.

The Party, he said, has analyzed the situation—on the battlefield and politically, within Vietnam and through the world. This is our conclusion:

The people now face the historic opportunity to liberate the south completely. The people have the opportunity of achieving revolution for the entire country, and fulfilling the task of the third Party Congress. Hard fighting lies ahead but we will absolutely win, the enemy will absolutely be defeated. The time has come when we have the conditions to ensure a complete victory.

Our army and people, led as always by the correct decisions of the glorious Party and fighting under the banner of the beloved Uncle Ho, have come to an historic strategic decision to open a general offensive and uprising, a large-scale strategic, decisive battle throughout the battlefield of South Vietnam. This offensive will be aimed at eliminating and disintegrating the entire puppet army, crushing the entire puppet administration, and securing the entire government for the people.

In other words, Le Duan and the Communist Party had decided to go for broke. There were no more limits on battlefield goals, and the aim was no longer to force negotiations for a coalition government. The aim was victory.

The applause could be heard a block away.

The dedicated leaders of North Vietnam, by the way, do talk in this stilted way, even to one another in informal discussions.

The decision to go for broke had not been made lightly, despite Le Duan's expressed optimism and implication that it was the only decision possible. Offensives were nothing new for Vietnamese Communists, and they were singularly unsuccessful before 1975. Giap's heralded offensives in the north in 1951 and 1953 were neatly turned back by the French and failed to gain the expected victory. Similarly, general offensives in the south in 1968 and 1972 had gained ground but had won little more than slightly increased areas of control. The Tet offensive of 1968 was a disaster of immense proportions in one sense. The Viet Cong as an army and organization was all but wiped out, and from 1968 on, only the North Vietnamese army was capable of winning the war.

Yet each offensive had gained intensely important victories in South Vietnam. The Tet offensive was responsible for taking the United States out of the ground war, although American combat participation dragged out through mid-1971. The 1972 offensive, while causing unbelievable strategic damage in North Vietnam because of the U.S. retaliatory bombing raids, had resulted in the Paris agreements, which removed the American air threat.

The last interest of the American public in participation in Vietnam fighting was taken away when the POW's were released. Those few Americans who cared about what happened in Vietnam after that were largely uninterested. Only a handful of Americans cared what happened in Vietnam or who won the war. The story was removed from Page 1 in newspapers, by general agreement of both editors and readers.

After each offensive, the leaders of the Party had reviewed their plans. New political decisions were made, which in turn led to new military decisions. Simply put, the decisions after 1972 were to build the North Vietnamese military into a fully armed, formidable main force army. Guerrilla warfare was all but forgotten. Big guns were moved south and surface-to-air missiles ringed the now-Communist stronghold at Khe Sanh, where U.S. Marines once went through a 77-day siege. North Vietnam had abandoned the idea of popularly supported jungle fighters—farmers by day and soldiers by night. The new army would be supplied by truck, not by donations from the population.

Military victory became the ultimate goal. Le Duan's announced decision to go for a purely military victory made this clear at last.

Finally, General Giap retook the podium at Ba Dinh to lay out details for the March 22 conference. The fighting in South Vietnam would be immediately escalated into an offensive. Everyone, everywhere, would be pressed into action. Directives already had been passed down the chain of command to military and political officers in the south. The end of the war was coming.

But even now, just 12 days into the offensive, Giap had no way of telling how long it would take to complete the victory in the south.

The general told the assembled leaders of North Vietnam that things were going more quickly than expected. But there was no real timetable for victory. A participant in the meeting said the general indicated that it probably would be about six months before control of Saigon could be wrested from the Thieu government and its American bosses.

Private Duc was lazily watching the My Chanh River just a few yards east of Highway 1 when the attack began. He remembers no panic anywhere. He is not sure whether bravery, training, or the knowledge that the attack was inevitable kept panic out.

Again, it was the tanks. The North Vietnamese had outflanked the Marine brigade, 2,500 men and the only decently organized Saigon force between Quang Tri province and tensed-up Hue. From east and west along the south edge of the My Chanh came the tanks, their clanking treads clearly audible in the clear night air, still cool in the spring.

Duc could see guns all around him spitting fire. Saigon artillery, back down Highway 1, was firing randomly around the Marines. The gunners were using maps marked with hastily drawn plotting lines around the Marine positions. But the artillery did little good and there was virtually no chance for air support.

The North Vietnamese tanks, T54 battle tanks and PT76 amphibious vehicles from the Soviet Union, were firing point-blank into the Marine lines, although for the moment doing little real damage. Machine gunners with .30-caliber and .50-caliber guns poked their heads out of the tank turrets, spraying the Marines.

Marines fired back, with machine guns and rifles. The antitank squads along the flanks rose out of the trenches, Marines gripping the single-shot M72 bazookas, firing at the lumbering tanks bearing down on them. One of their shells hit a tread, and the tank went into a wild spin, running out of its track before the driver got stopped. The machine gunner on top whirled his gun around and kept firing.

There would be no easy retreat this time, Duc thought. Last time, the tankers had stopped firing and turned on their lights so the Marines could get south of the My Chanh. Now, it was going to be a matter of fight and perhaps die, or retreat with a hail of bullets on one's back.

Duc was not shooting yet. He was closest to the western perimeter, but had a couple of hundred men—a company and a half of Marines—between him and the tanks, almost half a mile away. A tank shell whirred toward him. He ducked into his hole at the sound. The shell exploded, throwing a little dirt on him. Duc was unhurt, but his ears rang for a couple of minutes.

As his hearing returned, he heard a new noise, in front of him, across the river. The tanks were approaching from the north. This would be a problem. The antitank guns were on the flanks, with only a few of the single-shot weapons at the riverbank. With a good base of fire, the Communists could button themselves inside the floating PT76 tanks and drive across the river, landing virtually at the headquarters of Duc's force.

And that is what they did. The tankers pinned Duc and his riverside defenders into their holes with direct fire from the 76-millimeter guns and machine guns, especially the wicked 12.7-millimeter, equivalent to the Western .50-caliber. The huge green tracers from the big machine guns floated up to the Marine lines, then suddenly burst by, ripping the air. Duc knew the floating bullets only seemed to hang in the air. Any of them, hitting almost any part of the human body, is a killer.

People were getting killed on the perimeter, Duc could tell. The screams of the wounded were carrying back to him during the lulls in shooting that always punctuate even the most intense battles. A Communist tank went up in flames from an antitank weapon. Another was hit with a lucky artillery round by Saigon troops six miles back down the road.

One of Duc's buddies yelled at him that the brigade commander was frantically calling for airstrikes against the tanks. Duc felt that even in the unlikely event that Da Nang-based warplanes came, they would be too late, given the 100-mile flight necessary to reach My Chanh.

This Communist tank force clearly was even larger than the one that routed the entire Marine division from Quang Tri.

The Marines had two choices, fight or run. Unlike many other Saigon units, few individual Marines and no Marine units thought of two more possibilities, surrender or defection to the Communists.

Duc thought later that he was perhaps the 25th man in his unit to begin to retreat. No order was given. The mass retreat of a 350-man militia battalion to the east may have started the Marines in motion. The militia battalion was hacked up. The Marines remembered their training, stayed disciplined, but pulled back all the same. Advancing to the rear, Duc thought.

Small units, squads, platoons, even a couple of companies stayed together. Duc found himself with about 50 men from his unit. They leap-frogged backward, by instinct, reversing the procedure for attack that they had learned in training. Shoot. Rise up. Hunch down and run. A dozen steps, two dozen. Fall flat, turning back to the battle zone as you fall. Get ready to shoot again, covering the men you pass as they in turn retreat.

One mile, two. Many, many Marines fell, Duc said. Few were picked up. Few were even examined to see if they were dead or wounded. Men able to run ran. Others were left. It was said the Communists were humane to the wounded. Duc hoped tonight those stories were right.

The battle for Hue had begun from the north.

It began within hours from the south, as well.

Captain Tran Ba Phuoc listened to the Marine retreat on his radio tuned to the command net. The shooting on his own perimeters picked up. Phuoc took another look at his Jeep, the possible key to safety. Could he run on Highway 1 south to Da Nang? Shelling was heavy along the road, he could see. But the highway was technically open. With the flow of refugees southward trailing off because of the shelling, Lieutenant General Ngo Quang Truong had ordered tanks north from Da Nang to Hue, still hopeful of making a stand at the former imperial capital.

Phuoc now was very frightened. He walked out of his command post tent so that the radio operators and runners would not see his hands shaking. He spent about 10 minutes or so outside, trying to compose himself. He gulped, took large mouthfuls of chilly night air.

It was past midnight now, another day, March 23, a Saturday. Phuoc called his companies for status reports. Commanders were calling back, telling him that their troops were edgy, that several small units of Communist troops had been spotted. Shooting was frequent, although so far there had been no casualties among the men guarding the perimeters. The Communists appeared mostly to be bypassing the battalion for the moment.

Warning calls were made to the Highway 1 units, militiamen for the most part. Phuoc put in a special call to the militia company guarding the Thua Luu bridge just outside Phu Loc district town and the most important bridge within 30 miles. Thua Luu was a frequent North Vietnamese target. Successfully dropping the bridge—something the Communists managed every so often—meant long delays in Highway 1 traffic to Da Nang.

Phuoc, with his eye again to his Jeep, wanted no delays in Highway 1 traffic. So he told the militia commander by radio that Communist units had been spotted working their way toward the highway. Possibly, he said, they were commandos headed for the bridge. The militia commander, a sergeant, apparently had been awakened to take the radio call. He grumpily commented that maybe the Communists were headed elsewhere, but that he would have his men keep an eye out. Then he curtly signed off.

The bridge went up about 20 minutes later with a roar that startled everyone for miles around. A sheet of flame was visible for at least 15 miles. Phuoc, as a matter of form, tried to reach the militia unit on his radio, but there was no answer.

Highway 1 now was cut. If Phuoc was going to retreat, it would have to be to the north, into Hue. A bad choice. The reluctant battalion commander began to think of the possibility of fighting and dying.

The North Vietnamese knifed through the two Ranger battalions supposedly guarding Phuoc's western flank, like a shark through water. And like a shark, the Communist force struck out to the sides, ahead, and behind as it overran the 700 Rangers. Phuoc's unit now was in a bind. But still the Communists, apparently intent on wiping out the Rangers, held back the attack on Phuoc's battalion.

Tran Ba Phuoc thought of home and rice fields and living. He had reached 31 on his last birthday. He had a lot of living to do.

At 4 A.M. Phuoc's battalion came under attack from the north and the south. The assault from the north took the unit off guard, since it meant that the Communists had outwitted Phuoc and infiltrated between his men and Hue.

Now there was no retreat and the fighting was getting heavier.

Phuoc was giving orders mechanically, trying to move some of his forces from the western perimeter to the north, at the same time attempting to avoid stripping the very exposed western side completely.

Here, as at My Chanh, the green tracers of the Communist machine guns and rifles were floating through the air, although here they were doing more damage to the smaller 1st Division unit.

Company commanders' reports by radio indicated that at least two North Vietnamese battalions were attacking, one from each direction. Phuoc was switching from one radio frequency to the other, trying to keep up with the reports coming in.

Suddenly, the radio operator on one of the instruments stopped turning the dial. Phuoc heard an unfamiliar voice giving attack orders. He realized with a start that it was an officer of the opposing force, a North Vietnamese officer, and probably a battalion commander by the authority in his voice and the type of orders he was issuing.

Actually, coming across North Vietnamese and Viet Cong tactical units on the radios was not an unusual event. On many occasions, officers from the opposing armies even talked back and forth to each other, sometimes philosophically, sometimes hurling propaganda and invectives, before one cut the other off.

Phuoc listened to the other officers for a few moments, trying to detect the pattern in the orders of his opposition. What he heard was chilling. Though talking in code, the North Vietnamese apparently was telling his units to hold their positions while awaiting still other battalions or companies—it was not clear which—to come up and renew the frontal assault on Phuoc's perimeter.

The others in the command tent heard what Phuoc heard. One man, a young private, began shouting at Phuoc. He said they were all going to die. Phuoc said later he "had to subdue him," although he tried not to maim the young man as he knocked him unconscious. He happened to agree with the conclusion of the young private.

The pistol-whipping of the private kept the other men in the tent quiet. But panic could become general at any time, Phuoc realized.

Phuoc picked up the handset of the field radio, clicking it several times. The North Vietnamese officer, all business, demanded to know who was on the network. Phuoc did not answer. He was suddenly thinking the unthinkable.

Captain Phuoc did not know months later whether he did what he did to save his own skin or because he felt responsible for men like the young private. He said he would not have done it had it not been for the brief drama of the hysterical young man who was so afraid of dying on the battlefield.

Phuoc clicked the microphone once more, took a deep breath and coughed twice.

Depressing the "talk" button, he began speaking. He said he could recall the exact words.

"This is Captain Tran Ba Phuoc, battalion commander of the Army of the Republic of Vietnam. You are attacking my position. I wish to surrender."

There was silence for a moment. Phuoc repeated his statement, again releasing the "talk" button on his microphone to give the North Vietnamese officer a chance to reply. Outside, the battle continued. Phuoc was about to talk again, when a voice came on the radio. Presumably, the Communist officer had informed his own superior officer of the sudden call from the enemy and the more senior man was to give the answer.

"This is Mr. Ba [the word means three; Communist pseudonyms, used for security reasons, almost always are numbers] of the People's Liberation Armed Forces," the man said.

Mr. Ba informed Phuoc he was not able to accept his surrender. That would take a more senior officer than he. But Mr. Ba had been instructed to receive to the fold of the patriotic forces all those freedom-loving Vietnamese who saw the errors of their ways in fighting for the American imperialists and who earnestly desired to join the fight for freedom from foreign domination.

It may sound like double-talk to the Westerner, but Phuoc understood immediately. He asked Mr. Ba to wait for several minutes. Mr. Ba said he would wait for days if necessary, but that in the meantime, the attack would continue.

Phuoc hastily got on the radios to his company commanders. He outlined the situation to each and recommended the roundabout Communist surrender terms. Three lieutenants agreed with Phuoc within five minutes. They were losing men to mortar attacks on their exposed flanks, and had—like so much of the Saigon army—lost their taste for battle, especially when outnumbered.

Another company commander, a second lieutenant, differed with the other company commanders. He would not surrender, he said. Phuoc pleaded with him. Retreat was cut off, he pointed out. The North Vietnamese were bringing up more troops. That the battalion would be overrun, there was little doubt. There would be no air support before dawn. Dawn was a good two hours away.

The second lieutenant disagreed. His troops would hold, he vowed. Surrender meant death and—more significantly to this man—surrender meant dishonor. And furthermore. . . . Suddenly, the young officer's radio went dead. Phuoc was about to try an alternate frequency, when an unfamiliar voice came on.

A sergeant blandly informed Phuoc there had been an accident at the company command post. The young second lieutenant was temporarily out of action. In fact, on second thought, it appeared the man was out of action permanently. But he, the sergeant, now in charge of the company, had happened to hear Phuoc's proposal to surrender. The company accepted.

Phuoc returned to Mr. Ba's radio frequency. His battalion, he said, was prepared to surrender. Mr. Ba repeated that only if Phuoc and his men agreed to cross over to "the revolution" could he consider the offer and guarantee the safety of Phuoc and his men. Phuoc agreed.

HANOI, Vietnam News Agency, March 26—A battalion of the First Regiment, 1st (First) division of the Saigon army in Thua Thien province crossed over to the revolutionary side Saturday, bringing along all its weapons, according to the Giai Phong Press Agency.

The Saigon battalion was besieged in Phu Loc district when Captain Tran

Ba Phuoc, its commander, succeeded in getting contact with the People's Liberation Armed Forces and decided to change sides together with the whole unit.

Whether surrender or defection, it was the first mass crossing of the lines by a Saigon army unit in many years.

Phuoc's showing of the white flag was of course not publicized by the Saigon army or the American propaganda machine, and in fact was highly classified information. But the word got around just the same, thanks to the Communist propaganda outlets, including word of mouth by Communist agents and sympathizers.

Phuoc saved the lives of most of his battalion, of that there is no doubt. But by surrendering as a unit, Phuoc's battalion provided heady propaganda for the North Vietnamese and the Viet Cong.

First, the mass surrender of one of the elite battalions of *the* elite infantry division was another major step in the demoralization process of the Saigon army.

Second, it gave the first early indications that there was to be no blood bath by the Communists in South Vietnam. This, in turn, provided surrender and survival as an alternative to fighting and dying. Phuoc's battalion, it was known generally in the Hue-Da Nang area, suffered no reprisals. The men received treatment far superior to that of even a prisoner of war. They were removed to Quang Tri province, where they slept in abandoned homes of residents.

While kept under guard, Phuoc and his men were free to walk around. Their interrogation sessions were short and calm affairs, and their indoctrination lectures—always a feature of newly captured areas of people —low-key. Phuoc, like thousands after him, said the first few weeks in the hands of the North Vietnamese were some of the best he spent in Vietnam.

Phuoc did not resent the propaganda lectures. He felt he learned much from the Communist officers and officials who "explained" to him their view of the war. He was not converted to the North Vietnamese viewpoint, he insisted, but by the time Saigon was captured he had come to the point where he felt he understood. And he said he never again could fight against Communist forces.

Panic built slowly in Vietnam during the offensive. Often there was none, so quickly did the Communists move from this point on. Although it had two more days to live as part of the Republic of Vietnam, Hue was calm.

A militiaman in the Citadel said he was glad the civilians were leaving. It did not bother him at all. Now, the soldiers could fight for the city without worrying about killing and maiming women, children, and old people.

In Da Nang, however, panic was definitely building. The Air Vietnam office, too small at the best of times, cramped into the ground floor of the magnificently misnamed Grand Hotel, closed its doors because of crowds trying, begging to get a ticket to Saigon. All flights were overbooked, of course. Extra planes were put on the Da Nang-Saigon route, but there was no hope of flying to the capital everyone who wished to go.

From Da Nang, there was only Saigon to head for. The second largest city in the south was clogged with refugees. Now there was a definite movement south. With roads toward Saigon blocked by fighting, with no commercial shipping to speak of available to the population, Air Vietnam represented the last hope. Some staff members of the airline black-marketed tickets. Others tried to help friends get aboard the planes.

In Saigon, life went on. Not a shell had hit the city proper in four years. Saigon always was an island in the war zone, anyway. Seldom had the full shock of warfare been felt in the capital, and its residents had a tremendous ability to forget quickly those few occasions when they had seen war.

Saigonese told a newsman he was crazy to take his family to Phnom Penh in February, because the Cambodian capital was under constant rocket attack. They had forgotten that they had lived with the same daily threat of rockets for more than a year, and as late as 1970, rocket attacks were frequent.

American intelligence sources, however, were picking up some disturbing rumors. The stories had it that Americans now were stuck in the middle. Viet Cong units supposedly were entering Saigon, and were going to hit out at United States citizens, the natural enemies of the Communists. Other stories had it that formerly pro-American organizations—the police and the Saigon air force in particular—were setting up volunteer assassination squads to liquidate Americans.

The reason for the anti-Americanism by Saigon military and paramilitary units was the obvious cut or halt in American military aid to South Vietnam by the U.S. Senate and House of Representatives. None of the stories of Saigon assassination squads ever was confirmed, before or after the Communists took over Saigon. But two days before Hue fell, American officials were warned to stay off the streets of the capital except when it was unavoidable. After dark, Embassy and military officials were told, it was best to travel in pairs of Americans, if travel could not be avoided. Travel on foot was not recommended.

In fact, there was surprisingly little anti-Americanism among the Saigonese while supporters of the Republic watched the crumbling of the Saigon army. Maybe for them, too, the collapse came too quickly for an outraged reaction.

As for the supposed Viet Cong terror squads, there never was a confirmed report of a Communist attack on any American individual or installation in South Vietnam during this period. Publicly, the Viet Cong and North Vietnamese vowed over and over again to allow United States citizens to leave Vietnam unmolested. And that is what happened. Americans caught in the middle of the war, of course, received no special treatment during the battle. Two Marines died in the shelling of Tan Son Nhut air base the day of the American evacuation from Saigon, for example. But there never was an attack targeted against an American or a U.S. installation during the 1975 offensive.

The warning to keep off the streets, and a highly publicized grenade attack on an American bus in April, caused a certain tension among Americans as the offensive continued. Few Americans receiving pay from the U.S. Treasury gave much thought, ever, to remaining in South Vietnam much longer.

As Hue was surrounded and prepared for the last-ditch stand, the first American families—wives and children of Embassy and military personnel—left Vietnam. The U.S. evacuation of Vietnam had started. At this point, there was no reason for the U.S. Embassy officially to order an evacuation. If anything, Embassy officials opposed an evacuation as being harmful to the morale of the Saigon allies. But the wise Americans began getting ready to pull out if and when the helicopters came.

Nguyen Van Hao was another example to Americans of what the Vietnamese could become. A rich businessman by inheritance, Hao was considered a topnotch economist by the Americans and by many Vietnamese. In Nguyen Van Thieu's last cabinet shuffle, he became a super-Economy Minister, responsible for all parts of the economy. The Harvard-trained economist was assigned the tremendously difficult task of somehow getting South Vietnam's economy on the march.

Thieu was facing the fact of a cut in U.S. aid. Even with the aid dollars pouring in—at a much reduced rate from the boom days of the late 1960's—the nation was suffering from severe "stagflation." With foreign exchange holdings of something under $50 million, Vietnam was, essentially, broke. Hao was to do something about it.

Hao probably could have helped South Vietnam. Since the nation was irrevocably tied to the United States, only American-type fiscal policies could help. But the French-trained economists in the civil service opposed virtually every directive of his. Hao's policies were instituted only bit by bit, with a struggle over even the most insignificant of directives. The already molasses-slow civil service dug in its collective heels and opposed, often for the sake of opposing.

Nguyen Van Hao was chosen for the economy job partly because he was rich. Corruption was a serious problem in the nation. Thieu's fingers were believed to be stickier than most, but corruption in general was the single largest public issue in the nation. Would *you* fight for a man or a system that drained your income in straight shakedowns, knowing that your taxes were going, not to the nation, but to a man for his personal pleasure?

Hao was above reproach in this regard, went the official line, and many Vietnamese believed it as much as the Americans. The Americans, often slow to catch on to corruption, always thought the best of Saigon government officials. And so they were delighted at the choice of Hao to head the Economy super-ministry.

On March 23, Hao coerced businessmen from the Chinese Chamber of Commerce in Cholon into gathering 300 million piasters, more than $425,000. He said the money was for refugee relief. Although Chinese businessmen were the victims of constant government squeezes, in this case the money was given almost willingly. Newspapers were filled each day with stories and pictures of the tragedy of the Convoy of Tears and of overflowing Da Nang. Thousands of people wanted to help as best they could. For Chinese businessmen, the shrewdest and best in the nation, the easiest way to help refugees was by giving money.

Hao held a brief ceremony in his office to accept the 300 million piasters from the president of the Chinese Chamber of Commerce. Within hours, his office had issued a press release, praising the Chinese businessmen for donating 100 million piasters to the refugee relief program.

Where had the other 200 million piasters—just over $275,000—gone? Privately, Chamber of Commerce leaders said the check for 300 million piasters had been made out to Nguyen Van Hao personally. The president of the Chamber had commented that this was a strange procedure, but he could not believe anyone would steal money from refugees. All of the people are innocent some of the time.

Hao was made a semi-hero of the revolution by the victorious Communists when facts emerged proving he had personally prevented Thieu and his wife from absconding with all the money in the National Bank. (They got 15 tons of gold out when they left, but Hao saved another 15 tons.) He chose to remain in Vietnam after "liberation" and was unofficially named to be an economic adviser to the government during its first year and before the North Vietnamese completed the takeover of South Vietnam in July 1976.

Pham Van Song was asleep in his tiny room in Tam Ky early March 24. Song was an itinerant, fired a year before from his job with the American Army at Da Nang because of the U.S. troop cutback. He had picked up odd jobs here and there, but was unable to afford the cost of living in the nation's second largest city. Here in Tam Ky, he could get room and board—breakfast and dinner—for about $15 a month. When he heard of a job in Da Nang, or when there was nothing to do in Tam Ky, he hitched a ride or rode a bus to the bigger city to look for work.

Song was one of the human tragedies of the war. He spoke fluent English. He was two years short of a high school diploma and there was not a chance in the world that he would receive more formal schooling. His work for the Americans was not particularly appreciated by his own government in Saigon. That, combined with the lack of formal schooling, ruled him out of a civil service job.

The 33-year-old Song had received a draft deferment while he was working for the American military. Now he was technically a part of the million-man army, a member of the Popular Self-Defense Force, the home guard. But his pay went to the ward chief of a Da Nang district where Song maintained his official residence. In return, Song received the papers necessary to keep him from being drafted into the regular army.

The man had gone without work for about three weeks, and there was a desperation in his job searching now. Song was caught in a vicious circle. Unable to live in Da Nang, where the jobs were, he was forced to remain in Tam Ky, where odd and permanent jobs were equally few and far between. He had stayed up late the night of March 23, largely unconcerned about the war, drinking rice liquor with friends.

Skirting the street patrols, he had made it through the Tam Ky shacks and houses well after curfew, and had fallen onto his sleeping mat on the floor of a dismal room he had on the second floor of a small building in "downtown" Tam Ky.

The town was the capital of Quang Tin, the first province south of Da Nang. In atmosphere and distance, Tam Ky and surrounding Quang Tin were much closer to Quang Ngai, the next province south, than to the big city and port to the north. Viet Cong, and for the past few years the North Vietnamese army, always were close to Tam Ky's outskirts. The town was run-down mainly because the people felt there was no sense in building nice homes or businesses when the war would surely destroy them.

But unlike many other towns in South Vietnam, Tam Ky was the actual home of most of its residents. Refugees did not flock to Tam Ky, but rather to Da Nang, or even south to Quang Ngai. The 75,000 souls who lived in Tam Ky town really claimed it as a permanent home, not a temporary shelter from the war.

The defenses of Tam Ky were not exactly the best in South Vietnam. No regular troops garrisoned the town proper, and only a single regiment of the 2nd Division was assigned to the entire province.

A good guess was that about 75 to 80 percent of Quang Tin province was under total Communist domination. In 1974, Viet Cong forces overran the two western districts in Quang Tin, driving the small militia force from each with ease. Most of the population fled before the Communist attacks. So, with perhaps 80 percent of the province under their control, the Communists could claim only 5 percent of the population.

The single regiment of the 2nd Division assigned to Quang Tin was in the northern part of the province. Military commanders of South Vietnam knew for a certainty that any attack aimed at Tam Ky would have to come from the jungles west and southwest of Da Nang. In other words, the attack would have to angle at Tam Ky from the northwest. The 2nd Division troops were set out in a screen to the northwest of Tam Ky to guard against that very real possibility.

There were those in Vietnam who argued that the 2nd Division had come a long way since the late 1960's, when it was one of the worst. The 2nd Division of the Saigon Army, in fact, was many times worse than the Americal Division, demonstrably the worst division America fielded in Vietnam. The argument now went that the 2nd had vastly improved. The argument was three years late. In 1972, under the lackluster Brigadier General Phan Hoa Hiep, the 2nd Division had somehow performed well, fighting head-to-head with the North Vietnamese army and losing little ground.

Now, in 1975, the division was atrocious. Morale was bad and falling. The 1972 fighting had cost the 2nd Division many good men, and the junior leadership was well below the standards of three years before. Saigon had largely ignored the needs of the 2nd Division.

Pham Van Song awoke at 6 A.M. on March 24. The Communists were hitting Tam Ky with rockets. Not a large attack, Song estimated later; maybe 50 or so rounds hit the town. Too tired to move, Song listened to the rockets smash into the town. The attack stopped about 20 minutes after it began. Song listened, but heard no particular excitement, and certainly no shooting.

He went back to sleep.

Around 10 A.M., Song awoke again. Groggily, he walked to his second-story window, which overlooked a side street of "downtown" Tam Ky. He did a classic, movie-style double take, glancing out the window, turning back to his room, then suddenly wheeling back to the window as he realized what he had seen.

Under his window, parked on the street, was a tank. It was dark green, darker than the tanks of the American and Saigon armies. On its long radio antenna, and just below the level of Song's window, was a flag—red on top, blue on the bottom, a gold star in the center. The Viet Cong flag.

Song turned from the window for the second time, his drink-blurred mind starting to function. Non-American-style tank. Viet Cong flag. Street quiet. Hey! The VC have captured Tam Ky.

They had indeed, without a fight. The home guard and police, terrified by rumors making the rounds of every village, town, and city, of an imminent Communist attack, had fled at the first rocket. The single regiment of the 2nd Division, so cleverly placed northwest of Tam Ky, was caught totally out of position as the North Vietnamese tanks and infantry moved on the provincial captial from the west and southwest.

Pham Van Song, even with a rice liquor hangover, possibly the world's worst, had no particular desire to remain in Tam Ky with the Viet Cong and/or North Vietnamese authorities. Already dressed, he picked up the few things he owned—a comb, a bottle of rice liquor, his sleeping mat—and headed downstairs. He got out of the building by a side exit and simply walked out of Tam Ky. Others were walking out, too.

Song saw a few Communist soldiers, standing close to buildings. They appeared slightly tense to him, but not overly so. They made no effort to stop Song or any of the others walking away. None of the fleeing residents were in military uniform. The Communists, Song thought, were still interested in fighting the war, and had little or no interest in civilians for the present.

Song walked straight north from Tam Ky, figuring, correctly, that the North Vietnamese attack had come from the west. The usual way out of Tam Ky was straight up National Highway 1, but the Communists apparently had that road blocked, to prevent a counterattack by Saigon army reinforcements. Up tracks and so-called roads Song made his way, headed northwest after about an hour and at midafternoon hit Highway 1 well above Tam Ky. There, he joined a small tide of refugees headed for Hoi An—capital of Quang Nam province—and Da Nang itself, 15 miles further north.

It was after he arrived in Hoi An and found a place to lay his sleeping mat that Song discovered the North Vietnamese and Viet Cong had taken control of more than just Tam Ky. With their attack out of the west, the Communists had overrun all of Quang Tin province and all of Quang Ngai to the south.

There had been brief resistance by the 2nd Division garrison at Quang Ngai. The only place the Saigon army had put up any kind of decent fight was at Chu Lai.

Chu Lai was the headquarters of the 2nd Division. It was, until 1971, headquarters of the U.S.A.'s Americal Division, perpetrator of the My Lai massacre and some of the most poorly conducted operations of the U.S. war in Indochina. Chu Lai's military history went back to 1967, when Marine pilots flew fighter-bomber strikes into North and South Vietnam from a runway only several hundred feet long. An aircraft carrier-type arresting gear had made it possible to utilize the small base. In late 1967, the base was turned over to the U.S. Army and the units that formed the Americal. By then it was huge, with a two-mile runway.

Chu Lai was the site of the first U.S. offensive operation of the war, Operation Starlite, or Starlight, depending on whether a public relations specialist or a literate officer was writing. U.S. Marines, by the official version, had badly battered two battalions of Viet Cong, killing approximately 700 of the 400-man Communist force.

Now it was Dunkirk. But the "defenders" of Chu Lai were more interested in getting out themselves than in shielding an organized retreat of civilians and fellow soldiers. Boats took off thousands of persons from the Chu Lai beaches, but tens of thousands more were trapped in Quang Ngai city and the Chu Lai base. By late afternoon March 24, the Communists had taken two more provinces in the easiest battle of the war. Hardly a shot was fired.

The official version, understandably, was something else again. Lieutenant Colonel Le Trung Hien, from his podium in the press center in Saigon, acknowledged the attacks on Tam Ky and Quang Ngai.

Heavy fighting in the streets was under way, he said. The towns were in danger of falling. But at Quang Ngai in particular, government forces were fighting valiantly, although badly outnumbered. Casualties were heavy on both sides.

The news agencies in Saigon, with veteran staffs and excellent military sources, reported otherwise. But the valiant struggle for Quang Ngai and Tam Ky made a large number of the world's newspapers. Hien's word was accepted by the "tourist" newsmen, who had no one but Hien to provide information.

The Saigon government never did directly acknowledge the loss of Tam Ky and Quang Ngai. A week later, after Da Nang itself was captured by the North Vietnamese, Hien simply stopped reporting news of I Corps, the northern five provinces. He answered questions pertaining to that part of the country with no comments.

North Vietnamese and Viet Cong troops now had total control of 10 of South Vietnam's 44 provinces. The province around Hue—Thua Thien —was in their hands, although Hue itself was two days from falling. Da Nang was in severe danger, as were two provinces in the Central Highlands south of Ban Me Thuot.

More important from a strategic point of view, the capture of Quang Ngai had cut South Vietnam in two. This was something the Americans and

Saigon had been trying for 10 years to prevent. The Da Nang area was completely cut off from Saigon by road, a heavy psychological blow to men who believed they could not prosecute the war with the nation cut in half.

Three of South Vietnam's 12 fighting divisions were totally wrecked —the 2nd from Quang Ngai and Chu Lai, the 23rd from Ban Me Thuot, and the impotent 3rd from west of Da Nang. The Marines were no longer combat effective as a division, although about a third were holding together and fighting. The Saigon Rangers, which included many good battalions but more poor ones, had been virtually destroyed. Most units were in the boondocks well outside cities, and most of them in the highlands and I Corps had been wiped out. Casualties, by Saigon command count, were 5,800 killed, seriously wounded, and captured since the offensive had began. Almost all of the casualties were infantry troops.

The North Vietnamese had lost few men, by their standards. The Saigon command claimed 8,000 had been killed in two weeks. They were on the attack and were winning. Morale was high.

Communist morale got higher that evening. Field commanders were given the word on the offensive. At Hue, troops were told they were about to liberate the former imperial capital, then move on Da Nang. All over South Vietnam, the propaganda officers were busy whipping up enthusiasm. This could be the victory of victories, the offensive that would liberate the south. Every soldier must fight as hard as he could, and be prepared even to die for the motherland. Total liberation was at hand.

If the Communists were doing well March 24, the Saigon forces in I Corps were falling into hopeless confusion.

Who issued the various conflicting orders remains unknown. The suspected culprit was the deputy commander of I Corps, Major General Lam Quang Thi, assistant to Commander and three-star General Ngo Quang Truong. On the other hand, Truong himself may have done it. In fact, it could have been almost anyone, including some Viet Cong agent working in the Saigon military, attempting to destroy completely the last chance of defending Hue and Da Nang.

On the morning of March 24, as Tam Ky and Quang Ngai fell, the naval operation to pull tens of thousands of refugees and soldiers from the beach at Hue finally was falling into place. Tank Landing Ships (LST's), smaller troop carriers, and escorting warships—combined with large civilian cargo ships based at Da Nang—began heading out of Da Nang harbor at dawn for the trip to Hue. It should have taken them well into the coming day, and it would have been at least the next morning before refugees were all loaded.

The A37 Dragonfly jets flew out of the rising sun. The Da Nang-based warplanes, once criticized by Nguyen Cao Ky as a "plane for ladies" and unfit for men of war, circled out over the South China Sea and came in on the warships as they left the harbor. They had no bombs, or at least dropped none, but they strafed the leading escort ships in the convoy, HQ14, a patrol craft escort, and HQ609, a patrol gunboat. Six crewmen aboard the boats were wounded and small fires started by incendiary-tipped bullets caused light damage.

The naval convoy did not halt, and began arriving at Hue's port at sunset.

Pilots told commanders when they returned to Da Nang air base that they had orders to strafe the ships. That much is known. Truong, at least publicly, ordered an investigation into the incident. What remains unknown to now is almost everything else. The man who signed the supposed orders was never identified. The orders were never seen by an officer outside Da Nang air base. The investigation never took place, because Da Nang was in panic within three days and Truong himself was "sick" for the remainder of the war. At least he was sick and remorseful, contemplating suicide, until U.S. helicopters began evacuating Saigon. Then he made a rapid recovery.

The best guess that students of the war can make at the present is that an agent of the Communists, probably an officer in the Saigon air force, ordered the attack. It is possible, although more unlikely, that the pilots involved were themselves Viet Cong. Or it could have been simply an officer of the Saigon armed forces who viewed the evacuation of civilians from Hue as a cowardly act that was merely the prelude to a military evacuation. An attempt to stop the evacuation, in the mind of such a man, would be a noble deed. It would force soldiers to fight and force civilians to help in the fight.

There were many men who thought that abandoning land and cities was a cowardly act. There were already hundreds of officers and thousands of soldiers in the Saigon army who were calling for Thieu to resign because of the humiliation he had caused in handing the Central Highlands to the Communists. It is unlikely we ever will know who gave the order for the planes to strafe the Navy ships.

Private Duc of the South Vietnamese Marines could see Hue now. He had run, retreating, for more than 24 hours. He had not slept. He had eaten, twice, on the run, once stopping for cold rice and some meat "liberated" from a hastily abandoned home in a town on Highway 1 north of Hue.

Duc was at the rear of the Marine force retreating from the My Chanh River defense line. The retreat was once again fairly orderly, more orderly than the pullback from Quang Tri. One reason for this was that most of the retreat was conducted in daylight. Another was that the men now retreating were the best of the Marines, ones who had not panicked in the first retreat. The Marines were not panicking now.

The retreat was not easy. The Communists kept up their fire, but South Vietnamese airstrikes, artillery, and a few truckloads of the M72 light antitank weapons had slowed down the North Vietnamese and their armor. Men on both sides were dying. They were dying well, fighting for their lives. Few were shot in the back while running.

And now Duc could see Hue. It was a couple of miles away. His unit, kept at 50 men despite a few deaths and quite a few wounded by replacements from other units, was still together. For the moment, at midafternoon, Duc's unit had stopped. The sergeant who was their commander for now had a radio. Earlier that morning, on the command network, the sergeant and all his men had heard the orders.

General Truong, from his I Corps headquarters in Da Nang, had ordered an all-out defense of Hue. All troops in Thua Thien province were to gather in the imperial capital and prepare defenses. Hue was not going to be given up. There was to be a battle for the city. No more land would be given up without a fight. That was the order from the President and from the general. Duc and his men cheered.

On other radio frequencies, the Marines got their specific orders. They were, as quickly as possible, to make it to the walled citadel on the south bank of the Perfume River. Other units were to report to other areas of Hue. A fast count estimated that up to 25,000 gun-bearing troops of the Republic of Vietnam could make a stand in Hue. Warplanes were available at Da Nang. With the fall of Quang Ngai and Quang Tin, the planes could concentrate on the Hue area exclusively.

Huge, self-propelled, tracked 175-millimeter guns, able to fire 15 miles (about as far as the Russian-made 130-millimeter guns the Communists had), were set up in Hue. Even now, their shells were firing over Duc's head, whirring as they passed, crashing into—he hoped—Communist troops to his rear.

From the south at Phu Bai, from the north at My Chanh and Camp Evans and the district capitals, from the emperors' tombs and the villages, the troops of Thua Thien and the survivors of Quang Tri trekked to Hue that afternoon, prepared to fight almost to a man. The commanders' decision a week earlier to allow any soldier who wanted to flee Hue had paid off. The soldiers, militiamen, police, and home guard left in Hue were ready to fight. Those who did not want to fight were not there any longer. Tens of thousands were on a beach only six miles away trying to get out of Hue, but they might have been a thousand miles away so far as the troops in Hue were concerned. They were away from the battle scene; that was the important thing.

The battle for Hue, pitting up to 40,000 North Vietnamese troops against 25,000 Saigon defenders, appeared to be nearing. The lines were drawn.

Private Duc was one of the last Saigon troops to make it into Hue. He picked up ammunition for his M16 rifle and a flak jacket and helmet to add a little protection against the shelling that would have to precede the Communist onslaught.

He took up a position on the wall of the Citadel, 20 feet thick in places, able to shelter three Jeeps end-to-end in its entrances. Less than 200 yards away, the largest South Vietnamese flag in the nation flew. This was where the Viet Cong flag had fluttered for a month in 1968. Duc, the three men in his position with him, and virtually all of the 25,000 men in Hue, were determined that the Communist flag would not fly there again for a long time.

Private Duc slept well that night, in the two-hour bursts of a 50 percent guard alert. He felt he needed all the sleep he could get. The wall was hard, but he fell asleep on his flak jacket, using the helmet as a pillow. U.S. Marines have no patent on that trick.

The Saigon retreat from Hue was orderly.

No one, least of all Lieutenant General Truong, would admit to giving the order to abandon the imperial capital without a fight. But the expert retreat indicated it was a well-thought-out plan, ordered by an extremely high officer, and the result of a plan in the works for days. The American command at Da Nang knew of the orders as they were made, meaning they were issued from the I Corps command down the road.

As Duc alternated sleep and watchful guard duty on the Citadel wall, the first hint of withdrawal came.

First to be ordered out was the Quang Tri command post, an already small and largely disorganized headquarters. In effect, it had been the military government of Quang Tri province. Its withdrawal from Hue made some sense. It was made up largely of officers, many of them effectively, if not medically, shell-shocked from the events of the past week.

Then, around midnight, the order was relayed from Da Nang to Hue for police and civil servants to head for the beach at Thuan An and try to get aboard the large flotilla there. Again, a sensible tactical decision. Although almost all the police and government workers still in Hue were there voluntarily, their effectiveness as fighting men in an all-out battle could be questioned. Better to clear them out.

The Hue command post got its orders to move out shortly after that, and now there was more of a stir. Word of the various small withdrawals was spreading, as trucks moved out of Hue onto the six-mile two-lane highway to the sea. Soldiers and some senior officers were wondering just what was going on.

An officer protested, by radio, the pull-out of the Hue command post,

CP in military jargon. He was told the Hue CP was small and unneeded in close combat. Each force—the Marines, the infantry, the Rangers, the militia—had its own command. They were linked to one another by radio. That would be sufficient to defend the city.

The officer argued that whatever sense that made tactically was lost on the volunteers manning the Hue parapets. He described morale as "devastatingly low" (an exaggeration according to Duc, but not by much) and said the withdrawals now taking place could only hurt it more.

The Da Nang duty officer manning the radios on the graveyard shift told the Hue-based officer to mind his own business. The order had been given, he said, and should not be questioned. He then went off the air to cut off further Hue protests.

Still there was no troop panic. The would-be defenders of Hue were thinking evil thoughts of generals and presidents and other high-ranking people, Duc said, but they also were prepared to fight.

The sun had just finished its daily spectacular climb over the horizon the following morning, March 25, a Wednesday, when the order came to abandon Hue to the Communists.

Private Duc could not believe it, even as he watched the evacuation. Officers openly wept. Soldiers, even though relieved that they apparently would not die in Hue, were bitter. Their complaints were of the moving, of the right hand's not knowing what the left was doing—typical soldiers' complaints. But they were disillusioned.

South Vietnam's third largest city was to be handed up without a fight. Some very high-ranking officer or politician, somewhere, had decided Hue could not be held, and it was better to save the troops to fight another day.

But Duc and officers alike wondered: when would the stand be made, if ever? Ban Me Thuot had been overrun two weeks before in one of the last real battles of the Vietnam war. Three provinces in the Central Highlands had been handed to the Viet Cong and North Vietnamese without a fight. That retreat was a rout. Quang Tri had not held even for a night. Quang Tin and Quang Ngai had not resisted. And now, under a shelling barrage by the Communists that was heavy but certainly not devastating, Hue was being handed up.

Troops were being saved for a big stand, Duc thought. But where will we stand? And when we do, for God's sake, will we be too tired of running even to make a creditable stand?

Duc turned away from the wall of the Hue Citadel for the last time. The big yellow flag with the three narrow red bars of the Republic of Vietnam was still flying high. Duc knew it would not be there for long, and would not fly from that flagpole again for a long time, if ever.

There were enough ships for just about everybody at Hue, including civilians. That kept panic to a minimum. Still, confusion was the order of the day. The artillery left first, along with other vehicles. That type of equipment was valuable and, given the cut in U.S. aid, might never be replaced. Ships loaded on a more or less orderly basis, packed gunwale to gunwale with people who had no space to sit or lie down. Men were in the rigging.

The 1st Regiment of the 1st Infantry Division was the last unit to leave Hue, its job being to screen the departure.

The retreat was well planned. If it had begun a day earlier, it might have worked flawlessly. The late decision, however, would cost lives.

The North Vietnamese began their attack that afternoon, March 25. A retreat by 25,000 soldiers and a beach evacuation of 100,000 persons or more takes more than the few hours the Saigon army had to accomplish it.

The heavy shelling continued, as the vanguard North Vietnamese troops entered Hue from the north and south. Other units, including some guerrilla forces, swept around Hue and tried to cut off the road to the sea. The Communists had no intention of allowing anyone out of territory they captured in the Hue area, if they could help it.

Some guerrillas thought they knew how to stop the evacuation and retreat. As thousands of persons tried to sweep past them, the Viet Cong singled out five uniformed policemen and an 18-year-old police cadet. The cadet had just begun school, had volunteered to try to defend Hue. His brother, helpless to do anything, watched as the Viet Cong lined up the six men at the roadside. Screaming at the fleeing humanity from Hue, the guerrillas said the police were enemies of the people. They insisted that the revolutionary authorities guaranteed everyone's safety, and that the evacuation should halt.

Those trying to flee, the guerrillas said, would be shot down—like these police. They aimed their automatic Chinese-made rifles at the police and pulled the triggers. The six men, including the 18-year-old cadet, fell dead.

The fleeing people, many of them civilians, kept going. The brutality was exactly what they were running from.

A North Vietnamese officer, in uniform, lectured the guerrillas and informed them that shooting people—even enemies of the revolution —was not a way to win friends. He ordered them to stop. There were not enough Communist troops to stop the evacuation, and civilians and military continued their flight to the sea.

From the west, the south, and the north, the Communists moved into Hue. There were battles as they entered the outskirts of the town, the 1st Regiment of the 1st Infantry Division fighting to cover the retreat of the others. It took time for the North Vietnamese to get into Hue. Thousands escaped because of their last stand. Casualties of the 1st Regiment were officially "heavy," meaning more than 15 percent of the 2,000 men were killed or wounded seriously and the unit was destroyed as a fighting force.

From the south, up Highway 1, came Mr. Phuoc, formerly Captain Tran Ba Phuoc of the Army of the Republic of Vietnam. While the rest of his battalion was sent north behind the lines after Phuoc "returned to the side of the people" two days before, Phuoc himself was kept with the onrushing North Vietnamese forces.

Phuoc was their guide and, once, their propaganda agent. Only slightly unwillingly, Phuoc pointed out various approaches to Hue's center to the commander of the North Vietnamese battalion he was with. Mr. Ba (he gave no other name and did not speak of personal matters to Phuoc) kept the former captain with him.

Phuoc told no lies to the Communists. He revealed what he knew about the Hue defenses, the minefields, the garrisons at bridges, and the militia camps at the city's outskirts. Whether his information helped the North Vietnamese advance, he did not know. Mr. Ba had bluntly told him what he already suspected—one bad piece of misinformation, one attempt to lead his battalion into a trap, would cost Phuoc his life.

Mr. Ba's battalion headed straight into Hue, fighting most of the way, but blasting Saigon troop positions with a fire power that impressed even Phuoc, who had seen the American military in action. Phuoc still wore his Saigon army uniform, but had removed his pips of rank himself, in a sort of self-shaming ritual for surrendering. He had no weapon.

At 8 A.M., Mr. Ba personally roused Phuoc from a light sleep next to a stone wall in the inner suburbs of Hue. He gave Phuoc his instructions, and Phuoc agreed.

Phuoc picked up the handset on an American-made PRC25 radio about 4:30 in the morning, March 26. He called the Hue command post, now simply a battalion of the 1st regiment. Phuoc spoke to the major, who was called by a surprised radio operator in the Hue Citadel, only half a mile from where Phuoc and Mr. Ba stood.

Phuoc knew the man who was now the Hue garrison commander, but only slightly. He could not remember his name. Phuoc told the major who he was and how he had returned to the side of the revolution. He said he and his men had been well treated, and how he was better off for having made the decision to stop fighting for the Americans. Except for that line, Phuoc stayed away from Communist propaganda.

He told the major on the radio that he knew firsthand that Hue was surrounded. He himself, former Captain Phuoc, was standing within sight of the Citadel. The weapons the Communists possessed were formidable and the force backing the North Vietnamese was irresistible.

The Peoples' Liberation Armed Forces were not calling for surrender. Rather, they desired that the major and his men see the error of their ways and return to the side of the people of Vietnam. If the major wished, the commander of the battalion with whom former Captain Phuoc stood would facilitate the return of the major's battalion to the revolution.

The words surrender and defection had no meaning, Phuoc said. But in returning to the people, the major and his men would be guaranteed good treatment. They would not be prisoners of war, but patriots.

The major in the Citadel agreed at 9 A.M.

One hour later, at 10 A.M., Mr. Ba's deputy accepted the M16 the major handed him at the gate of the Hue Citadel.

Mr. Ba was too busy to accept the weapon himself. He was running up a huge Viet Cong flag on the Citadel flagpole.

The flag was bigger than the yellow standard with the red stripes that Mr. Ba's soldiers took down from the pole. It had been made as a village project in a hamlet of Quang Tri province a month before. Its actual dimensions remain unknown, but witnesses say it was about 25 feet by 15 feet. Maybe bigger.

BEGINNING OF THE END

Flight From Da Nang

In retrospect, the loss of Hue was the single greatest trauma for the Saigon government in the war. From the day Mr. Ba raised the Viet Cong flag over the Citadel, South Vietnam was doomed.

South Vietnamese who had never traveled to Hue considered the city the cultural and intellectual center of the entire Vietnamese nation. And the people of South Vietnam began to think like Private Duc: if the Saigon army would not defend Hue, where would a stand be made?

Every Vietnamese knew about Hue. It lay almost in the exact center of the nation, and was home to hundreds of revolutionaries of all political persuasions. Its French-run high school had turned out almost every educated person of note in the nation in the 1930's and early 1940's. Hue, with its emperors' tombs, its girl students in white tunics bicycling to school, its Perfume River, its museums—was well known to millions of Vietnamese who never had visited the city.

Saigon might be the capital of South Vietnam and Da Nang a more important city commercially, but many Vietnamese left their hearts in Hue.

So the anti-Communists and pro-Saigon residents of South Vietnam were severely shocked by the loss of Hue. As a tactical victory, the North Vietnamese forces had done well at Hue. But psychologically, the capture of Hue without a fight was the most important victory of the war. That the Saigon military was ordered to retreat from the city without a fight was doubly shocking, and only showed that there was no chance of regaining

Hue in the foreseeable future. It was another sign of the weakness of the Saigon government and of President Nguyen Van Thieu.

Thieu showed no sign of weakness outwardly. Inside the councils of the Saigon power structure, however, there was seething trouble. The military, the base of Thieu's government, were becoming more angered by the day. The idea of giving up large chunks of land and important cities without a fight was repugnant to the generals who ran the Joint General Staff and subordinate commands in Saigon.

Thieu was no dummy. He had power and intended keeping it. Thieu believed with the fanaticism of the just that only he could save Vietnam from itself and from the foreigners who wished to see its downfall. He included the Americans with those foreigners.

Two days before Hue fell, Thieu's strong man prime minister, the dour ex-Four Star General Tran Thien Khiem, submitted his resignation and those of the entire cabinet. Friends of the taciturn Khiem said the resignations were intended to prove to Thieu he was in deep political trouble.

The President's answer was to accept all the resignations but Khiem's. He ordered the Prime Minister to form what he called a fighting administration to meet the needs of the nation. With South Vietnam threatened, Thieu said in his order to Khiem, all members of the government had to devote themselves to saving South Vietnam from the Communists.

Alas, there were no fighters around to take over the cabinet positions. A new line-up of the same old faces who had dominated South Vietnamese politics for the past 10 years was Khiem's idea of fighting government. No prominent oppositionist—right or left wing—was even considered. The status quo was maintained.

And now the Americans began the first stage of their three-stage, panicked evacuation. Still without the leadership of the autocratic Ambassador Graham Martin, who was preparing to accompany General Weyand to Vietnam the following day, the U.S. establishment in Vietnam tried to cope. These are a few of the confusing and sometimes tragic decisions American officials made around the time of the March 26 fall of Hue:

• U.S. Embassy officials said American merchant and military ships would be used to help in the evacuation of Hue. None was close enough to Vietnam to help.

• The U.S. Embassy, through its official spokesman, announced that a chartered Boeing 747 Jumbo Jet would begin flying refugees from Da Nang to camps further south. The Jumbo would be augmented by other American jets. In fact, the 747 never arrived in Vietnam. A single 727 began flying about 200 persons per flight from Da Nang south the day Hue fell. Many of the persons on the 727 flights did not want to go, and thousands who did want to go south could not get to the plane.

• The U.S. "consulate" in Da Nang, the advisory and aid mission, ordered all "nonessentials" of the American staff out the day Hue fell. There was no explanation of why nonessential personnel were at the Consulate in the first place.

• Because it would supposedly hurt the morale of an already stunned ally, senior American officials refused to speak of the possibility of evacuation from Saigon. No help was given to any American, including the families of U.S. officials based in Vietnam, who wished to leave the country. Saigon immigration authorities were allowed to continue their delays in granting exit visas, delays that were at best bureaucratic and more often aimed at extracting bribes for the documents.

In Da Nang, the panic was growing and becoming ugly.

The accepted count of refugees in the second largest city of South Vietnam was 500,000. Some very conservative estimates said it was more like 300,000. And many others said there were one million homeless persons in Da Nang. There were, in the final analysis, a lot of refugees in Da Nang. The number of refugees was probably more than the population of Da Nang, which had been 458,000.

The Saigon government, to its credit, somehow got things about as well organized as could be expected—better than expected from the bureaucratic mess that disguised itself as the Republic of Vietnam, in fact. Dr. Dan, the Minister of Social Welfare, outdid himself in organizing a credible refugee program in Da Nang. Dan also pushed approval for foreign volunteer help for the refugees through the bureaucratic lines of his ministry and government.

Schools were closed and they, churches, pagodas, and abandoned U.S. military camps were used to house the homeless. Meals were churned out, as rice came out of the well-filled Da Nang warehouses. A real and amazingly successful effort was made to segregate refugees by grouping them with people from their own villages, the real administrative divisions in Vietnam. Public address systems blared incessantly the names of lost and separated family members. Families were reunited, often tearfully.

But as much as was done, it was not enough. With the fall of Hue and of Tam Ky and Quang Ngai, the refugees in Da Nang, now joined by the population of that city, wanted out again.

For a week, there had been little theft and virtually no looting by the refugees. Troops stuck to the business of preparing to fight the war, setting up Da Nang's defenses. But as Communist troops gobbled up territory north and south of Da Nang, the city became more anarchic almost by the hour. Soldiers fleeing the North Vietnamese and Viet Cong arrived in Da Nang with only their guns. They had no unit commander, no food, no equipment, no home. Soldiers were turned away from refugee camps and military bases alike. There was no room for them.

That they turned to violence to obtain food and more was understandable. But it sparked the anarchy that was to speed Da Nang to its downfall.

A Vietnamese newsman had to plead for his life with five Rangers when they pulled pistols on him. He was given his life, but stripped of his cameras, watch, and money, including $300 in American currency. He was holding the American money for a U.S. newsman who thought it would be safer in the hands of a Vietnamese. But there was no racism in the violent crimes now. Soldiers were stealing for survival. With guns, their success ratio was very high.

Da Nang was the gathering point for a million or a million and a half people who had nowhere else to go. The ships from Hue and from Chu Lai came here, to the bastion of the Saigon army in the northern part of South Vietnam. There was at first a confidence that Da Nang would hold. But with the abandonment of Hue, there was a growing feeling of helplessness.

The war had been close to Da Nang for almost a year. Heavy shelling attacks followed up by ground assaults had put the district capital of Thuong Duc in Communist hands in July 1974. Only the last-minute efforts of General Truong—his personal battlefield visit at midnight—had saved nearby Duc Duc. Front lines were within 25 miles of downtown Da Nang.

In reality, the war had been even closer than that for years. Rockets were a regular feature of life for those who lived around the Da Nang air base. Once the busiest airfield in the entire world, Da Nang was quieter now. But it was the main war base in the northern part of South Vietnam. For that reason, it was a frequent Communist target.

The day Hue fell, 14 rockets hit Da Nang air base. Six persons were killed and 34 others were wounded. These people lived around the periphery of the air base in slums like the one nicknamed Dogpatch, after the cartoon slum home of Li'l Abner. Many residents made their living from the base, directly as employees or indirectly by catering to the needs of the airmen. They bled and died along with the soldiers when the rockets crashed in.

This day's rocket attack killed an entire family of five. Their bodies, amazingly whole, only nicked in vital places by tiny slivers of white-hot metal, were stretched out in the ruins of their shack for all to see. It was a part of the propaganda war. Look, see what the Communist barbarians do to children and women.

Da Nang was where the United States entered the Vietnam fighting war.

U.S. Marines on March 8, 1965, 10 years previous, had stormed a beach near the city. It was not a very secret operation. Vietnamese girls were there to garland the Marines with leis. Which, even after 10 years, was about as secret as any operation in Vietnam had ever been kept. The Marines were to defend Da Nang air base, but they had to move far out to patrol the "rocket belt." Then they had to launch spoiling operations to keep the Viet Cong off balance. They later had to go on offensive sweeps to keep the rocket belt, and then the rocket belt's rocket belt, clear. So the U.S. combat role had escalated.

The best study of the role politics played in the escalation of the war is the collection of documents and commentary produced by the U.S. Defense Department and nicknamed the Pentagon Papers. Even the massively edited versions presented in the daily newspapers give a tremendously illuminating view of American decision making on Vietnam. The unedited, 12-volume version available from the U.S. Government Printing Office for $50 is even more of an education.

The Pentagon Papers show the decisions to escalate at each stage in the war, beginning in 1946, when President Harry S Truman turned down the recommendations of field agents to back Ho Chi Minh. That decision was a political one, to show U.S. support for demoralized colonial allies—in Vietnam, specifically, the French.

Decisions made in Washington concerning Vietnam after that were almost purely political, although the results in Vietnam were almost always military in nature, and so perceived by Americans in Saigon. Many of the most important military decisions of the war, according to the Pentagon Papers, were made for the specific political purpose of showing support for, and boosting the morale of, authorities in Saigon. This was especially true of the Marine landing at Da Nang, and the beginning of regular airstrikes against North Vietnam in February 1965, a month earlier.

When the decisions were being made, U.S. escalation seemed to follow in steps. Not until 1971, however, was it clear that each step had been carefully planned well in advance by American officials, including the Presidents involved.

Unfortunately for those involved, the final step out of Vietnam had not been so meticulously planned. The panic, the treachery, the inability either to improvise or to form contingency plans began in Da Nang. It was then repeated in Nha Trang and Saigon.

Shortly after Hue fell, the man who ultimately would have to accept all or nearly all the blame for the American role in the Vietnamese tragedy of April 1975, was about to arrive for the last time. Ambassador Graham Martin was flying to Saigon with General Frederick C. Weyand.

And in Saigon, a perfectly sensible decision was being made. The United

States Information Service employees, especially including men in the field, were launching a search for Communist "atrocities" in newly captured areas. The blood bath theory, one of the most arguable policies of the United States, was to be reinforced with facts. Any and all reports of killings by the Viet Cong and North Vietnamese were to go to USIS and the Embassy as quickly as possible. This perfectly sensible decision to look for an anti-Communist propaganda weapon would unfortunately help deepen a tragedy a month later.

Refugees and what to do about them were the big questions of the war now. They were in the way of the fighting. They were causing near-panic in Da Nang and in Nha Trang along the central coast. Their suffering, particularly that of the children, had reached the senses of the American people, who now began clamoring for the beginning of an evacuation to the United States.

Ed Daly, millionaire, airline owner, hard drinker and harder talker, was not a likeable man. His intensely loyal staff, however, said that it was necessary to get to know Daly. Those who met him usually declined getting to know him better, so bad was the first impression—and the second and the third.

But Daly, unlike thousands of those who reviled him, decided to do something about Vietnam.

Bruce Wilson of the Melbourne, Australia, *Herald,* wrote and printed perhaps the most unkind stories of Daly, following the near-catastrophic flight from Da Nang just hours before that city fell at the end of March. "Mr. Ed," Wilson wrote April 3, ". . . is not personable. He has a face like a red beacon fed by 100 bulbs, 30 of which have ceased operation." Daly most certainly was flamboyant, and his language was not always above reproach. At a formal press conference following the Da Nang flight, he took a pistol from beneath his clothing, placed it on the table beside him and said he would "shoot the next God-damned man who talks while I'm talking." There was a hush in the room. On April 2, after he had abandoned plans to fly orphans to Australia when the cabinet at Canberra barred such flights, Daly told newsmen at Tan Son Nhut airport: "If he (Australian Prime Minister Gough Whitlam) tries to tell anyone he didn't stop me from flying those babies to his God-damned country, then he is a lying bastard."

The day after Hue fell, a 727 tri-jet of Daly's World Airways flew to Da Nang and picked up 200 persons, almost all of them women and children. Packing the 200 aboard the jet, Daly's pilots and crew flew south to Nha Trang.

The plane was carrying almost exclusively the wives, mothers, and children of South Vietnamese air force men. Air force personnel, notably the air police stationed at Da Nang, refused to guarantee the safety of World Airways planes unless their dependents were taken out first.

There was atrocious organization to the World Airways flights, although this was not the fault of Daly or his airline employees. The first plane from Da Nang landed at Nha Trang at midmorning March 27, the day after the Viet Cong flag went up on the Hue flagpole. The first two persons off were children, boys, about 10 or 12 years old. Their parents were not on the flight. "Where do I go now?" asked one of the brave little fellows as he walked down the steps.

Third off was a woman. She thought she was on a plane to Saigon. She demanded of refugee officials who met the plane that they fly her to the capital. They refused. She demanded to be allowed back on the plane returning to Da Nang, where, she said, part of her family remained. They refused again. The 200 were loaded onto buses and were driven to a refugee camp.

Such scenes were helpful to the Viet Cong and Hanoi propaganda machines. All along (and to this day) the Communists insist that no one —save some senior military and government officials—ran away from their forces. Rather, the Saigon government and its American henchmen "forced" patriotic people at gunpoint to leave areas about to be "liberated."

The opposite, of course, was the truth. There was a mass movement to get away from the approaching Viet Cong and North Vietnamese forces. It was neither the forced evacuation of the people that the Communists so fervently believed it to be nor the fear of a blood bath that the U.S. Embassy portrayed. The reasons for fleeing "liberation" were varied. The most common, by 1975, was pure pressure and panic. And the fear of the war—not of the Viet Cong nor the Saigon army, but the planes and artillery they brought with them to do battle.

By 1975, the Communist side was no less destructive than the Saigon forces. Fearsome artillery barrages and fire power at least matching those of the South Vietnamese troops were employed by the Communists. People fear that. If you have ever been under a heavy—really heavy—artillery barrage, you know why.

People fled toward Saigon-controlled territory rather than toward the Communist lines for various other reasons.

Toward Saigon, there lay known certainties. Toward the Communists lay not only uncertainty, but the probability of some bombing attacks. Few peasants in Vietnam voted with their feet, although city dwellers did from time to time. There was not, however, the fear of the Viet Cong and North Vietnamese that the simplists of America and Saigon liked to believe. By fleeing, and especially by running toward Saigon, the people had a better chance of living. It was as simple as that.

And panic builds by itself. Panic was building in Da Nang now, and there was nothing anyone could do about it.

Thousands of residents and refugees jammed the entrances to Da Nang air base. The air police, reinforced by soldiers, closed down one entrance entirely. At the other, they put up barbed wire barricades. From time to time, the barricades would come down, one layer at a time, for a VIP or an American limousine to pass through.

Buses carrying passengers for the Air Vietnam and World Airways flights were delayed time and again getting to the airport. But there was no violence on the part of those being left behind—yet. The first shots in the battle for Da Nang had not yet been fired. It was only ironic that when they were it would be Saigon forces who fired them.

At the Da Nang docks, the scene was something else. There was no central gate to the mile-long port area, and most of the port had only a single fragile link-metal fence line between the river and the main road of Da Nang. The docks were jammed as civilian and military ships loaded for the runs to Cam Ranh Bay. Here at the docks, people demanded space. They pushed and fought one another to get on the boats.

Vietnamese Boy Scouts, some of the heroes of the Da Nang operation, politely but effectively kept some loading areas clear. They also helped unload the ships from Hue.

By midafternoon, there were 100,000 Vietnamese at the gate of the air base. The crowd, jam-packed, stretched from the gate itself back half a mile. The airport entrance was within the populated suburbs of Da Nang city, making access to its gate easy. The afternoon of March 27, flights of Air Vietnam and World Airways were canceled until further notice.

The first foreign nation to come to the aid of the sea evacuation of Vietnam was the Philippines. The least effective ally on the U.S. side in the war now became the first to answer the call for humanitarian aid. A Filipino Navy LST stood just off from the mobbed docks and took on human cargo from sampans and tiny lighters. By evening, the LST was filled with about 3,000 persons and it pulled out of Da Nang for the trip south to Cam Ranh Bay.

Cam Ranh Bay was a testament to America's earlier professed intent to remain in Vietnam until the war was won.

Here in 1969 ships unloaded at a magnificent floating dock, ammunition was stored in the most secure dump in Vietnam, fighter-bombers took off from the undulating airstrip. A tribute to American excellence in planning. The first place where soldiers in Vietnam could drink fresh milk. Where water skiers could watch the ammunition boats come in.

It was the base where security was so good that American President Lyndon Johnson could visit just before Christmas in 1967 and not fear for his life, though the war was at its height and killing 200 GI's a week. And the guards were so lax in 1969 that Viet Cong commandos could creep inside an American hospital and wound 100 American patients with mines and grenades.

Cam Ranh Bay. Built on the hot sands of one of the most beautiful beaches in the world, where the sand entered the soldiers' teeth the minute they landed and stayed in their teeth for days after they left. An R and R center and a major war base.

Now it was deserted, its buildings falling apart, sand covering the runway. Grass didn't grow through the runway only because grass didn't grow anywhere in Cam Ranh Bay.

Cam Ranh Bay was a center of controversy from time to time in its short history. A young airman named Ned Posey received six months in jail for refusing an order to cut his hair. While Posey sat in the slammer, a three-star general named John Lavelle was asked to resign—with no loss in permanent rank and no loss of benefits and pension as a loyal veteran —because he had disobeyed the highest order in the land and bombed North Vietnam.

The U.S. Navy trained dolphins to attack frogmen in Cam Ranh Bay's harbor. There was an outcry from animal lovers when the highly classified program was revealed, because the dolphins, it seemed, would be killed along with the enemy.

Now decaying Cam Ranh was to be a refugee center. The great opportunity to use this base as an industrial base—General William Westmoreland's great dream—was really gone by the boards now. Waterless, foodless Cam Ranh, where the only industry had been war, now would house the men, women, and children who had fled their homes.

In defense of Dr. Phan Quang Dan, there was little option to using Cam Ranh Bay. There were buildings of a sort, still standing, abandoned by withdrawing American soldiers, sailors, and airmen. There was space. God knows there was lots of space. The trouble was, there was little else. Even the security that had marked Cam Ranh Bay as the safest place in Vietnam was gone.

Nha Trang was too full of refugees. The plan was to move refugees from Nha Trang—survivors of the Convoy of Tears—and Da Nang into Cam Ranh Bay, where they would be safe behind Saigon army lines. It was a plan that just might have worked, except that there was never time.

Lieutenant General Ngo Quang Truong was still working the day after Hue fell. His movements begin to become hazy about this time, and it is not clear when he gave up. But now he was trying to realign his battle formations.

The evacuation of Hue, so far as the military was concerned, had gone well. Only hours after Mr. Ba ran the flag up the Citadel flagpole, the first Saigon army units began arriving in Da Nang by ship. They came off the vessels in an orderly manner. The first units back brought their trucks and guns. Newsmen on the docks watched as soldiers drove off the 175-millimeter guns. Within minutes, the self-propelled guns were moving on their tracks up Bach Dang Avenue, heading out Highway 1 north of Da Nang to set up new defensive positions.

The Marines came in from Hue, packed on an LST, most of them. They were armed. They had all their equipment. Those meeting the boats say the Marines were more angry than downcast. Sad that they had been ordered out of Hue, this elite fighting force now wanted to do battle. Their commander, Brigadier General Bui The Lan, another good fighting man of the Saigon forces, watched his Marines unload and saddle up with pride.

Like the artillery and transportation men, the Marines moved north. There, according to Truong's plan, new lines were to be set up. About 2,500 of the Marines had fled Quang Tri but had not stopped at Hue. They had reformed at the Hai Van Pass, south end, about 15 miles or less north of Da Nang. The Marines from Hue were to join them, along with the artillery. This would be one part of the new line. About 7,000 or 8,000 men, already beaten in one or two battles, were to hold the Hai Van Pass.

Truong wanted to move the survivors of the 1st Infantry Division to the west and southwest of Da Nang. Here, the shattered 3rd Infantry Division held the line only because the Communists had not yet attacked. Here, too, the front lines were 12 to 15 miles from Da Nang.

To the south were to go Rangers and other supposedly elite units, many already assigned there. It was here that the airborne division was once based, until the previous autumn, when Nguyen Van Thieu ordered it back to Saigon as a reserve force. Now it was the weakest link in Truong's planned new defense.

It was not Truong's fault that his plan never got a real chance to work. To the north went the Marines and artillery as planned. They came off their assigned ships from Hue in good shape, bitter at the generals who had twice ordered their retreat. Their morale was low, but they were ready to prove to all that they could fight.

But the rest of the Hue evacuation and landing at Da Nang was pitiful. Soldiers threw off their equipment under the Communist fire at the Thuan An beachhead in Hue. Or they threw it over the sides of the packed boats on the way to Da Nang. Many of those who still had their arms now tossed them over the sides of docks in the port city. One rifle discharged as it hit the dock, the M16 bullet whining harmlessly into the air.

It was no military force that unloaded under the name of the 1st Infantry

Division in Da Nang. It was a mob. Boy Scouts did not have to clear a way for the soldiers to disembark. The crowds naturally shrank back from the disorganized, bitter men of what had been the Saigon army's best fighting force.

President Ford saw off General Weyand to Saigon, announcing that the general would report directly to him what was wrong in Vietnam. Ford aides made it clear that the envoy would find that the reduced U.S. aid to Saigon had caused things to go wrong, had tipped the balance of forces to the Communists. It was clear that Weyand would report back to Ford how much more ammunition and equipment the Vietnamese would need to beat back the Viet Cong and their allies from Hanoi. Congress, in turn, could be pressed even harder to provide more.

On this day following the fall of Hue, Saigon was busy too.

President Thieu, sensing that his head was on the block, began his repression. He sent his police and secret police to the streets during the nighttime curfew, and about 15 or more civilian political opponents of Thieu heard the midnight knock on the door.

The government said the men arrested—it would not name them—were "short-sighted elements" who were plotting to bring down the government. As indeed they were. The men were all anti-Communists, holding no elective office. They included a few civil servants, a couple of teachers and professors, some businessmen, and—mostly—lawyers. They felt that with Thieu in power, South Vietnam was doomed to a Communist takeover.

Not that they went to the streets or organized a coup or anything of the sort. They met socially from time to time, and their views were no secret to Saigonese who cared. This day, they would go to jail.

Government sources let it be known that the men were planning a coup d'état and that their arrests were the only thing that had saved the Saigon administration.

The rumors, thanks to the attempt at thought suppression by the Thieu government, began to fly immediately. The most common (which was completely wrong) was that former Premier and self-styled Air Vice-Marshal Nguyen Cao Ky was behind a military plot to overthrow Thieu. Ironically, the arrests and the resulting rumors were what gave Ky, always ambitious and with a burning personal dislike for Thieu, the opportunity to speak out.

That very afternoon, March 27, with Hue fallen, Da Nang in a near-panic, and General Weyand on his way to Saigon, Ky took the opportunity.

Air Force police guarded the Tan Son Nhut air base officers' club as Ky drove up. The army, which basically supported Thieu, could do nothing about the press conference.

There, in front of the club, sat Ky. At his side, the bitterly anti-Thieu, anti-Communist priest Father Tran Huu Thanh. While supporters cheered and applauded, Ky and Thanh denied any knowledge of the coup. In fact, Ky said later, the first he heard of the arrests was when he was roused from his sleep by an American Embassy political officer trying to get some facts on the alleged plot.

But now that you mention it, Ky said, I am indeed for the removal of Thieu. He has proved himself incapable of leading the nation. His decisions, political and military, have led South Vietnam to the brink of defeat by the Communists.

The military in particular, Ky said, has no confidence in the Thieu leadership. Ordered time and again to retreat, the armed forces want instead a leader who will order them to fight, and then back the fight to the best of his ability.

Father Thanh went through the litany of alleged corruption in the Thieu regime, particularly the corruption of the President himself. Thanh was an author of "Indictment No. 1," a document outlining Thieu's alleged dishonesty, which was printed in several Saigon newspapers in 1974.

Both then called for replacement of the Thieu government. Ky carefully and specifically said he was not under any circumstances calling for a coup d'état against the President. Such a change in administrations, he said, could only harm South Vietnam, taking its few remaining allies (specifically the United States) away from Saigon.

Rather, the two right wingers called for Thieu to step down, and for his succession to be smooth and—they only hinted at this—made up of competent military officers with some political experience. Left unsaid was that Ky himself was one of the few men in the country with those qualifications, other military-political leaders having mostly been forced into exile.

Shortly after midnight, early in the morning of March 28, the senior Communist command in the Da Nang area gave the order. It was passed to the lowest units quickly. By nightfall, the order was no longer secret, and was being broadcast by Communist radio stations as propaganda.

> The Revolutionary People's Committee in the province of Quang Da and Da Nang city appeal to the people to rise up and, together with the Liberation Armed Forces, seize the right to decide their destiny.
>
> The Saigon troops in the province of Quang Da and Da Nang city are already encircled and under attack. In great panic, they are seeking to retreat.
>
> The time to liberate Quang Da province and Da Nang city has come. The people must resist the enemy deportation (evacuation). Officers, men,

> policemen, and other personnel of the Saigon administration: Cross over to
> the people's side. The rural population must smash the enemy's machine and
> rapidly organize their forces to liberate and defend their native villages.

The order was simple in its meaning. The North Vietnamese high command felt victory in Da Nang was so close that it could afford to eliminate
the usual tight security around attack orders. It also felt that publication of
the order could cause even more panic—and more surrenders, in and
around Da Nang.

In addition, the high command was giving its codes for just *how* Da Nang
would be captured. The Liberation Armed Forces would fight only if
opposed. At Da Nang, the order said between the lines, there was to be no
massive softening up of the city by artillery attacks. The order also said that
captured countryside areas were to be put under the control of local
Communist committees of Viet Cong, and the troops were to keep moving
on Da Nang. Personnel of the Saigon army, police, and civil service were to
be allowed to surrender and not shot on sight.

The order for battle went to the lowest levels in the Viet Cong organizations in the Da Nang area. It went to the troops and political cadre by radio,
including by the night of March 28 by Radio Hanoi; by courier; and by
Morse code.

In Da Nang, some heard the order on the radio. But broadcasting it
failed to increase the panic noticeably. In the first place, the panic was
already almost unimaginable. In the second place, the people in Da Nang
knew the city was under attack. The Communists were closing in. That
much everyone knew. The order of the day only confirmed what was
already known.

Leonard Dow Judson had retired in South Vietnam, and made his home in
Da Nang with his common-law wife. A world traveler with the U.S. Mer-
chant Marine in his youth, Judson had more or less fallen in love with
Vietnam when he worked in the Da Nang area as a contractor for U.S.
military forces and the U.S. Agency for International Development
(USAID).

He was not the kind of man who depended on others, this Floridian. But
now he was legally blind and actually almost totally blind. He had undergone one operation in Bangkok on a cataract in his left eye in January, and
was due to undergo surgery again in Bangkok in April. In the meantime,
he was, to his supreme disgust, partly dependent on the woman he lived
with.

Judson lived comfortably in a walled villa in Da Nang, a fact that would
become important within a day of this March 28.

He was temporarily without his woman. A native of Hue, she had gone to watch the evacuation ships unload at Da Nang port, to see whether she could find part of her family that she hoped had managed to flee. Judson says he had been assured by personnel of the American Consulate in Da Nang, those in the final analysis responsible for his well-being, that he would be looked after in any evacuation.

At 10 A.M. Judson felt his way to the front gate of his villa and stepped to the street outside. He could see only light and movement, and a servant had to fetch a pedicab for him and direct the driver to the American Consulate. When the pedicab driver heard the destination, his fare instantly shot up, from the normal 100 piasters Judson was used to paying to 1,000. The driver felt he was taking a chance by going to the Consulate at all, and expected to be rewarded for his bravery.

Grumpily, Judson got into the pedicab and sat back for the 10-minute pedal to the White Elephant. The name borne by the Consulate had been handed to it by an employee of the U.S. government years ago, when the riverside building was the headquarters of the CIA-dominated organization called Civil Operations and Rural Development Service (CORDS). CORDS chiefs always were career CIA men. William Colby, later the director of the CIA (his title on this particular day) had once run CORDS.

Feeling his way with his feet, Judson mounted the steps of the White Elephant. As usual in this building which supposedly catered to Americans and the general public, there was no way to get past the front door. Judson talked to an amiable but tense U.S. Marine on guard. It looked as though, Judson suggested inquiringly, everybody should start thinking about getting out, maybe. The Marine, Judson remembers, was polite. The U.S. Embassy was running special flights into Da Nang to take out nonessential personnel, some Vietnamese employees of the consulate and their families, and those American citizens who wished to go.

How and where, Judson asked, should he go to catch such a flight? No problem, said the Marine. Go to the airport any time. Special permission had been obtained from the Vietnamese Air Force to allow any passport-bearing American and his family through the gate. Flights would be frequent.

Judson gave the Marine his address in downtown Da Nang and said that he probably would go to the airport that evening or the next morning. The Marine, on cross-questioning, was sure there would be no problem getting Judson's "wife" and her family into the airport, and certainly none boarding the U.S. Embassy plane to Saigon once inside.

Reassured, Judson caught another pedicab. He could tell pedicabs, also called cyclos, by the speed and motion at which they moved. He stopped off to talk to an Indian friend and coincidentally to change a few dollars with the man, because he was running out of piasters. Throughout most of Asia, Indian businessmen are always good, honest moneychangers. Judson got three times the legal rate of exchange with the man.

That shook him, Judson said later. The money exchange rate, a sure guide to the confidence of the people, had more than doubled in 24 hours. Judson now started to have second thoughts about the confidence of the young Marine. Helped by the Indian, Judson caught another pedicab back home. He decided he would leave Da Nang as soon as his woman came back from the docks.

Ly Suong was 25, and her daughter, Ly, three. Her husband, Lyndsey Davis, was a 22-year veteran of two wars and the U.S. Army. Davis was retired and lived in Da Nang with Ly Suong and Ly and their 25-year-old maid Thung. Only this day Davis was in Saigon on business. He made his living "doing this and that." He didn't want to talk too much about it, but it seemed clear that whatever it was was not against the law.

So Mrs. Davis, the maid, and the daughter were by themselves. This morning, Ly Suong was getting a little desperate. Yesterday, having heard of the fall of Hue, she thought it was time to get out of Da Nang. She had no contact with her husband, but felt that if she could get to Saigon, it was the proper thing for her to do.

Ly Suong packed up Ly and Thung. Each clutching a bag, they headed for the Da Nang air base. The crowd of 100,000 was not unruly at this point, although there were occasional shoving matches between the more desperate persons in the mob and the air police. The police had their orders: Keep everyone out, with certain hand-picked exceptions.

Mrs. Davis was clearly an exception. The legal wife of an American, she was under the protection of the U.S. Consulate. The problem was that there was no way to prove that to the policeman on guard duty at the gate. She got close enough at one point to scream at the guard, but he just stared at her blankly.

Expecting she was not sure what, Ly Suong, Ly, and Thung curled up on the grass a quarter-mile from the main gate to the air base and slept fitfully. One of the women tried to remain awake at all times in case of a development, but nothing hopeful happened.

Early this morning, March 28, the mobs pushed the gates back briefly. Reinforcements arrived to shore up the air police patrol. The mobs pushed. Shots were fired. People in the crowd began screaming.

Ly Suong watched all this. She had not seen an airplane since the previous afternoon, it suddenly occurred to her. She circulated on the edges of the crowd where, so far, there was no panic. She could not confirm the truth. But it was common gossip among the crowd that all flights had been canceled. Thousands of persons thronged the runway, making the landing of airplanes impossible.

The wife of the retired American sergeant thought hard. Looks like no more flights, she thought. She discarded the idea of even trying to get to any American officials. She felt, rightly or wrongly, that the Americans would never help her.

One other chance, she thought. The boats. Packing daughter and maid aboard a pedicab, she headed for the docks. The two women and the little girl pushed their way to the riverside. It was crowded, littered really, with humanity.

Ly Suong and Thung, alternating carrying Ly now because of the press, moved downriver a couple of hundred meters. Here, it was not so busy.

Mrs. Davis was lucky and intelligent. Her survival depended on an excess of both attributes. She was intelligent enough to pack up all the money in the household before she left. This, of course, would be a normal thing to do. She was lucky husband Lyndsey had left her with a lot of piasters when he took off for Saigon.

Ships had stopped loading refugees at the Da Nang docks. It was too dangerous. There was a very great danger of the crush of people causing deaths. Sampans were ferrying those with money to the ships and barges from the Da Nang riverside. Sampan operators were being selective as to whom they took. Only those with money were eligible. Ly Suong waved 25,000 piasters under the nose of one of the profiteers. He nodded and the two women, Ly Suong holding the baby, clambered aboard the flimsy craft. Seven others who passed the sampan owner's fiscal muster also got aboard.

The sampan headed, almost indiscriminately, for a barge. It seemed hundreds of other sampan operators had the same idea at the same time. The barge was already packed. There was not room for one more person. Yet there were hundreds of Vietnamese scrambling to get aboard.

Ly Suong Davis, 25, weighing 110 pounds, fought beside a fragile maid holding a suitcase and a three-year-old child. For the first time in her life, she scratched and kicked and hit and fought for a handrail on the barge, fought and kicked to get her feet to the rail. Struggled and elbowed to climb over the rail and claim her daughter from the maid, who then fought her own way aboard.

Within hours, the barge was being towed out of Da Nang, leaving behind some of the most horrifying scenes of the Vietnam war.

After only four flights by the chartered 727 jetliner of World Airways, U.S. officials in Saigon ordered the airline to halt operations into Da Nang. Reports from the port city said 100,000 persons had flocked onto the runway and there was no way to land a plane. Even if a jet could land, the reports said, it would be mobbed.

World Airways' chief pilot Ken Healy, who was in Saigon mainly to fly a DC8 to Phnom Penh with rice three or four times a day, was called into conference by his boss, World president Ed Daly.

At midafternoon, Leonard Judson's woman came home. Her brother, a soldier, had arrived on a ship from Hue. The rest of the family, so far as he knew, had got out all right and would be along on other boats and ships. Judson told her what had occurred at the Consulate and the Indian shop.

Together, but unpanicked, they agreed it was time to get out of Da Nang. Not that either of them was particularly afraid. Judson wanted to make sure he made an April date with the eye surgeon in Bangkok. His woman simply wanted to be with Judson. They packed their suitcases, three in all. Judson's common-law wife told her brother to watch the house. He invited other soldiers from his 1st Infantry Division unit into the home. The men still had their rifles, ammunition, and hand grenades. But their taste for battle was gone.

At the last minute, the two decided to leave one of the three suitcases behind. No sense getting bogged down with bags, Judson said.

Into a pedicab. Now it cost 2,000 piasters each for the two pedicabs to the U.S. Consulate. This, Judson thought, is ominous. It's about time we were getting out of here. This town is going to fall.

Judson and his woman did not have to get out of their pedicabs when they got to the ugly White Elephant. The mobs were already tearing it apart. She yelled to the almost blind man just behind her at the roadside: "They've gone." "Who has gone?" Judson yelled back at her, annoyed by the noise and the crowds of people passing him, and by their stupid statements. "The Americans have gone," she shouted.

The retired American, blind and largely helpless without his woman, had been dealt the fate due the helpless in Vietnam. He had been abandoned. There was no known attempt to find him, even though the Americans had a record of exactly where he lived and what his physical condition was.

The Marine who had so calmly told him there was nothing to worry about would become a feature of discussion during the following month. The effective refusal to help a fellow American, even one without Judson's handicap, would rankle many when Judson's story became known.

For 10,000 piasters, the pedicab drivers agreed to take Judson and his woman to the Da Nang airport. That place, as Ly Suong Davis had already found out, was in chaos.

Half a mile from the airport gate, with only a mob between them and the entrance, Leonard Judson gave up. He decided that if his fellow citizens were unwilling to help him, could he do worse by staying in Da Nang? The answer he came up with was no. Twenty-four hours before the first Viet

Cong flag went up in Da Nang, Leonard Judson took a 500-piaster pedicab ride back to his walled villa, his home.

No one who was at Da Nang, and certainly no one who was not there, has been able to explain why not a single American would tell Judson, Mrs. Davis, or others about the flights from Marble Mountain.

Marble Mountain was on the other side of Da Nang from the air base. It was one of a string of bases down the South China Sea coast, most of which had been built by and for U.S. Marines who had their headquarters at Da Nang between 1965 and 1972.

Technically known as the Marble Mountain Air Facility, it had been used by all the U.S. services as a base for their smaller planes. With a short runway hard by the hill of marble that gave it its name, Marble Mountain was able to handle hundreds of daily flights by spotter planes, helicopters, and the like, flights that simply could not be handled at the busy air base across town.

With the U.S. withdrawal from Vietnam, Marble Mountain was unnecessary as an airfield. Now, with the main air base closed by the mobs, Marble Mountain was worth its weight in—well, marble, if not gold.

C46's, C47's, the two-engine planes of Air America, were able to slide into and out of Marble Mountain with ease. And for the last American citizens in Da Nang on March 28, the airfield was a godsend. Four flights and four Air Vietnam DC4's took out the fortunate who were informed of the planes' arrivals.

They were the last airplanes but one to make it into and out of Da Nang before the gold-starred flags went up.

Lyndsey Davis, native of Walhalla, South Carolina, husband of Ly Suong, father of Ly, employer of Thung, watched one of the Marble Mountain planes land in Saigon. Off strode an American woman, an employee of the consulate in Da Nang. She carried two small dogs.

The ex-sergeant was, to put it mildly, slightly angered. "They can get a God-damned dog out of Da Nang," he told Charles R. Smith of UPI that night. "But they couldn't go and get my wife." Davis detected more than a trace of racism in the action. The U.S. Embassy and the entire Da Nang consulate staff, of course, denied all such charges.

And now, on the afternoon of March 28, a Friday afternoon elsewhere in the world with a weekend coming up and nothing else, Da Nang was in its final throes of panic.

The troops from Hue, with the exception of the Marines who had headed north to the Hai Van Pass, were in revolt. The scene, it is said, was indescribable.

No military officer could control the mobs of survivors from Hue, from Quang Ngai and Tam Ky, from Quang Tri. Many of the garrison troops in Da Nang—and many of them were the dregs of the Saigon army, the 3rd Infantry Division—had joined the lawlessness. The shooting was like fire-crackers on a Chinese New Year. Most of it was into the air to intimidate, but some of it was not. The death toll is unknown.

Murder and rape were common. Robbery was the order of the day. The smart residents of Da Nang got behind the steel shutters of their homes or the homes of friends. But even that was not protection. On the side streets of the main business district, shutters were pried off, fired through, or scaled for a second-story entrance.

Leonard Judson, in his home on just such a side street, could hear girls being raped, cars being stolen, Jeeps being blown up just for fun.

General Truong, in his last known coherent order, put the tanks of the South Vietnamese Army on the streets with instructions to restore order. He also ordered a 24-hour curfew, broadcasting the order over the Da Nang radio station. It did no good. Many of the soldiers on the tanks joined in the looting spree. Others were afraid to oppose it, having no desire to die on what appeared to be the last day of the war. And having no desire to die in battle with men wearing the same uniform.

Tran Ngoc Binh, a private in the South Vietnamese Rangers assigned to a headquarters battalion in Da Nang, watched the men in his unit head out, in twos and threes, and join the looting spree.

Finally he said to hell with it, got one friend, caught a pedicab to the home of some relatives in the Chinese section of Da Nang, and proceeded to get very drunk. When he woke up with his hangover, there was order once again on the streets.

Leonard Judson, if he wasn't scared that evening, was concerned. The sounds of violence were all around him. Judson needed neither his own eyes nor those of his woman to tell him of bad vibrations in Da Nang that evening.

His savior was the brother of his common-law wife, the deserter from the 1st Infantry Division. With five of his friends, this man stood guard in the courtyard of the villa. Once, soon after dark, a hand sneaked over the wall.

Snicking the bolt on his M16, Judson's woman's brother said in a not-too-loud voice: "Go pick on another American. This one is a good man and he is under our guard." The hand disappeared and no one bothered Judson's home again.

The *Pioneer Commander* had dropped anchor off Da Nang and was taking on 10,000 persons. Among them was the almost-last of the foreign community, including the final "nonessential personnel" of the U.S. Consulate. U.S. Marine guards were no longer needed, there being nothing left for them to guard.

The ship was one of three that had been promised by the White House and the Saigon Embassy of the United States to help in the evacuation of Hue. It had arrived a little late to help the survivors of that city. What its 37-man crew would do in the next month would make most forget its late arrival.

Right behind the *Pioneer Commander* in arriving at Da Nang was a sister cargo ship, the *Pioneer Contender*. And right behind her, the U.S. Navy ship *Miller*, with a crew of civilian merchant marines.

On the afternoon of March 28, the military situation around Da Nang was bleak. Hoi An, the provincial capital 15 miles south of Da Nang, had been abandoned by its militia garrison, leaving the Communists with a clear shot at the bigger and far more important city of Da Nang.

The 3rd Infantry Division, a division of draft dodgers and deserters, minor thieves, and criminals, just couldn't make it as a Dirty Dozen. Assigned to protect the western and southwestern flanks of Da Nang, it once again proved useless. The Division, known as the "Fleet-Footed Third" after the 1972 rout from the demilitarized zone, had collapsed in the face of only the lightest North Vietnamese attacks that morning. Which was predictable and surprised few.

All but about five Americans, including their leader Albert Francis, the "Consul-General," had left Da Nang by plane from Marble Mountain or aboard the *Pioneer Contender*. Many Marines and tankers who should have been manning the approaches to Da Nang were instead inside the city trying to put down the military anarchy.

The warplanes—more specifically, the pilots of the warplanes—had either fled Da Nang or were trying desperately to get out. Many had been ordered out. Others had simply left the air base to pick up their families. To them, family was more precious than the saving or losing of Da Nang. In any case, there would be little air support, if any, for the battle of Da Nang.

And once again, it was generally believed that there would be a battle, this one for Da Nang.

Wolfgang J. Lehmann, America's second ranking representative in South Vietnam, donned his rose-colored glasses as the panic-stricken searched for a way out of Da Nang.

Lehmann was Deputy Ambassador and more often than not chargé d'affaires during the absences of Graham Martin. Lehmann was generally known as the player of the nice guy role behind Martin's Mr. Nasty image. He was well liked, if not particularly well respected, around the Embassy and Saigon diplomatic circles.

No one could accuse Lehmann of being uneducated in matters of Vietnam. He had served as Consul-General in the U.S. headquarters at Can Tho in the Mekong Delta before Martin hand-picked him for the Saigon job. But he was, rightly or wrongly, accused of being a yes man to the Ambassador. Martin dealt directly and only with Lehmann during his frequent trips abroad, and Lehmann always kept the Ambassador's trust.

A week before, in a conversation in his office with a newsman (unlike Martin, Lehmann was not comfortable with newsmen), the Deputy Ambassador had been sanguine about the situation in Vietnam. But it was true then that the only serious setback had been the loss of Ban Me Thuot. The full extent of Thieu's horrible decision to abandon the highlands was not evident. Lehmann used the conversation mainly to lobby for more U.S. aid to South Vietnam. He hoped the newsman would point out how the Saigon government was the victim of an aggression.

Now, two days after the fall of Hue, with Da Nang in panic, the Vietnamese army in retreat, and Thieu under severe attack from his former supporters, Lehmann was going to lay facts on the line. He chose as his audience a carefully picked delegation of the American Chamber of Commerce in Saigon. Newsman members of the Chamber were carefully excluded from the potential audience. This would cause a row within 24 hours.

It was a fairly representative group of business people who met with Lehmann, some of the cream and some of the lesser lights. American business people ran the gamut from oil company executives to successful entrepreneurs to outright war profiteers operating, at best, on the fringes of the law.

Lehmann's talk with the business people—naturally enough it was labeled a briefing; most discussions in Vietnam were called briefings—was lengthy. Most of the Americans there were astounded, shocked, or on the verge of a severe case of giggles.

The second-highest ranking American in Vietnam told his fellow citizens that the situation at present was not, of course, too bright. But he saw no reason for pessimism. The Saigon government had been forced to give up certain areas of the nation, but there was little choice. South Vietnam was the target of outright aggression by North Vietnam. America had chosen not to give the Saigon government enough aid to defend its entire territory. President Thieu had made what in retrospect was a wise decision in abandoning the highlands.

But, Lehmann said, Thieu had made it clear there would be no more retreats (this was two days after Hue fell in another advance to the rear). Government lines now would stiffen, there was no question of it.

Business may be down in Saigon right now, Lehmann conceded. But things are going to get better. No, one could not rule out a "lucky" rocket attack on Saigon. But government forces were deployed to prevent even that, and so far as an outright Communist assault on the capital—well, there just was no chance.

Lehmann urged business expansion. He urged the business people present to pour their money into Vietnam and to urge friends and acquaintances to get into business in South Vietnam.

On very good authority (the impression was that the authority was Thieu) the Americans knew Saigon armed forces now were preparing an "aggressive defense" of all remaining territory, north and south of Saigon, he said.

The American Chamber of Commerce representatives gave Lehmann a full hearing. There were not many questions. They thanked the Deputy Ambassador very much, and left.

Within minutes, one of the group—by prearrangement—was on the phone to the UPI office. This man, one of the most honorable among all the small businessmen in Saigon, cautioned me at the beginning of the conversation that what he was going to say was no joke. It sounded like a joke, he said, but the following was what Lehmann actually said on the afternoon of March 28. Then he gave me the gist of Lehmann's talk.

Having been purposely excluded from the invitation list, UPI felt no compunction about running the story, quoting Lehmann by name. The English-language Saigon *Post* ran it on the front page. It did, after all, make the Thieu government look good. The Americans still believed in the President and in his policies. The Embassy was obviously backing the call for more aid to Saigon.

Not long after the paper appeared, Alan Carter, chief of the U.S. Information Service in Saigon, began leaving calls all over town for me. When I finally returned home to a very late dinner, I decided to wait until after I ate to return the call. Carter called in the middle of the meal.

Polite but obviously upset, Carter complained about the story. The briefing, he said, was "for background only," a technical term in the news business meaning that the speaker—in this case Lehmann—cannot be named.

Very tired and not quite so polite as Carter, I said that since UPI had not received an invitation to Lehmann's briefing, since we had not been told in fact that it would take place, since no Embassy official at any time had attempted to give us any information on the Lehmann briefing, there obviously could be no such ground rules. Carter pointed out that I had not requested any briefings lately. I told him the point was extraneous, since as a member of the Chamber of Commerce I should have been invited, and the conversation was ended.

To me, the point of the phone call from Carter was that, as it had done for the past five years, the United States wanted to keep a low profile in Vietnam. But because I represented an American news agency and because I believed the United States profile was very high in Vietnam the story was not only news, it deserved telling.

There was another briefing the same day from behind a rose-tinted glass. The Defense Attaché's Office, formerly called the military command before the American withdrawal in 1973, assigned officers to tell Americans what was going on. Again, the news media were excluded. At this one, a friend, a retired U.S. lieutenant colonel, carried a tape recorder and taped the entire briefing.

To name the briefing officer would be unfair, since he was merely a representative. Unlike Lehmann, he held no high rank and received instructions on what to say. He was a U.S. Army major.

But he would prove, as did Lehmann, one of three things: U.S. operatives were woefully uninformed of the situation in the field; high-ranking officials were not reading their field reports; or briefers lied. The briefing was upbeat, with just enough pessimistic news thrown in to make it believable. In short, it was the standard briefing, Number 1A in the Vietnam briefer's handbook.

The major said that because of the cut in U.S. aid, South Vietnam had been forced to adopt a new military strategy. Instead of holding outlying areas, the armed forces had decided to concentrate their efforts on holding populated areas. He did not mention the fate of Hue, third largest city in the nation.

Abandoning so many parts of South Vietnam had been a bitter pill to swallow for Saigon, he said. But the new strategy was the result of a realistic assessment by the government that it did not have assurances that it would have all the resources needed to defend all areas.

The retreats are finished, but there is no reason to think Communist attacks will stop, the briefer said. For example, a North Vietnamese division was poised southwest of Da Nang, and a major attack was anticipated. Recent intelligence reports indicated, although it was not confirmed, that another two divisions of the North Vietnamese Army were being gathered and would soon move—if they had not already—into the south.

But all in all, pessimism was not justified. Saigon was well defended. There would be heavy fighting in many areas of the country in coming months. But as of March 28, there was no danger of the government's collapsing, nor was Saigon directly threatened by the Communists.

Since newsmen were excluded from this briefing, we were not subject to any rules on reporting it. We combined the two stories—the Lehmann briefing and the statements of the U.S. military representative—into a single piece, and moved the story to UPI clients.

The panic in Da Nang was growing. The curfew was totally ineffective and troops assigned by Truong to get rebellious soldiers and panicking civilians off the streets made almost no headway. There was an understandable reluctance on the part of the Marines and tankers to fire on their own soldiers and civilians. There were fire fights from time to time in the streets, but most were between factions of rebellious soldiers fighting over food or money.

Civil servants were afraid to come out of their homes and report to work, since government offices were hardly the place to be. Workers refused to report to the post office building, which housed the communications network, because it was in an open area on the riverfront, and undefended. All communications between Da Nang and Saigon, with one exception, were cut during the afternoon of March 28. The exception was a Telex line manned by the lone Da Nang employee of the government news agency, Vietnam Press. This man would provide the only believable information on the situation until the city fell to the Communists.

Consul-General Albert Francis in Da Nang was trying to work some order into the city's evacuation. But he had waited till too late. It was to become a habit of the Americans in this last month of the Vietnam war.

U.S. policy was caught between two disagreeable alternatives, so far as the evacuation was concerned. Officially, the Americans had no business declaring a city such as Da Nang, Nha Trang, or Saigon lost. To do so risked the likelihood of Vietnamese commanders, troops, and civilians agreeing—too early—and abandoning the places before they were lost.

But on the other, unofficial, hand, American representatives and indeed the nation had their own honor to uphold. The Americans had given their word to Vietnamese employees that they would not be abandoned in any U.S. retreat. The employees, virtually all of them, believed the blood bath theory. The Americans did nothing for many years to dissuade them.

Now, leaving behind Vietnamese employees of the United States and their families was just as morally unthinkable as causing the loss of a city.

Albert Francis faced this problem. Many believe he faced it badly, as —they contend—did Moncrieff Spear, the Consul-General in Nha Trang, several days later. The Americans who were with Francis this last day that U.S. officials would spend in Da Nang do not agree. John Swenson, a U.S.

Nguyen Cao Ky told a rally of thousands of Catholics in Saigon to "let the cowards run away with the Americans," and said he would lead a final defense of the capital. During the next four days, Ky worked on plans for the flight of the Saigon air force—and himself. When this rally occurred, his wife had already left Vietnam.

As the war moved toward Saigon, authorities ordered military police to keep refugees out of the capital at all costs, in order to avoid the type of panic which hit Da Nang. Two days before the U.S. evacuation, Vietnamese troops were threatening women with their weapons in order to keep the hordes from Saigon.

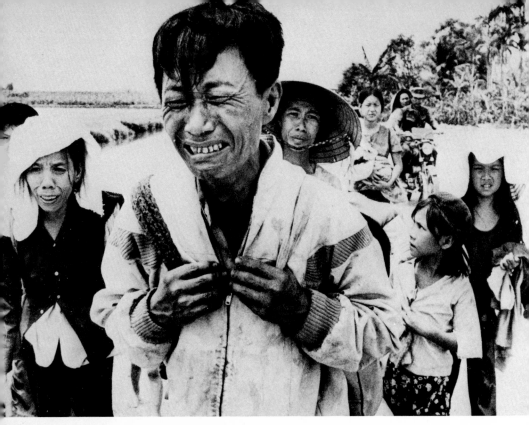

Vietnam suffered tragedy for 30 years of war within its borders. But the Convoy of Tears from the Central Highlands in late March 1975 staggered even the hardened.

The battle for Xuan Loc marked one of the most gallant stands ever by a South Vietnamese armed force, but the attempt to stiffen resistance and make a propaganda coup with sheer gallantry was overshadowed by other events. ARVN soldiers celebrated a victory at Xuan Loc with captured flags April 13. Eight days later, survivors were fleeing the town, President Thieu had resigned and plans for the American withdrawal were completed.

Hoping for a ride from the encircled, embattled and levelled city of Xuan Loc in late April, civilians huddled on the Highway 1 "landing zone." Few made it out to join the hundreds of thousands of other refugees wandering the ever shrinking area controlled by the Saigon army.

An American punches a Vietnamese man in the face trying to break him free from the doorway of an airplane as the man was attempting to climb aboard an already overloaded evacuation plane from Nha Trang.

There were supposed to be only orphans and U.S. government employees on the C5A "Operation Babylift" flight which crashed April 4. But persons digging in the wreckage found many "orphans" were the children of rich or influential Vietnamese officials or officers.

U.S. President Gerald Ford, with U.S. Army Chief of Staff General Frederick Weyand, and U.S. Secretary of State Henry Kissinger, conferring in Palm Springs, California, April 5, 1975, on Vietnam problems.

A week before his April 21 resignation, South Vietnamese President Thieu (left) picked congressman and national unknown Nguyen Ba Can for his prime minister and ordered a fighting government. The move brought an open split in the army, and public calls for Thieu to step down or face a military coup.

South Vietnamese President Nguyen Van Thieu speaks to his people on television on April 21 saying that he resigns.

Stopgap presidents who ruled
briefly after the resignation of
Nguyen Van Thieu. Two days
before the Communist victory,
Duong Van (Big) Minh, on the left,
takes power from ailing Tran Van
Huong, who was president for a
week. Forty-three hours after the
picture was taken, Minh
surrendered.

The United States
Embassy in Saigon.

Graham Martin, last American Ambassador
to South Vietnam.

Ten days before the "hard pull," the lines at the American consulate were long but orderly. Five days before evacuation, there was a smell of panic in the air and it was virtually impossible for a Vietnamese to get inside unless he had an American friend who could go through the special American-only entrance.

By evacuation day, April 29, harassed and overworked U.S. Marines were forced to try to keep off the buses to the helicopters even those Vietnamese clutching American air tickets out of Vietnam. Many made it anyway, by a variety of means.

The first tank down Thong Nhut Boulevard passed the American Embassy. Flying a Viet Cong flag, the North Vietnamese vehicle crashed through the Independence Palace gates, symbolically completing the Communist victory.

North Vietnamese Defense
Minister Vo Nguyen Giap.

The front lawn of Independence Palace, where
citizens never trod before, was the gathering place for
government-organized demonstrations following
"liberation" April 30. The building then sported a
picture of Ho Chi Minh and the flags of the Viet Cong
and North Vietnam.

About three weeks after the war ended, the freighter
Tam Nam Viet landed at Guam. On board, for
shipment to Montreal and a former Thieu aide, were
antiques from the Saigon museum, shipped out by
President Thieu's wife. As it turned out, most of the
"antiques" were fakes, replacements by thieving staff
workers at the museum.

Information Service man from Saigon assigned temporarily to Da Nang during the downfall, defends Francis staunchly.

Certainly Francis was cool until the end. He got out most of the U.S. citizens known to be in Da Nang, and all of the Consulate staff, on planes and ships. He did not get out Leonard Judson. He did not, so far as is known, attempt to help Ly Suong Davis.

He also did not get out more than 100 U.S. employees and their families—men, women, and children he was pledged to help. Some of them got out by themselves. Many others will spend the rest of their lives as Vietnamese rice farmers, more bitter than any Viet Cong at the treatment that Americans dealt them. Francis and his defenders claimed they did not have the time to evacuate. Critics, many of them within the U.S. establishment in Vietnam, said he had plenty of time to organize an evacuation, but he did not.

The fact remains that when the last ship pulled out from Da Nang, Francis was aboard. A U.S. citizen named Judson was not. Another U.S. citizen whose skin was yellow had not been helped. Many Vietnamese totally and irrevocably committed to the American cause were not. There was, in the final analysis, only one man who could have made sure they were evacuated. Albert Francis.

Rockets began to hit Da Nang about 9 o'clock at night. Southern and western defenses had collapsed. The Marines and artillerymen to the north were holding their lines. They were organized. They were fighting. Their communications were intact. Rockets hit the air base and the I Corps headquarters, a not-infrequent occurrence during 10 years of warfare in and around Da Nang.

Lieutenant General Ngo Quang Truong, hero, soldier, digger of last ditches, pulled out for an offshore ship. Albert Francis went with him. From the beach on the east side of Da Nang, where U.S. Marines used to swim in the surf, Truong and Francis and their staffs headed to safety. Truong maintained the fiction that it was too dangerous in town, that the marauding troops posed a danger to his command. He said he would take command of the battle for Da Nang from offshore.

Truong couldn't swim, it quickly became evident, or at least he could not swim well. The surf was gentle, but breakers were rolling about 100 yards offshore. The first one knocked Truong over and a second poured over the general. Albert Francis grabbed Truong and held him afloat for the quarter-mile walk and swim to the ship.

In Saigon earlier that day, General Frederick C. Weyand, a towering American, stooped and shook hands with President Nguyen Van Thieu. Photographers recorded the scene and then were taken out. Weyand had flown in very early Friday morning, received a short briefing from senior Americans, then had gone straight to Independence Palace and the Thieu meeting.

When the doors shut on Thieu, Weyand, and the few aides each had, Thieu got directly to the point. He wanted U.S. air support, the return of American combat fighter-bombers. Weyand told him he hoped to have a realistic talk with the President and to discuss U.S. fighter-bombers was not realistic. The United States, he told Thieu, had no intention of fighting in Vietnam ever again. That word, the general said, was directly from President Ford.

Now, he said, exactly what was the situation and what did Vietnamese —repeat, Vietnamese—forces need to defeat the Communist attacks?

The rocket attack on Da Nang that Friday evening was slightly heavier than those of the past year, but only slightly. About 70 rounds hit, virtually all of them on military targets. A significant number, perhaps a couple of dozen, hit the evacuation beaches along Da Nang's east coast.

There was no ground attack that evening, that night, or the next morning.

The city was in total chaos now. An estimated 100,000 troops were in the area. The best estimate was that 80 percent were trying as hard as they could to get out or to loot what was available in the orgy of shooting and stealing under way. But there were 20,000 men ready to fight a Communist attack.

Whether Truong could have restored order to Da Nang itself was questionable. Many of those who spent these days in Da Nang say that it *was* possible to restore order.

All of those in Da Nang at the time now say that order or no order, the city could have been defended. One Ranger said later that if one man had picked up a weapon in the city and gone to its perimeter, Da Nang would have held back any North Vietnamese assault for at least a month.

With Truong gone, and with other generals planning two secret predawn flights from Marble Mountain Saturday, Da Nang was handed over. It was gone, finished, given to the North Vietnamese and Viet Cong.

Through the night, the destruction, looting, pillage, and rape continued. The U.S. Consulate, the White Elephant, was stripped to a shell.

A crowd of about 100 gathered on the banks of the Da Nang River early Saturday morning and tried to put the building to the torch. Screaming oaths against the Americans who had "abandoned" them, they set a gasoline-aided fire to a corner of the White Elephant. The fire sputtered, smouldered, and went out. No one tried to relight it.

Captain Ho Van Hoa of the Army of the Republic of Vietnam was the last man who would speak to Saigon as a member of the pro-American administration. Eight o'clock Saturday morning: The generals and senior officials have fled. The Americans, those who can, have gone. Captain Hoa is still at his desk.

Hoa was at his desk all night Friday, had been for 48 hours. He did not know whether his family in downtown Da Nang was safe or dead. Whether his wife, his parents, and his four children had fled on the ships or had remained at home. Captain Hoa knew his duty was to remain at his desk. His exact job will not be revealed here. But it was not all that important a job. Not as important, say, as that of a commanding general who had received a direct order from his President to remain on the job and defend Da Nang, as had Lieutenant General Ngo Quang Truong.

Different men have different ideas of duty. Hoa, a friend to many Americans and always a credit to his own armed forces, had his idea of what the word meant. It meant, to him, carrying out the job to the best of his ability.

In a Saigon office, the telephone rang. An army captain, a far different man from Captain Hoa, answered the phone. The Saigon captain did not speak, except to say hello. What he heard was this:

"This is Captain Hoa. I think this is the last call from Da Nang. Take this message. Effective March 29th, I am no longer a soldier in the Army of the Republic of Vietnam. I am now a soldier of the other side. I have no choice. I tried to lead my men out. We fought to the perimeter, but we could not escape. I am bringing disgrace on my head and on my family's head. But it is this or death."

The telephone line went dead.

The city of Da Nang, second largest in South Vietnam fell. It was the most heavily defended of any city in the entire country, and was led by the best general in the Saigon army. Its warehouses were packed with food for months and ammunition and weapons for 60 days.

Two truckloads of guerillas, more than half of them women, captured the city.

The trucks drove in from the southwest just after dawn. Each flying a Viet Cong flag, they drove on main streets, past still-looting soldiers, to a central part of town. In groups of twos and threes, they spread out over a three-square-block area. They told soldiers to throw down their guns, and the soldiers did so.

Two women, dressed in black pajamas and carrying American-made M16 rifles, walked up to a now-abandoned three-wheeled Lambretta, rigged out as a sound truck. One of the two blew into the microphone, flipped a switch inside the vehicle, blew again, and heard her breath over the loud speaker on the Lambretta's roof.

She said Da Nang had been liberated. There was no need for anyone to have fear. Revolutionary authorities and soldiers would be arriving soon. In the meantime, the people were to put up flags of the revolution to welcome the comrades when they made their appearance. Those not having flags of the revolution should hang flags of their religion. Turning to a gaping but nonhostile crowd of mostly men, one of the women asked who could drive the Lambretta. A middle-aged man raised his hand to shoulder level. The woman told him to get in and start driving. Where, asked the man. Around Da Nang, the woman answered, seemingly exasperated. Everywhere. She must tell the rest of the city that the revolution was successful.

Within half an hour, flags of the Buddhist Church of Vietnam— multicolored standards of red and orange and blue and yellow and white in a patchwork design—were flying from 75 percent of the homes and buildings in Da Nang.

Leonard Judson, unafraid, listened to much of this in his villa half a block away from where the Lambretta had stood. He could not believe it. His woman and her brother told him of the occupation force of men and women guerrillas. He snorted and asked for some bacon and eggs for breakfast.

Once again, the Communists had won their victory almost without firing a shot. Almost.

And not exactly all of Da Nang was out to greet them. Many thousands were on the beaches and on the airport tarmac, willing to fight for a way out. Their way would be shameful, although some would make it.

The *Pioneer Contender,* her sister ship *Pioneer Commander,* and the Navy ship *Miller* had dropped 28,000 souls at Cam Ranh Bay and were back at Da Nang for more.

In Saigon, there was a last-minute rearrangement of the schedule of General Frederick Weyand. Weyand wouldn't be able to go to Da Nang as planned. So he was taken out to the Bien Hoa area to lay a wreath on the grave of one of the few Vietnamese generals killed in the war, the heroic Lieutenant General Do Cao Tri. That was close to Saigon, and probably safe.

The Communists now had 13 provinces of South Vietnam under their control. This included the entire I Corps, the five northernmost provinces. This area, while the smallest corps in the nation, had more combat troops on both sides than any other.

Virtually without firing a shot, without a single stand by the Saigon armed forces, the Communists had taken the entire corps area. They also had more than half of II Corps, the Central Highlands and the coast.

With the capture of Da Nang, the Communists had exactly 50 percent of South Vietnam's land area behind their lines.

Ed Daly, president of World Airways (the most profitable airline in the world during March of 1975), was flamboyant, pistol-packing, foul-mouthed, and filthy rich. He came to Vietnam for reasons of compassion and publicity. He was trying to get permission for a low-cost cross-country flight in the United States.

His planes already had been hired for the Da Nang-Cam Ranh Bay refugee flights and to carry rice to besieged Phnom Penh.

On the morning of March 29, after a fruitless all-night session with Vietnamese and American officials, Daly decided to hell with bureaucracy. He asked chief pilot and World vice-president Ken Healy how he felt about flying to Da Nang. Healy knew his boss and knew the answer wanted, and he gave it to him.

Just after noon, a startled air controller in the Saigon airport tower watched two World Airways 727's roar down the runway and leap into the air. When airborne, Healy told the controller he was heading for Da Nang. The controller, although he had full authority to do so, neither ordered nor recommended that fighters be scrambled to knock the 727's out of the sky.

Da Nang airport was overrun with people, perhaps 100,000 of them. But the runway was clear. Healy dropped down to a couple of hundred feet and made a pass down the 10,000-foot asphalt strip. It looked okay. Five minutes and a turnaround later, he was flaring his tri-engine jet for a landing. And a nightmare.

Healy, with the backup 727 still in the air, taxied quickly, very quickly, off the runway. He headed for one of the smaller groups of people near the old Air Vietnam parking ramp. He did not go off the wide taxiway that paralleled the Da Nang runway.

Paul Vogle, speaker of the language, lover of the Vietnamese customs, and former Daly employee, was aboard. Vogle worked for UPI mostly, but since he was a stringer he also held jobs with the American Broadcasting Company as a radio reporter, the *Daily Express* of London as a writer, and the German Press Agency DPA as a newsman.

Vogle had spent 18 years in Vietnam. He was to describe the next 90 minutes as the most terrifying of his life. He had a tape recorder with him. It was malfunctioning, but the snatches of his report were later transcribed.

> Mobs of people are pushing and shoving, thousands trying to get aboard. The plane is taxiing away from the mob.
>
> The crew is scared. The mob is panic-stricken. There's a man with an M16 (rifle) pointed at us, trying to get us to stop.

We're loading (people). The panicked crowds are running at us, with Hondas. We just passed a rocket hole. A Jeep, a pickup truck, right under the engines . . . ignore engines . . . people grabbing at the plane.

Soldiers are rushing the plane now. Daly is at the bottom of the ramp trying to push the people back. We're mobbed. (Vogle in Vietnamese. Please line up. It's all right. It's all right. We've got room for everybody. Please don't push.)

Men with guns are fighting each other. The pilot gooses the engine. (Roar of screaming jets in background as Healy keeps the plane moving quickly down the taxiway to avoid being overwhelmed by people.) Panic-stricken people are grabbing at the plane.

People are storming aboard, shouting . . . pushing . . . soldiers, civilians. People climbing up on wings, falling down off wings.

Soldiers are firing in the air to frighten other people away . . . no control at all.

. . . women and children lying on the ground. Some people trying to lie in front of the wheels, some are being carried aboard. Some have literally run 100 miles (from Quang Tri) to get here. The engines are being kept on high. People falling off ramp . . . last man aboard fell off the landing ramp . . . all blood.

Two men and a woman are holding on outside (to the plane fuselage) . . . woman climbing up outside.

(Crew voices, especially high but amazingly calm women stewardesses, can be heard yelling, "go, go, go." The engine noise picks up even more. Vogle now is screaming into the microphone.)

The pilot gooses the plane. They'll die when the plane takes off. People are still on the landing ramp as the aircraft picks up speed . . . fall off on the ground as it goes, pulled out by suction.

In the cockpit, Healy, picture-pluperfect ideal of an airline pilot, calmly pointed his plane down the taxiway. Told by intercom that the plane was full, Healy now felt his only responsibility was to those aboard. Under full power and already taxiing at a brisk 15 or 20 miles an hour, Healy threw the throttles just about to the fire wall. The 727 surged easily into the air.

But there were some problems. A distraught soldier hurled a hand grenade, which had blown off part of the wing, badly damaging the flaps on the right side. The landing gear would not retract. There were people inside the wheel well.

Stunned stewardesses, Daly, an American security man, and Vogle began to make the rounds of those who had made it aboard. Two women, one child. The child's mother did not make it. The baby was thrown aboard. About 150 soldiers. All members of the best single unit in the entire Saigon army, the Hac Bao, Black Panthers. A 200-man company whose members for 10 years were fearless in the face of the enemy. A legend. Better than the best American troops ever in Vietnam. Disciplined. And now, as Vogle wrote in the most memorable story of 1975, they had proved themselves the "toughest and meanest" and made the last flight from Da Nang.

One made it on by kicking a woman in the face. She was left, badly bleeding, on the taxiway.

The soldiers were armed. Vogle and Daly moved up and down the rows of people, stepping over the troops. Vogle asked a man for his rifle. The soldier looked at him blankly. Vogle realized he was stunned, virtually comatose. The newsman reached down and plucked the rifle away. He made his way from man to man, taking rifles, pistols, grenades, ammunition. There was a silence throughout the aircraft.

As the 727 took off, one of the men hanging on to the wheel well could not maintain his grip. From the backup plane, a UPI photographer snapped, sickened. His pictures showed the desperate man plunging to his death. Four others rode to Saigon in the wheel wells. One died.

In the backup plane, the copilot crossed himself. "Please, God, help them get down okay," he said.

Wheels down, the damaged wing fluttering from time to time, with unknown but obviously crippling structural damage, the unauthorized flight winged south now. It followed the coast, much of which was already in Communist hands, south to Phan Rang, a major air base still in the hands of the Saigon forces.

From the backup plane, the Vietnamese-speaking photographer spoke to Phan Rang ground control. He said there was an emergency, that a 727 was going to land. Phan Rang controllers, however, were aware of possible political problems. They had listened to the Saigon controller order Healy not to land at Da Nang, to return immediately to Saigon. Phan Rang told the interpreter they did not have the equipment to handle an emergency landing. It was an obvious lie, but Healy had better things to do than argue. He pointed the jet for the Saigon approach, 165 miles to the southwest.

Over Bien Hoa 15 miles north of Saigon, lined up with the Tan Son Nhut runway, Healy felt rudder problems, and he wanted to land the first time; he wanted to be right on line with the runway. If the rudder would not function, there would be no room for last-minute course correction. If the flaps on the damaged wing failed or fell off, there would be more problems. Healy wanted a runway under him, and fast.

> The (Da Nang) airport was being shelled as we left. There was machine-gun fire at the plane. There's a body hanging on our landing gear. The pilot says we can't get the gear up. The pilot says the plane is badly damaged. We landed. We landed.

Vogle was as completely wrung out, emotionally as well as physically, as any human being could be when he returned from the last flight from Da

Nang. Other UPI newsmen debriefed him and did stories on the flight and the continuing Saigon setbacks.

By late afternoon, Vogle was fairly composed again, and in lots of time for Sunday morning papers throughout the world he was able to put together the single most memorable story of the 1975 Vietnam offensive.

ZCZC VHA093 NXI
UU HNA HED
WITNESS 3-29
A PERSONAL REPORT
BY PAUL VOGLE
DA NANG, MARCH 29 (UPI)—Only the fastest, the strongest, and the meanest of a huge mob got a ride on the last plane from Da Nang Saturday.

People died trying to get aboard and others died when they fell thousands of feet into the sea because even desperation could no longer keep their fingers welded to the undercarriage.

It was a flight into hell, and only a good tough American pilot and a lot of prayers got us back to Tan Son Nhut air base alive—with the Boeing 727 flaps jammed and the wheels fully extended.

It all started simply enough. I asked World Airways Vice President, Charles Patterson, if he had anything going to Da Nang. He said, "Get on that truck and you've got yourself a ride."

It was a ride I'll never forget.

World Airways President Ed Daly was aboard. He was angry and tired. Daly said he had been up all night arguing with American and Vietnamese officials for permission to fly into besieged Da Nang to get some more refugees out.

Daly finally said to hell with paperwork, clearances, and caution, and we were on our way.

It seemed peaceful enough as we touched down at the airport 370 miles northeast of Saigon.

Over a thousand people had been waiting around a quonset hut several hundred yards away from where we touched down.

Suddenly it was a mob in motion. They roared across the tarmac on motorbikes, Jeeps, Lambretta scooters, and on legs speeded by sheer desperation and panic.

Ed Daly and I stood near the bottom of the 727's tail ramp. Daly held out his arms while I shouted in Vietnamese, "One at a time, one at a time. There's room for everybody."

There wasn't room for everybody and everybody knew damn well there wasn't.

Daly and I were knocked aside and backward.

If Ed Daly thought he'd get some women and children out of Da Nang, he was wrong. The plane was jammed in an instant with troops of the 1st Division's meanest unit, the Hac Bao (Black Panthers).

They literally ripped the clothes right off Daly along with some of his skin. I saw one of them kick an old woman in the face to get aboard.

In the movies somebody would have shot the bastard and helped the old lady on the plane. This was no movie. The bastard flew and the old lady was tumbling down the tarmac, her fingers clawing toward a plane that was already rolling.

A British television cameraman who flew up with us made the mistake of getting off the plane when we landed, to shoot the loading.

He could not get back aboard in the pandemonium. In the very best tradition of the business he threw his camera with its precious film into the closing door and stood there and watched the plane take off.

We heard later that an Air America helicopter picked him up and carried him to safety.

As we started rolling, insanity gripped those who had missed the last chance. Government troops opened fire on us. Somebody lobbed a hand grenade towards the wing. The explosion jammed the flaps full open and the undercarriage in full extension.

Communist rockets began exploding at a distance.

Our pilot, Ken Healy, 52, of Oakland, Calif., slammed the throttles open and lurched into the air from the taxiway. There was no way we could have survived the gunfire and got onto the main runway.

A backup 727 had flown behind us but had been ordered not to land when the panic broke out. He radioed that he could see the legs of people hanging down from the undercarriage of our plane.

UPI photographer Lien Huong, who was in the cockpit of that backup plane, saw at least one person lose his grip on life and plummet into the South China Sea below.

There were 268 or more people jammed into the cabin of the little 727 limping down the coast.

Only two women and one baby among them. The rest were soldiers, toughest of the tough, meanest of the mean. They proved it today. They were out. They said nothing. They didn't talk to each other or us. They looked at the floor.

I saw one of them had a clip of ammunition and asked him to give it to me. He handed it over. As I walked up the aisle with the clip, other soldiers started loading my arms with clips of ammunition, pistols, hand grenades. They didn't need them anymore. In the cockpit we wrapped the weapons and ammo in electrical tape.

There was no more fight left in the Black Panthers this day.

They had gone from humans to animals and now they were vegetables.

We flew down the coast, the backup plane behind us all the way. Healy circled Phan Rang air base 165 miles northeast of Saigon, hoping to put down for an emergency landing.

On the backup plane Lien Huong served as interpreter, radioing Phan Rang control tower that the Boeing had to land there in an emergency. The reply came back that there was no fire fighting equipment at Phan Rang so Healy aimed the plane for Tan Son Nhut.

I heard Healy on the radio, telling Tan Son Nhut, "I've got control problems." The backup plane was shepherding us in.

Huong, in the cockpit of the backup plane, told me later when we touched down safe the pilot and cabin crew on his plane pulled off their headphones, some of them crossed themselves, and all thanked God for a small miracle delivered this Easter weekend.

When we touched down the troops who had stormed us were offloaded and put under arrest. They deserved it.

A mangled body of one soldier, M16 rifle still strapped to his shoulder, was retrieved from the undercarriage. He got his ride to Saigon, but being dead in Saigon is just the same as being dead in Da Nang.

Over a score of others came out of the baggage compartment, cold but alive. Somebody told me that four others crawled out of the wheel wells alive. One died.

The last plane from Da Nang was one hell of a ride. For me. For Ed Daly. For Ken Healy. For the Black Panthers. And for two women and a baby.

But the face that remains is that of the old woman lying flat on the tarmac seeing hope, seeing life itself, just off the end of her fingertips and rolling the other way.
(UPI) PV
PN/1908
NNNN

It was the perfect news story. And it was that dream of reporters—the exclusive that could not be matched by anyone else. Over Easter Sunday breakfasts throughout that part of the world where editors are free to choose their own stories, Vogle's tale was on Page 1. Vogle got dozens of letters of congratulations, virtually unheard of for a writer for the largely anonymous wire services. From the southern United States, he even got an oblique marriage proposal from one amorous fan.

Private Duc was weary, tired of it all. If he had been alone, he would have thrown down his rifle, shed his uniform, and surrendered. But he wasn't. There were about 3,500 Marines now, ready to fight. In hastily contrived battalions and companies for the most part, held together only by the single radio frequency of the Marine command, Duc and his friends and others like them were once again preparing to defend a city.

On the evening of March 27, two days after the retreat from Hue, Duc's combat group—it could not literally be called a company or a battalion —was told to head up Highway 1 from Da Nang. Straight from the Da Nang docks into trucks and Jeeps and even a couple of buses went the Marines. Over the Nam O bridge and up into the southern slopes of the Hai Van Pass, South Vietnam's highest—724 meters, 2,377 feet—went Duc and a thousand other Marines from Hue.

Another thousand or so of the survivors from Quang Tri were already there. These Marines had not stopped to help in the defense of Hue.

Largely on their own, they had simply passed through Hue and joined the lines of refugees fleeing what had then seemed the inevitable battle for the imperial capital. Sergeants and junior officers had pulled the Marines out of the 250,000 or 300,000 refugees, formed them into makeshift combat groups, and put them here at the south end of the Hai Van. Some had begun at the north end, but retreated quickly as North Vietnamese troops cut across Highway 1 and "liberated" territory south of Hue.

The exhortations of officers, in person and on the radio, to prepare to defend Da Nang now fell on largely deaf ears. Duc had heard it all before. Now he might fight for his life, for the life of his buddies around him. He would fight because he had been trained to fight. During the training, he had been taught, as all soldiers are taught, that it is often safer to fight than to run. So no, Duc would not run. But there was no thought of fighting for Da Nang or for South Vietnam. Certainly, after the government-ordered retreats at the Central Highlands and Hue, after the lack of support given the Marines at Quang Tri, Duc would not be fighting for the Saigon Government of Nguyen Van Thieu.

Duc and his fellow Marines fought their hardest battle of the offensive the night of March 27. North Vietnamese tanks drove at them from the north, over the Hai Van pass. Enormous fire power from the tanks, the infantry, and the North Vietnamese artillery with its 130-millimeter guns crashed around Duc.

The North Vietnamese infantry launched two all-out ground assaults against the Marines. But the Communists had limited movement. They were attempting to fight this offensive by simply overwhelming the opposition. But first, in this tactic, the North Vietnamese had to be able to encircle the Saigon army enemy. The night of March 27 and the morning of March 28, they were unable to surround the Marines.

Blocked to the sides by the natural barrier of the Hai Van Pass, the Communists could not outflank Duc's force. Supplies of ammunition were flowing to the Marine positions up Highway 1 from Da Nang. The army artillery, sitting just behind Marine lines, was firing for all it was worth. The tanklike 175-millimeter guns, moving constantly to prevent the Communists from zeroing in on their positions, duelled the 130-millimeter guns of the North Vietnamese, and battled them to a draw or better.

Duc managed a couple of hours' sleep because he was so tired. Time after time, firing his M16 rifle, he was forced to stop when the barrel became too hot. Both sides were using American-style tactics now, trying to overwhelm each other by sheer numbers of bullets. Outnumbered, Duc and the Marines fought hard anyway.

There were amazingly few casualties. The artillery mostly was fighting the other side's artillery, instead of concentrating on the ground troops. But in the darkness, few guns were hit by either side.

Sometime during the night, the Communist command for Tri-Thien, the senior headquarters in the area, ordered the 324B North Vietnamese division into battle. One and possibly two of the three regiments of the 324B moved out of the jungle northwest of Da Nang and came straight from the west at the Marine flank. On the evening of March 28, as other Communist units moved on Da Nang, most of the 324B division began pushing the Marines off the slopes of the Hai Van Pass.

Once again, the Communists left an escape route for the Marines. They took it with alacrity, mostly in buses and Jeeps. Duc scrambled aboard a six-by-six truck that was following others into Da Nang. On suburban streets, the Marines skirted the downtown area and made for Son Tra, China Beach. All agreed they had had enough. Da Nang was falling, doomed. The Marines were on their third retreat in a week. No other force was willing to back them up. It was definitely time to leave.

The Marines now were no longer a group. They were 2,000 or 3,000 individuals, armed, determined to get out of where they were. They were bitter men. They felt (with some justice) abandoned by their government, their people, their supporting services. Deprived of a chance to do battle, the Marines were angry. The only groups now existing were small cliques of friends who would protect one another against anyone and anything.

Down to the beach, looking for ships they went. The sands where GI's and Vietnamese once lay between refreshing dips in the South China Sea was now itself a sea—of humanity. Everyone who was able to do so stayed clear of the bitter Marines. Not everyone was able to.

By chance, the Marines wound up on two ships—a Vietnamese naval vessel with no name and the *Pioneer Commander*, back from dropping off refugees at Cam Ranh Bay to pick up another load. About 1,000 Marines jammed the Vietnamese ship. Another 2,000 or so made it to the *Pioneer Commander*.

Others tried to make it to the Vietnamese ship. Duc, still on the beach, watched the fights break out. They were one-sided. Marines killed to get on the ship. They killed to prevent others from getting on with them.

Duc was one of the lucky ones who got a huge, inflated inner tube to float out to the *Pioneer Commander*. Others swam, some came out in sampans and lifeboats, motorboats and fishing boats. On nets and stairs, they scrambled aboard the big American ship. Perhaps 50 persons died when they made the mistake of trying to clamber on the ship in front of armed Marines. Marines opened up with their M16's and fought with their hands to kill. The toll of those who drowned or were crushed between the *Commander* and smaller boats is unknown. But it is high.

Through the morning of March 29, as the Communists took over Da Nang and Paul Vogle got ready for his flight on World Airways, Marines took over the two ships. There was nothing to plunder on the Vietnamese navy ship. Defiant Marines stood on every square foot of railing space and made sure no civilian or army man got aboard. More were shot and killed.

Duc watched, sickened. His Marines were turning into animals. Seemingly so frustrated by their inability to hold any line on land, the Marines were almost thirsty for the blood of anyone who challenged their "lines" on board the ship.

Duc did not know, and probably would not have believed, that there would be two more major battles in the Vietnam war, at Phan Rang and Xuan Loc. He would participate in one, almost by accident. But now he was running from nothing, toward nothing more than battles with himself.

March 30, the day after Da Nang fell, was a Sunday. On Sunday, there was no morning briefing for newsmen by the Saigon command. But Lieutenant Colonel Le Trung Hien, the spokesman for the command, was in his office this Sunday morning. Hien had worked seven days a week for virtually all of his life. He was trying to figure out what to say about Da Nang at the afternoon briefing.

On this day, Hien would not lie. He was in a quandary over what to say when he took the podium that afternoon. Whether or not Da Nang had actually fallen was in doubt. That it would fall, there was no doubt at all. Hien's job was to be careful not to give public credit to the enemy before the enemy deserved it.

At the Associated Press office in the Eden Building eight blocks from Hien's office, there also was no desire to give the Communists credit for anything that was not theirs. Here men worked 24 hours a day and seven days a week, probably longer hours than Hien, man for man. And here very early on this Sunday morning—just in time to make the first editions of the Sunday morning newspapers in the United States—George Esper got the information everyone had been seeking

Esper was a nervous nail-biter, an all-business newsman whose likely greeting to another correspondent was, "Got any biggies today?" meaning big news stories. His in-trade fame came mostly from what newsmen call "angling"—subtle writing of the first paragraph of a news story so that the story appears bigger than it actually is. The purpose of angling in the case of AP was to have editors use the AP story rather than that of UPI, its chief competitor. UPI feels no differently.

But the AP bureau manager needed no angling. From military friends, Esper received confirmation that the city of Da Nang was in Communist hands. Convinced by his sources that government resistance had stopped, he bulletined the story to the United States and around the world.

As such stories often do to spokesmen in general, the AP story touched a nerve in Hien, the ARVN spokesman. It raised a hackle, so to speak. Hien felt himself privy to all information, although he was not. He felt the AP story was premature and therefore phony. So when a newsman telephoned Hien and asked for reaction or more information based on the AP story, the colonel said, about 16 hours after Da Nang fell and 26 hours after the last call from Captain Hoa:

"As far as I can determine there still is very heavy fighting going on in the city. It is true that some elements of the Communist forces, even some tank elements, have been in the city since late yesterday. But my latest information indicates there is heavy fighting in the administrative center of the city.

"I know there are some like AP who may say the city has fallen. But I personally tend to doubt it because I don't think they have any better information than we do."

Hien then presented a reasonable argument to the reporter on the telephone. The problem was that his argument did not work in Da Nang, nor in Hue, nor in Nha Trang, and eventually it did not work in Saigon. Except that Hien was not there to see the final breakdown of his theory. He left in the American evacuation for the United States just before the final showdown in Saigon. His argument at this time was:

"I think that when Communist elements enter a city, some people just tend to draw the conclusion that the city has fallen. I think this is not necessarily true. I still believe there is some heavy defense of Da Nang and it is not yet in enemy hands."

All of this was very reasonable under ordinary circumstances. But it was too late for logic, platitudes, and the rest of what spokesmen had been getting away with for years. Other newsmen did not print Hien's statement and AP had no reason to do so. In the view of most correspondents, the war had reached the stage where the Saigon command would have to prove its every statement. And of course Hien simply could not prove Saigon troops still held Da Nang, since they did not.

It was only half an hour after Hien told newsmen of heavy fighting that the rest of the press corps had ironclad confirmation of the AP story. It came from Social Welfare Minister Phan Quang Dan, who interrupted his own news conference appealing for refugee aid to tell reporters Da Nang had come under Communist control.

At the afternoon briefing, Hien would not discuss Da Nang. It was on this day that he himself realized that the state he supported was going to lose the war. Embarrassed and sympathetic reporters for the most part avoided questioning him about the loss of the northern city.

"A VERY FINE PER- FORMANCE"

Private Duc was aboard the Vietnamese naval ship that was commandeered at gunpoint off the Da Nang beach March 29, as the city was being taken over by Communist troops. There were perhaps 2,000 other Marines on board, standing for the most part. There was literally no place to lie down.

The crew of the ship, a small crew, had locked itself in its quarters to prevent the Marines from stealing their valuables or perpetrating other crimes of violence. One or two Marines made attempts to get into the crew's quarters. Luckily, they listened when others pointed out that violence on the crew could mean the Marines would have to take over the ship. No one, it was quickly determined, could run the ship. So the crew was left in isolated peace.

On March 31, two days after leaving Da Nang, Duc's ship and its cargo of Marines steamed into Cam Ranh Bay. On this day, one of President Gerald Ford's emissaries was making a fact-finding tour in the area. David Kennerly, Ford's photographer in name and adviser in fact, was looking around.

Kennerly made his reputation in Vietnam, based mainly on the Pulitzer Prize for feature news photography that he won early in 1972. The prize came from a montage of pictures Kennerly shot in Vietnam, Cambodia, India, and Pakistan in 1971. Shortly after he won the prize, Kennerly quit United Press International and went to work for *Life* magazine. After an even shorter time, when *Life* folded, Kennerly went to work for *Time* magazine, left Vietnam, and returned to the United States.

He had become friendly with Ford while covering the then Vice-President during the last days of the Nixon regime. The two were unlikely friends—the bearded, mod, girl-seeking Kennerly, known to smoke funny cigarettes from time to time, member of the "now" generation, and Ford, the politician from Michigan, Mr. Middle American, Mr. Status Quo.

Flying around the United States refusing to defend Richard Nixon, Ford came to like and respect the brash Kennerly. The photographer was not above making "friends" who were in high places. He liked to impress. Ford was not above flattering people; no politician is. Yet there was something between Kennerly and the President and the Ford family. They respected each other, and even liked each other.

When Kennerly asked the President if he could go along on the Weyand trip to Vietnam, he pointed out that he had spent a year or so in the war zone, knew people there able to give him more viewpoints than Weyand could get, and could better reach the younger field officers, and, yes, newsmen, who had a good idea of what was going on. Ford gave his blessing, and it became known that Kennerly would make his own report to Ford when he returned from Vietnam. Not only Weyand's viewpoint would be weighed.

At 2 P.M. Kennerly was in an Air America helicopter over the South China Sea. The purpose of the trip was to watch the poor souls who had fled Da Nang come to Cam Ranh Bay. There were many ships. Kennerly asked the pilot—or rather instructed him—to swoop in on a Vietnamese Navy ship jammed with humanity. The photographer wanted some pictures to document his trip and his views.

The silver whirlybird dipped toward the ship. On deck, Duc's friends who were armed raised their M16's and fired. It was an expression of outrage. The helicopter with the American flag was mocking them, they felt. Those who were unarmed yelled at the chopper, cursed the men inside, raised their fists in defiance. The helicopter banked and surged away. There were no casualties and so far as could be determined the chopper itself was not touched.

That night, after returning to Saigon, Kennerly mentioned the incident to old friends who still worked for UPI in Vietnam. The shooting had not particularly scared him, since the chopper could only have been brought down by the greatest piece of luck. Rather, Kennerly was shocked. This was the highly touted Marine division, best or second best division in the South Vietnamese armed forces, which had tried to kill him.

Kennerly said the incident had given him great insight into the morale of the Saigon army. In short, it apparently had none.

U.S. spokesmen did not release the incident to the press. When asked about it by newsmen from other agencies, newspapers, and networks, the spokesmen said they knew nothing about it. This was not quite true, of course. The U.S. Consul-General in Nha Trang, highest ranking American in the central area of the nation had been aboard the chopper with Kennerly. Moncrieff Spear had seen the shooting, and had reported it. The spokesmen did not know about it because they did not want to know about it and have to answer questions. Allies shooting at high-ranking Americans make good news copy but bad publicity.

So the spokesmen made no attempt to confirm or deny the incident. Other officials who knew privately blasted not the Marines, not the lack of discipline, not the lack of morale. They criticized Kennerly as a publicity grabber who was not toeing the line in reporting the news as the establishment wished it reported.

On March 30, the day after Da Nang fell and Vogle took his last plane from that northern city, General Frederick Weyand stood on the beach at Nha Trang, 200 miles to the south. Nha Trang used to be one of the prettiest places in Vietnam, with one of the best beaches in the world. The town itself had grown as Americans moved in, and in the late 1960's, although still pleasant, had taken on many of the trappings of a military base town anywhere in the world. It got better after the Americans pulled out in 1971, although the town itself still was dirty compared to many other resorts.

Weyand was taking his first-hand look at what was left of the II Corps area of South Vietnam, the central part of the country. The commander was Major General Pham Van Phu, a brave soldier and a tested combat officer. It was Phu who had stood up to Thieu alone on March 14 when the President ordered the evacuation of the Central Highlands.

The U.S. Army Chief of Staff knew that Da Nang had fallen. He had all the facts on morale, desertions, and abandonments at his fingertips. But for some reason, he was unworried. Nha Trang was peaceful this day. There was no sign of panic and almost no sign that residents were moving out. Even the American Consulate, for some unknown reason, had not seen fit to order the evacuation of those "nonessential personnel" who always were herded out of a threatened enclave.

General Phu, moreover, was a tough commander, subject of many a glowing report by U.S. advisers. He had served as chief of staff and commander of the 1st Infantry Division, the best army unit in South Vietnam. Phu was ill with tuberculosis, but the change from the damp cold of Pleiku to the warm beach climate of Nha Trang had revitalized him.

The refugee situation was going as well as could be expected. Cam Ranh Bay was no heaven, but there was food. Water was hard to find, but arrangements were being made.

Phu briefed Weyand on the situation. It was not optimistic, of course. But in the eyes of the intelligence and operations officers—and Weyand agreed—it was not critical. The main reason for the limited optimism was the belief that the Communists, having captured huge tracts of land and many population centers, would have to halt their advance to consolidate their gains and regroup their forces.

Weyand, Phu, and their intelligence officers couldn't have been more wrong.

In any case, the facts and assumptions Weyand absorbed in Nha Trang enabled him to stand on the beach and tell Matt Storin of the Boston *Globe* and Ron Yates of the Chicago *Tribune:* "South Vietnamese forces are not demoralized in any sense. [Saigon army troops will stand and fight north of Nha Trang and] are determined to slow the Communists down. They are giving a very fine performance.

"Things now are stabilized," Weyand went on as the reporters scribbled. "I'm heartened by what I've seen of the ARVN troops now. They are performing well."

Weyand told the two newsmen Saigon had decided to defend only "viable portions" of Vietnam, and "viable portions" include Nha Trang and areas south of it. General Phu had declared that Qui Nhon, two provinces north of Nha Trang, also would be defended, although Weyand himself was not that optimistic.

Phu was able to include Qui Nhon—fourth largest city in South Vietnam—in his defense lines, because the full 22nd Army division was stationed there. It had fought hard losing battles for the northern part of Binh Dinh province above Qui Nhon, but was still basically intact. As for Nha Trang itself, there was little available force to defend it, a vital part of the equation ignored by Weyand, Phu, and other officials in Nha Trang and Saigon. Estimates of what could and what could not hold were all too often based on guesses of *enemy* ability, rather than hard looks at the available resources of the Saigon armed forces.

The threat to Nha Trang came from the west, from the Communist troops who had massed around Ban Me Thuot in early March and had overrun that town March 10. It also came from the northwest potentially, from the Communists who had followed the Convoy of Tears from Pleiku-Kontum to the coast. An estimated 25,000 North Vietnamese soldiers thus were available to attack Nha Trang.

Saigon forces, meanwhile, had lost their only crack unit available for the Nha Trang defense. On March 27, two days before Da Nang fell, a brave brigade of about 2,000 paratroopers had finally been overwhelmed by a superior Communist force at Khanh Duong district town, 25 miles west of Nha Trang. Loss of the town not only wiped out the paratroopers—most of whom never returned to Saigon lines—but eliminated the only important government stronghold on the western flank of Nha Trang.

The only other defense forces available for Nha Trang were scattered Ranger units, most of them stationed at and around the Ranger training base of Duc My, eight miles north of Nha Trang. Not only was the Ranger force relatively small—perhaps 2,500 front-line troops at the most—it was also a question mark in battle. Ranger units had fought well in some cases, but the battalions had been diluted with raw recruits and most Ranger groups were far from the elite units they once had been.

These facts Weyand and Phu apparently failed to take into account when they made predictions about last ditches and valiant stands.

The U.S. and South Vietnamese officers were making other plans as well, of course. They were not entirely blind to the fact their troops were outnumbered on the battle maps. The plan was to regroup the overrun and defeated units from the Da Nang, Hue, and Central Highlands areas and throw them into the defense of the central coastal enclaves like Nha Trang. The fallacy of this plan was that the Communists would move much too quickly. There was no contingency plan involving the rapid movement of North Vietnamese forces.

Instead, the planners took as gospel what had gone before. Communist troop units had never been able to move quickly. Their own battle plans were limited in scope, and left no room for field command decisions. The intelligence officers and planners felt now that Communist tactics would remain the same. Having achieved basic initiatives at Ban Me Thuot, Pleiku, Hue, and Da Nang, the North Vietnamese would have to halt. Supply lines would have to catch up to the infantry and the tanks. This was the way the Communists had always fought.

Little or no thought was given to the possibility that the North Vietnamese Army had refined its methods and indeed had given more decision-making power to the field commanders. There was no planning for the possibility that the supply lines were now moving with the North Vietnamese forces, that they were not stationary behind the lines.

Long experience and good planning by Generals Giap and Dung would expose the fallacy in the Weyand-Phu statements that Nha Trang could and would be held.

There also appears to be little doubt that Weyand and the Americans especially, and Phu and the South Vietnamese as well, greatly underestimated the giant fall in morale among all residents of the Republic of Vietnam. The people and the soldiers alike felt betrayed, not only by the Americans, who were no longer pouring in aid, but also by their own leaders, and especially President Thieu. The entire nation felt helpless, and most believed the North Vietnamese soldiers were some sort of supermen.

What the nation needed was not brave speeches by those behind the lines. It needed some examples. Between Ban Me Thuot and the April 16 battle for Phan Rang—37 days—there was virtually no resistance to the

Communists. There was no actual bravery, although there was talk of it. No general fought to the death. No soldier was cited as a hero.

Its leadership bankrupt and its people demoralized, the Republic of Vietnam was doomed. Weyand, an experienced battlefield commander, for some reason was blind to this, as were most American leaders. The attitude would cause much suffering in the following 31 days.

The way Da Nang fell showed it could happen in Saigon. The nonbattle for Nha Trang proved it almost certainly would. It was neither a surprise nor a tragedy that the coastal enclave fell April Fool's Day, without a fight, in panic.

But without a shred of Monday morning quarterbacking, it became obvious with the fall of that Corps headquarters that plans should be made in Saigon. American intelligence officers pressed for—no, demanded—the drawing of contingency plans for the evacuation of Saigon. Many of their plans now are public. They were written a month, sometimes two months, before Nha Trang fell.

The argument is made by Graham Martin and others involved in the defense of Vietnam that they walked a tightrope, and an exceptionally dangerous one. They talked about rocks and hard places, about irresistible forces and immovable objects, about tightropes in which a fall would bring death and remaining on the rope brought one into a den of hungry lions. This is specious.

Contingency plans do not involve action. They involve only one or more persons' sitting down, thinking up adverse situations, and recommending ways of meeting those situations *if* the situations actually arise. The fall of Nha Trang caused the writing of such plans. Senior U.S. officials refused to consider them. Graham Martin would not allow their consideration in the Embassy, and refused to allow their transmission to Washington.

One Nha Trang veteran, Anthony Lawson, became so frustrated by the lack of contingency planning that he wrote his own plan to handle refugees. Blocked by his own superiors in the military and by Graham Martin from sending it on to Washington, the young defense intelligence specialist became so enraged that he went outside normal channels. He talked to staffers of the U.S. National Security Council and sent a copy of his plan, with a cover letter, to President Ford.

This, of course, cost Lawson his job and probably will blackball him from U.S. government service for the rest of his life.

Martin was right in one thing he said. He was walking a tightrope so far as overt action was concerned. An early U.S. evacuation would doom South Vietnam before the final battle was fought, because the Saigon army would not fight if it was clear that it would not be backed by Washington. A late evacuation, on the other hand, could doom many Americans and loyal employees to capture and possible death at the hands of the North Vietnamese.

His refusal to allow planning was something else. Waiting too long in Da Nang had cost many Vietnamese what they considered their freedom. Now the experience was to be repeated in Nha Trang. And later, it would happen again in Saigon.

A combination of factors caused the panic in Nha Trang. First, there was the loss of Qui Nhon. The banks closed and money was flown out. The Duc My Ranger camp eight miles north of the city came under Communist attack. Refugees from the north got into Nha Trang despite Phu's orders to keep them out, and they—especially armed soldiers who looted—added to the panic. Phu's headquarters began to pack, an obvious sign that it would move south again. And the Americans began on March 31 to evacuate those "nonessential personnel."

Qui Nhon fell early in the morning, April Fool's Day. There was little fighting. The Binh Dinh province capital was simply abandoned by the Province Chief and the commander of the 22nd Division. The stationing of the U.S. merchant ship *Trans Colorado* offshore from Qui Nhon made the abandonment easy. About half of the 10,000-man division, fully equipped for a fight, instead fled the scene in boats.

North Vietnamese troops estimated at only about regimental strength began their assault on the Duc My camp before dawn April 1. The Rangers fought well, although the camp commander ducked out with the firing of the first shot. Carrying the entire payroll for the Vietnamese Ranger force, the colonel would hightail it to Saigon and eventually bribe his way aboard a flight for the United States, supplied by the U.S. Air Force. The men he left behind fought bravely, and were still fighting the day after Nha Trang itself had been abandoned without a battle. In Nha Trang on April 1, the sounds of battle at Duc My could sometimes be heard.

Not, however, in the areas where the panic was building. In downtown Nha Trang, small bands of armed soldiers roamed the streets. At those soup stalls and small restaurants that kept their doors open, the soldiers "bought" food with their guns. On this Tuesday morning, crowds started to gather at the gate to the Nha Trang air base, formerly used as an air force training site and now the obvious evacuation point. Army and air force military police were put on full alert, and dragged dozens of stands of barbed wire across the base entrance, keeping the crowds out but causing bigger panic.

The panic fed on itself. First there were rumors that Phu's II Corps headquarters, much of it still unpacked from the March 15 retreat from Pleiku, was repacking for another flight. Soldiers going in and out of the headquarters confirmed the reports. Although Phu had not yet ordered another retreat for his headquarters, it was soon obvious that it was only a question of time before he did so.

Graham Martin reluctantly ordered the nonessential Americans out. By midday, when the panic rally got going, there were but 75 Americans left. Some hard decisions were called for from the U.S. Consul-General, Moncrieff J. Spear.

Military police of the Saigon army met the *Pioneer Contender* and the unnamed South Vietnamese Navy ship when they dropped anchor at Cam Ranh Bay April 1. But the normally tough and swaggering police took one look at the Marines and decided discretion was definitely the better part of valor. Having no personal reason to tangle with the Marines and seeing no particular professional advantage in challenging them, the military police absented themselves quickly.

Duc and his buddies commandeered sampans and a couple of fishing boats to get to the bright white sandy beaches of Cam Ranh Bay. One sampan that came a little too close to the navy ship was grabbed, and others were rounded up quickly at gunpoint. The Marines wanted ashore.

And they wanted more. They wanted out of Cam Ranh Bay. That was a place for refugees, for the nonelite. Marines deserved better. They had fought and been betrayed.

Arriving on the shore, the Marines began piling into trucks. Some drivers fled. Those who did not and who indicated that they were not happy about carrying Marine passengers soon found themselves at gunpoint, with four tires flattened by M16 bullets. The others got the idea, and the Marines loaded into trucks, jeeps, and cars and ordered the drivers to head for Nha Trang.

A very few of them made it. Those who did arrived just in time to see the utter panic in the city. Duc was in a six-by-six truck, commonly called a deuce-and-a-half by Americans, since its capacity was two and a half tons of cargo. Just outside Cam Ranh Bay, on the road to Nha Trang 30 miles to the north, the Marine convoy met the vanguard of the refugee convoy southward from Nha Trang. The Marines learned quickly that Nha Trang was now or soon would be in Communist hands.

The vehicles carrying Marines turned back south, to Cam Ranh Bay. Many of them, the drivers still at gunpoint, kept going south, the object being to get to Saigon. More than half let the Marines out exactly where they were picked up—on the beach. Duc was not among them. The Marines again commandeered ships, but their mood was less rough. Strength and anger had been sapped from them. Marines, soldiers, and civilians piled back onto the ships, many of them the same ships they had ridden from Hue to Da Nang, from Da Nang to Cam Ranh. The ships turned south again. The passengers did not know their destination, but it was Phu Quoc Island, in the Gulf of Thailand. Duc and thousands of others turned south on Highway 1, the direct road to Saigon.

About 100 Vietnamese employees of the United States Consulate-General in Nha Trang had been promised evacuation to Saigon, along with their families if the Americans had to leave. Americans who worked with these people had promised all, at some time or another in the past week, that if they went the Vietnamese would go with them.

The problem was that the evacuation contingency plans did not include the possibility of panic. Each plan was based on the assumption that evacuation would be calm and orderly, sort of like a fire drill in an office building or a school. None allowed for opposition by any segment of the Vietnamese security forces.

Most of the plans considered evacuation as more or less a lazy exercise, probably lasting a few days or so. Aircraft from Saigon, planes from outside Vietnam, helicopters, and ships were all considered in various of the plans. One reason opposition from the Vietnamese army was not considered was that there would be little that the Nha Trang-based Americans could do. There were so few of them.

Logistics planning was something Americans were always good at in Vietnam. Soldiers at the front lines could receive mail from home in a few days. Hot food and PX goods reached the men in the field. Evacuation was simply logistics in the minds of the planners, moving people instead of ammunition or pizza.

The breakdown came with the realization that people were not chattels. And Moncrieff Spear faced the agonizing decision April Fool's Day of having to decide about people. He also had to make his decisions with Graham Martin looking over his shoulder and offering "suggestions" from 188 miles away in Saigon.

Late in the morning, Spear decided Nha Trang was lost, no matter what. It was time to get out. The next decision was just how to proceed. The best plan was to drive to the air base and board airplanes. That was impossible, because of the barbed wire barricades at the entrance to the base. Spear ordered up Air America helicopters, with a capacity, if pushed to the limit, of maybe a dozen Americans, perhaps 15 Vietnamese.

The choppers clattered into the downtown Consulate grounds shortly after U.S. Marine guards closed the front and rear gates to the compound. There was a moment of panic, pushing, and shouting by the few Vietnamese employees inside when the helicopters first set down. That moment passed as the Americans began loading the Vietnamese onto the helicopters first. Locked outside were 100 other Vietnamese and their families who had been promised a ride out.

Then the real panic began. Air American C46 and C47 airplanes were to be used for the flights to Saigon. They were small. With no seats, they might hold 60 to 70 people, but that was all. The sealing of the air base was too late. There were hundreds already inside the field when the barbed wire was strung at the entrance. As the Air America twin-engine planes began to load, the real panic began. A few Vietnamese, loyal employees and their families, were loaded onto the first plane, but they were the last to fly out.

Now, at midafternoon, there were 75 Americans in the compound downtown, including Spear. All had weapons, including the only U.S. newsman there, free-lancer Chad Huntley, who was working for UPI.

The front gate of the Consulate began to give under the pressure of Vietnamese troops outside. United States Marines and others designated as security guards thought, naturally enough, that the Vietnamese were out to do harm to the Americans, or at least to stop the evacuation and force U.S. citizens to go down with the Vietnamese ship. The guards shouted out for the Vietnamese to stop banging down the gate. They said it would be opened shortly. The troops stopped pushing, but did not go away.

With only about a dozen Americans left, and as the last two helicopters were chattering in for the final loads of men at the Consulate, the back gate of the compound burst open. A Marine fired five shots in the air. But the crowd of mostly Vietnamese troops had no designs on the Americans. Some ran for the U.S. vehicles, hot-wired them, and drove off. Others began looting the Consulate office.

The Americans were loaded on the helicopters and took off for the air base.

The scene there was even worse. As the planes were loaded, a Vietnamese airman with a child in his arms pushed through the mob to the American security guard aboard one and pleaded with the man, "Can't you at least take the children?" The American shook his head. "If one Vietnamese is allowed on the aircraft we'll never be able to stop the rest of them." No children were permitted aboard. No Vietnamese at all, including the employees of the U.S. government.

One young Vietnamese, claiming he was a Consulate employee, gripped the side of the open door of a C46. U.S. Embassy security guard Joe Hrezo was unable to pry loose the fingers of the desperate man. The burly Hrezo let fly a punch and smashed the young man in the face. At that instant, a UPI photographer caught the punch on film. It was to become a famous picture. Neither the photographer nor the desperate young man, both Vietnamese, made it onto the airplane.

There was also a plan to fly to Nha Trang, a DC8 charter aircraft, a plane that could have carried perhaps 300 or more persons from that city. The plane was available from among the four based in Saigon and flying rice daily to the besieged Cambodian capital of Phnom Penh.

The excuse given later for the plane's not flying to Nha Trang was that there was no loading ramp to allow passengers to board. But the actual reason was that the pilot of the plane insisted, quite rightly, on an American ground controller who could guarantee that the base was safe for landing and loading. He did not want a repeat of the last-plane-from-Da Nang episode. But the evacuation was so confused that apparently no thought was given to requesting a volunteer to stay and guide the DC8 into Nha Trang.

There would have been such volunteers, beyond doubt. II Corps more than any other area had battle-experienced and brave young Americans who felt deeply about leaving Vietnamese behind. In fact, most claimed later that they left Nha Trang only because they were assured by senior Consulate officials, including Monty Spear, that all Vietnamese employees had been taken care of. Senior Americans say that is not true.

The last American officials left Nha Trang just before nightfall. The Communists were already in the city proper, although it would be another day before the air base itself was captured. Nha Trang fell like Da Nang, to a tiny advance force of Viet Cong soldiers, some of them women. Tanks were at the city's outskirts, but did not enter the provincial capital until the infantrymen arrived the next day.

Thousands of persons fled south toward Cam Ranh Bay, including General Phu and his II Corps headquarters. Thousands of others, including most of the Vietnamese staff of the American Consulate, managed to get fishing boats out of Nha Trang to Saigon. Two Americans who understandably would not leave without their Vietnamese families, were able to catch fishing boats. The American Consulate would not take their families aboard U.S. aircraft.

And a bewildered American official close to the Consul-General, speaking of the abandoned Vietnamese, told a newsman, "We had it all planned, but when people started to panic we had to let them go." It was similar to American statements after the Da Nang fall. And it would be repeated after the evacuation of Saigon in exactly four weeks. The truth was that "it" was not "all planned" at all. The fatal flaw was that America had precious few plans, and officials in charge would not allow plans to be written until it was too late.

Free-lance reporter Chad Huntley was in the Nha Trang evacuation. Because friendships made under adverse conditions are deeper than normal acquaintances, Huntley was close to the disenchanted young American intelligence officials who had been at Nha Trang and now were criticizing the debacle.

Only one of these men had total courage of his convictions. Anthony B. Lawson was persuaded by Huntley to talk to UPI. Two days after Nha Trang fell, Lawson wrote his letter to President Ford, criticizing the typical U.S. representatives in Vietnam as "bureaucrats . . . inadequate" to the task. Lawson told the President: "Your mission here has performed poorly, and in spite of glowing reports you may hear, both planning and personal performance have fallen short, with every indication that they will continue to do so. The Consulate staffs in both Da Nang and Nha Trang panicked and lost control. From all indications Saigon is no better prepared."

Others agreed. But many, of course, did not. Senior Americans praised the bravery of Al Francis and Monty Spear. Their reports put the blame for tragedies at Da Nang and Nha Trang squarely on North Vietnamese invading forces. Few, if any, reports by ranking U.S. government servants pointed to a lack of planning.

Lawson was seething, and with the encouragement of Huntley brought both his letter and a seven-page plan on refugee evacuation and care to UPI. He wanted to see it in print, because he was sure the "vast staff, the layer after layer of middle managers" who protected the President from time-consuming matters, would prevent the plan from reaching Ford. At first, he didn't want his name used. But it was pointed out to him that without a name, the plan and criticism meant nothing. So Lawson agreed to let his name be used in the story. What he did, with full knowledge, was to throw away his job. The plan was printed, and the only action taken was to declare Lawson nonessential to any U.S. government department, ship him to the United States, and sever him from government service.

Graham Martin would refuse for a week to hear of evacuation plans. His staff was refused permission to draw up, for example, a contingency plan that took into account possible Saigon army interference with an evacuation. This was despite the fact that U.S. law *requires* every U.S. Embassy in the world to have updated evacuation plans, just in case. In Saigon, of course, it was more than a matter of "just in case."

Lawson's friends from II Corps, who watched the Da Nang evacuation from afar and the Nha Trang evacuation from up close, were highly critical of this. Morris McDaniel, Ed Sprague, and others would sit over drinks in the eighth-floor bar-restaurant of the downtown Saigon Miramar Hotel and tell whoever was there that in effect Martin was a fool. "The Embassy is handling this in the usual fashion," said one. "If we ignore it, the problem will go away."

It seemed then and it seems now that there was no excuse for the Embassy to refuse to make contingency plans. After Nha Trang fell and

Saigon held only one third of South Vietnam, the Embassy press officer issued a statement strongly denying rumors that the Embassy was even recommending partial evacuation. Americans who wanted to send out their families could do so, of course, the statement said—at their own expense. And many were doing it. The day Nha Trang fell, and every day for the rest of the life of the Republic of Vietnam, every airline flight out of Saigon was fully booked.

Persons who in the past had not even considered sending their families out of Vietnam now were doing so. I gave no thought to leaving Vietnam, or having my family do so, during the Tet offensive of 1968 or the Easter offensive of 1972. Indeed, I scoffed at those who did leave. But now, my family was obtaining exit visas. Before the panic hit, I wanted my family out.

There was another reason for moving the families out: an almost universal lack of faith in the evacuation planning of the U.S. Embassy. Whereas in the past Americans had felt that their representatives would go to any length to evacuate them if necessary, the faith was missing now. Not only the Vietnamese mistrusted the Americans—their fellow citizens did, too.

The large American community in Saigon knew that U.S. citizens and dependents had been left behind in Da Nang and Nha Trang. Most were particularly bitter at American officials for treating the Vietnamese and Chinese dependents of Americans as "second-class citizens." Most now began planning to move their dependents out by means independent of the U.S. Embassy.

As with Da Nang, the fall of Nha Trang was confirmed by a telephone call to the military headquarters in Saigon. The Khanh Hoa Province Chief called from Nha Trang in the late afternoon. To the startled officer who answered he shouted, "I am leaving. The situation is hopeless." He then hung up.

Exactly half of the so-called million-man Saigon armed force was destroyed now. Six and a half divisions were euphemistically termed "combat ineffective." None would fight again. Of what was left, only half the paratroop division and the 18th Division were considered of any worth in the immediate future. The 5th and 25th Divisions had been combat ineffective for a year, their commanders in jail on charges of corruption, selling material to the Viet Cong. Three others, of questionable ability, were in the Mekong Delta and could not be moved toward Saigon.

Two other provincial capitals fell to the Communists the day Nha Trang was captured, Qui Nhon and Tuy Hoa. In all, 15 of the 23 provinces north of Saigon were irrevocably in North Vietnamese and Viet Cong hands. In Da Nang alone, 100,000 troops had been captured. The estimated total of forces lost to North Vietnamese attacks was about 300,000. This included many troops neither killed, captured, nor wounded, but totally disorganized and thus "unavailable for combat." Three of the four largest cities in South Vietnam were in Communist hands. Perhaps a million road-clogging, food-using, time-consuming, resource-demanding refugees were on the Saigon side of the lines.

In Phnom Penh on April Fool's day, President Lon Nol was helped aboard an aircraft and flown out of the country. His fall from power was desired by his own supporters and by the Americans, who were trying desperately to open negotiations to end the war and the siege of the Cambodian capital.

The move gave further heart to the growing anti-Thieu movement in Vietnam. It was on this day that Thieu's backbone, Prime Minister Tran Thien Khiem, served notice he intended to resign. He told Thieu flatly that the President had lost the confidence not only of influential politicians but also of the military. Khiem, one of only two four-star generals in Saigon (the other was Joint General Staff Chairman Cao Van Vien), was a main reason Thieu was in power. So long as Khiem supported Thieu, most generals would do so as well.

An open split between the President and the Prime Minister, however, could produce a political battle that would make the coups of the mid-1960's look like practice sessions.

Thieu, trying to avoid reading the handwriting on the wall, cancelled his 5 P.M. farewell appointment with General Weyand April 1. He would work frantically to try to repair the political damage.

Without knowing this, influential opposition Senator Vu Van Mau, a former foreign minister, joined the growing list of public figures calling for Thieu to step down. And in the Senate, men who were now former Thieu supporters drew up a resolution that would pass unanimously the next day.

The Vietnamese Senate said there must be, with all possible speed, "a change of policy and leadership which will base its policy on freedom and justice." Thieu would survive for another three weeks less one day. That he could hold out even that long, with his conservative Senate political base destroyed was testament to his political acumen.

Thieu had rescheduled his meeting with Weyand, Martin, and General Vien for Wednesday morning, April 2. Weyand was becoming eager to pack up and leave to make his report to the President. But Thieu cancelled again. Still beset by political problems, he was not ready to see the American. Finally, they met at 5 P.M. It was far from a satisfactory conference.

According to the official U.S. notes of the meeting read to me later, an obviously agitated Thieu berated Martin and Weyand, as Vien, now a political enemy of Thieu, sat and watched. The President said he was no longer willing just to listen to Americans. It was necessary to speak out. He did something Martin had long hoped he would not do. The President pulled out a letter from former President Nixon.*

The letter, sent just before the Paris agreements were signed January 27, 1973, promised U.S. reaction in the case of another Communist offensive. There is little doubt that Nixon meant that U.S. air raids would be resumed, although the letter was purposely vague on just what the reaction would be. Weyand knew in general about the letter, and was able to point out to Thieu Nixon had given no promises of armed support.

Weyand argued that the support the U.S. was providing was what Thieu could expect. First of all, Nixon was no longer President. More important and more to the point, the American public would not take intervention by American forces in the Vietnam War. The day before, Weyand pointed out, a C5A U.S. Air Force transport had lifted 14 artillery pieces to the Saigon army. More C5A's, with more aid, were on the way. The aid airlift would continue indefinitely. Thieu and his generals, Weyand hoped, were working on a list of priority equipment needed.

Thieu was not in the mood to listen. He blasted the American administration, told Weyand directly and bluntly that so far as he, Thieu, was concerned, he had been sold down the river by Henry Kissinger. Kissinger had sold Thieu a bill of goods with the Paris Accords. The meeting went back and forth like this until it ended.

Weyand and Martin more or less agreed with Thieu, or at least sympathized with him. The Paris Accords were opposed by most strong supporters of the Saigon government as a sellout. Now, with the North Vietnamese on the offensive, with American forces unable to help for mainly political reasons, and with the U.S. Congress approaching the time when all aid to Saigon would be halted, the meaning for the Saigon government of

---

*This is one of two "secret letters" believed written to Thieu and Prime Minister Pham Van Dong at about the time of the Paris accords. The one to Thieu, referred to here, has never been made public. On April 15, Thieu had almost decided to release the text of his Nixon letter, and asked the U.S. Embassy for permission to do so, according to UPI correspondent Robert C. Miller in a story that day. The Embassy response, if any, was never revealed, but Thieu actually read the letter in a Vietnamese translation the night he resigned, April 21. Unfortunately, when he read it he was out of range of television and radio microphones, although those listening said they heard phrases indicating that Nixon had promised Thieu a hasty military response by the United States in case of serious North Vietnamese violations of the cease-fire. "Immediate and vigorous reaction by the United States" was one key phrase.

The other secret letter, to Dong, was released in part by Hanoi April 16, 1976, in a story by *Nhan Dan* newspaper and translated and broadcast in English by official Vietnam News Agency the same day. Nixon's letter stated, said the newspaper: "1. The government of the United States of America will contribute to postwar reconstruction in North Vietnam without any political conditions," and, "2. Preliminary United States studies indicate that the appropriate programs . . . will fall in the range of 3.25 billion (dollars) of grant aid over five years. Other forms of aid will be agreed upon between the two parties."

the accords was exposed for what it was: a piece of paper providing no protection for the anti-Communists of South Vietnam.

Thieu did say the required thing at the meeting: that he would continue to fight the Communists until death. He also said he had no intention of resigning. General Vien's reaction was not noted. The twin vows were dwelt upon by Martin and Weyand in their reports. They would recommend, on the basis of the reports, a massive step-up in military aid deliveries to Saigon.

On April 1 a sign went up at Tan Son Nhut air base that was not a Fool's Day joke. Erected at the military post office in the buildings called Pentagon East and occupied by the massive Defense Attaché's Office, it banned shipment of ceramic elephants.

These elephants are not important to those who have not been in Vietnam. But so far as Americans were concerned, they probably were the single biggest export item from Vietnam. Just barely small enough to meet U.S. postal requirements, the elephants were known as Big Ugly Friendly Elephants, acronym BUFE, pronounced buffie.

The reason their shipment by post was banned was that Americans were lined up about a block deep to mail home household goods, the post office being cheaper than the shippers. The loads of household goods were taking up so much space on outward bound U.S. aircraft that no more BUFE's could be accommodated.

It was a sign of the times. Americans really were getting out of Vietnam, in a hurry. Packing and shipping companies had a week's backload of orders, and within a few days they would be booked through the end of the month. Officials could deny it until they were blue in the face, but an evacuation of Vietnam was underway.

The senior American publicity man in Saigon, Alan Carter, chief of the United States Information Service station, would say later he did not realize Saigon was in trouble until April 8, when a South Vietnamese Air Force plane bombed Thieu's palace. He was right. That was the tragedy. With the country falling about their ears, senior Americans refused to accept the facts.

As of April 1, the U.S. Embassy refused to:
• Help Americans obtain visas to leave Vietnam.
• Help Americans obtain visas for their dependents to leave Vietnam with them.
• Warn businessmen in any way, shape, or form to be cautious of their investments.
• Influence the Saigon government in any way to change any of its losing policies.

• Provide transportation for dependents of its own employees to leave Vietnam and thus reduce the number of "nonessential personnel."

• Cut back its staff.

• Consider contingency plans for evacuation, other than those updated four months previously and three months before the Communist offensive began.

On the contrary. Rosy pictures were painted to those who asked. And for those U.S. citizens requiring the services of their Consulate-General, the lines stopped moving for two hours every lunchtime, so that the unaugmented staff could enjoy the Vietnamese siesta break. Not that consular officials didn't deserve the break. They worked hard, very hard, on endless paper work. But as the lines outside got longer and longer, there was no sign of extra help forthcoming, although dozens of people had been put out of jobs by the loss of I and II Corps and could quite effectively have been put to work.

More than three weeks later, Vietnamese secretaries with ironclad promises of evacuation if they volunteered were put to work in the Consulate-General. Most of them were left behind.

Optimism was a façade and little more. The tragedy was that everyone knew it, at least everyone outside the walls of the various Vietnamese and American ivory towers around Vietnam.

With the fall of Nha Trang, the piaster lost 80 percent of its value on the free money market. The exchange rate went from 725 to 1,300 per dollar overnight.

In Singapore, representatives of the three U.S. companies directly involved in oil exploration got orders from their head offices to close up shop, and passed the word to Saigon. Global Marine (leasers of oil rigs, and exploration companies), Mobil, and Pecten—a Shell Oil subsidiary—got out within 48 hours.

Vietnamese employees of Americans watched their bosses like hawks. Virtually every American promised at least one Vietnamese he would guarantee evacuation if it was at all possible.

The tension began, really began, with the fall of Nha Trang. Rice prices rose a bit in the market, reflecting the stockpiling mentality of the day. There was no panic evident on the surface in Saigon. Only a long-time Saigon resident, in fact, would notice the tenseness. It was there. The panic lay just below the surface, as did the barely latent xenophobia of the Vietnamese, which translated these days into anti-Americanism.

Now all the moves belonged to Hanoi.

And now the target was Saigon, excited members of the North Vietnamese leadership learned. With General Van Tien Dung, Chief of Staff of the armed forces, directing the day-to-day planning of the offensive personally from the south, Giap told the Hanoi hierarchy of his plans.

The generals were sure their troops could take Saigon. Giap avoided predicting when. But that South Vietnam would soon be Communist, he had little doubt.

At this first Politburo meeting after Da Nang fell, Giap laid his belief out in the open for senior officials. The meeting took place in the first couple of days of April, probably on April 1, according to senior informants. Giap told the attentive audience:

> Thanks to the solution by our Party of the problems of military art, during this offensive we have dealt the enemy lightning and powerful blows. Continuously building our speed, tempo, and scale of attacks, we have created huge, continuous chain vibrations. They have become stronger and stronger, day after day. We have sown confusion and so shaken the entire force of the enemy, and its troop bases, it has had no time to fight back and has collapsed totally.
>
> Before the enemy recovered from the loss of the Central Highlands battles, while it tried to draw up plans to withdraw (from the highlands) and gather its forces to better defend the coastal region of central Vietnam, it was dealt a blow at Hue, then at Da Nang.
>
> Now, while it is still in a state of extreme confusion and bewilderment, and while it is urgently patching up a new defense line for Saigon, our great army is already rushing from all directions to the gate of that city.

There was more, much more. Giap is not a scintillating speaker, and like most Communists he tends to ramble on. But his presentation was staged to encourage the Politburo to approve an all-out drive on Saigon. He raised, and dismissed, the argument that it was unseemly for Hanoi's army to take Saigon.

Giap laid out his new plans and tactics. The new strategy, he said, was to combine speed with concentration of forces. If the North Vietnamese Army was kept on the move, Giap argued, it could overcome the Saigon forces in a matter of weeks. It might, just might, be necessary to besiege Saigon, but Giap did not personally think so.

Swift movement, said Giap under questioning, could transform a small force into a large strength; a large force into a larger strength. Vietnamese history, going back 1,000 years to a famous battle with the Chinese at Tay Son, showed that mobility could ensure victory. Strike, win a battle, and move. In commerce, one says that time is gold. In warfare, one can say that time is troops, Giap said.

And Giap had more. For the battle around Saigon, he asserted, he intended to form—for the first time in the history of the Vietnam People's

Army—a task force, a multidivisonal unit combining infantry, tanks, transportation, and signal troops under a single command. And it could be done, the general argued, despite the fact that it had been less than 30 years since the daring idea of forming an entire division had been tried.

Communications lines were already established, Giap declared. Roads built by the Americans in the south would carry most of the traffic. The immense numbers of trucks captured by the North Vietnamese army from Saigon troops would be put to work immediately, carrying soldiers from one battle to the next, eventually to converge on Saigon. Commanders would be instructed to utilize captured equipment, to turn Saigon guns around on the troops who had formerly used them. They would also use prisoners as guides, as propaganda agents, and for information on local military positions.

Hanoi's leadership, of course, was made up of many individuals, and most decisions, like this one, were compromises. The argument was made and accepted that North Vietnam still was working under the Paris agreements. This was true, even though the enemy was daily violating the cease-fire and other provisions of the Nobel Peace Prize-winning accords.

But the Paris agreement provided, in purposely vague wording, that a coalition was to be formed in South Vietnam. It was not called a government. It was to bear the name National Council of Reconciliation. The Communists had become angry when Saigon blocked formation of this council, and had decided on an offensive. But they also were aware of responsibilities—in particular to Russia and China, guarantors of the Paris accords. Because of détente, these giants had made it known that they favored an end to the war short of outright military victory.

The Politburo in early April thus came down slightly on the side of moderation. The following instructions went out to the generals and the civilian leaders of the Communist side:

• Hanoi's aim was a negotiated settlement of the war. Conditions were the political death of President Thieu, removal of his cabinet, a resulting government that would give the Communists at least a 50-50 say in the running of South Vietnam, and an end to all American presence except for diplomats, and especially including military aid officials and their money.

• The military campaign would continue up to the perimeter of Saigon, but would not continue into the city until the Politburo specifically ordered it. Fighting was approved only as a method to force negotiations.

• Giap's new military tactics would be adopted wholly in bringing the army to the doors of the southern capital.

• Southern Communists were to remain alert to the day-to-day political situation in Saigon and be ready to step in, in the very possible likelihood that the Saigon government collapsed entirely from within.

Giap was to instruct his troops to take care in attacking cities. The decisions had been made earlier that when possible population centers were to be taken intact, the troops were to preserve as much of the industrial infrastructure as possible.

A good political student himself, Giap saw the reason for the decisions taken. In any case, he could foresee an internal collapse in the Thieu administration. And he could also foresee that his forces might yet be allowed to capture Saigon if Thieu and the Americans refused to negotiate. He could wait for word to launch the final attack on Saigon. For now, he would capture as much of the rest of the country as possible and put Saigon under siege. Orders were sent south to Dung.

By the morning of April 3, through casual discussions here and there in the diplomatic corridors of Hanoi, Moscow, and Peking, the gist of the North Vietnamese decision was made known to friendly Communist governments. The Eastern European governments were happy to hear the decision. Never great supporters of the North Vietnamese style of Communism, and believers in the advantages of détente with the United States, these governments were happy to hear that Hanoi favored a negotiated settlement.

A friendly official of the Polish peacekeeping team in Saigon telephoned me on April 3. In a most unusual act, he asked me to be sure to come to a cocktail party his delegation was giving that evening. I didn't ask him why, and in fact felt he was trying to tell me that Viet Cong and North Vietnamese officials would be there, a common occurrence, and one way Communist delegations helped the press.

In fact, I had almost decided not to go. The working hours had lowered my resistance, and I was feeling slightly ill, as well as tired. A cocktail party was not really what I was looking forward to that Thursday evening.

Intrigued by the unusual telephone call, however, I went. I was in the villa housing the Polish Ambassador only about two minutes before I was spirited to a corner. A senior Polish official conducted little of the usual chit-chat, and got right to the substance. Did I realize that North Vietnam was not trying to win the war militarily? Could I accept the fact that Hanoi wanted very much to negotiate—but not with Thieu, never with the present administration? Almost anyone else would be acceptable. The offensive could end quickly if only Thieu would resign and a replacement be found. He added that U.S. military aid need not end, at least until after negotiations were concluded.

Feeling quite ill, I left the party early and telephoned the story to UPI deskman Joe Galloway from my home before getting a good night's sleep. Galloway ran the story out under my by-line. I thought myself it was quite exciting, and expected much speculation over this revelation from "a senior Communist diplomat," as I called him.

Neither the U.S. nor the Saigon governments showed the slightest interest. Not for three weeks would the negotiating approach be tried, and then it would not work, because it was too late. On April 3, the United States was not prepared to undercut Thieu. Thieu was not prepared to resign. The Polish Connection became the last of the long list of chances for peace in Vietnam that went unexplored between 1966 and 1975 and therefore were missed.

Not that there was any guarantee, of course, that Hanoi would have kept its word on negotiations. I, and many other people, felt that trying negotiations, however, was always a good idea. But for now, the officials involved had no interest in talking to the Hanoi enemy. By the time they did, the war was one day from completion, and Hanoi had decided it did not want to talk.

PLANES AND BOATS AND THINGS

The battle for Saigon began the day after the evacuation debacle at Nha Trang, although few realized it at the time. It ended exactly four weeks later, a few hours after the evacuation debacle at the U.S. Embassy.

For those in South Vietnam during those four weeks, events are a blur. Hours were long, suffering was great, and memories were not totally reliable. The writer trying to document that month must rely not only on his own memory. The best documentation of that time is in the notes taken by newsmen and cables sent by diplomats directly involved.

For the foreigner in Vietnam now—particularly the newsman—it was like combat to an infantryman, an Olympic final to a sprinter, a typhoon to a sailor of a three-master. In a word, as events happened to and around him, it was exhilarating. It was constant motion, a speeded-up movie in which each person was a star. Helpless to influence most events, merely trying to keep on track, each person had the task only of doing a job as well as his or her training, upbringing, and circumstances allowed.

To the citizens of Vietnam, there was more. There was tragedy. There was fear. There was hopelessness.

Foreigners had no worry, in the main, of losing their country, splitting their families. One existed on sandwiches, booze, and adrenaline. Yet one was never hungry or drunk. One was never tired, although a six-hour sleep was an unthought-of luxury. The newsman was conscious of tragedy, but the adrenaline channeled it into extreme uninterest during the offensive.

Only in the days following "liberation" was one able to begin to fathom and understand the other feelings. As the Communist express hurtled down the track, it was merely a case of getting on with the job.

For a newsman, it was almost impossible to keep up with the pace of events. News agency and television bureau staffs doubled and redoubled. Newspaper reporters found their stories out of date before they were printed, so quickly did things happen.

The four-week battle for Saigon involved two heroic battlefield stands and a political war inside the capital. Rumors were rampant, and often by the time they were checked out and found to be false, wonder of wonders, they had become true. Vietnam was a perpetual-motion machine.

April in Saigon was the entire 30-year Vietnam War in microcosm. Everything that had gone before now came again—from Americans dying in battle to coups to bravery and to cowardice. The U.S. Marines came and went in less than two weeks. American planes bombed only for a few hours and "rules of engagement" occupied the planners. U.S. officials first defended and then, in total frustration, flouted the laws of the sovereign nation of South Vietnam. The Vietnamese Army fled, then on two cases put its back to the wall and fought like the tigers Americans had long declared them to be.

There were the missed chances for peace, at least two of them. There were the U.S. Congressional hearings, the executive-legislative battles, the rifts within the U.S. Embassy. The French were involved. Faces from the past like Big Minh and General Nguyen Cao Ky appeared. General William Westmoreland, now retired, managed to be heard, briefly, with his calls for big sticks against Hanoi.

Yet at the time, there was no sense of déja vu. On the contrary, at least for the newsmen, it was the most galvanizing time of the eighth decade of the twentieth century. Later there would be heartbreak, desolation, a realization of tragedy, bitterness, self-serving statements. But as Cam Ranh Bay fell on April 2, and for the next four weeks, there was only the sheer excitement that comes with participation in the making of history.

The children of Vietnam, pictured by the world as uncared-for waifs, often hungry, were the catalyst for the evacuation mania that began with the fall of Nha Trang. The people who ran the orphanages in the Saigon area made it known that they wanted their children out. This provided a ready-made propaganda issue, and not only for the well-meaning workers who helped the children.

The cynical and the selfish who were in no small number in Vietnam found it a delicious moment.

Among these last must be classed Graham Martin, who told one of his

Embassy aides in a not very discreet moment that the issue of evacuation of children was marvelous propaganda. The Ambassador's feeling was that full publicity on a children's evacuation program would help direct American public—and more importantly, Congressional—opinion toward Saigon. In turn, Martin's reasoning went, Congress would vote the money so badly needed by Saigon to shore up its defenses.

And there was Ed Daly back. Still looking for publicity, the World Airways president thought the only thing better than evacuation of Vietnamese adults was evacuation of Vietnamese children.

The orphanage directors were, for the most part, willing to take help where they could get it. So a couple of them snapped at Daly's offer of a Boeing 747 to ferry children out of Vietnam illegally. World Airways spokesmen announced that 458 orphans were to leave April 2.

Martin, or one of his aides, was not happy about Daly's plans. U.S. officials considered Daly himself a pain in the neck, a publicity seeker who was motivated by nothing other than winning approval for his proposed U.S. coast-to-coast airline service. U.S. employees of the Embassy and the U.S. Agency for International Development visited the main mover in the orphanage evacuation in an effort to dissuade her from using Daly's airliner.

Rosemary Taylor, Saigon representative of the Friends for All Children, was receptive to the U.S. "suggestion" of turning down the offer of World Airways. Miss Taylor, who shunned all publicity normally, was persuaded by American officials to call off the World Airways flight. The reason, she told Daly, was that the 747 was not properly equipped to handle the children.

Miss Taylor was told by USAID officers that the 747 would be without seats—true, because Daly wanted to jam in 458 children plus adults to look after them. She was told the plane would be unheated—untrue. She was told the plane would be unsafe when set up without seats—a debatable point that became moot within a day.

So the influential Miss Taylor removed her blessing from Daly's efforts at evacuation. She did so mainly because of the alternative U.S. officials offered her. They told her Air Force jumbo jets, C5A planes, the biggest in the world, would be at her disposal for the evacuation of her children and those from other orphanages. The big planes were flying in daily or more frequently now with equipment for the South Vietnamese Army, and they were flying back to the United States empty. It would be no problem, officials told Miss Taylor, to put her children aboard these flights.

At the same time, the U.S. Embassy began evacuating Americans from South Vietnam. It was now 48 hours after Embassy spokesman John

Hogan had denied categorically in a written statement that any evacuation was under way or being planned. Yet many Americans received orders April 3 to leave Vietnam within 24 hours.

The orders went out first to those who had only a month or two left in Vietnam. This was to maintain what U.S. officials called "plausible denial." The official, or cover, reason men and women were now receiving orders to get out of Vietnam was that they were getting "drops" on their tours. "Drops" are a kind of official present to American soldiers and officials in hardship tour posts that allows them to go home ahead of the official end of their tours.

Another cover was that the orphans needed adults to accompany them, to feed them, change the diapers, and so on. This also was true. Plausible denial was at work, twice over.

The Americans went to the trouble of securing legal papers to take the orphans out of Vietnam. Officially, the children all had foster parents awaiting them in the United States, and the U.S. government was merely aiding in speeding up the normal paperwork of absentee adoption, a process that normally took a year or more. What actually happened was that Martin sold the idea of the children's evacuation to the Saigon government, and particularly to Social Welfare Minister Phan Quang Dan.

Daly's DC8 (he didn't need a 747 for the smaller load) flew out on the evening of April 3 with a reduced load of 85 orphans and a small assortment of newsmen. One of the writers, Associated Press correspondent Peter Arnett, had to return briefly to the United States anyway. By leaving before the scheduled April 4 flight of the C5A, Daly managed to attract a lot of publicity. With no problems and a lot of good will, the World Airways jet headed for the United States.

The C5A, so big it looks slow when it flies, landed at Tan Son Nhut early on April 4, and workers unloaded tons of military supplies for the beleaguered army. It was scheduled to take off that afternoon with the first "official" load of orphans and a number of Americans, the latter supposedly guardians for the children in flight.

Newsmen dutifully trooped out to Tan Son Nhut around noon for pictures and interviews as the children loaded onto the plane. The giant clamshell doors at the rear of the plane gave most of them entrance to the three decks inside. The C5A was like some giant liner of the sky. It had few comfortable places to sit, but it had a lot of room.

The mootness of sitting on the floor of Daly's airplane came to light now, when Miss Taylor and others discovered that just about everyone on the C5A was to sit on the floor. The C5A, for some reason, was considered safer than a 747 in such a situation, according to Air Force officers. Cargo straps were pulled tight across the width of the plane, and passengers slipped under the straps and sat up during landing and takeoff. The common safety strap was said to be as safe as the regular seat belt. Daly's planes, of course, had the same cargo straps for passengers.

A few lucky ones got the top-deck airliner seats on the C5A, but the great majority of the 300 or so persons on the plane got under the straps. In typical military fashion, it took a long time to load the plane. The newsmen didn't help, jumping from place to place for interviews and pictures.

Finally the huge doors of the plane closed on the crew and passengers. It received clearance from the tower to taxi to the head of the 11,000-foot Tan Son Nhut left runway. Brakes released, its four huge jets whining, the plane gathered speed and took off after using only about half the runway. Newsmen, clearly aware that the American evacuation of Vietnam had begun, stayed to watch the takeoff. Television cameras rolled, and a number of photographers took pictures of the plane as it stood momentarily on its back wheels before clearing the ground. Then they headed to Saigon with the pictures and the story.

At 4:45 P.M. the plane was high in its climb to cruising altitude, past the coastline of Vietnam, over the South China Sea. It was four miles high, headed for eight. Its interior was pressurized to 1,000 feet high. Because the plane was still climbing, passengers were still strapped down. For the children who were not infants, an adult was sitting between every two children. This was to calm the children, most of whom had never flown before, as well as to look after them for more normal needs like eating or going to the toilet. Most of the adults had crossed hands to hold on, making a game of the flight. Some were singing songs.

Then the doors blew out. The suction stripped the plane's interior of everything that was not strapped down, including some infants. Twenty minutes later, with a desperate pilot unable to keep the plane on line for an emergency landing, the huge jet hit a rice paddy hummock, skimmed over a creek and came to a grinding halt in the next paddy. The crash was less than two miles from Tan Son Nhut.

Fire broke out and smoke killed some aboard. The crash killed some instantly, and still others died when they were sucked out over the South China Sea. But, miracle of miracles, there were survivors of the crash. And more amazingly, many of those who survived were relatively unharmed physically.

Martin took the phone call telling of the crash in his Embassy office and he received the news calmly. "The C5A has crashed," a U.S. official told him during a brief emergency phone call by Embassy radiophone. "Yes," said Martin. "There are survivors," the aide said. "Yes," said Martin. "Thank you." Then he hung up.

No thought was given to ending Operation Babylift. The Air Force ordered C5A's grounded for a time to determine the cause of the crash, but 19 hours after the plane flew into the ground, a Pan American World Airways jumbo jet took another 400 children out of Vietnam, and a day after that another U.S. Air Force plane—a smaller C141 jet—flew more than 100 others out.

"It is the least we can do," said President Ford in speaking of his decision to order South Vietnam to cut out the red tape and get the orphans on the way.

But despite the evacuation of the children, and despite the covert evacuation of some "nonessential" Americans from the official community, the U.S. Embassy would not help other Americans. U.S. citizens married to Vietnamese were told by American officials that they would be given no help in breaking through the bureaucratic wall. Martin was willing to help the children because the orphans "helped" him. But for his fellow citizens, the Ambassador remained firm that the law would have to be followed.

In a sidelight to the crash, the United States proved it had improved the old, distasteful job of "graves registration" to the science many men said it was. Army Lieutenant Colonel Howard Tucker, a 53-year-old soldier who doted on physical culture, received news of the crash as he was doing his daily exercises.

Tucker, an up-from-the-ranks officer without a political bone in his body, was commander of the Central Identification Laboratory at Samaesan, Thailand. The CIL was established following the 1973 Paris agreements to identify the remains of Americans missing in the war, who were to be exhumed and returned to American control. This part of the agreement worked no better than any other, Tucker's hand-picked staff had a lot of time for training.

The crash was the CIL's first big job, and it proved itself capable. About 30 hours after learning of the crash, the CIL teams had identified virtually everyone who died, and the bodies and remains were prepared for shipment back to families in the United States or burial or cremation in Vietnam. Tucker and his dedicated staff were happy with the job they had done. They wished only that North Vietnam would begin returning remains so they could do the actual job for which they had been trained.

The South Vietnamese Army now abandoned Dalat. This hill station city a mile up in the southern highlands of South Vietnam had lost its civilian population in March. The Saigon military ordered the officers' university—South Vietnam's West Point—closed even before April came.

Dalat was abandoned by its would-be defense force April 3. The Communists were unable to get a soldier into the town until 28 hours later.

In Saigon, one wondered when, if ever, the line would be held.

Prime Minister Tran Thien Khiem made his last public appeal on the Saigon army radio station April 3, as Dalat was being handed over to the Communists by its defenders. He had already tendered his resignation and had told President Thieu he and many of the other generals had no intention of supporting Thieu.

But the former four-star general found it easier to abandon Thieu than he did to give up the anti-Communist fight. In addition, Khiem was basically a soldier, despite having technically given up his stars to take over the nominally civilian role of Premier. Speaking in his usual monotone, the lackluster Khiem gave his version of a fighting speech during the siesta hour. It was not announced in advance and it was doubtful that 10 percent of the population ever heard it.

Khiem beseeched his fellow soldiers to stop retreating. "Stand and fight for the part of our country that still remains," he said. He confirmed that field generals had been given permission to execute military deserters or others "causing trouble." He did not speak of politics, but of war.

His fears were well founded, even from a purely military standpoint. North Vietnamese troops were headed for Saigon down Highway 1. About 5,000 regular Saigon army soldiers stood between Cam Ranh Bay and Saigon as of April 3. The Communist strength was just unknown, a matter of guesswork. The estimate most often quoted was perhaps seven divisions—about 50,000 troops, more or less.

April 4 was a busy day for President Thieu, even without the C5A crash, which after all did not affect him. He launched another midnight crackdown on his political opponents, he made a promise to General Frederick Weyand just before the general left for Washington, and he accepted Khiem's resignation.

Early morning knocks on the door for the loyal opposition had almost halted in South Vietnam by 1975. Thieu revived them, claiming civilian members of splinter parties were out to get him and launch a coup d'état. Without presenting a shred of proof to his people, Thieu had his spokesmen announce the arrests of certain "short-sighted elements" who were plotting his overthrow. The impression he wished to create was that generals had attempted a coup. Newsmen quickly found out otherwise, as the families of the men involved contacted friends in the press corps and told them of the Gestapolike raids.

The men arrested may have been short-sighted in believing they could force any change in Thieu's policies. But other than that, they were less than harmless. The lawyers, teachers, and professors Thieu ordered incarcerated were at least anti-Communist. More to the point, they were harmless to Thieu, as they were unable to act on their theories, which ranged from digging in for a long military fight to making peace by negotiation.

Saigon's overnight curfew was custom-made for the midnight door-knocking, and the men fingered by Thieu had no chance of escaping. Most were idealists who considered themselves realists. The main point was that they posed no threat to the Thieu government. There was a theory that Thieu was trying to intimidate his more important political-military opponents by arresting the small fry. In any case, the men were jailed.

Shortly after the roundup, Thieu met Weyand in a short conference just before the American went back to make his inevitable upbeat report to President Ford. Weyand told Thieu the issue of Vietnam aid was in trouble. In effect, he told the Vietnamese leader that wholesale retreats were losing the Congressional votes of even the pro-Saigon Senators and Congressmen.

Weyand was not harsh with the Vietnamese President. But he was shocked at the fall of Nha Trang, where he had told newsmen there would be a fight. Now the general told the President gently it was time for a stand. Somewhere, before the Communists reached the Saigon area, Thieu's forces had at least to fight, and preferably to win, a single battle. Thieu promised such a battle would take place.

Weyand told newsmen at Tan Son Nhut airport he was not concerned about Saigon's holding, although the war in the countryside was going poorly. With the correct aid from its allies—are you listening, Congress?—South Vietnam could defeat the North Vietnamese army.

Thieu took all this, not surprisingly, as American backing for himself and his policies. He also took as a veiled threat Weyand's plea for the Saigon army to make a stand somewhere. Thieu called in his palace military advisers and decided Phan Rang would be the place. He racked his brain briefly and decided Lieutenant General Nguyen Vinh Nghi would be the man to lead the stand.

Most South Vietnamese generals were corrupt in one way or another, sometimes simply using their ranks in influence-peddling or allowing their wives to use their ranks to get special favors. Nghi was so blatantly corrupt that it was embarrassing even to the Americans, who pressured Thieu to fire him as commander of IV Corps in the Mekong Delta in 1974. According to several Embassy officials in Saigon, the publication of the so-called

Indictment No. 1 by anticorruption forces in Vietnam so compromised Nghi that Thieu was forced to dismiss the general.

With the publication of the indictment, Saigon newspapers were emboldened to print other allegations against Nghi—that he owned at least three homes and villas in Saigon with an estimated value of close to $1 million; that his wife controlled distribution of beer and soft drinks to the 300,000 armed forces members in the delta; that he was somehow (the newspapers never said exactly) linked to the alleged sale of delta rice to the Viet Cong, a matter under public investigation at several levels in Saigon. In short, Nghi was accused of overstepping the bounds of what had become accepted use of a corps command to attain personal advancement.

The three-star general had no battle record to speak of, according to his official biography. He was rich, came from a good family, had good political connections. But his greed was coarse, and became too openly known. Unable to find a battle command for a three-star general, and unwilling to place him in a staff position because of the graft opportunities, Thieu had given him a staff title but no job. But Nghi, according to those who knew him well, had a personal loyalty to Thieu and the anti-Communist fight, which in 1975 could be utilized.

Now Thieu came back to Nghi for the job that was to be the most important of his life. He gave Nghi command of Phan Rang and Phan Thiet, the only two towns left to the Saigon army in II Corps. Technically, Nghi would report to III Corps headquarters at Bien Hoa, but in fact he was to take whatever force he could scrape up and fight for the two towns. Phan Rang, 165 miles east-northeast of Saigon, was the northernmost, the site of a major air base, and the most easily defended. Therefore, Phan Rang was to receive priority as a defense line.

Nghi scraped the bottom of the barrel for men. He took the Phan Rang defense force, most of the real fighters being air force police. He intercepted soldiers fleeing down Highway 1 to Saigon and turned them around to Phan Rang. He swept up dregs of survivors from Hue, Da Nang, and other overrun spots in the northern areas. In days he built a fighting force and on April 10 he arrived in Phan Rang to set his lines.

Thieu's third act came on the evening of April 4 and was more eyebrow-raising than the first two. He went on radio and television and announced he had accepted Khiem's resignation. Then he proceeded to set out his two chief enemies—greater, if one accepted the tone of his speech, than the forces of North Vietnam.

The American people: "The spirit of the people of South Vietnam has been undermined for more than one year. The Vietnamese people see the people of the United States not only refusing to take action, but contributing to our problems by letting the Communists infiltrate here. The loss of support has caused a loss of morale. . . . The U.S. government and Congress has cut down on aid. They are letting the North Vietnamese bring all their men and arms into the south for the offensive against South Vietnam. . . . Having allies who are ready to let us down brings about a corresponding drop in morale. When soldiers lose their morale and confidence the people lose their confidence in the soldiers. How can we trust the Americans?"

And the press: "I call on the military, on the people, on all cadres and civil servants not to listen to untruthful propaganda from the Communists or news reports, whether by local or foreign journalists. There are a number of people in the news agencies and radio and television stations who have been bought off by the Communists to help undermine our fighting spirit. The BBC (British Broadcasting Corporation) and the VOA (Voice of America) have particularly spread these reports. These foreign news agencies which purposely distort the truth will be punished."

Thieu was passionate in flailing military commanders who had refused to stand and fight, although he did not name any. His plan to abandon the Central Highlands he defended as a brilliant military campaign poorly carried out by his military forces. He did note that civilian panic helped hinder his officers.

The President then was unable to name a place where a commander should have fought. Hue had fallen to a superior force, he said. At Da Nang, there was not time to set up a viable perimeter with the troops available and given the panic. He did not discuss Nha Trang except to criticize civilians for panicking by "rushing to the airport" and not giving refugee workers time to organize an effective evacuation.

There was the usual Thieu claptrap about more last ditches. "With or without foreign aid," Thieu vowed he would continue as President and his army would fight.

On the political side, it was not Thieu who was quitting, although there had been rumors to this effect before the speech. Rather, he said he had accepted the resignations of the entire cabinet, including the Prime Minister. Khiem's successor as Prime Minister was to be Nguyen Ba Can, a 45-year-old hack politician who had stood at the wallflower line of power for several years without being asked for a dance.

Known for neither his administrative ability, his political canniness, nor his popularity, he was an odd choice. But he had one thing in his favor, unwavering support for his President. Thieu supported Can in a knockdown contest for Speaker of the House in 1974 and there was no question of the new Prime Minister's loyalty.

Thieu was not shaking up his cabinet so much as he was serving notice that he was not afraid of Khiem. Most of the key ministers were kept in their posts and continued their jobs while reporting directly to Thieu, rather than going through the Prime Minister. Can knew few if any of the key decisions made by either Thieu or his ministers.

In retrospect, the ploy worked in that it kept Thieu in power. His opponents were still looking around for support when, just over two weeks later, it was time for Thieu to resign. In the short time that remained to the Republic of Vietnam, Thieu's indication that he would fight Khiem and all the generals if necessary caught his opposition so short it was unable to act to force him out of office. If it had not been for U.S. Ambassador Martin and French Ambassador Jean Marie Merillon, Thieu could have stayed President until the end of the war. As it was, he lasted longer than most people believed possible.

As a sidelight, Thieu received public backing for his anti-American tirade from only one Vietnamese official. Viet Cong Senior Colonel Vo Dong Giang, the suave and urbane deputy leader of the Communist delegation to Saigon, told newsmen the United States was indeed to blame for the situation. Giang, of course, blamed Washington for the whole war, as well as developments in the Ho Chi Minh campaign.

Thieu followed up his harsh speech by ordering the arrest of three generals, while a fourth he dearly wanted to jail lay in his sickbed. Major General Pham Van Phu, who had argued with Thieu about the Central Highlands evacuation; Major General Pham Quoc Thuan, who was supposed to defend Nha Trang, and Lieutenant General Du Quoc Dong, whose troops lost Phuoc Long province in January, were incarcerated at the Joint General Staff jail. Lieutenant General Ngo Quang Truong, who was unable to hold any city in the northern sector, was in a military hospital suffering mostly from shame.

Truong was on a hunger strike. Family friends indicated that he had no desire to meet or confront Thieu. He did speak with members of his immediate family, although they did their best to indicate that the general was mad. He was not. When the end came for the Republic of Vietnam, Truong was one of the first aboard a U.S. helicopter.

Marine Private Duc came driving down Highway 1 from Cam Ranh Bay April 6, four days after the port had been abandoned to the Communists. Not really hurrying and not at all desperate, Duc reached Phan Rang in four days. This is an almost phenomenally slow time to go from Cam Ranh Bay to Phan Rang, but the truth was that Duc stopped off for a couple of days of "relaxation" with a couple of bottles and some friends.

Duc had stayed on the army truck as it pulled out of the beach at Cam

Ranh Bay April 1. And it was obvious that Cam Ranh would fall soon. But about 25 miles south of Cam Ranh, Duc's truck broke down. The riders walked only about half a mile before they came to Du Long, a village of perhaps 5,000 persons. Du Long was a district headquarters, and as such had troops, radios, and the like. Having troops, of course, it also had girls for hire. With no obvious threat to the town, Du Long also had Duc and his friends for a couple of days of fun.

It had been a long time coming so far as the Marines were concerned. The last time they had been free of the pressures of battle was the day before the North Vietnamese swept through Quang Tri province March 21. Duc had fought twice and run many times. So far as he was concerned, a couple of days at Du Long were his due.

So he enjoyed. And when four giggling Marines including Duc hot-wired a Jeep and headed south for Saigon again on April 6, they were refreshed and not even thinking about the coming hangovers. The euphoria lasted about 15 miles, when Duc and his companions ran into the Military Police checkpoint and were impressed into the armed forces again.

The MPs were working for General Nghi, charged by Thieu with holding Phan Rang, or at least with making a heroic stand. Nghi took the job seriously, for once, and the police were obeying his instructions to build up the Phan Rang defense force as quickly and as strongly as possible. Anyone who appeared able to fight was to be impressed or re-impressed into the armed forces of South Vietnam.

One of the reasons—many say the only real reason—Thieu picked Phan Rang as a defense post was that it was his hometown. The President was born just outside Phan Rang near Ninh Chu village, not far from the South China Sea coast. His mother had lived there until the early 1970's, when Thieu brought her south to join him in his Saigon triumph. The President visited the Phan Rang area more often than any other part of his country. Thieu was a converted Roman Catholic, in deference to his wife. His Buddhist upbringing dictated regular returns to Ninh Chu to visit the graves of his ancestors.

General Nghi, no political fool, planned his defense of Phan Rang to include Ninh Chu. Located about five miles north and slightly east of Phan Rang city itself, Ninh Chu was not totally defensible. Tacticians have questioned the defense of the town by Nghi. In fact, it appeared that there was a very proper reason to defend it. Ninh Chu was near the beach, and therefore controlled an escape route. Also, it was well within gun and rocket range of Phan Rang itself. Capture of Ninh Chu would put the provincial capital directly under Communist gunfire.

Private Duc and his three Marine buddies went to Ninh Chu. Other Marines were there, along with Rangers, soldiers, militiamen, and even a few air force men, some of whom had trouble telling from which end of their rifles the bullets exited. Airborne troops overrun west of Nha Trang a week before were on the line at Ninh Chu. About the only thing common to the Ninh Chu defense force was that virtually all of them had fled fighting at one time or another during the previous three weeks.

The actual Ninh Chu defense force was a militia battalion. Four days before Nghi took over defense of the Phan Rang area, its men had fled, frightened by the huge refugee columns snaking down Highway 1 to Saigon from points north. The town was also deserted by its civilian population. Ninh Chu was a dead village guarded by troops who were running. Few believed their running had stopped.

Lieutenant Colonel Bao appeared on the scene the afternoon of April 7 to take charge of the defense of Ninh Chu. He reported directly to General Nghi, he told the troops, and he intended to hold Ninh Chu for the general and for the President. He was a striking man, leading the only troop with new fatigue uniforms, and shined boots. He never said where he came from, although Duc and his buddies thought it was likely he had come from a Saigon command and was hand-picked by Nghi.

In two days, Bao made as much sense of his ragged defenders as he could. He set up listening posts, perimeter posts, and regular patrols. He formed fire teams of any size, from half a dozen to 50 men each. He picked his subordinate commanders by instinct rather than rank, since there were almost no officers and very few sergeants anyway. Duc became deputy leader of a 50-man team assigned to reserve force duty inside Ninh Chu. It was the cushiest job available. For three days, Duc's team did little more than forage for food for other members of the defense force on station farther out of town. Ninh Chu's defense perimeter extended only five kilometers from the central market—not nearly enough for a good defense of the town, but the best Bao could do with the limited number of troops at his fingertips.

There was one other notable addition to the Phan Rang defenses before the battle for the provincial capital and air base began. He was James Lewis, former captain in the U.S. Army, native of California. Lewis was one of those shadowy men of the Vietnam War, certain to be identified in Communist propaganda as a military adviser in civilian clothes. He was not. He was a reporter, although not a newsman. For some reason he was sent to Phan Rang to watch the battle there from the viewpoint of General Nghi.

There was no question of a man like Lewis advising Nghi. Even his civilian rank fell well below that of the three-star general. Lewis' paycheck came from the U.S. State Department, and he was officially assigned to the U.S. Consulate-General at Nha Trang. Whether he was an intelligence officer is impossible to say, since active spooks do not identify themselves.

Lewis says he was not, but he would say that anyway. In any case, here he was a reporter only. He was to observe the battle for Phan Rang and report back to the U.S. Embassy the results of the battle. The assignment was to cost him dearly, although when he left Vietnam six months after the "liberation" of Saigon he still had his sense of humor and his health.

It is difficult to pinpoint the actual date the battle for Phan Rang began. The city was being shelled and its civilians were fleeing even before Nghi arrived to take up its defense. But the North Vietnamese took better than a week to roll up their lines at Nha Trang and Cam Ranh Bay and Dalat in the Central Highlands. There was no serious Communist attempt to overrun Phan Rang until after April 7, a week after Nha Trang was abandoned. The first big ground attack came April 9.

While Phan Rang received a heroic defense, other events overshadowed what was taking place there. As it turned out, there was no opportunity to publicize the defense of Phan Rang. Nguyen Van Thieu's fortress was being bombed and another battle, which would dwarf Phan Rang both in heroics and importance, was getting under way.

Nguyen Thanh Trung was a confused young man in early April. He had successfully fled Da Nang air base when the Communists were closing in, flying his multi-million dollar F5E out of the besieged city. The F5E was the newest toy in the arsenal of the South Vietnamese Air Force, and American-trained Trung was one of the first pilots to take it up.

Many argued that the fighter was ill-suited for the Vietnam war. It had a light bomb load compared to other planes, and was designed mainly as an interceptor. Its critics in Vietnam claimed that the Americans had given it to Saigon only because the Vietnamese insisted on having a supersonic plane—which was true—and that the Americans were not willing to give Saigon what it wanted—F4 Phantoms. The F5E's came to Vietnam with great publicity about their bombing accuracy and their suitability to the Vietnam war. The critics laughed. As it turned out, the bombing accuracy was not all that great.

Just who Nguyen Thanh Trung was will not be known for quite some time, if ever. The South Vietnamese Air Force said he was a distraught pilot who bombed Thieu's palace because he felt he and he alone was upset with the way the President was running the country. Other sources said he held Thieu personally responsible for the fact that his wife and son were left behind in Da Nang during the retreat.

The Communists claim he was a lifelong member of the Vietnamese Communist Party, then called the Lao Dong. They claimed he was a "sleeper," one of the many Communists inserted into the Saigon administration to stand by for future orders.

Both claims are simplistic and highly unlikely, the Communist claim more so than the Saigon one.

Trung's bombing of the palace was pivotal. It was, in a trite phrase, the turning point of the offensive. Before the bombing, the optimists believed that a last stand for Saigon was possible, that Thieu might survive, that Americans could remain in Vietnam indefinitely. The bombing symbolized dissatisfaction with Thieu, made it clear that problems within the armed forces were serious, and meant that there would be no stand for Saigon, and that the Americans were finished.

But all these facts became evident only *after* Trung's attack on the Independence Palace. No strategist or politician could know that a single attack by a lone pilot could catalyze virtually every force in the Republic of Vietnam and so change the course of battle. This is what makes the North Vietnamese claim that Trung was a "sleeper" so difficult to accept. Clasping him to their bosoms was great Monday morning quarterbacking by the Communists, but it is impossible to believe anyone would have foreseen the palace bombing as a great catalytic event.

Sources in Saigon after the end of the war give a different and more credible version of the bombing and just who Nguyen Thanh Trung was. This is their theory, backed, as usual, with just enough facts to make it credible.

Trung, like most servicemen, lived in a slum area of town, in his case Da Nang. The slums were breeding places of discontent in Vietnam, as in any country in the world. The cadre of the National Liberation Front and of North Vietnam found propagandizing in the slums of Da Nang relatively easy.

The son of a Viet Minh who died in combat against the French, Trung listened to the soft-core propaganda he heard in the coffee shops and grog stores of his Da Nang slum. He listened to it enough, and he was smart enough, to realize that the Communists of Vietnam did not have horns growing out of their heads. He accepted very little of what they actually said about the golden streets of postliberation Vietnam. But other points made—the corruption of the government, the poor leadership of Thieu and his generals, even the ultimate victory of the Communists—made some sense to the pilot.

Over a period of years, Trung formed his own ideas about the Communists. He traveled in the United States for a year and found the American people pleasant and infinitely richer than those of his country. At heart, Trung was a capitalist. But the propaganda of the Communists also struck a nerve. He came to believe that he could accept a socialist government in South Vietnam. In a word, he was confused. His political thinking ran in two directions at the same time.

There was a man who lived in the Da Nang slum who probably was a Communist agent. He and Trung lived next door to each other, the man being a motocycle repairman who spent his time at his home-shop. Trung liked the man and talked often with him, sometimes about politics. They agreed that the political situation in South Vietnam was bad. From time to time they talked about the Viet Cong and the North Vietnamese. They agreed that there was some justice to the Communist fight.

The pilot was not distraught after the Da Nang retreat. He was angry, however. His family was not taken care of and he did not know whether they were dead or alive—in Da Nang or on a ship or in a refugee camp. He blamed his generals for loss of face, for retreat, for his family's situation, whatever that was. He blamed Thieu because Thieu was the leader of the generals and of the nation.

At some time, the man gave Trung a name and address in Bien Hoa. He gave him some other names and addresses in other places. He told Trung they were names of friends who could be counted on in an emergency. The Viet Cong was never mentioned, but Trung knew the men had to be Communist agents. The man in Da Nang was taking a chance giving Trung the names and addresses, of course, but apparently felt he could trust the pilot.

On April 6, the sources said, Trung had decided he could not fight for Thieu any longer because the President was personally sinking the Republic of Vietnam. He went to see the man in Bien Hoa whose name and address he had kept in his wallet. They had a beer, two beers, in a Bien Hoa cafe. Trung let his vitriol flow. He said he would kill Thieu if he had a chance. He would bomb the Independence Palace. The man told Trung to come for more beer the next day.

The plan, of course, was Trung's so far as the pilot was concerned. This was essential so that the catalyst would believe completely in what he was doing. Viet Cong agents were trained to appear never to think up plans, to guide rather than to lead.

The next day, the agent had a couple more beers with Trung at the Bien Hoa cafe. Obviously having checked with his superiors, the agent told Trung to go ahead. "Friends" of his, the agent said, had informed him they would guarantee Trung's safety if he was able to fly his plane behind Communist lines. With enough fuel, Trung could head for Da Nang, where he would be greeted as a hero. One jet, and one alone, would be allowed to land. The Viet Cong made this stipulation to rule out the possibility of a double cross by Trung.

For a couple of days, news had been slim in South Vietnam and early on April 8 newsmen were rehashing the early April developments. Robert C.

Miller of UPI had been to the upper Mekong Delta April 7 and wrote that the approaches to the capital were manned and the soldiers might possibly fight a Communist advance. The flight recorder of the orphans' C5A had been found in the South China Sea. Neutralists were calling for Thieu's resignation, but with rightists and former supporters of Thieu doing the same that story was a nonstarter.

Americans continued to flow out of Saigon under the guise of escorts for the orphans, who also continued to leave by the hundreds. One plane landed in the Philippines with more escorts than orphans, finally destroying the U.S. Embassy's claim that no evacuation was under consideration.

Perhaps the greatest topic for discussion was the evacuation on April 4 of American managers and staffers of the three U.S. banks in Saigon, the Chase Manhattan, First National City, and Bank of America. Their flight had not been discovered until Monday, April 7, when their banks, staffed by Vietnamese, opened to the announcement that no more foreign currency transactions would be allowed. Senior Vietnamese employees said the American managers, before leaving on their chartered airliner, had taken all dollars, checks, and other foreign currency instruments with them. This outraged local foreign businessmen and left hundreds of residents temporarily stranded and dependent on the evacuation planes and helicopters, because the travelers' checks they held were worthless in Vietnam. On the other hand, they needed the checks to buy airplane tickets, which had to be paid for with foreign currency. The Vietnamese kept the banks open only to manage accounts in piasters, the local currency.

Most correspondents who had been chained to the job for a month managed drinks and dinner at a restaurant the night of April 7. The office-openers on April 8 were more relaxed than they had been for weeks, and in fact for the first time sat looking at their piles of notes and wondering just what they could write about for the afternoon newspapers, which demanded front page copy every 24 hours.

Nguyen Thanh Trung solved the problem at 8:25 that Tuesday morning. He took off from Bien Hoa airport 15 miles northeast of Saigon with two other F5E pilots for a preplanned strike against Communist positions west of Phan Rang. Still in his climbout from Bien Hoa, Trung simply left the three-plane formation, reporting to his flight leader that he had engine trouble. The leader accepted the explanation, because it was common. He and the other pilot continued on to make the strike.

Trung did not return to Bien Hoa, and there was nothing wrong with his plane. He dived to less than 1,000 feet and headed straight west to Saigon. He came over the capital at about 400 miles an hour, spotting the Independence Palace in its parklike setting about the time he swept over Tu Do street.

He made a screaming right-hand, climbing turn, pulling about 5 G's, heading north of the city and gaining altitude at the same time. He made a tight left-hand turn as he reached about 3,000 feet not far outside Saigon, a 180-degree turn.

The nose of his plane pointed directly at the Saigon zoo, another park oasis in Saigon. The zoo was a great landmark for the palace, because it was at one end of Thong Nhut (Unification) Boulevard. About a mile down the street, at its southern end, was the palace. Trung brought the nose of his plane up slightly as he continued his bombing dive. He swept over the zoo, over the U.S. Embassy halfway down Thong Nhut, and released a 500-pound bomb even before his plane reached the palace.

His aim was good, but not excellent. The bomb trajectory dumped it just outside the palace wall, rather than on the eastern wing generally known to house Thieu's office.

He peeled left over the downtown area and sped back to the north, climbing as he went. Barely below the speed of sound now, he dived again at the palace, loosing his other bomb. (The plane carried only two bombs, a main criticism of those who said it was not suited to its attack function in Vietnam.) Again he just missed the east wing.

The damage of his attack was not great, considering what a half ton of explosives could have achieved. Windows cracked and the inside staircase of the palace collapsed. Two palace guards were killed by concussion. Nguyen Van Thieu, who had taken to sleeping elsewhere because of the possibility of a military coup d'état, was not even in the palace when Trung made his two fast runs.

Poor defenses were also shown up by the Trung attack. He was over the palace three times, but only at the end of the third run was there any antiaircraft fire. The F5's supposedly on station at Tan Son Nhut air base to intercept Communist planes were not on station at all. They were parked, their engines shut down, and their pilots nowhere to be found.

And no one had any idea of what was happening. Radio Saigon broadcast blithely along as if nothing had happened, as did the American radio station. A press aide woke Air Vice Marshal Nguyen Cao Ky to tell him of the attack, although many assumed Ky was behind it because of his almost total control of air force loyalty. A block and a half from the palace, at the American Embassy, no one had the slightest idea of what had happened.

The Saigon military went half-mad in its typical approach to the unknown. The palace, naturally enough, was sealed off, as was Tan Son Nhut for some unknown reason. Instant curfew was declared, and Saigonese rushed home under the eyes of heavily armed troops.

In a doorway just off Tu Do, the main street, a pathetic policeman asked Vietnamese-speaking Paul Vogle what was going on. Without waiting for an answer, he said he didn't know what to do, nobody told him anything. "If it's really a coup, I should be getting out of this uniform."

By midmorning, it was becoming clear that it was no coup. American radio broadcast bulletins saying that all evidence "indicates that the event of this morning [never named, of course] was the work of a single individual." Americans and Vietnamese alike were told to keep off the street.

Thieu himself, under heavy guard, drove to Radio Saigon and taped a brief message saying he was alive and well, as was his family. Apparently truthfully, he said he had the assurances of all military commanders of their support. By midafternoon, the curfew was called off and the military alert status lowered.

Nguyen Thanh Trung by midafternoon was posing for publicity pictures with North Vietnamese soldiers at Phuoc Long. He had landed there with no trouble and been disarmed and debriefed. His story of bombing the palace was quickly and easily checked, and Trung was welcomed as a defector. He was *not* welcomed as a returning comrade, however. The high command of the People's Liberation Armed Forces gave him a paper promotion from lieutenant to captain and announced the award of a hero's medal.

At his headquarters at Loc Ninh, the so-called Viet Cong "capital" north of Saigon, General Dung received word of the palace bombing and Trung's defection. He formed the idea of using Trung as a training pilot and issued an immediate order by coded radio message that the pilot be sent to Da Nang. Dung ordered Trung to help form squadrons of A37 and F5 jets using North Vietnamese MIG pilots as fliers.

But Trung was not allowed to carry arms and was not allowed to fly a plane unaccompanied by a North Vietnamese. He did work hard and he did continue to fly. He had participated in a turning point of the war. He was to be the catalyst again in less than three weeks. He would lead the attack that brought about the final surrender of Saigon.

The palace bombing was the turning point. Alan Carter, chief of the United States Information Service station in Saigon, remembers it this way:

> . . . somehow, April 8—the day of the bombing attack on the Presidential Palace by a South Vietnamese pilot—looms as the point at which we felt evacuation became an inevitability.
>
> The USIS office compound was so close to the Palace (about three blocks) that our windows were rattled by the roar of the plane as it swept close enough to cause anxiety; and the chatter of small-arms fire was frighteningly close. Within a few hours, the 24-hour curfew that followed was lifted, and within another 24 hours we had begun to stock large quantities of food in the main compound, the Binational Center, the USIS Annex, and the VOA office. We

had been close enough to being trapped in our building by a bombing and a curfew to warrant taking all possible measures to prepare for another episode. From this point on, more importantly, the thinking and planning of the mission veered sharply toward an evacuation, one which we knew would be unlike any other evacuation faced by an American Embassy. . . . A repeat of the panic-stricken evacuation of Da Nang was likely.

We were already in the process of thinning down the American staff. There were, as of March 31, 5,800 Americans in Saigon for whom the Embassy had a responsibility. It had still another responsibility: not to withdraw in such numbers and with such speed as to trigger panic in the streets or the collapse of the South Vietnamese government, a balancing act of such delicacy and importance that no ambassador could welcome it or avoid it.

There is only one major fallacy in Carter's article, which appeared in the USIS staff publication in June, a month after the Saigon evacuation. In it, he refers to his belief "that the North Vietnamese were intent on the military and not the political solution." Carter was writing with hindsight, correct in the belief that planning for an American evacuation should proceed on this "worst possible scenario and the most likely one." But there was opposition, both to the presumption that the North Vietnamese were trying for a military victory, and to planning an evacuation based on that presumed fact. The opposition came from Graham Martin. Martin believed the Communists would eventually make a political settlement, rather than embarrass themselves with a military victory march down Saigon streets. He was right, but that was beside the point on April 8.

Carter and many other high-ranking Americans in the Embassy establishment believed evacuation plans should have been drawn up *in case* of a military attack. Martin still disagreed. A believer in self-fulfilling prophecies, Martin wanted no negative thinking.

Nevertheless, prodded by Carter and CIA station chief Tom Polgar in particular, Embassy security chief Marvin Garrett took it upon himself to start revising evacuation contingency plans. He paid particular attention to the plans to be used in case of a military attack, and worked hard on outdated plans that assumed resistance to the evacuation by Saigon forces.

Martin had discussed virtually nothing about Vietnam with any of his Embassy staffers for more than a week. He had talked to them; he had asked questions. But there was virtually no intercourse between the Ambassador and the hundreds of men paid to advise, guide, and inform him.

The day the palace was bombed, Martin did little apparent work apart from assuring himself that Thieu was unharmed in the attack. It was on this day that a correspondent referred to "madman Martin" and criticized the Ambassador's rejection of any discussion of any evacuation plans. It was the day an Embassy staffer in the upper ranks of the establishment said he believed Martin wanted to "go down with the ship. If Vietnam falls, Martin wants to go with it."

Ironically, the bombing of the palace ended the factionalizing within the U.S. Embassy establishment that had been a major problem for 15 years. Finally, in adversity, the CIA, the military, the Foreign Service officers, the young staffers and the older ones, USIS, USAID, and the other agencies stopped their internal squabbling. They were talking to one another, openly, in a refreshing change from the bureaucratic methods of before. Tragically, only the man who had to make the decisions wasn't talking to anyone.

Refusing to take persons below him into his counsel was nothing new for Martin, as it turned out. He had a reputation in the Embassy in Bangkok for doing the same thing.

DIGGING A
LAST DITCH

Although the battle for Saigon was already under way, most people realized it only on April 9, the day after the bombing of Thieu's palace. When realization came, Saigon was in an uproar. Thieu had yet to name his new cabinet. The old was holding out in a caretaker status. Enraged by the attack on his palace and the lack of response, Thieu had ordered the Tan Son Nhut air force commander arrested, then released only hours later. The deputy commander of the III Corps area around Saigon, two-star General Nguyen Van Hieu, was dead. The story was he had committed suicide at his Bien Hoa office after arguing with his boss, three-star General Nguyen Van Toan, about defense of the capital area.

To the south of Saigon, the attacks were just probes, although there was a heavy battle in the small and lightly defended district capital of Thu Thua, 12 miles from the capital. Commandos also broke into Tan An provincial capital on Highway 4, the "rice road," and held up traffic for half a day.

To the north, the battle around Phan Rang began to get hot. Private Duc, out at Ninh Chu, didn't see a shot fired, but shelling picked up in the provincial capital and at the air base nearby.

But the biggest battle was in Long Khanh province, centered 38 miles northeast of Saigon. An entire Communist division swept down on the capital of Xuan Loc, setting off the toughest battle of the entire Ho Chi Minh campaign and marking the beginning of the single most gallant stand of the South Vietnamese army. Truly, one last ditch was being dug.

Xuan Loc is on Highway 1. By Vietnamese standards on April 9, it was neither large nor small (population 38,000), capital of a province that was similarly neither large nor small, rich nor poor. There was a rubber plantation just outside the town on Highway 1, which links Saigon and Hanoi. Other than that, there had been little to recommend Xuan Loc for 3,000 years, when it apparently had been the site of an important Malay-Polynesian tribe during the Neolithic Age of history.

In the early morning of April 9, in a surprise attack, a full division of North Vietnamese soldiers backed by an artillery battalion hit Xuan Loc with 2,000 shells, more or less. No one was counting, that was for sure. Then the ground forces hit the outnumbered Saigon defenders and fought into the middle of the city.

The defenders of Xuan Loc, in addition to the usual provincial militia units assigned at any capital, were members of a 2,500-man regiment of the 18th Division. This was once the worst division in the entire Saigon army, which is saying a lot, or rather very little about its capabilities.

When it was formed, it was called the 10th Division. This inevitably and deservedly earned it the title "Number 10," Vietnamese pidgin English for "the worst." Because of the insults heaped on the "Number 10" soldiers of the division by the population, it was redesignated the 18th. But in the mid-1960's it was stationed in the Saigon area because it was such a poor division that it posed no threat to coup-fearful generals.

Something happened to the 18th Division on the way to the Paris peace talks. Specifically, just after the Paris agreement, the 18th was handed a new commander—newly promoted One-Star General Le Minh Dao. He was a rarity, a general who had worked his way up from lieutenant by ability, not by politics. Dao had actually fought for and earned most of the medals he never bothered to wear on his chest. His uniform was fatigues, not whites. He was a fighting man.

When Dao took over the demoralized and really not very good 18th division in 1973, it was as if the whole unit started eating pep pills instead of food. It did more fighting than any other division in the armed forces during the two years after the Paris agreement. The 18th Division became the single most dependable and most important of the Saigon defense forces.

Dao was not at Xuan Loc the night the 2,000 rounds came in to open the battle for Saigon. He was quickly there shortly after first light, however, as his soldiers battled on the streets for control of the town. He ordered another regiment into the battle, which meant that better than two thirds of his unit was fighting for the small town. He now had about 2,500 men inside Xuan Loc fighting for the town itself and another 2,500 just outside trying to protect the flanks of the provincial capital.

The shelling was heavy, but caused few casualties. The Communists came on the receiving end of airstrikes. These, too, were limited in their effectiveness. In the streets, the market, and the bus station, it was another story. The fire power of both sides was brutal, and the discipline a joy to military hearts. The Communists and the 18th Division stood and fought. The 18th fell back in order during the first hours of the battle, giving up most of Xuan Loc. Then it pressed forward again. By nightfall, the soldiers of the 6th division of the People's Liberation Armed Forces were themselves pulling back to regroup for fighting another day.

The battle went another day and another and another. Dao and his soldiers put up a fight few had thought them capable of. The Communists threw another division at Xuan Loc. The 18th held. But the North Vietnamese commanders had other cards.

On the Catholic Church at Trang Bom village is a sign saying "Tan Binh." It means "New Peace." The church was built by the Vietnamese and Chinese Roman Catholics who settled in the town in 1954 when the propagandists were saying that Christ was fleeing North Vietnam. The settlers wanted peace in their new village and named their church after their hope.

Because of the town's strategic position about halfway between Bien Hoa and Xuan Loc, Trang Bom usually was peaceful. The war seldom intruded. Heavy truck and military traffic along Highway 1 through the village was a greater complaint than warfare in the new town.

All that changed April 10. The North Vietnamese generals had made one mistake that was to cost them a few extra days of fighting, although it had no effect on the result of the offensive. In the initial attack on Xuan Loc, the commanders apparently underestimated the determination and ability of the 18th division. The first attack came from two directions, leaving the other two—and specifically Highway 1—free as a route for retreat.

The 18th did not retreat; it stood and fought. And it used Highway 1 early on April 10 as a route for reinforcements. Faced now with a stand by General Dao and his forces, the Communists moved out along Highway 1, then pinched in and cut the road to prevent another reinforcement. There were two dangers in this, and the North Vietnamese commanders knew them well. First, there was the possibility of a pincer attack on the roadblock by ARVN soldiers inside and outside the road cut. Second, it cut off an easy escape route for Dao and his men, which probably would mean they would fight all the harder in an attempt to save their necks. It was what an American strategist once unkindly called the "trapped rat theory": an encircled force fights harder.

The theory was correct this time. On April 10, the Communists punched to the middle of Xuan Loc and the 18th pushed them back. On April 11, the Communists pushed slightly into Xuan Loc and the 18th repelled the assault. On April 12, the North Vietnamese were unable to get into the town proper. The two ARVN regiments not only were holding, they were fighting better each day.

At Trang Bom, now, there was heavy fighting and shelling each day. The residents pulled out, trying to get away from the fighting. Barred by armed police from Saigon itself, most ended up on Highway 15, the road to the coastal resort of Vung Tau. Many hoped to catch a boat out of the battle zones.

The war became accessible to newsmen again, and they journeyed out from Saigon each day by car to get first-hand stories and battle pictures. There had been very little up-close coverage of the war during 1975 because of the new North Vietnamese tactic of siege. Even on the first day of fighting at Trang Bom, three photographers were caught by a Communist-fired mortar round and were wounded.

ARVN troops fought hard at Trang Bom. They were unable, however, to reopen Highway 1 so that convoys could safely travel it to Xuan Loc. The Saigon soldiers were backed by good, low-level airstrikes, and big guns fired in support of their stand at Trang Bom. The airstrikes could be seen from rooftops in Saigon. From the UPI office on the sixth floor of a Saigon riverside hotel, one could see the tiny specks of planes and the huge plumes of black smoke from the bombs.

That this was the start of the battle for Saigon there was no doubt in anyone's mind. And as the ARVN fought and held at Xuan Loc and Trang Bom and Phan Rang, there was renewed optimism inside the capital itself that Saigon would hold. North Vietnamese soldiers were streaming into the Saigon area from the north, however, hopeful that sheer numbers could settle the battle.

The United States was rushing emergency military aid to Vietnam, paid for with money from aid appropriations as much as two years old but never before used. Despite all the official American calls for more money from Congress, there was more than enough in the coffers to keep equipment and ammunition flowing to the Saigon army for months.

As the battle for Trang Bom broke out, a C5A landed at Tan Son Nhut as the morning mist was burning off, with 27 tons of steel helmets and flak jackets.

As the plane was landing, Radio Saigon was informing the Vietnamese that President Ford, on the other side of the world, had during the night asked Congress to give Saigon 722 million dollars for military aid, and another 250 million dollars in economic aid. In promoting the programs,

Ford stressed America's responsibility to the anti-Communist Vietnamese. He verbally pictured the plight of the refugees, who could be helped with the economic allotment.

But many Vietnamese were unimpressed. While the leadership in general welcomed Ford's show of moral support for Saigon, others wanted something more. The anti-Communists who were slightly to the left of Thieu wanted peace. One of their major spokesmen, Tran Van Tuyen, a former Speaker of the National Assembly and a leading anti-Communist Thieu opponent, said there was "another totally different thing that we need—a diplomatic effort, not military aid, to end the war." He said U.S. failure to implement the Paris agreement had brought a stalemate and, ultimately, more war.

It wasn't money the ARVN needed, it was leaders. An incredibly bad decision was made on April 11 which showed that the battle for Saigon had little hope of success for Thieu and his followers, even as the hopes were rising.

Thieu and his generals were holding back two brigades of paratroopers in Saigon. The President wanted them as much as an anticoup force as for a reserve for the battlefield. On April 11, he agreed that one of the brigades was needed.

The paratroopers were considered by many to be the best soldiers in the Saigon army, as they are in many. Volunteers to the man, trained to the élan common to parachutists throughout the world, the Saigon airborne division was a good force. Man for man, it certainly could defeat most armies of the world.

A North Vietnamese Army division had mauled one brigade of paratroops in late March west of Nha Trang. And now one of the remaining two brigades was ordered into combat by Thieu and his Joint General Staff. There was no disagreement that Xuan Loc was the key to Saigon's defense now. Loss of that town would open the capital to direct attack. Just as important, loss of the town would demoralize Saigon so badly that surrender would have to be considered actively.

The brigade was trucked to Long Binh, 15 miles northeast of Saigon and on Highway 1 directly west of Xuan Loc. There, it was loaded onto huge Chinook helicopters for what was to be the men's last air trip of the war. The ultimate target was Xuan Loc, but the heavy fire in that town made it impossible to airlift troops directly into the provincial capital.

A landing zone was picked, therefore, in the French-owned rubber plantation about five miles east of the town proper. The plantation had not been worked for several years, and its trees were intertwined with the weeds and jungle growth that sprang like magic from virtually all of

Vietnam's untended, fertile soil. The lead company was landed and the troops spread out, ready for combat. Not a shot was fired. The helicopters shuttled back and forth between the plantation and Long Binh, bringing in more paratroopers.

Officers in Saigon and in the field congratulated themselves on the surprise operation. The lead company warily walked through the planta-tion into Xuan Loc, encountering not so much as a single shot by its enemy. Senior officers of the brigade moved in, established a base camp, and set up the radios that would link it with Saigon and with Xuan Loc.

Just before dusk, the North Vietnamese division ringing the rubber plantation sprang its attack. The Communists had let the single lead com-pany go by their positions in order to lull the rest of the brigade into a false sense of security.

The paratroopers never really had a chance. The adrenaline of the combat assault had worn off. Totally surprised, outgunned by perhaps three to one by the Communists, and lulled by the apparent lack of Com-munist activity in the plantation, the airborne troops were defeated before the battle really was under way.

It was one of the largest ambushes of the war, perfectly executed by the North Vietnamese division involved. The death toll was not all that great, but the paratroopers were on the run, some heading towards Xuan Loc, others in other directions. Some stood and fought, but communications were not good and they received little support from airstrikes or artillery. The airborne brigade was wiped out as a fighting force.

Just as significantly, the ambush meant that another North Vietnamese division now had joined the fight for Xuan Loc. Attacks now were from the north, the northwest, and the east. To the west, Highway 1 was cut and with it the only dependable line of retreat.

General Le Minh Dao stayed with his men at Xuan Loc, directing the continuing battle for the town. As the paratroopers were scattered and killed to the east of him, Dao commanded his forces in the running battle for the town proper. And the 18th continued to hold. One regiment with Dao in the town was fighting attacks to the north and northwest. Outside the town, another regiment held off Communists attacking from the west, along the general Highway 1 route.

Another 2,000 artillery shells, more or less, tore apart Xuan Loc as the paratroopers tried to get out of the well-laid ambush. But Dao held on, although he knew there would be no reinforcements for his men. The soldiers of the 18th worked to build fortifications, laboring to erect them faster than the Communist shells could knock them down. The town crumbled around them. Outmanned at least two to one, the 18th held on.

On April 12, the Communists again concentrated on the town proper, and overran a battalion of the 18th division north of Xuan Loc. But the attack, Dao noted, was lighter than before. He smelled a possible victory. He reported this to Saigon at midafternoon.

Saigon badly needed a victory, even a paper victory, for propaganda purposes. Stunned and even shamed by the fleet-footed retreats of its soldiers for a month, official Saigon needed to show its people and the world that victory was possible. So victory was proclaimed at Xuan Loc and a press visit was set up.

On a Sunday morning, April 13, correspondents and photographers, clad in helmets and flak jackets, clambered aboard a Chinook helicopter at Long Binh for the frightening trip into Xuan Loc. At full speed, the unwieldly twin-rotor chopper headed into a makeshift landing zone on Highway 1 just outside the provincial capital.

Once over the North Vietnamese siege lines, the correspondents relaxed slightly. Few of them had not been under fire before, and the occasional screech of an artillery shell or the whoosh of a rocket did not bother them much. It bothered the Xuan Loc commanders even less. Proudly, they escorted the newsmen on a tour of their town, now blackened, its buildings riddled, its civilians either gone or mobbing the helicopter pad to leave.

Corpses littered the streets, and the newsmen saw that most of them were North Vietnamese soldiers who had been cut down while storming the city. The church was all but destroyed, but its steeple stood. Newsmen saw that the defenders appeared still fresh. The 18th division, it was clear, was not yet ready to imitate other Saigon units in turning tail. The battle was not yet over, but the 18th was claiming victory because it had not been defeated.

The newsmen were human. Although most could see that Xuan Loc eventually would fall to the North Vietnamese, they wrote well of the defenders. Essentially sympathetic to the underdog, the newsmen who visited Xuan Loc that day accepted the slightly unusual definition of victory. One wrote that Saigon "needed the victory it claimed Sunday in this destroyed province capital." Another, slightly more optimistic than his fellows, said, "The magnificent defense of Xuan Loc by the 18th division, which clearly has taken the North Vietnamese Army completely by surprise, has won Saigon the time it so urgently needed to finish regrouping."

But the regrouping was not going well. There were bright spots, it was true. Plans had been made in most cases to rebuild battalions, not divisions, to throw them into battle as quickly as possible. In one case, a division-sized force of battalions was rebuilding south of Saigon. Open revolt among the troops had ended in most places, and soldiers were being reimpressed.

Just 15 miles south of Saigon that Sunday, another group of newsmen was visiting the site of another claimed Saigon victory. It had much less validity than the Xuan Loc claim, and most of the correspondents were unimpressed, despite the large numbers of bodies of Communist troops they had seen. And even the small amount of good impression gained was wiped out on the automobile ride back to the capital.

The correspondents passed a large fire. A Vietnamese photographer stopped his car and talked to the guards at the gate of the military camp where the fire was burning. The blaze was an ammunition dump, the guards said. Communist saboteurs had got in sometime during the night and set off time bombs, which destroyed the dump. Ammunition and equipment ruined in the fire was meant to reequip 15 battalions of South Vietnamese troops. Now they would have to wait for new shipments.

And the next night, a lucky artillery shot landed in the center of a huge ammunition dump at Bien Hoa, setting it off with a whoomp heard and felt in Saigon. This ammunition was needed for the Xuan Loc battle. It included bombs and artillery shells, as well as ammo for smaller infantry weapons. It marked another serious blow to Saigon's chances.

By the third-last week of the Vietnam War, President Nguyen Van Thieu was in trouble. Under attack by serious political opponents for a year for being too hard or too soft on the Communists, he now was the President of a rapidly shrinking nation with little hope for survival.

The calls for his political head came of course from Hanoi and the Viet Cong, who had switched from outright attacks on Thieu to a slightly softer form of propaganda. What Radio Liberation and Radio Hanoi now were saying as their troops swept toward Saigon was that peace was impossible with Thieu in office. Under no circumstances, the Communists said, would they deal with Thieu or with members of "the Thieu clique," loyalists who owed their positions to the President.

Saigon's self-styled neutralists, who claimed to favor neither the Communists nor the anti-Communists, wanted Thieu out. Without him, they believed they could take the reins of the Saigon government and negotiate a peace with North Vietnam and the Viet Cong. They intended, they said, to set up a coalition including all political factions in the country. When pressed, neutralists envisioned a political path leading undoubtedly to a Communist victory, but at a slower pace, without the bloodshed brought by the continuing war.

Ultrarightists wanted Thieu out. Ironically, with their public attacks on the corruption of the President, his family, and his retainers, the holders of some of the best anti-Communist credentials in South Vietnam were admittedly giving heart to Hanoi. They attacked Thieu's military decisions and blamed Thieu for the loss of two thirds of South Vietnam. Three hundred Roman Catholic priests, many of them refugees from North Vietnam, had publicly released "indictments" outlining corruption by Thieu, and Saigon newspapers printed them.

As the Communist hierarchy met in Hanoi in the fall of 1974 to plan this final offensive, Redemptorist Father Tran Huu Thanh had formed in Hue the "People's Anti-Corruption Movement for National Salvation and Peace Construction." In September 1974, this group released "Indictment Number 1," which contained seven specific charges of corruption by Thieu and his wife and influence peddling by both of them that allowed corrupt acts by others, including their families. Saigon newspapers that printed the indictment were seized after they hit the streets, but only after hundreds of copies had been sold and passed among the population throughout the country. The following charges were devastating and documented:

• Thieu, with an income of only several hundred dollars monthly, had two Saigon homes valued at more than $150,000; a riverside home just north of Saigon; "a magnificent villa" in Switzerland, and plots of land in numerous provinces, all specifically named in the indictment.

• Thieu's brother-in-law, with the knowledge and protection of the President, was guilty of speculation, hoarding, and price fixing of American-supplied fertilizer, with the dual result that farmers were made to pay outrageous prices for the fertilizer and there were many crop failures when they couldn't pay.

• Mrs. Thieu had built a so-called hospital for the poor, using smuggled goods to finance its construction, and siphoning foreign aid to outfit and maintain it. Into this hospital the poor could not enter. [This case will be examined further shortly.]

• Thieu, his chief aide General Dang Van Quang, and Prime Minister Tran Thien Khiem were involved in the drug rackets to a greater or lesser extent, and the documentation for this charge, the book *Politics of Heroin in Southeast Asia,* was banned in Saigon.

• Thieu's aunt was guilty of hoarding and price fixing government rice and pocketing government subsidies for transport. This had caused the deaths of a number of Vietnamese from malnutrition or starvation.

• Thieu was guilty of misappropriation of property of the armed forces and the nation, including acceptance of "gifts" of land, use of armed forces engineers for his private homes and estates, and appropriation of land reserved for Vietnamese peasants under the land reform program.

• Thieu had acted against the country's anti-Communist constitution by agreeing to sign the Paris agreements, which in effect allowed North Vietnam to station its 300,000 troops in the south.

The charges were bombshells. Most South Vietnamese had been prepared to accept the fact that their President was corrupt before the publication of Indictment Number 1, but it was only with its publication that the populace had "facts" of Thieu's corruption with which to argue. As in most other countries, what was true in Vietnam was not so important as what appeared to be true. And with the publication of Father Thanh's "indictment," Vietnamese were prepared to accept the fact that their leader was wantonly corrupt.

Father Thanh released his second indictment just before the end of 1974, even as the North Vietnamese were getting their troops into position for the capture of Phuoc Long province. It charged that Thieu accepted a bribe of seven million dollars from the Americans to sign the Paris agreement. This particular charge also was printed in the local newspapers, which were duly seized. Several journalists were arrested on charges of pro-Communism. It did not create the stir of Indictment Number 1, but was widely circulated and widely believed nevertheless.

So the moralists of the right wing wanted Thieu's political blood, just as the Communists did, if for entirely different reasons. The documented, detailed corruption charges had caused Vietnamese in general to lose faith in Thieu and they did not support him personally. They had no particular say in the decision-making process but their voices were becoming stronger, and lent weight to those of the more influential.

The military to a large extent wanted Thieu out in the second week of April 1975, and this was a crucial vote against the President. The main complaint of the generals was the mishandling of the military situation in South Vietnam, for which they laid the blame directly on the President. Most generals believed they could do better than Thieu in running the country and the battlefield. Most of them probably could have. A coup was discussed, often and at length. Discreet and not-so-discreet inquiries were made to the American establishment in Vietnam, most often by Nguyen Cao Ky, who was by his own admission willing to replace Thieu. These were met by blunt refusal or a gentle turning aside by Martin and the other Americans in Saigon. Ky and other generals were told, apparently on orders from Secretary of State Henry Kissinger, that a coup would bring the immediate end of U.S. aid to Saigon.

Graham Martin did not want Thieu out. In the words of one of his aides, the U.S. Ambassador believed that "Thieu is the only President we've got." What Martin hoped was that Thieu would open negotiations with Hanoi and sue for peace. Thieu refused, but that is beside the point. Martin spent hours trying to convince Thieu to take a course that was totally unacceptable to the Communists. Thieu could have begged for negotiations on bended knees and Hanoi and the Viet Cong would have spat on him.

After 10 years in the highest office in South Vietnam—eight of them as President—Nguyen Van Thieu in 1975 was the richest and most corrupt man in the country. By Vietnamese standards, he was born of middle-class parents, which is to say he came from a poor family. He was a career army man, with no business career on his record, no rich relatives. He never was authorized by his position to receive more than $600 a month in salary and perhaps another $300 to $400 in side benefits during his entire life. Still, by any standards, he was and is rich.

How he became rich is an intricate and devious tale, and what follows here is undoubtedly incomplete. What is known is that with two exceptions—the villa in Switzerland and a bankrupt Saigon bank—neither Thieu's name nor that of his wife has been found on any document concerned with any business, legal or illegal. Yet they became rich. According to interviews, documents, and other investigative sources, Thieu, his wife, close friends, and top aides stole hundreds of millions of dollars. Much of it came from American taxpayers and most of the rest from their own citizens.

Not surprisingly, Thieu's moneymaking depended on the war and the circumstances bred by the fighting and American aid. To put it kindly, this represented a conflict of interest. Thieu may have honestly believed he could never negotiate with the Communists, never give an inch. But because he believed this, the war continued. And because the war continued, Thieu and his friends and family got richer.

At the bottom, corruption in Vietnam was simple. At its upper and middle levels, it was a complex web. And like the Mafia, it had as a main aim shielding the head man.

At the bottom, it was petty influence peddling, protection, and extortion. A drugstore on Tu Do Street supplied American GI's openly with amphetamines and barbiturates because its owner had police protection. When U.S. military authorities put the store off-limits to the troops, the drugstore supplied the drugs to bar girls and pimps, creating peddlers. Linda's Surprise Bar on Saigon's outskirts could put on its sex shows for Americans because the right payoffs were made to authorities who looked the other way and ignored the puritanical laws. Civilian loggers in the Central Highlands could operate only because the army commanders were paid a percentage of the profits. When the payments stopped, the logging convoys were ambushed by "Viet Cong guerrillas."

Immigration police collected under-the-table fees on visas in Vietnam, and soldiers set up free-lance "checkpoints" on the highways to shake down drivers. The amounts involved were small, sometimes as little as ten or fifteen cents.

But as corruption got more important, and the sums involved got higher, the system became a pyramid. At the top of the Vietnam corruption pyramid sat Thieu. The pyramid was an organization tool, not necessarily a funnel for payoffs. By allowing persons on the sides of the pyramid to work out their own deals, Thieu gained favors, debts, and power. Favors must always be paid back in the Orient. Between 1965 and 1975, Thieu had done thousands, perhaps tens of thousands, of favors. He rarely called for repayment until necessary. Until he did call for repayment, he was one up on everyone down the scale.

It is necessary first to understand that South Vietnam was a nation of patronage. Even if the constitution was followed explicitly, the President had enormous power. Thieu had even more than the constitution allowed. He was chief of the Council of Generals, an extraconstitutional body set up in 1971 to resolve political differences among the military hierarchy, with Thieu holding by 1975 virtually all power within its ranks. He was military Commander-in-Chief and head of the civil service. Through these quite legal power bases, Thieu controlled more than three million jobs directly—half the jobs in the nation—and had exclusive right to appoint, promote, demote, or fire the three million job holders. He delegated very little of the power.

There were webs of corruption in Vietnam in which money filtered from top to bottom, or vice versa, with each echelon skimming off its share. Most foreigners in Vietnam believed, for example, that the immigration department worked this way. Bribes were tendered to the police clerks in most cases, and it was generally assumed that the bribes were split and passed on up the line. Successive chiefs of immigration were fired and shake-ups of the department were announced from time to time by various Saigon governments in order to eliminate the corruption.

So far as I have been able to learn, Thieu was not part of any such ring. Payoffs made by bar owners, illegal immigrants or favor seekers did not, so far as I and any of my acquaintances have been able to determine, work their way up to Thieu. Rather, the Saigon President collected favors instead of money, and used those favors to help himself to riches in separate schemes.

A method of collecting favors can be illustrated from U.S. government files.   Edward G. Lansdale, then a   major-general, returned to Vietnam in 1968 and wrote a series of special reports for his government and the U.S. Embassy. One, classified Secret and later included in the Pentagon Papers, was written for U.S. Ambassador Ellsworth Bunker. It was called "Nationalist Politics in Vietnam" and detailed how patronage allowed corps commanders to become virtual warlords:

> . . . the civil apparatus and armed forces in most of the country have operated more on the basis of a system of the patronage revolving around each corps commander . . . each has appointed and replaced virtually all province and district chiefs and to a considerable degree division and regimental

commanders. . . . Certain facets of this system have also led to considerable
corruption within the government.

By 1975, not only was Thieu appointing the corps commanders—there
were four in the nation—but he was firing them with some regularity. He
also was handling most appointments of division commanders. He had
thus refined and taken more control of the system that Lansdale in 1968
said was already causing much national corruption.

A specific example of how Thieu worked is this. In 1973, he promoted
General Nguyen Vinh Nghi to three-star rank and appointed him chief of
IV Corps, the Mekong Delta, or South Vietnam proper. Nghi was free to do
his best to become rich in the corps. In mid-1974, U.S. Embassy sources told
newsmen that 8,000 radios and 25,000 rifles and other small arms had
disappeared from Saigon army stocks in IV Corps during the time Nghi
was commander. When the publication of Indictment Number 1 put the
public heat on Thieu shortly after this disclosure—and only after circumstances forced him to make at least a token gesture of cleaning up
corruption—Thieu fired Nghi from IV Corps. No charges ever were
brought against him, however, and Nghi was retired to a staff job, from
which he was resurrected later in the war for a last-ditch stand at Phan
Rang. Despite the available evidence that Nghi was selling equipment
either to or for the Communists, Thieu still felt Nghi was a good enough
commander to take charge of troops in an important battle.

Two other generals in III Corps surrounding Saigon were sacked in
1974 when investigators of both the Saigon army and the U.S. Embassy told
newsmen in off-the-record sessions of alleged selling of rice to the Viet
Cong. The two were Tran Quoc Lich of the 25th division just northwest of
Saigon and Le Van Tu of the 5th division to the north of the capital. The
selling off of food, military equipment, and deferments from duty from
these two divisions during the time Lich and Tu served as commanders
made both divisions combat ineffective. By the time they absolutely had to
be thrown into the battle for Saigon in April 1975, the 25th division was still
unable to field a fighting force. The 5th division, although it went to the
field, fought no battles of note.

These appointments and scores of others like them were made by Thieu,
particularly after his clever manipulating of the 1971 elections when he was
the only candidate. After that, he held power that could not be checked by
any of his political opponents. President Nixon once called Thieu "one of
the best four or five politicians in the world," and this 1969 accolade from
Nixon was not so far off base. Thieu by 1971 had out-maneuvered all his
notable opponents and had the others checked or cowed, or both.

So generally speaking, Thieu was able to make at least some of his appointments with a view to collecting favors later. A general appointed with the backing of Thieu was free to build his own web of corruption, limited in his ability to enrich himself only according to his own wickedness and cunning.

A general made money by padding his division payroll with phantom soldiers, for example. Evidence made available to newsmen by staff members of the U.S. General Accounting Office in 1974 indicated that this was one method used by Lich and Tu to build their bank accounts. A general could sell safe jobs away from the battlefield to soldiers willing and able to pay the price. He could sell equipment meant for his unit on the black market, or even to the Viet Cong. Most generals, according to available evidence, stayed away from arms sales because Americans, if they got a whiff of such a deal, could force an investigation that would end all rackets for the general involved. But mess kits, uniforms, Jeeps, knives, and boots brought in much money, and the numbers available on the Saigon black market indicated that high-ranking officers had to be involved. Gasoline became a fine product for the black market sale after the Arabs raised their prices in 1974. Some generals apparently ran protection rackets on other black marketeers or smugglers.

The way of making money—with the one stipulation, that the person must stay out of rackets controlled by the President, his family, and his close friends—was immaterial to Thieu. And although Thieu had not benefited from an appointment by a straight cash payoff, as far as can be learned, he was owed a favor, and we shall see how some of those favors were called in.

Many of Thieu's appointees were delegated the authority by the President to appoint their own subordinates in turn, and here cash often changed hands. Following the mythical Thieu-appointed Corps Commander down the line, the general was often free to sell positions within his area to the highest bidder. The national police chief of Vietnam could and sometimes did throughout the history of the Republic of Vietnam sell lucrative positions to policemen who desired a sinecure or a title to conduct a shakedown racket or a protection scheme.

The highest-priced job known to be for sale in South Vietnam was Police Chief of Cholon, the Chinese section of Saigon. Nguyen Cao Ky* said during his days as Prime Minister in 1966 that the position was for sale for 15 million piasters, about $130,000 at the rate of exchange of the day. In the early 1970's, according to other informants, it cost $100,000 to the major or lieutenant colonel who could raise the cash to buy it (and a

*In his book *Twenty Years and Twenty Days,* published in 1977.

surprising number could). So lucrative was the job that the officers had recouped their payment within two to three months and after that were able to clear about $50,000 a month. That is net profit, after paying subalterns involved in the shakedown rackets among the Chinese businessmen who would rather pay than fight—either the war or city hall.

It cost army colonels $80,000 to become Chief of Chau Doc province on the Cambodian border in the Mekong Delta. A chief industry there was cattle smuggling and province chiefs collected a fee for each head of beef crossing to Vietnam, where there was not enough to feed the population. Again, it took about two months to get back the fee for the job, and after that it was all profit.

Spreading upwards into the government, most cabinet ministers through the war years managed to get rich on corruption in South Vietnam. As one example, mentioned earlier, Pham Kim Ngoc, an Economy Minister highly admired by the Americans, managed to build up a cash balance of eight million dollars in Taiwan. Americans in a position to know said Ngoc charged "commissions" for securing contracts for their companies to do work in Vietnam. This was particularly galling to many of the contractors, because the projects on which they were working were being paid for by the U.S. government in the form of aid. The companies passed the "commissions" along to American taxpayers in the form of higher bids for the jobs.

But all these were minor deals compared to those managed by Thieu, his family, and a small coterie of friends, many of them related by marriage. No one, needless to say, competed with this inner circle of presidential dealing.

Two persons fronted Thieu's multimillion-dollar corruption—his wife, Nguyen Thi Mai Anh, and the Chinese husband of her adoptive sister, Ly Long Than. There was a supporting cast of scores, but the big money went to Thieu bank accounts in Singapore and Switzerland and silent-partner investments made in Taiwan, Guam, and Hawaii through the Chinese man.

Mai Anh's involvement in the corruption was considered normal in Vietnam. In matters other than war, the Vietnamese often are matriarchal. Women control the purse strings, always at home and often in business. Vietnamese women are tough, conservative, parsimonious. The fight for equality of women was not a big movement in Vietnam. As one once told me, Vietnamese women do not want equality; they always have been content simply to remain superior to men.

Mai Anh's direct involvement in the rackets is almost impossible to document. She was a known diamond fancier, and at parties would discuss diamonds and the markets knowingly with diplomatic wives and other guests. She wore one particularly large stone often in public, and had either a rotating supply of other diamond jewelry or a very large collection. According to Vietnamese newspaper gossip columnists, whose reports never were challenged, she had one of the best diamond collections in Asia, both in quality and quantity. Like Thieu, she had no known legal source of income.

The other main schemer in presidential corruption was seldom mentioned in the press, and unlike the Thieus he had numerous legitimate sources of income. Ly Long Than (called Ly because he was a Fukien Chinese who had Vietnamized the spelling of his name) "had bought off the mouths" of the gossipy Chinese newspapers in Saigon, according to several editors I talked to in 1974, and was seldom mentioned at all. He is, probably, the second richest man ever to come from South Vietnam, Thieu being the richest. He was the President's silent partner because he was an extremely rich, influential businessman in his own right; because he had excellent ties with the rich of Saigon, most of whom happened also to be Fukien Chinese, and of course because he was a member of Mrs. Thieu's family by marriage.

Before 1967 and Thieu's election as President, Ly was known as a rich businessman, and his name appeared from time to time in the newspapers. After Thieu began solidifying his power base, Ly became "the man to know if you want to do business here," according to one American businessman who knew the power structure and did very well in Saigon.

One of Ly's better deals involved cheating the Americans directly. It is not generally known that the United States once paid for the right to destroy and kill in South Vietnam, but Ly knew. In 1968, his Vinatexco (Vietnam National Textile Company) plant was destroyed by American helicopters when Viet Cong soldiers took it and used it as a command post in the Tet offensive.

Au Ngoc Ho, the Minister of Finance at the time and generally considered a scrupulously honest man, said in a 1974 interview he was rather surprised when Ly's claim for 200 percent of the cost of the plant was channeled through his office on its way to the U.S. Embassy. Ho said that with the claim was a note from Thieu. It had two instructions: to submit the claim forthwith despite the obvious fact that it was excessive; and to destroy the accompanying note. Ho, needless to say, complied. And predictably, the Americans paid off, in full, in short order. Ly rebuilt his plant with half the check and pocketed the rest, according to Ho and other Chinese-Vietnamese sources also in the textile business. Today, that plant—under a different name—is the largest textile plant in Vietnam. It is under workers' nominal control and, according to Hanoi statements, is earning foreign exchange for the Communist government.

Ly, according to reports from the Washington area, has bought a home valued at $300,000 in Langley, Virginia.

Like the Mafia, Ly felt a need to launder his money made from corruption. Through middlemen, he bought land in Taiwan. He became a silent partner in some of Guam's largest developments and land holdings just as that island began to skyrocket into the economic twentieth century in 1969 and 1970. He bought several hundred acres in Hawaii, which he still owned in 1975, according to sources in Honolulu. The land was bought relatively cheaply, and increased in value almost immediately. Since then, the same officials say, the value of the land has dropped slightly, but Ly still would stand to gain millions of dollars if he sold now.

Thieu's major source of revenue was smuggling, both into and out of Vietnam. What went out directly broke American and Vietnamese law, because Thieu never bothered with the formality of the export permit required by the laws of both countries. It robbed South Vietnam's treasury and indirectly looted the U.S. government. What went in through the Thieu network sapped the morale of his people and directly aided the Viet Cong.

Scrap metal—brass and iron, but especially brass—was the most lucrative export item. The brass was the residue of tens of millions of dollars' worth of shot-away bullets and artillery shells. The iron came from the ruins of war-wrecked tanks, planes, trucks, and the like. Scrap has been a growing market throughout the world, particularly in Japan, because of rising steel prices.

A million soldiers shoot a lot of ammuniton and leave behind mounds of brass at each battle. They also use up many tanks, crash a fair number of aircraft, and wear out large numbers of trucks and Jeeps and radios and typewriters. Much of this was left on the battlefields during retreats. But what could be recovered was scooped into the scrapyards to begin a new life as moneymaker for Thieu.

The smuggling operation itself was simple. Not too many persons were involved. Those who were all owed favors to Thieu. For it was at this stage in the operation that the President began calling on the generals and colonels who owed their positions, standards of living, and favors to Thieu. Even the favors were simple, in most cases meaning only looking the other way at the appropriate time and ordering underlings to do the same thing. The fact that Vietnamese and U.S. laws were being broken was less important.

An American involved for a while in the smuggling business has outlined in an interview how the operation worked. In his case, the operation actually began at the Tham Thuy Ha ammunition dump just across the Saigon River from the capital city. During the illegal shipments of scrap, access roads to the dump were blocked off. This caused huge detours for the local people trying to get from one town to the next, but kept the smuggling secret by using national security as a cover.

The scrap was carried in army trucks, covered with canvas so no prying eyes could see what was in the back. Usually, the shipping point was the Saigon docks. The President could easily demand that officials here look the other way. At other times, the trucks carried the scrap to lighters on branches of the Saigon, Dong Nai, or Mekong Rivers, then to a waiting ship lying offshore.

When necessary, Ly's shipping and stevedoring companies could be utilized, but according to the American businessman it seemed that army troops and chartered ships were used more often. The ships used usually were registered in Panama and crewed by South Koreans. Details of shipment, once the smuggled scrap was on the high seas, were taken care of by the buyers or middlemen, which is where the American businessman first was involved. (Later, he was able to follow several shipments from scrapyard to final destination and thus provide some details.)

This source and others all agree that payment was taken usually either by Ly or Thieu's wife personally, in U.S. dollars when possible, but from time to time in other hard currency. Ly flitted around the Pacific—one of an extremely small number of Vietnamese citizens permitted free travel —arranging financial details of laundering in Taiwan, Hong Kong, Singapore, the Philippines, Guam. Mrs. Thieu sometimes used the cover of visiting her children in Europe to bank the money or convert it into jewelry as another laundering technique.

It was on such a trip in 1972 that she bought a villa in Switzerland and put it under her own name. An alert newsman discovered this, and began making inquiries in Geneva and through UPI in Saigon. Several days later, he said, the villa was switched to another name, that of a man believed to be a Swiss banker.

In 1974, a high-ranking American official bragged to me that the American-controlled computer contained thousands of names of influential Vietnamese, with dossiers on their lives. He said he would be willing, if asked, to run through the machine the name of any person on whom I wished further information. I gave him Ly Long Than's. He did not call me as I expected. When I met him about 10 days later, he was obviously shaken when I brought the subject up, and he told me never to give him such a name again. He could not tell me anything that was in the file, he said, and did not want to know himself what was contained in Ly's file. It concerned Thieu, he said, and he would divulge nothing further. But other U.S.

officials told me in a series of 1974 interviews that what is written here of the President's dealings was well known to them. One harried investigator with wide knowledge of the scrap deals asked a senior American diplomat why no action was taken against Thieu in the matter. Because, it was explained, Thieu was an indispensable part of U.S. policy in Vietnam.

This same investigator said that when he or others got close to fully documenting their cases, there were ways of dampening down the situation short of violence. The most common and frustrating was the South Vietnamese habit of keeping stocks of scrap on the move from yard to yard, mixing one shipment with another, then dividing again. Paperwork was often "lost." In 1971, when Saigon tax investigators and their U.S. advisers began looking into the tax returns of Ly and other influential citizens, the main tax office in Saigon was "unluckily" fire bombed, and burned to the ground. Viet Cong sabotage was entered on the police report that closed the case.

The outward bound smuggling was reprehensible enough, but it had little effect on the war until Thieu was publicly charged as a corrupt person in late 1974. The inbound smuggling was something else. It resulted in killing, prolongation of the war, and direct aid to the Viet Cong.

The front and reason for this incredible program was the fine-looking hospital just outside Tan Son Nhut airport in a Saigon suburb. With a bucketful of irony, it was called *Vi Dan*—Hospital for the People. In fact, as Indictment Number 1 made clear, it was the most expensive medical facility in Vietnam. It was modern by Saigon standards, although much below Western standards. It maintained a few beds for indigent patients, but in fact catered almost exclusively to the well-to-do.

Mrs. Thieu was, publicly, the patron of the Hospital for the People. It was her idea to build it, and she took full credit. It was built via smuggling, a fact known to many in the early 1970's, when it was constructed, but not general knowledge until Father Thanh made it a point of his indictment against Thieu.

Mai Anh's idea was that Thieu's office would seize smuggled items caught by customs inspectors, sell them at auction, and use the proceeds to build the hospital. Besides being a breach of the law stating proceeds of such auctions would go to the public treasury and their disposition settled by Congress, there were other twists along this road.

According to agents of U.S. customs stationed at Tan Son Nhut airport, Mrs. Thieu herself was believed to be the person who arranged for most of the smuggled goods. These agents, backed by sources inside the airline, said that Air Vietnam was the main conduit, replacing the Saigon air force as a means of transportation because the air force still was largely loyal to Thieu's political opponent, Nguyen Cao Ky.

Air Vietnam flew to 11 Asian cities from Saigon. The "airline with the charming tradition," as its advertising said, was run by Nguyen Tan Trung, a friend of Thieu's. Trung's son was the husband of Thieu's daughter. In Asia, much more than in Europe or America, marriage binds in-laws closely. Trung himself, according to airline spokesmen and press reports, fled Saigon just before the end of the war carrying with him six million dollars' worth of various payment orders. Payment was stopped in time by some of Air Vietnam's creditors, but many of the checks and travelers' checks were cashed. Trung reportedly now lives in comfort in France. Because the international airline cartel apparently closed ranks on the matter, it is not possible to say just how much Trung gained from this.

In any case, Air Vietnam's cargo holds were filled in Tokyo, Hong Kong, and Singapore with goods for the Saigon black market. Cognac and cigarettes were staples, according to airline stewardesses on the flights. Cosmetics, electronics goods, bolts of clothing material, dinnerware, and practically any item that could fit through an airliner's cargo door made their way to Vietnam aboard the jets, reportedly at the behest of Mrs. Thieu.

An Air Vietnam public relations representative was himself aboard one flight from Hong Kong that was diverted to Bien Hoa military air base. There, soldiers surrounded the plane. While passengers watched from the windows, troops unloaded dozens of cases of French brandy and cigarettes from the jet and to military trucks. After this, the plane flew to Saigon and the public relations man and other passengers disembarked.

The planes were met in Saigon often by persons known to customs officials to be friends of the presidential family. While customs officers watched—or turned their backs—the smuggled goods were loaded openly into cars and trucks and driven out of Tan Son Nhut airport to warehouses and marketplaces around Saigon. There was no auction and no tally of money gained by sale of the smuggled goods.

Nevertheless, the Hospital for the People was built. Saigon army engineers were dispatched by the Commander-in-Chief to do the work. U.S., Japanese, and South Korean aid paid for most of the furnishings and medical equipment.

In what they regarded as payoffs for silence, the air crews and some customs officials were told by their superiors that they could take advantage of their positions to do minor smuggling of their own. Many claim they did not do so, but say others of the Air Vietnam and customs staffs did. This, they say, allowed Mrs. Thieu to make her split with Trung, Ly, or whoever else was involved in the racket and still emerge holding a large amount of money. The normal black market markup was in the neighborhood of 100 percent.

The problem was that the money gained from this was almost all piasters, the internationally worthless South Vietnamese currency. The Thieus and their partners now held more of the piasters than could be spent in Saigon, and the money changers of the capital were unable to convert such large amounts into dollars or other hard currencies. So the Thieus turned to Hong Kong, Asia's money market headquarters, where just about any currency is available for a price.

A special kind of bank was offering good exchange rates for South Vietnamese currency during the Vietnam war, the chain of banks run by Communist China. U.S. investigators on several occasions followed known associates of Mai Anh to these banks, where they reportedly saw exchanges of piasters for Hong Kong and U.S. dollars. On at least one occasion, an agent followed one of these Vietnamese to a jewelry store, where he viewed diamonds, Mrs. Thieu's known passion.

. The Chinese-run banks offered a rate noticeably better than the capitalist banks and money changers for piasters, because China was helping Hanoi and the Viet Cong.

North Vietnam maintained an office in the main Bank of China building in Hong Kong, and this mission was apparently used to facilitate the flow of the piasters from the Communist banks. In any case, the South Vietnamese currency exchanged by the agents of Mai Anh went to the Chinese mainland and on to North Vietnam, where they then were passed to the south. And, back in the only country where they could be spent, the piasters went to work for the Communists.

With the millions of dollars in genuine piasters in their hands, the Viet Cong and North Vietnamese did the following: they paid their agents and troops in contested and Saigon-controlled areas, where only the piaster was acceptable to local merchants; they bought rice and other food at village and town markets for the Communist army; they purchased hundreds of thousands of dollars worth of medicine, most of it donated in the first place by the United States and then placed on the black market by corrupt officials; they obtained on the black market whatever military hardware and software had been placed there by corrupt Saigon officers; they recruited more and better agents; and they bought into legitimate non-Communist enterprises. Depending on the situation, the Communists could either wreck the businesses from the inside and harm the general economy or build the enterprise to provide profits or a product to the Viet Cong.

There is no way of computing Thieu's personal wealth, other than to say he is a very rich man. His deals were myriad, his partners many, his middlemen tight-lipped.

He is believed to have major investments in Singapore and Malaysia with his drug dealing military aide, former three-star General Dang Van

Quang. It was in fact Thieu who resurrected Quang, after the general had been cashiered from all responsible positions in 1966. Ky had recommended to the U.S. Embassy that Quang be sacked, and Thieu signed the order dismissing him from command of the Mekong Delta. But when Thieu became President in 1967, one of his first orders was to assign Quang as his personal aide.

Thieu is said by other acquaintances, including Ky, to have a massive account in a Swiss bank. And there was that Swiss villa, which at one time bore the name of his wife, only to change legal ownership when a newsman began inquiries about it.

Public investments of Mrs. Thieu, through her own friends, were in two Saigon banks. One of them, the Nam Viet Bank, declared itself bankrupt in 1972. The director of the bank, a close friend of the Thieu family, was under investigation for fraud in connection with the incident, and Saigon newspapers charged that he had made millions through the bankruptcy. No charges were ever brought, however.

Thieu's corruption was particularly harmful to his country from 1972 onward, as South Vietnam itself teetered on the edge of bankruptcy. Congressional aid from the United States dropped, and prices of food, fuel, and the thousands of tons of other necessary imports rose. The nation's foreign currency holdings dipped well below 50 million dollars.

In early 1974, a reputable American businessman visited Saigon. In his pocket was an open letter of credit for 200 million dollars. The man wanted to buy 200 million dollars worth of scrap metal at current world prices. His reputation was investigated and found impeccable by the U.S. Embassy in Saigon, and American officials later confirmed this story.

The man spent a month in Saigon, trying to see the men in government who could deal with him. He was received instead by low-ranking economic officials. One was indiscreet enough to tell the man that "a very influential Chinese businessman" in Saigon opposed the scrap sale. A senior official for the U.S. Agency for International Development said he was sure the Chinese was Ly, backed to the hilt by the Thieus.

A few days after the man left, after telling his story to U.S. Embassy officials, American Ambassador Martin went to Washington. He did not go there to discuss nor to expose this scandal. He went instead to form plans for an administration assault on Congress to increase aid to the Thieu government by a vast amount because South Vietnam was in desperate financial straits. He was backed by President Ford, Secretary of State Kissinger, and Defense Secretary James Schlesinger.

There were other important, although smaller, examples. Hilton wanted to build a hotel in Saigon, but Ly and his Chinese group also wanted to build a luxury hotel and Hilton never got past the planning stage. A Tucson,

Arizona, businessman wanted to build a factory to manufacture coin-operated machines—not slot machines—and could not even get an appointment to see the appropriate officials who could authorize his spending two million dollars in Vietnam.

There were two prerequisites for doing business in South Vietnam, despite the fact that the country had one of the most liberal foreign investment laws in the world. First, bribery to the senior officials was necessary. Second, there had to be assurances that the new industry would not conflict in any manner with the schemes of Ly and the Thieus.

Of all this American officials were aware. Yet they did nothing to halt it. The line was that Thieu was the only viable leader in Vietnam. No one in the U.S. Embassy could think of a way to stop the corruption without toppling Thieu. There were actually several, although none was ever tried.

Thieu and his friends and supporters got richer and richer. And the people lost faith in their President. By mid-April, as Thieu passed his tenth anniversary as Chief of State of South Vietnam, the pressures had built too far. It was no longer a question of whether Thieu would go, but when and how.

Private Duc was getting back into the war four days after the opening of the battle for Phan Rang, April 9. He was not enjoying it, but at Ninh Chu April 13, he felt he once again had a purpose in life. The North Vietnamese fire was heavy here, but Duc could see and hear that it was much heavier at Phan Rang, five miles down the road. The heaviest fighting, he could hear, was at the air base, where General Nguyen Vinh Nghi and James Lewis were at the command post.

The ground attacks at Ninh Chu were probes. Duc saw that the lines of his makeshift force would hold for a while. But they were not extended enough. There was little purpose in staying in the village, Duc thought. With a shortage of men, Duc's force could not get out far enough to stop the North Vietnamese shelling on Phan Rang.

Duc and his companions stayed on full alert for six nights. There was a lot of shooting around Ninh Chu but few casualties. Lieutenant Colonel Bao, the Saigon-based officer who had looked so sharp when he arrived, now looked like the rest of them—tired, dirty, rumpled. He had hit the ground often to escape the incoming shells.

The Communists were pouring more and more men down Highway 1. General Dung's tactic of speed, hitherto all but unknown to the North Vietnamese, was being pursued with a vengeance. On tanks, trucks, buses, and any other vehicle that could be scooped up along the way, the green-clad North Vietnamese army poured southward, leaving the newly captured areas mostly in the hands of local troops. They came south down main highways and jungle trails, but always quickly. Excepting only the helicopter-borne operations of the American era, no army in Vietnamese history had moved as quickly as the North Vietnamese force now was moving.

General Nghi, in his Phan Rang air base command post, felt that the situation was hopeless. He did not even know exactly how many men he had under him. He estimated that there was the equivalent of a division or so, perhaps 7,000 to 8,000 combat troops, or at least men with military training and rifles. Many were not combat experienced, of course. But truck drivers, clerks, and militia forces all had been impressed. There was a general feeling that they were fighting for their lives. Certainly there would be no escape by land. Only the sea to the east held a hope for those who were contemplating running.

And Nghi's defense force was shrinking, along with the civilian population of the Phan Rang area. As the civilians fought for places on the fishing boats, which in turn were running for the U.S. evacuation fleet off the coast, many soldiers went with them.

Most of the defections came from Phan Rang city. The air base was under a virtual siege, and at Ninh Chu and other villages most troops held their ground. The fighting was not very heavy, and local commanders were able to convince soldiers like Duc that they had a chance of victory.

Communications between Nghi and his surrounding positions were fair. The general had a good idea most of the time of what was going on, and what his weak spots were. This fact also helped shore up the men, because they knew that until the general left, the situation was not hopeless.

Duc, on guard duty, was paired with one of the few militiamen who had not run from the Phan Rang area. The man mentioned to Duc during a conversation that the Thieu family graveyard was only about 300 yards from where they were hunched in a shallow hole. Duc remarked sarcastically that he now understood why they were defending Ninh Chu, but after what he had been through in three weeks, even his sarcasm was weak.

In Saigon, there was a new government, a "fighting administration" in the words of the President, who was on hand for the swearing in April 14. It was, lamentably, anything but. It had taken Thieu well over a week to form the new government, because few of the capable men in South Vietnam wanted at this point to be identified with Thieu.

A general was removed from the showpiece task of chief armistice negotiator (the talks hadn't taken place for a year) and made Information Minister. He called in a newsman and told him he would be candid with the press, but he expected newsmen to stop printing untrue stories. It was the closest to action that any cabinet minister ever came.

Thieu's speech to the nation following the swearing-in ceremony was typical and was widely scoffed at by his citizens. The new cabinet would deal mostly with the refugee problem, caused by the massive Communist attacks. He made no mention of the part he played in creating refugees by his orders to retreat. The country was in a battle for survival, said the President. He would never surrender to the Communists. All peace-loving Vietnamese could look forward to the day when the troops of the Republic of Vietnam would recapture territory seized by the Communists.

The anti-Communists were heartened slightly by Thieu's hard line. They and many others were perked up even more by that day's military activity. The perimeter at Xuan Loc had actually been enlarged measurably on Monday, as the 18th division went on the attack and pushed back elements of the 6th North Vietnamese division. A few optimistic military analysts in Saigon said they believed the Communists might actually be pulling back, defeated by the 18th.

But it was a short-lived theory. For at Bien Hoa, only 14 miles from Saigon, the Communists were making advances. For a couple of weeks, their 130-millimeter guns had been firing a few shells a day into the most important airbase in South Vietnam. They had scored a few hits, but none was serious, except to the morale of the 200 American advisers there. Most of them pulled out.

On the night of April 14, the gunners hit the ammunition dump. And the next day, the zeroing-in completed, the North Vietnamese artillery went to work on the Bien Hoa base. When pilots reported for work at dawn on April 15, one of the twin runways was unusable because shells had gouged holes in the concrete.

The bombing strikes at Xuan Loc and Phan Rang had to be halted for a crucial half day while engineers filled in the holes. And during the repairs, more 130-millimeter shells pounded the air base. Most of the firing was random, and apparently for terror purposes only. Grounding the planes at Bien Hoa was a serious matter. Half the planes in the Saigon air force were at the base, and there could be no airstrikes around the capital at all.

That afternoon, army trucks began a shuttle from Bien Hoa to Saigon, moving bombs and rockets from the air base to Tan Son Nhut airport just outside the capital. Planners were looking ahead. It was obvious there was no way for the Saigon army to patrol a 30-mile circle around Bien Hoa and stop the shelling. Therefore, as a last gasp, the Saigon air force would be moved to Saigon.

There were several disadvantages to this, even if there was no alternative. Saigon was a little farther from the battlefields than was Bien Hoa. Tan Son Nhut was already a fairly busy airport. And airline pilots didn't exactly enjoy seeing fighter-bombers landing beside their planes that were full of passengers. Tan Son Nhut was also—because it was a civilian airport —more open to the public, and thus to saboteurs, than the more tightly controlled military base at Bien Hoa.

Without Bien Hoa's airstrikes that Tuesday morning, a North Vietnamese force estimated at a full division—perhaps 8,000 men—swept down on the regiment just outside Xuan Loc. The battle lasted about an hour. The regiment was routed. Most of the men were unable to make it into the city, and were forced to take off through the jungles. The Saigon army had lost one of its best units. The fate of Xuan Loc now depended on a single regiment. Four Communist divisions encircled Xuan Loc. General Le Minh Dao and his men fought on. But now they were trapped and fighting for their lives.

GOOD-BYE, AMERICAN...

That night, as Saigon slept and soldiers in the field watched, President Ford was acting in Washington. The criticism of Graham Martin had reached a peak, from within and without his Embassy and the administration. The charge was foot-dragging on evacuation.

Martin argued that evacuation of Americans or public evacuation of Vietnamese would panic the country and make surrender inevitable. At least, it would hasten a Communist victory; at worst it would bring total collapse and cause a panic that would make Da Nang seem calm by comparison.

On that issue there was little argument. What other Americans in Saigon and in Washington believed, however, was that Communist victory was inevitable. Chief military man Major General Homer Smith had reported to the Defense Department that the time to begin evacuation was already past. CIA station chief Polgar agreed. No matter what Martin said, ordered, or believed, all Americans in Saigon were making their plans to get out. Almost all were concerned about getting their staffs out with them, believing in the possibility of a blood bath.

Until now, Henry Kissinger had supported his man in Saigon. He believed Martin should make the decisions on when and how, or even whether, to leave, because the Ambassador was the man "on the ground," in a position to feel when evacuation should come.

But there were many facts against this theory. Some of the strongest

opponents of Martin's policy of a low-key, slow evacuation of some Vietnamese and a few Americans believed the Ambassador was out of touch
with reality. "Madman Martin" now was a phrase heard often. The propo-
nents of an immediate start to evacuating all but a hard core of American
officials and newsmen believed it might already be too late to get everyone
out who should be out.

On April 16, in an attempt to stop some of the criticism, Martin ordered
his Security Chief Marvin Garrett to update the contingency plans for
evacuation. Garrett waited for a pause in Martin's instructions, then told
the Ambassador gently that the plans were complete. There were several
versions, of course. The ones on the top presupposed opposition from the
South Vietnamese military and police and a possible panic by the civilian
population.

Martin told the security chief he wanted a plan for evacuation if there
were an intense shelling attack on the capital, followed by a Communist
ground attack. Garrett told him bluntly there was no way everyone would
be able to get out of Saigon if that happened.

Americans now were figuratively coming out of Saigon's woodwork. The
Embassy officers believed there would be perhaps 6,000 Americans to
evacuate if it began in mid-April. But as the North Vietnamese blitzkrieg
advanced, more and more U.S. citizens appeared.

Many were military retirees, who had chosen to live in Saigon for various reasons, usually having to do with cheap liquor and a surfeit of available
young women. Others were naturalized Americans of Vietnamese origin.
And there were the deserters.

No one ever knew how many Americans had walked away from the
armed forces in South Vietnam. Those who investigated at all usually came
up with an estimate of about 300 men who lived in Saigon by their wits and
off their women. Many were directly or indirectly tied to the drug trade,
usually as small-time pushers. But others had managed to get passports and
live useful lives in Vietnam, often marrying and raising a family, undetected by the official American community. Veto Baker, a Hawaiian with
no identification papers, lived in Da Nang for more than three years. He
was teaching English at the Embassy-sponsored Vietnamese-American
Association when the northern city was "liberated."

Between April 15 and April 28, 277 persons presented themselves at
evacuation sites and claimed they were American citizens. They held no
identification whatsoever. All were Caucasian or black and spoke American English. Officials asked no questions in Saigon, but put the men—and
their families if they had any—aboard the evacuation planes and flew them
to the United States. The FBI and military police were alerted and met the
planes with those men aboard. What became of them is unknown. Officials

have so far refused to answer questions on the 277. On the final day of evacuation, no identification was required for Caucasians or blacks boarding evacuation helicopters. How many others over and above the 277, with no identification, left Vietnam by chopper is unknown.

Security Chief Garrett informed Martin that Americans and their dependents by the hundreds were appearing and asking for evacuation. Instead of the 6,000 to 7,000 Americans the Embassy had planned on for evacuation, there were more likely double and perhaps even triple that number who would have to be taken out.

Martin was undaunted, but Garrett was worried enough about evacuation to make his views known, through Embassy friends, to influential officials in Washington. And President Ford, with the reluctant but full support of Kissinger, issued orders.

Ford's public order to get all "nonessential" Americans out of Saigon (no one ever explained why unessential American officials were there in the first place) was not issued only in the heartfelt interest of saving lives. Congressional leaders in both houses of the U.S. government had made it clear to the President that there was not a hope in the world that any kind of aid bill for Saigon would reach a vote unless most of the Americans in the war zone were removed expeditiously.

The offices of Congressmen and Senators were being flooded with cables, letters, and telephone calls from constituents asking for help in getting friends—usually Vietnamese—out of Vietnam. Inquiries to the State Department made it obvious that there was foot-dragging on all types of evacuation from the war zone. With voters on their tails demanding action, the congressmen in turn demanded action from the administration.

During the Saigon night of April 16-17, Ford told newsmen in Washington he was ordering Martin to speed up evacuation immediately. There would be no more delay and no excuses should be submitted, the President said. American officials necessary to U.S. operations in Saigon could remain. But all other American officials were to get out.

Martin didn't like it. But there was little he could do. Every senior official in the American establishment in Vietnam would work to implement the plan.

On Tuesday, April 15, U.S. military authorities in Saigon announced the end to PX Commissary and post-office privileges for retired military men living in Saigon. The men complained. General Homer Smith and his staff explained the order by stating they wanted the men to leave Saigon. The retired personnel replied that they could not leave with their families because the Vietnamese would not issue exit visas to their Vietnamese wives and children. And they would not, of course, leave without them. Smith went to work.

On Wednesday, at the movie theater in the Americans-only compound inside Tan Son Nhut airbase, Smith laid it on the line. The general thought it was a secret meeting, but a retired officer taped his speech for UPI. The way Smith built up the crowd was like real theater. The men grumbled, and only their respect for the two stars on Smith's lapels kept them from shouting out as he began his spiel with the same old line the retirees had heard before: it's time to leave. You should get out now while the getting's good. We cut off privileges, he said, because this would mean a lot of retirees would leave Vietnam. He appeared almost argumentative, holding back the punch line, never volunteering it in his speech. He opened the floor to questions. An almost combative Navy veteran arose and demanded of the general whether he expected retirees to leave without their Vietnamese families. Smith sprang his surprise.

He had made certain arrangements, and beginning the very next day, April 17, these retirees and their Vietnamese families would be leaving without paperwork. Planes would be available at no charge. Red tape would be at the absolute minimum.

> We'll process you and take you out and put you on an airplane. That's what I'm going to do. I'm going to do it the military way and get it over with.

There were a few seconds of silence as the statement sunk in. Then there were wild cheers. Patriotic Americans and believers in the military system, Smith had them charmed.

> I think very seriously that you should think very seriously about leaving South Vietnam [he said when the cheering died down]. Never before have you had a better opportunity, because never before have you been offered free transportation for you and your families.
>
> I'm not suggesting it [Communist victory] may happen, but hell, anybody who's got any smarts at all can look at the situation and figure out what kind of risk there is involved.
>
> In my considered judgment you should very seriously consider moving you and your family out of here.

The Tan Son Nhut American movie theater had shown its last picture. Within a day, the theater chairs were moved out and it became part of a huge evacuation operation, where instant marriages were legally (and often bigamously) performed; where clerks typed in minutes papers that used to take days; where the laws of Vietnam were totally overlooked and the laws of the United States were shunted to the side with official blessing from the Ford administration.

Graham Martin had lost a battle. He was later to claim credit for the airplane evacuation that followed Ford's order and Smith's speech, but he deserved little. By April 17, as the evacuation swung into full, overt action, Martin was not even being consulted on most points. Officials in the American community were solidly behind the order to evacuate. Martin was able to slow the evacuation of a few hundred Americans and Vietnamese, and to order his officials not to use the word "evacuation" in connection with the evacuation. But the "drawdown" began and continued on its own inertia and Martin in any case was soon busy frying other fish.

Leon Daniel of UPI wrote an analysis that began: "If this war were a Western movie, the good guys in the white hats would now drive their wagons into a circle and fight like hell for survival."

There were briefings on Friday, with evacuation as their main theme. One was at the U.S. Embassy, where Security Chief Garrett met American newsmen in an "off-the-record" discussion. The newsmen, Embassy officials knew full well, would stay at least until the end of American involvement. Some would stay even later.

The final evacuation (unlike the "drawdown" already under way) would be for Americans only. Updated contingency plans mostly revolved around having either an airport or a seaport, or both, open for use. But these plans appeared outdated. New plans had been drawn up for use in the likely event of a helicopter evacuation. Contingencies were written that presupposed resistance to the pull-out by South Vietnamese military or police forces.

The modified plans would provide for the evacuation of up to 10,000 foreigners, including Americans and eligible diplomats and others. The Embassy security office had compiled a list of 13 assembly points at which those who wanted to leave would gather to sweat out the pull-out. The 13 locations were American-controlled establishments where security was available in case of resistance. They were handy to the various living areas of most foreigners, and could handle small 12-passenger helicopters on their roofs or in their courtyards.

Garrett, who was tired, slouched in the briefing room chair where Martin sat during higher-level meetings. The ideal final evacuation would begin after the nightly curfew, at 10 P.M., say. Americans would gather at their assembly points, and then be taken by bus to the airport or the main Saigon port, called Newport. Ships or planes would begin ferrying the Americans out of Vietnam about 6 A.M.

The "worst possible case," a phrase of contingency planners, would mean the battle for Saigon under way, some panic in the streets, and resistance to the evacuation from the Saigon armed forces. In that case, helicopters would be used, Marine choppers able to carry between 20 and 50 persons to 7th Fleet ships offshore. The Marine pilots had already visited Saigon clandestinely to take a look at possible evacuation sites, particularly the Embassy grounds and the U.S. military compound at Tan Son Nhut.

In case of trouble, the Green Berets were in town. Teams of Special Forces soldiers had entered Saigon secretly and had mapped out and patrolled various routes to Tan Son Nhut airport on dry runs. The men had small submachine guns. The Green Berets, Garrett said, were to be used at any signs of trouble from the South Vietnamese. They would seize the one and only entrance to the airport if Saigon forces attempted to block it to departing Americans or dependents.

(Whatever happened to the Green Berets is an unsolved mystery to most Americans who were in South Vietnam at evacuation. The Saigon forces blocked the airport gate, as expected, but the Special Forces were not around to take it. Neither was there any security for the scores of buses for the Americans and Vietnamese.)

Evacuation was set up in four phases. We now were in Phase 1, a "drawdown." Phase 4 would be the final "hard pull." We probably would go from Phase 1 to Phase 4 in a matter of hours. Once the North Vietnamese artillery gets in range of Saigon and they start popping shells in, Garrett thought, we'll have to go immediately to try to avoid the panic situation.

Air America had at least 25 helicopters available, each capable of taking a minimum of eight persons with hand luggage from the roofs of buildings where some Americans inevitably would be trapped. Garrett recommended wearing a back pack rather than trying to clutch a handbag, for greater ease in boarding the helicopters. Under no circumstances, it went without saying, would suitcases or other large luggage be taken on any final evacuation.

Garrett concluded by handing around a mimeographed copy of the worst kept secret in a war of ill-kept secrets:

> Should it be felt necessary for U.S. personnel to report to their designated assembly areas, a coded message will be broadcast over American Radio Service. This message will consist of a temperature report for Saigon of "105 degrees and rising" followed by approximately the first 30 seconds of "I'm Dreaming of a White Christmas." This message will be broadcast every 15 minutes for approximately two hours.

Garrett said he didn't plan to use the coded broadcast because too many Vietnamese already knew about it and were listening to the Muzak over the

American station 24 hours a day waiting for word to evacuate. The whole succeess of an evacuation depended on keeping it secret from the Vietnamese.

At some other American offices around town, there were other briefings, smaller, more informal, but just as important. American officials were telling their Vietnamese staff members about getting out of Vietnam.

Those Americans who were not "nonessential" and who would remain to the end appealed for understanding. At the U.S. Agency for International Development, an American appealed to his secretary to remain with him to handle the paperwork necessary for others wishing to leave now. The secretary was a fast and accurate typist. At the U.S. Information Service office, other Americans were appealing to their workers to remain until the end. "You will definitely go with me on the helicopter when I go," one secretary remembered her boss telling her.

In return for shows of loyalty, the employees would be allowed to take their families with them—spouse and children if married; parents and brothers and sisters if they were not. Almost all pledged to stay until their bosses left. Most of those who were nervous were put in the waiting lines for evacuation, and taken out of Vietnam over the next week or so, with their families.

As the panic built, more and more persons showed their true mettle. Pressure separated the good from the bad.

At a USAID office, American architect Fred Gulden was ordered to leave Vietnam because he was nonessential. He disobeyed the order because no plans had been made for evacuation of the staff by the panicky American workers in the office. He remained in Saigon and arranged for the evacuation of many of the workers. Others never did get out.

At Tan Son Nhut, an American had a particularly attractive secretary, who was married. Instead of arranging for evacuation for the couple, the American army officer told the handsome Vietnamese woman he would arrange for her trip to the United States, but would not help her husband. Unfortunately, the woman, like most Vietnamese, was afraid of the man and did not report the case to his superiors. She and her husband took a hand grenade home the night of the American evacuation, and vowed to commit suicide if the Viet Cong came into their home. Luckily, Communist soldiers stayed away from the area for a couple of days, and the woman and her husband survived "liberation."

While the briefings were under way Friday around Saigon, and as C141 and C130 transports began the serious business of evacuating unessential personnel from Saigon, U.S. Embassy officials began discarding unessential papers. Hundreds of pounds of documents and secrets were shredded, burned, or both.

Panic was building, but interestingly enough few Americans were panicking. First, few of the Americans in Saigon had seen war. And there was an abiding faith in Martin and Ford to get them out if the going got tough. The "drawdown" was well under way and U.S. citizens in Saigon saw no particular reason they would not be able to leave.

For the Vietnamese who worked for Americans, it was different. They sensed, then saw, abandonment by the men and women they worked for. There was a very real fear of a blood bath among American-associated Vietnamese. It was a fear that had been nurtured by U.S.-inspired propaganda for more than 20 years, and backed up with not inconsiderable facts. Now, as Americans daily walked out of their offices in the evening, never to return, the Vietnamese employees were getting edgy, and even downright panicky.

President Ford's public order for a speed-up in evacuation was censored from all Vietnamese dailies, some of which were appearing on the streets with more empty columns than news. But through the radio and imported newspapers—chiefly the U.S. military's *Pacific Stars and Stripes*—the evacuation was well known.

Huge lines formed in front of the U.S. Consulate daily, as thousands of Vietnamese asked, begged, pleaded for a way out of the country. Many clutched identification cards showing that they had worked or worked now for the American government. Some clutched as their only proof of an American association, flaxen-haired babies and years-old love letters from boyfriends who had long since forgotten the names of the girls who held them.

Some were applying legitimately to leave. Inside the Consulate, there were stacks of letters and telegrams from American citizens and officials and congressmen who were agreeing to sponsor certain friends or former employees. But the lines were unmanageable and the harried and now beefed-up Consulate staff simply could not deal with each case.

Knowing an American in Saigon became the way to get out of the country, usually as a "dependent." And the venal among the American community began to show up everywhere.

A crewman deserted the merchant ship *Green Wave* , itself involved in evacuation, and canvassed the long lines of desperate Vietnamese in front of the Consulate for several days, auctioning his services as a temporary husband. He bragged he got twelve thousand dollars from the daughter of a rich Chinese family and took her out.

A well-known Saigon merchant who peddled his hand-made wares to Americans at honest prices said he was approached at least three times in two weeks by three different U.S. citizens offering to take him out of Vietnam as a "dependent" for between six and ten thousand dollars. The man, who had no desire to leave his country, turned them down.

Within a week, there were few beautiful prostitutes in Saigon. Young Americans made the rounds of virtually every bar and whorehouse in the capital to round up the women and sponsor them out of the country. One man claimed he made four trips in and out of Saigon, each time leaving with another "wife" and several "sisters-in-law." One prostitute who turned down the offer to leave said her would-be "husband" told her he planned to start an all-Vietnamese whorehouse in Honolulu. She said he worked for the CIA.

The men and women authorized to leave Vietnam were dependents of American citizens and those who held sensitive jobs and whose lives were clearly in jeopardy in any change of government from the present to Communist. But newsmen covering the daily evacuation flights saw who was leaving and reported that the plan was not working.

The wealthy, many of whom had become wealthy by preying on their countrymen, bought their way out. Many women paid with their bodies. Many of the truly endangered were considered "essential personnel," and they were to remain at their desks. Many of them were left behind on the final day.

America received many decent immigrants among the 140,000 who eventually arrived in the evacuation. But large numbers of corrupt men and undeserving women were among them. Most of the cutthroats who worked with the Phoenix Program for the CIA managed to get seats on specially-designated CIA aircraft. And some of the most decent, dedicated men and women in South Vietnam were left behind when the Americans finally panicked on the second-last day of the war.

At Xuan Loc, General Le Minh Dao knew that at least three (actually, it was four) North Vietnamese divisions threatened his single regiment inside the provincial capital. Dao ordered his third and last regiment into the battle, sending it down Highway 1 from the west toward Xuan Loc. The regiment, he hoped, could take some of the heat off Xuan Loc itself, and give Dao and his men inside the town a fighting chance.

In a way, you could say the tactic worked. Part of the Communist force broke off from Xuan Loc itself and met the oncoming regiment head-on near Trang Bom. Heavy fighting broke out, with the North Vietnamese trying to push the regiment back and the relief force trying to break through. With some luck, it was hoped, the third regiment—bolstered by some of the first regiment overrun earlier—could pierce the siege and get into Xuan Loc.

The battle was also taking most of the time of General Dung, who was, however, watching from a safer distance. He was at his headquarters at Loc Ninh, the Viet Cong "capital" 75 miles north of Saigon. Dung was faced with the sudden resistance shown by Dao's forces at Xuan Loc. He called in three-star General Tran Van Tra and others for a discussion on the situation. Then he issued orders.

Dung wrote later he felt he was in a winning position. Xuan Loc, however, was an unwanted thorn in his plan to storm the gates of Saigon. He now ordered his troops to stop the direct frontal assaults on Xuan Loc and pull back slightly into a tight siege of the town. Even with Saigon pouring new troops into the provincial capital for several days Dung felt that his superiority manpower and fire power would cause Xuan Loc to fall eventually. While the siege remained on, he ordered the other waiting forces to head for Saigon and simply bypass the town. Their advance would be slowed by having to use small roads and trails, but that was a small price to pay.

Tra went to the Xuan Loc area to give the new orders personally to the division commanders. Pham Hung, Number 4 man in the North Vietnamese Politburo and head of all Communist activity in the south, gave an impassioned speech to many of the cadre at Loc Ninh. With luck and hard fighting, he said, it would be possible to celebrate Ho Chin Minh's birthday in Saigon. Uncle Ho's 85th birthday was May 19.

The Communists continued to leapfrog, cutting Highway 1 again behind the advancing regiment. North Vietnamese forces now were west of Trang Bom, within 21 miles of Saigon.

Scouts were sent into the Saigon military region itself. They were messengers, harbingers of the big force that might come if the Communist command decided to wage the battle of Saigon. They discussed contingency plans with Viet Cong political cadre around the Saigon defense perimeter. Security forces for the scouts fought a couple of very brief skirmishes with Saigon militiamen.

Local Communist forces in the Saigon area got their provisional orders. It now was only a question of how and exactly when the capital would fall, they were told. Detailed instructions were issued, covering such matters as dress (as neat and clean as possible) and deportment (be wary, but no shooting unless life was endangered) for the day of "liberation." Code words for the attack were issued. They would be broadcast by Radio Hanoi.

By April 15, Phan Rang was lost. The largest North Vietnamese military force in the history of the war was all around the town. Gunners were blasting it apart with artillery, and the ground troops were taking their time. As the infantry and tanks moved up, there was little resistance. The town fell, and Viet Cong flags went up.

Inside the air base, it was a different story. Here, there were real defensive posts. There were no civilians to worry about. The base was small by the standards of air bases in Vietnam, but was still more than two miles long and about a mile wide.

In the command center were Lieutenant General Nguyen Vinh Nghi, the corrupt military man turned fighter, James Lewis of the U.S. Embassy, and a host of Vietnamese officers. On April 15, the situation did not look so bad in the air base. Nghi took the news of the fall of the town with some equanimity. He was not happy, but realized there had been little hope of the population's center holding out.

Over in Ninh Chu, Private Duc felt the loss of the provincial capital more personally than the general. He and the 400 or so men at Ninh Chu had not taken much incoming fire yet. The North Vietnamese were carving up the area, following their tactics by the book. Ninh Chu was an island unto itself. It was impossible to link up with any other Saigon forces from the village, although retreat to the sea was still a possibility.

General Nghi was in direct contact with Lieutenant General Nguyen Van Toan, the Saigon commander of III Corps, the 13 provinces surrounding Saigon but not including the capital itself. Toan told Nghi on the radio hookup that Phan Rang was to fight as long as possible, in an effort to slow down the huge Communist advance down Highway 1. The fall of Phan Rang shocked Toan, who was following the war only by maps in his office rather than from the field. He had hoped the town would be able to hold out for another week or more. Toan had planned to send reorganized battalions northward within a week to try to relieve the pressure on Phan Rang and block Highway 1 to the advancing North Vietnamese.

But Nghi's optimistic report on holding the air base cheered Toan somewhat. Toan told the chairman of the Joint General Staff, four-star General Cao Van Vien, he was hopeful the air base could hold out long enough for him to dispatch the troops reorganizing at Ham Tan, the small provincial capital of Binh Tuy about 100 miles south of Phan Rang. That would put Saigon soldiers between the advancing Communists from Phan Rang and the blocked North Vietnamese forces at Xuan Loc. It was a desperate plan, but it was a desperate time.

It was just after dark on April 15 those plans and that optimism began going out the window in the crashing boom of North Vietnamese guns.

The Communist 130-millimeter long-range artillery blasted Phan Rang air base with concentrated fire. Post after post along the air base perimeter was blown apart by the 40-pound shells, and the outer defenses of the now terribly small base crumbled. Soldiers retreated or were killed, panicked into running by the lack of cover. Many were cut down as forward artillery observers directed the fire closer and closer to the command post, where Lewis, Nghi, and the command staff waited underground.

The tanks and infantry began moving on the air base that night. Through the dark, patches of light appeared and disappeared as shells and tracer bullets lit up the scene. There were more green lines from the tracers of the Communists than there were red lines from the American-made ammunition of the Saigon forces.

Through the blackness of the hot, sticky night the battle raged. And around dawn, General Nghi decided the fight was hopeless. He radioed to his outlying positions and to Bien Hoa headquarters that he expected the command post to fall at any time.

Private Duc listened to the radio announcement from Nghi. The general was telling men at Ninh Chu and the few other areas not already overrun in and around Phan Rang to get out as best they could. There was no panic at Ninh Chu. North Vietnamese troops had all but ignored the village, and boats were available at the South China Sea beach which was so close that Duc could smell the water.

But for Duc, three Rangers, and a regular army soldier, the order to retreat was one too many. Duc had already retreated half the length of Vietnam. Would no one stand and fight?

There was a bulldozer at Ninh Chu, and one of the Rangers knew how to hot-wire the ignition. It roared into life, a Ranger in the driver's seat, Duc and the others on the hood, back, and blade of the machine. Lieutenant Colonel Bao, the officer from Saigon who was in charge of the Ninh Chu defense, ordered the men off the machine. Duc and two others pointed their weapons at the officer in a direct show of defiance. Bao retreated to his radio.

Straight to the Thieu family gravesite went the bulldozer. In five minutes, the tombstones were smashed, the ground was torn up. There was no longer any way of telling who, if indeed anyone, was buried there. The five men, emotionally exhausted, got off the bulldozer and began walking to the east, to the sea.

Bao reported their actions to a stunned Nghi and, after saying he was leaving Ninh Chu, signed off the radio and began walking to the beach himself.

Duc and many of the other men from Ninh Chu caught a fishing boat heading south. They arrived at the port of Vung Tau three days later after a leisurely trip, during which the boat owner stopped for more than a day to catch fish for food. Duc slept much of the way.

Lewis and Nghi got out of Phan Rang air base that day, with the North Vietnamese moving in and taking over the base within hours. Before he left, Nghi reported to Toan what had happened at Ninh Chu, and received permission to leave. He directed the blowing up of whatever military equipment and radios he had under his control, and he and Lewis set out. An exploding mortar shell spewed shrapnel into their bodies, slowing them up and causing tremendous pain.

There was no question of getting directly to the sea, as Duc and the men from Ninh Chu had done. They made it out of the air base through a gate, although for a while it looked as though they would have to chance going through a minefield to escape. Then Lewis saw more tanks and trucks and guns and troops than he ever knew the North Vietnamese Army possessed.

For 24 hours they escaped capture. They tried to make it to the seashore, but every route they tried was blocked. Highway 1 itself was impassable as an escape route, but the woods that paralleled the road provided some cover. Nghi, who could possibly have blended into the population, refused to leave the American. The kind of bond that often grows between commonly threatened persons grew between the wounded Nghi and Lewis. They would live or die together. After 24 hours of trying to make it south to Saigon, Nghi and Lewis were captured by Communist troops and made prisoners of war.

There was surprisingly little questioning and no brutality by the North Vietnamese toward either one of the high-ranking enemies. They were kept together, or at least close to each other. The Communists announced the capture of Nghi in a gleeful clandestine radio broadcast, but never mentioned Lewis during the more than six months he was their prisoner.

The two men were taken under guard to North Vietnam, with few stops along the way. There, they were escorted to the Son Tay POW camp, once the site of an abortive raid by Green Berets to rescue American prisoners who had already been moved to Hanoi.

Finally, Nghi and Lewis were separated. Lewis never talked to Nghi again. The day he was released, with the Ban Me Thuot 12, Lewis saw the general, pacing the compound at Son Tay. His head was still high. He made a small hand sign of goodbye to Lewis. It was the last known time he was seen alive. Presumably he still lives, although Lewis and others wonder whether Nghi was among the "small handful" of senior Saigon officers and officials the Communists told Senator George McGovern they executed. No one knows.

Two days after the fall of Phan Rang, its sister provincial capital of Phan Thiet, 100 miles east of Saigon, was captured by the North Vietnamese armed forces. The Communists now controlled 20 provinces, all of II Corps areas, two-thirds of South Vietnam.

Ambassador Martin was physically unwell, still feeling the ravages of the pneumonia he had suffered in the United States. Under normal circumstances, he would be in the hospital, or at least at home in bed. But Martin was not that sort of man. Now that dice were being cast and important decisions were being made daily, almost hourly, Martin insisted on being present. It was the way he operated. He was in full charge of his Embassy, demanding loyalty but making all decisions himself, often secretly.

"I'm no hawk and I resent being cast in the role of a hawk here in Vietnam," Martin told visitors to his third-floor office in better times. The word may be meaningless, anyway. There is no doubt he was a hard liner on Vietnam. He believed President Thieu was a popularly elected—if not popular—President and had a reverence for the Constitution. It was the tenth hour now, with the eleventh rapidly approaching, and Martin remained unshakable.

Strictly against his beliefs and his gut instincts, he was reluctantly carrying out the letter—if not the spirit—of the order from his President to step up the evacuation of Americans in Vietnam. Like a ship's captain, he ordered the women and children out first, then approved the paring of the Embassy staff.

As for American relations with the Republic of Vietnam, Martin remained in charge. He was convinced, and often said so at staff meetings, that the North Vietnamese could be forced into making a deal with Thieu. Most of the staff disagreed. They pointed out the apparently irreversible statements by the Communists that they would deal neither with Thieu nor with members of the President's "clique," a reference to almost every South Vietnamese official in the republic's government.

Martin's answer was that Thieu was President, like it or not. His term of office expired in October 1975, when voters would have the opportunity of turning him out of office. He was unfeeling to the argument that Thieu was elected in a one-man election in 1971. Similarly, he refused to budge from his position when staffers pointed out that Thieu was President of very little, thanks to the Communist offensive. The Ambassador insisted on following form. He would not press Thieu to resign.

He did talk to the President, several times. Thieu, in his last week in office, had few of his own citizens to whom he could turn. His officials and generals did not trust him, and were calling publicly for his blood. Only Martin's threat of a total cut-off of U.S. aid had held the generals back from a coup d'état.

Martin had a conspiracy theory, in which he held that the true enemy of

American and Vietnamese anti-Communist aims was the American left. This included newsmen, certainly. While Martin was more of a sophisticate than the myriad American officials who during the early 1960's had urged U.S. newsmen "to get on the (American) team," he had specifically called *The New York Times* correspondent David Shipler in 1974 "a conscious or unconscious dupe of Hanoi." Shipler had written extensively of the huge American presence and direct involvement in South Vietnam. The forces of the antiwar movement, particularly those who openly visited Hanoi, and authors and speechmakers who concerned themselves with political prisoners of the Saigon government were targets of the Martin theory. Much of the antiwar propaganda "was directed from Hanoi," Martin said on several occasions, and he had no compunction in having his spokesman in Saigon pass these words to other newsmen.

How much of a conspiracy there was, if any, is impossible to say. That the Communists drew support from so-called antiwar activities by Americans and critical stories by newsmen is above argument. North Vietnamese propaganda frequently used selected American events and opinions to buttress their own.

Martin unrealistically wanted a united American front against the Communist Vietnamese. Lacking this, he denied Shipler and other newsmen in Saigon access to information, and urged Secretary of State Henry Kissinger on March 21, 1974, in a cable to withhold "an honest and detailed answer" to a request for information by Senator Edward Kennedy. The Senator, Martin charged in the classified cable later leaked to Kennedy, "will spearhead this effort [to reduce aid to Saigon]," and detailed answers to his requests for information would give him "the tactical advantage" in an aid fight.

Given Martin's theory of a conspiracy by the American left, it is easy to see why the Ambassador was able to reject intellectually the Hanoi and Viet Cong statements that they never would negotiate with Thieu or Martin. America's man in Saigon fully believed that a unified front by pro-Saigon officials could force Hanoi into negotiations that would bring an end to the war, while maintaining at least the semblance of the Republic of Vietnam. There was no lack of advice to him, however, to encourage more honest and realistic South Vietnamese in the final anti-Communist showdown of 1975. This might have produced a less corrupt, more defensible South Vietnamese administration that could have dealt in some way with the Communists, or at least refuted the Communist argument once and for all that they preferred talking to fighting. Martin was not impressed with such advice.

There is no question that he misjudged the Communists. What he missed was the 30 years of historical precedent that Hanoi never retracted a public statement. Not once did the Communists take a step backward from their public positions. Now, when they said they would definitely not negotiate with Thieu or Martin, they meant it. Martin, for unknown reasons, firmly believed that was a propaganda statement, which could be weakened by firm diplomacy.

And there was the problem of where the firm diplomacy would come from. By April 16, Thieu himself was in deep depression, his officials were trying to get out of Vietnam to save themselves, his generals were in open revolt, and his people—all his people—openly reviled him.

Martin met Thieu about the time Lewis and Nghi were leaving Phan Rang as a lost cause. Himself physically ill, the Ambassador tried to bolster the President. He told him the United States had full confidence in Thieu, because he was the elected leader of South Vietnam. He encouraged Thieu not to resign. Discussions were underway with Hanoi representatives, Martin said, which could lead to a negotiated settlement. For the present, Martin counselled Thieu to remain firm. The Americans, he said, remained committed to the Thieu government and to the maintenance of the Republic of Vietnam. Military aid was continuing to flow to Saigon, and President Ford was lobbying hard with congressmen to send more.

Thieu thought otherwise. According to a cable to Washington detailing the meeting, Thieu said his Embassy in Washington told him there was little chance of Congress' voting more military aid to Saigon, ever. In a long monologue to Martin, he demanded that American warplanes enter the war. On his desk was a letter from Richard Nixon, written in 1973, promising strong U.S. responses to any Communist offensive. So where, he asked Martin, was the strong response? With no help from the Americans, Thieu said he might be forced to resign. And that would lead directly and quickly to a Communist takeover, because there was no one but himself who could lead the nation to victory over Hanoi.

Henry Kissinger had undermined Vietnam more than any other American by forcing the Paris agreement on a reluctant Saigon in late 1972, Thieu said. The Americans had promised them that aid and support would continue. They had promised direct military help if Hanoi broke the agreement. Where was it? Perhaps Martin should not be offering advice. It would be better if the Ambassador could come to Independence Palace with word that the B52's were again pounding Hanoi and Haiphong.

Martin agreed with Thieu, and had said as much to Americans in his office for more than a year. Being a good diplomat, however, he did not say so to the President.

Another diplomat was worried about a possible final battle for Saigon. Jean Marie Merillon, the French Ambassador, also was seeing his chance for reestablishing some French influence in Vietnam. He in Saigon and allies in Paris and other capitals, including Hanoi, talked now to Thieu, to members of his "clique," to former General Duong Van "Big" Minh, who was a possible Thieu replacement, and to the Communists.

Merillon had the vision of a new French order in Indochina. Big Minh was willing to talk to the diplomat, because he saw himself as the savior of South Vietnam now.

But the influential on both sides had little time for the French government and its envoy in Saigon. They listened respectfully as French officials rushed from one warring side to the other, trying to stress points of agreement between the two sides. But there was little respect for the French among the hierarchy, either in Saigon or in Hanoi. Too many on both sides had fought French colonialism too recently.

Merillon advised Thieu to resign in favor of Big Minh. Although the Communists had not said so directly, it was the belief of the Paris government that Hanoi would negotiate an end to the war with the hero of the 1963 coup against Ngo Dinh Diem. Such a move would restore peace and avoid a bloody battle for Saigon.

The first probe in the final battle for Saigon came April 18, two days after the loss of Phan Rang. A small commando band of Communist soldiers, estimated at about 30 men, attacked the Phu Lam signal site on the western edge of the capital. The assault by itself was a typical sapper attack, with some damage and a few casualties. Taken as a single incident, it meant little, except as a one-day headline.

But the assault on Phu Lam was much more than that, everyone realized. For one thing, the Communists were bringing the war close to the capital for the first time in a couple of years. For another, military men agreed it was actually a probe on the Saigon defenses, testing reactions and movements of the Saigon army.

The reaction, in fact, was good. Helicopter gunships got to Phu Lam quickly from nearby Tan Son Nhut and a couple of small ground units stationed near the communications station made good time in hustling to Phu Lam to help repel the small attack.

But Saigon was in trouble should the big battle come. The troop dispositions were no particular secret. The Saigon army had one brigade of paratroopers, a couple of Ranger battalions, the air force and little else.

Some Saigon officers and American advisers were making frantic efforts to reorganize some of the Marines and a couple of infantry divisions near the capital, but there was little progress possible inside a month. The only other units in any position to guard Saigon were:

• The 5th Division, stationed just north of Saigon, but considered combat ineffective, mostly because corruption had weakened the unit beyond repair;

• The 25th Division, in worse shape than the 5th, and stationed to the northwest of Saigon; and

• The 9th Division, a fair unit that guarded the northern Mekong Delta, beginning about 25 miles south of Saigon.

The Joint General Staff looked over what was available and issued a reluctant and highly unusual order to the 9th Division to move north toward Saigon. The division was to cross the border from IV Corps to III Corps. In the past, Corps borders had been considered almost inviolate. But JGS planners felt that the only chance of defending Saigon lay with the 9th Division, and so ordered the unit into a semicircle south of Saigon hard on the outer periphery of the capital.

A large area in the northern Delta was thus opened up to the Communists. Viet Cong units moved into many villages and took over, usually without a fight from the home guard militia. The noose on Saigon was getting tighter, and there was little maneuvering room left.

If Martin could not disobey his orders to speed up evacuation, he could perform what he felt was his main duty—to try to stem the obviously growing panic among large segments of the Vietnamese population. The Saigon government had censored all references to evacuation from its own press, but there were few Vietnamese who did not know that evacuation was under way.

Martin chose Alan Carter as his foil in not telling the Vietnamese the truth. It had to be done without lying. This kind of propaganda exercise is a peculiar American refinement. Americans believe their government should never lie, and it seldom does. Instead, the technique of partial truth and emphasis on misleading statements is used.

Carter was the Saigon chief of the United States Information Service, a usually important branch of any U.S. Embassy. In Vietnam, USIS (pronounced You-sis by most and Useless by the cynical) had been badly emasculated by Martin and his doctrine of one-man rule in his Embassy.

The goateed Carter had come to Vietnam the previous August after a particularly successful tour as chief of USIS in Tokyo, where both the Japanese and foreign press corps gave him high marks for his accomplishments. In its dealings with the press, the task of USIS is to push the American line and provide easy access to American officials for the opinion formers who work in the press corps.

Carter saw Vietnam as a major challenge. He had read of the wide chasm between Martin and the press in Vietnam and came to his new assignment in Saigon with the optimistic feeling that he could repair the rent. On his arrival in Saigon the previous summer, he had invited most of the Americans in the press corps to individual lunches and dinners at his Saigon home and had promised more cooperation.

The problem, however, was Martin. The Ambassador was simply not going to let Carter do the job the USIS chief thought he should do. Martin had a hand-picked press officer—Vietnam veteran John Hogan—who was under strict orders from the Ambassador to withhold most of the information available within the Embassy. What little Hogan was able to release to the press was personally approved by Martin.

Carter was astounded, angered, and finally depressed. Supposedly a member of the "country team" within the Embassy—the policy-making staff—he found he was not permitted even to read most of the message traffic in and out of the Embassy. Martin had found that the easiest way to maintain security—secrecy from the press—was to compartmentalize his fiefdom. No member, say, of the political section, could read reports from or to any other section. Only Martin and three or four other Embassy members had access to all information. Carter, the supposed policy maker, was neatly cut out.

The USIS chief fought the system, but with the complete support Kissinger provided Martin in running the Embassy by his own rules, Carter found himself unable to make headway. And slowly, it appeared to Carter's staff and outsiders who watched Embassy happenings and listened to gossip, Carter became resigned to his fate. As his job developed after his arrival in Saigon, Carter was given such heavy tasks as running a library and overseeing the straight propaganda program of distributing pro-American stories to the Saigon press.

To fight Martin, it became clear, would accomplish nothing, because Martin was backed by the U.S. Secretary of State. Carter slowly fell to his new task. Stripped of real responsibility, he stood aloof, and even on the occasions he talked to newsmen, I do not recall his giving any meaningful information.

On the second-last Saturday night of the war and under orders from Martin, Carter conducted a strange exercise for the first time ever in the Vietnam conflict. He arranged to be interviewed on Saigon Television and Radio. An English-speaking interviewer, reading questions from a script in Vietnamese and English, asked Carter about evacuation.

The session was one of America's poorest moments in Vietnam. The interview was so clearly staged and Carter's answers were so clearly uncandid and evasive that among those who cared there were only two reactions—hilarious laughter or sheer anger. The interviewer asked Carter about a "rumor" that all [not some, but all] Americans were at that moment evacuating Vietnam. [No one I knew had heard this particular rumor.]

Carter: This is the kind of unfortunate speculation which causes people to be more concerned than necessary. . . . There is absolutely no truth at all, not a shred of truth, to this rumor.

Q: There is a rumor that the American Consulate has been issuing passes to Vietnamese citizens for purposes of evacuating them.

Carter: Well, this is still another rumor to which there's absolutely no truth. The American Consulate in Saigon maintains what we call locater cards for every American citizen and his dependents. This is a matter of records and it's a function performed by every American Consulate around the world. Because many Americans, for example, came to Saigon from Da Nang and Nha Trang and still many others have failed in the past to file these locater cards, we've been busier than usual performing these routine functions of an American Consulate. [This is called not answering the question that is asked. In fact, such passes—called airplane boarding cards—were being issued daily and in large numbers.]

Q: Mr. Carter, the long lines that we see every day at the American Consulate have given rise to speculation that there is either an evacuation procedure or that many people are leaving the country.

Carter: Well, we're really talking first about normal functions performed by American Consulates. These include the filing of marriage papers, the recording of births, the issuance of visas to American citizens and all of their dependents, many of whom are Vietnamese. It's obvious the present circumstances have created some nervousness in both the American and Vietnamese communities. As a result, American citizens and their dependents are now updating their records with the Consulate, something they should have done much earlier. And in addition, many Vietnamese who had planned to go to the U.S. for study or for business have come to the Consulate for issuance of an American visa. But obviously they must first have received permission from their own government, your government.

[This was not a lie, although it was not the whole truth. The Consulate itself was not issuing visas to Vietnamese who did not have permission from Saigon to leave. That job was being taken care of by American personnel at Tan Son Nhut in the old movie theater.]

Some Americans have been leaving. I'm sure many of you have noticed that some of your American friends have gone. But given the circumstances, it's understandable that some Americans and their dependents would have wanted to leave somewhat earlier than they had originally planned. It's logical that we should have reduced slowly over the next—over the last few weeks, rather—and now on a somewhat accelerated basis, the number of nonessential Americans in the Embassy. But even when we've completed this process, we will still be one of the largest U.S. Embassies anywhere in the world.

It was one of those perfect interviews, where no lie had been told, although an impression other than the truth had been left on viewers and listeners. A week before, the interview might have worked. But with C130's and C141's pouring into Tan Son Nhut and lifting out several thousand persons a day, it didn't.

Critics of the interview, most of them employees of the U.S. government, blasted it as worse than useless and counterproductive. In their opinion, Carter's exercise merely proved that the Embassy was continuing to drag its feet on getting out of Vietnam those Vietnamese whose lives were endangered in a Communist takeover. There was truth in this.

The interview was played over official radio and television two nights in a row. The Saigon press did not pick it up even as a news story, so blatant did they consider it. Saigon editors knew full well that a large evacuation of Vietnamese and Americans was under way, and there was no question of bureaucracy involved.

Carter said that "if you were to visit Ambassador and Mrs. Martin's home, you would see that nothing whatsoever has been packed, and the same is true at my house." According to one of his secretaries, the packers arrived at Carter's home the day after the interview.

On Saturday morning, April 19, Viet Cong Senior Colonel Vo Dong Giang held his regular press conference at Camp Davis at Tan Son Nhut. His Provisional Revolutionary Government was ready to bargain, he told newsmen. But it would strike no deal with Thieu or his "clique." Any negotiations must be undertaken after both sides had agreed that all American advisers would leave quickly. The PRG would participate in national elections in South Vietnam and, following the vote, would dissolve itself to participate in a new Saigon regime.

Barring this, a smiling Giang told the newsmen in the packed former American mess hall, where he held his news conferences, the Communists would strive for a military victory.

"I'm sorry I cannot say in advance the date" of the final attack on Saigon, Giang said. Orders to prepare for an attack were issued April 4. In the meantime, Communist forces, while getting into position for an all-out assault on Saigon, were holding back, awaiting "an assessment of the chance which they consider best."

It was the closest the Communists had ever come to telegraphing their punches. Giang was saying that the Viet Cong wanted a political victory, but if worst came to worst—by their reasoning—they would take a military victory.

The lines were set. The Saigon army had been routed everywhere it had been tested, except at Xuan Loc, where the 18th was trying to hold but was badly outnumbered. At least 100,000 Communist troops—10 divisions of infantry and supporting forces—were within one or two days' march of Saigon. The capital was defended—with only a few thousand exceptions—by ragtag infantry units that most experts believed would fold shortly after the first taste of fire.

Thieu would not resign, he said, but in fact he was weakening. He continued to say he would not negotiate. Martin wanted him to stay on, to try to bargain. The Communists wanted him out, and had flatly stated they would attack Saigon if he did not leave. They would not bargain with him. Most Americans were worried only about evacuation and had almost no time for their jobs. The pro-American Vietnamese were in a partial state of panic and were not functioning well. All Vietnamese were capable of doing bodily harm to Thieu, so deep was their hatred of the man.

The Vietnam war, in other words, was near an end.

"YOU AMERICANS"

For three and a half years, since December 20, 1971, Saigon had been a curious island in the war. Untouched by bomb or bullet during these years, the largest city in Vietnam was a unique vortex. In some ways, it should have been 1,000 miles from the war zone, for it was not a battleground. Yet it should have been a battleground, because it was the center of the war zone.

While Hanoi took B52 strikes, Saigon basked in sunlight. While soldiers died all around it, Saigon was peaceful. It was no different a place to live from, say, Taipei or Colombo or Jakarta.

In April of 1975, it was a little more tense than ever before. The war was drawing to an end, it was clear, and at the very least, the Communists were going to end up in the driver's seat, if not owning the entire car. Several thousand Vietnamese and Americans, who wanted to get out before the end, were making the whole city tense.

But life went on. The only identification with the war for most of the three and a half million residents of the city was through the newspapers. Except for a few newsmen and photographers and fewer still of the American and Saigon military establishment who traveled regularly to battle fronts, there was no direct knowledge of war, and had been none for years. There was plenty of secondhand knowledge, but war raged around Saigon, not in the city. To mark the 1971 anniversary of the establishment of the

National Liberation Front, Communist gunners had fired three rockets into the city. Since then, peace.

As hundreds died every day in Vietnam of gunshots and bomb shrapnel and starvation and malnutrition and dehydration brought directly by warfare, Saigonese had other problems. The market prices were rising. The PX's were closing, and the commissary had little food. The French restaurants did not have the tasty lettuce from Dalat, and the city was missing the short strawberry season because the roads from the highlands growing areas were cut.

The middle and upper classes who wanted to get out had another fear: that the three million or so refugees on the road would get into Saigon. They strongly backed the high-level decision to keep them out of the capital.

The war was something vague to the long-time Saigon resident. Everyone had his or her own Tet offensive story, of course, but that was a long seven years ago by now. The short-term resident, usually a refugee, had fled to Saigon for the express purpose of escaping the war and attempting to forget about it.

But it was getting closer. The ammunition dump explosion at Bien Hoa could be heard. And the front-page maps in the Saigon newspapers showed graphically how close to the capital combat was coming.

There had to be an end to it all. And there was increasing concern in Saigon among the middle ranks of power, as there had been among the upper ranks for several weeks, that the main—perhaps the only—block to a peaceful settlement before Saigon erupted in the flames of war was Nguyen Van Thieu.

The cries for his political head were strident on this relatively peaceful Sunday. The French Cercle Sportif was busy, although some of the familiar faces weren't around, having caught a recent flight out of Vietnam. The swimming pool was bustling and white-clad waiters padded the terraces with trays of ordered drinks and what passed for delicacies in South Vietnam.

It was accepted almost everywhere except in a third-floor office of the U.S. Embassy that Thieu had to go. Officers at the Joint General Staff had made it clear to Thieu that they expected him out quickly. In fact, they only had hope and no power to threaten, because of the clear U.S. threat to abandon Saigon in case of a military coup. The right wing wanted the President out, and had done so for months. The Roman Catholic prelate, Archbishop Nguyen Van Binh, a political neutral, had called on Thieu to step down.

On this Sunday of the packed leisure clubs and movie houses filled to capacity, and strollers in the zoo, and an evacuation at Tan Son Nhut air base, which was running on its own inertia by now, one thing was perfectly clear. Nguyen Van Thieu was finished. If he stayed, it was obvious to almost all, the war would come to Saigon. There was no way, no way at all, that the Communists were going to negotiate with Thieu or his immediate supporters. And it was obvious that if Thieu stayed on, the Communists would simply win the war. The generals could not see how Saigon could defend itself for more than a few token days. One officer said Saigon was 36 hours from defeat in case of an all-out North Vietnamese drive on the capital.

Nguyen Van Thieu was in his bomb shelter under Independence Palace this Sunday, April 20. Although he had thought the previous week he might head out to the luxurious riverside weekend retreat he had built just north of Saigon, other things had intruded.

Like the helicopter that landed on his lawn Saturday afternoon. General Cao Van Vien, the only active four-star general in the Saigon military, and three-star General Nguyen Van Toan, commander of III Corps around Saigon, were on the chopper.

Toan came to the point as soon as they got inside the palace door to be greeted by an apprehensive Thieu. Mr. President, said Toan, the war is over.

Toan was in charge of the meeting. He had asked Vien to go along with him only because the President would better believe him, and as a witness. The general told Thieu that Phan Rang was gone, a fact that had been kept from Thieu for three days for reasons that are obscure. And Toan told Thieu what had happened at Phan Rang—his three-star general and friend, Nguyen Vinh Nghi, captured; the air base in Communist hands; the quick fall of Phan Thiet, which surely meant that the Communists would automatically turn down Highway 1, away from the coast toward Saigon.

Toan told Thieu what had happened to the family graves at Ninh Chu. The President, already wringing his hands, turned white when Toan, his eyes downcast, told Thieu this. The general had debated withholding this piece of information from the President indefinitely. But too many people already knew it. Nghi had radioed it to Bien Hoa just before he left Phan Rang, and the bulldozing of the graveyard was the talk of Toan's headquarters. Toan felt it was better that Thieu be told the information straightaway, rather than hear it on the grapevine.

To the surprise of both Vien and Toan, Thieu did not fly into a rage. The President was typical of many people in that when things went wrong, he tended to blame others rather than look to his own shortcomings. Vien was looking for a way to tell Thieu that what had happened was in great measure a product of the President's own acts. But without dismissing the generals, Thieu merely turned into the residential wing of the palace. Vien and Toan let themselves out.

That was Saturday. Now, on Sunday, Thieu was brooding still. He had not spoken, to anyone's knowledge, in about 24 hours, except to say he was unavailable to anyone for any reason. For Saturday, all of Sunday, and Monday morning Thieu stayed alone, most of the time in his bomb shelter. He did not, to anyone's knowledge, eat, although he may have snacked on the food available in the underground shelter.

His press office announced during the weekend that, as custom demanded, the President would appear at the King Hung Vuong celebrations Monday, commemorating the historical founding of Vietnam. The President had always appeared at the ceremony, a national holiday, usually to make a short, sharp speech pledging himself and South Vietnam to the fight against the Communists. Press badges were handed out on a rationed basis to newsmen and photographers. There was a scramble for the badges. In times of crisis, newsmen tend toward the leaders, no matter how nominal they are. And there were a lot of newsmen in Saigon now, perhaps 400 foreigners, ready to cover the last big story in Vietnam in their lifetimes.

The commander of Xuan Loc and the 18th Division, Brigadier General Le Minh Dao, knew the town was finished on Monday morning. Sunday night and early Monday it was apparent that the Communists were moving in for the kill. He had had two hopes of relief forces, and the North Vietnamese, with their superior manpower, had cut off both hopes. The paratroop brigade was bogged down in the rubber plantation in a fight for its life, and there was no hope it would reach Xuan Loc now. Relief forces from Dao's reserve regiment of the 18th clearly had no hope of punching through the siege along Highway 1.

After a night of the heaviest shelling yet on the battered provincial capital, Dao saw the fight was hopeless. He later estimated that two divisions of North Vietnamese troops took part in the final attack, which began just before dawn.

The fire power of the attacking Communist forces was enormous. Dao thought it was greater than any he had seen from any American infantry unit. The outposts around Xuan Loc began to fall one by one, with the men of the 18th falling back on the town in an orderly but inexorable retreat. The end was near, although the 18th fought on. No quarter was given voluntarily. The North Vietnamese fought for every inch, and the 18th division soldiers gave as well as took. The problem was the manpower. There just were not enough men in Xuan Loc to hold the town.

Shortly after dawn, Dao talked to Bien Hoa headquarters on his radio. General Toan was not available, he was told, but had issued contingency orders to hold Xuan Loc as long as possible. There was no Thieu-type order to hold at all costs. The generals who commanded field troops knew better than to issue that kind of order.

Dao was out among his men. There was little commanding to do, and a colonel—the commander of the 40th regiment, Le Xuan Hieu—did all of that. Dao moved around, ducking the frequent artillery and mortar shells, bobbing from foxhole to command post to bunker to half-blasted house serving as shelter for small groups of soldiers. He was almost melancholy as he saw his men fight on. Where the much more honored airborne and Marine and 1st Division soldiers had cut and run, the 18th was fighting on.

At midmorning it was clearly a hopeless fight. Xuan Loc, the only symbol of Saigon resistance to the North Vietnamese blitzkrieg was about to fall. Reluctantly, Dao gave the order to pull out. Four of the six battalions completed the retreat, edging between the town and the rubber plantation to the east where the airborne was trapped. They encountered only light resistance. Dao went with the fourth. Colonel Hieu stayed on with two battalions to cover the pull-out.

The North Vietnamese moved into the gap beside the rubber plantation and completed their siege of Xuan Loc, cutting off the last two battalions from retreat. For those 600 men, there were now two choices—surrender or fight on. On Monday, they chose to fight on, pulling in their lines and setting up a new, smaller defense perimeter of Xuan Loc. About 600 men with no hope of victory fought a combined tank, artillery, and infantry force of about 10,000 North Vietnamese.

Thieu, who was morose, came out of his bomb shelter early Monday morning. He had made his decision. He went to the east wing office and took out paper and pen and began to make notes for a speech to the nation.

He called in an aide and told the man he wanted a meeting of the very senior staff, no more than a half-dozen men, still trusted by the President. He issued orders for Martin to be at the palace within an hour.

Thieu told the aides he wanted to address the senior military and civilian officials in Saigon at the palace that afternoon. No, he said, he would not be attending the Hung Vuong ceremony, due to start within an hour.

He gave virtually the same speech to the senior aides and to Martin. Thieu said he had been betrayed by the Americans. Kissinger, in particular, had promised him aid in case of a North Vietnamese offensive, and the aid had not been forthcoming. The situation was almost hopeless. But there was a chance yet. The people must be drawn together to fight the Communist enemy. Bickering must stop immediately. There was a time to play politics, but now was not the time.

Thieu said that despite the reprehensible treatment of the Americans,

Vietnam would fight on for freedom. He had seriously considered resigning during the past two days of solitude. He was still thinking about it. But
he felt that only he of the available leaders could help Vietnam withstand
the Communist attacks. The survival of the Republic of Vietnam was the
most important thing. He would have more to say later that afternoon in his
address to a couple of hundred senior officials, Thieu said. He wanted TV
cameras and radio microphones to tape what he said for broadcast later
that evening. It probably would be a long speech.

The palace aides quickly spread the word that Thieu was going to resign,
probably that afternoon. The secondhand information reached tuned-in
newsmen, who worked frantically to try to get confirmation.

By midafternoon, with the rumors of resignation spreading by the minute, one American newsman tried again for some sort of confirmation.
This was not the sort of story one put out unless one was absolutely sure. A
newsman who said Thieu was resigning, only to have the President deny it
hours later, probably wouldn't be in Vietnam for long.

The American put a call in to Graham Martin, who surprisingly came on
the line immediately to chat. Martin had received the same Thieu speech
as the palace aides. But he had taken the President's words in exactly the
opposite way as the Vietnamese officials. He was seemingly less attuned
both to the nuances of Thieu's manner of speaking and the President's
mood.

The Ambassador told the newsman he would be making a very serious
mistake in printing even speculation that Thieu intended to resign. The
President had indicated, Martin told the newsman, that he intended to
remain in office and to fight all attempts to oust him. He intended to
demand, on television before the nation, a vote of confidence by virtually
every official in the Republic of Vietnam. Thieu would, Martin predicted,
receive the overwhelming vote and would stay to direct the final defense of
Saigon.

The newsman, impressed by Martin's firm denial of the resignation
rumors, held off on the story. It cost him a three-hour beat when his rival
news agency ignored the American Ambassador's guidance. UPI received
a telephone call from a senior officer present at the afternoon meeting
—later shown on television—and sent a bulletin around the world that
Thieu had quit. Trusting Martin had cost other newsmen the story.

Thieu's speech to his officials, shown on television just after the 8 P.M.
curfew gave him a captive audience, was the most vitriolic of his career.
And indeed, the first half of the talk was tough stuff, statements about last
ditches and fighting on and battling Communists and protecting the Republic of Vietnam. He spoke to the senior members of his Congress, the

Chief Justice of the Supreme Court, his entire cabinet, military and police commanders, and senior officials; in short, as a Vietnam TV reporter said, "every personality involved in the government leadership at present."

The President said he wanted to speak directly to those gathered at the palace, rather than through an interlocutor such as the Congress. The country was "in a period which has forced us to retreat almost to Independence Palace." The situation was urgent. When he became chief of state in 1965, Thieu said, 50 percent of South Vietnam was under Communist domination, and officials feared an imminent takeover. The United States and other "allied nations" intervened and the Republic of Vietnam gained strength.

In 1968, the Communists went to the Paris talks with the express and only purpose of forcing American withdrawal. In 1972, the North Vietnamese began forming more and more infantry divisions and tried for an all-out military victory. The attempt failed.

But then, declared Thieu, there were under-the-table agreements between Saigon's American allies and the Communist North Vietnamese in Paris. Thieu spent much time explaining this to his countrymen. He argued the Americans had sold out South Vietnam to the Communists. The Americans had demanded that Thieu agree to the Paris accords. Thieu called the Americans traitors and refused to sell out South Vietnam, rejecting the American plan. Thieu remained opposed to any reconciliation with "the government of the other side," Hanoi.

The Paris agreements in fact provided for North Vietnamese presence in the south. They gave no guarantee for the territorial integrity of South Vietnam. They encouraged Hanoi to take over the south. North Vietnam would accept only the total surrender of the Saigon government and army.

The most important thing, the President went on, was the Constitution. So long as the Constitution (actually written totally by Americans) remained, Thieu said, South Vietnam could survive. North Vietnamese promises, even signed promises, meant nothing. Hanoi never intended to respect the sovereignty of the south. Only with the support of the Americans could South Vietnam hold back the Hanoi military threat.

So the Americans promised military and economic aid in exchange for Thieu's signature on the Paris agreement. It was understood that America would not intervene in Vietnamese internal affairs. Richard Nixon personally sent a letter to Thieu stating that if Thieu signed the Paris Accords, not only would aid to Saigon continue indefinitely, but the United States would also come to the aid of Saigon if North Vietnam threatened to take over the south.

Thieu never thought a man like Henry Kissinger would deliver the South Vietnamese people to the fate of being overrun by the North Vietnamese. As he had said many times before, don't trust foreigners, trust only yourselves. This statement now was proving to be true.

Every day, Thieu said, the Chinese and the Soviet Union send more and more aid to Hanoi. But—and what should his listeners think about this —aid to Saigon from the west had been falling. Obviously, the Communists now were richer than the Saigon side. The Communists continued to send tanks and guns and men to the south in an attempt to overrun the Republic of Vietnam.

If only the Americans had intervened as they had promised, South Vietnam would not be losing district capitals and provincial capitals and would not be faced with the possibility of losing the national capital. Because of the lack of American aid, Saigon did not have the means to protect the Central Highlands, and Ban Me Thuot, Pleiku, and Kontum fell.

Here Thieu managed a straight-faced lie that provoked some nervous glances and querulous muttering around the room: "What happened in the highlands was the decision of leaders in Military Region II." He had apparently conveniently forgotten his fight with the commander of the region, General Phu, who had argued against Thieu's own order to abandon the highlands.

The orders of the Military Region II leaders to retreat led inevitably to the loss of Military Region I, insisted Thieu.

When the Americans withdrew from South Vietnam in 1973, the Saigon armed forces lost 63 percent—well, at least 60 percent—of their military power. (This, incidentally, was the same figure used by General Dung when briefing the Politburo three and a half months before.) It lost tanks and artillery because the Americans refused to replace equipment lost by the Saigon military. And why didn't the Americans help? They had promised to help.

Thieu had stood up the Americans and prevented them from interfering in Vietnam's business. Perhaps, he intimated, this was the reason Washington was no longer providing its promised support.

The President paused, biting his lip, apparently fighting back tears.

He had given the entire background now, holding back nothing, Thieu said. Stick with the President, he told his audience. Pleiku and Kontum could not be recaptured. They were lost causes. Quang Ngai was lost, and Hue had to be given up because it was surrounded. Those were facts the Vietnamese now had to live with.

But now, from this moment, Thieu said "we" are going to regroup and "we" are going to retain III Corps (around Saigon) and IV Corps (the delta south of the capital), even though others made stupid mistakes in the northern sectors. Soldiers should not lay down their arms; they should keep their weapons. Anyone making the mistake of abandoning outposts and surrendering would lose everything.

In front of the National Assembly, Thieu now stated, switching tacks quickly, "I announce my resignation as President." Tran Van Huong, the Vice-president, would immediately take over as President.

As something to remember him by, Thieu said, he would accept all responsibility for everything that had happened in South Vietnam during his terms as President, good and bad alike. He hoped that the new President could take over authority according to the Constitution and that the Congress and armed forces would accept Huong as Commander in Chief. He wanted to avoid political disturbances.

"Good-bye, my friends." But Thieu was not finished.

Thieu said his own flesh was worthless. But he was sorry for every casualty in the war, more sorry for the individual soldiers even than for the lost territory. He hoped success could be restored again.

In 1968, when the Paris talks had first started, Thieu had fought the inclusion of the Viet Cong in the talks. He had resisted talking at all. He had said that those who listened to Americans would be lost. Now, Vietnam was about to find out what he had meant back then.

In 1972, Thieu had his life threatened and it was suggested that he leave Vietnam. [He did not say by whom, the but indicating to the listener that American officials had issued the alleged threats when Thieu balked at signing the Paris accords.] Thieu was not worried about threats, only about safeguarding Vietnam's independence.

Now Thieu [who had just agreed to take all blame] was afraid history would judge him as the scapegoat for the loss of South Vietnam to the Communists. He could say only in his defense that Americans forced him to sign the hated 1973 Paris agreements, those agreements that were so traitorous to South Vietnam. Now the United States had gone to the extreme of cutting off their assistance which they had promised under those same accords.

There was a time in 1954, 1955, when perhaps North and South Vietnam could have gotten along. Then the Americans came and promised help and aid, and Hanoi and Saigon had split, had become enemies. Thieu said that with aid equal to that received by Hanoi, Saigon could win the war.

"But you [Americans] have not given us the aid you promised us. Given that aid, I would not be afraid of the Communists." So, Thieu declared Americans had cut down aid, saying they did not want to support Thieu. So, the President said, I'll go, all right. He would leave office while the army still was struggling along, however weakly. If the Americans did not want to support South Vietnam, let them go, get out; let them forget their humanitarian promises. But stabilization could come about only through arms.

From here, Thieu rambled on for another half hour, repeating himself. Later, some who watched him on television questioned whether he was sane at that moment. He waved his arms, pounded his fists, and rambled in a—for him—wild display. From his audience there was not a sound. After a painful 90 minutes, he stopped talking, turned, and kissed Vice-president Huong, and strode off. It was his last public appearance.

Among his people, there was a general sign of relief at Thieu's resignation. The most reviled man in the nation had stepped down, ending the need for a coup and, they hoped, providing the possibility of a negotiated settlement of the war. For that now was the best that could be hoped for. Thieu was right: there was no way to recover the lost territory. North Vietnam was in full control there, and there were few who felt the Saigon army could protect much, if any, of what was left of South Vietnam.

Even Graham Martin was relieved at Thieu's resignation, although he was totally surprised by the announcement. Martin now believed, fully, that the Communists would have to negotiate.

Huong, who, according to cruel jokes, had died 10 years before, was clearly incapable of handling any serious government business. On the thin knife edge of senility and a physical wreck, Huong was a definite non-starter. This alone, the pro-Saigon optimists felt, was a point in their favor, because bargaining Huong away in negotiations with the Viet Cong or Hanoi would be no loss at all to Saigon.

A second point bandied about by Martin and others who felt that peace talks now were inevitable was the Communist belief in "face." Communist diplomats both inside and outside Vietnam were telling Americans and others that Hanoi had no wish for a military victory. Rather, they said, Vietnamese Communists wished to win the war by political means. Automatically, the pro-Saigon optimists believed, this meant negotiations, a coalition government with Communist participation, and a try for an eventual power grab by the Viet Cong.

The optimists, however, had not been reading the propaganda from the other side. It is true the Viet Cong and Hanoi both had promised negotiations—but only if Thieu *and the Thieu supporters* ("the Thieu clique" in Hanoispeak) were removed from the Saigon government.

The first hint of trouble came within hours of the Thieu resignation. With the Viet Cong delegation at Camp Davis still working on its statement to the press, the office of General Duong Van (Big) Minh, an unabashed candidate for presidential appointment, issued a press communiqué of its own.

Thieu's resignation, it said, was all well and good. But Huong, a firm Thieu supporter, was unacceptable as a new Saigon administrator. The entire cabinet was made up of Thieu appointees, and was therefore unacceptable. There still was no one in the upper branches of the administration who favored directly implementing the Paris Accords, which in effect called for a coalition government.

But the definitive, meaningful answer to the question of whether there would now be negotiations came 20 hours later in a Radio Hanoi broadcast of the text of a newspaper editorial. Stripped of its rhetoric, the 600-word editorial made two points: that "Thieu and Huong differ in nothing," and that the United States had to end all military involvement in Vietnam immediately, specifically meaning that Hanoi was demanding an end to all U.S. military aid.

> Thieu and Huong differ in nothing. The former is a fascist militarist and the latter is a reactionary civilian traitor. Both are anti-Communist and have been opposing the homeland and the people by stubbornly continuing the war.

This statement was about the most important public pronouncement by the Communists during the offensive, until the final few days. Analyzed by those who understood and could cut through rhetoric, the short editorial from the North Vietnamese Communist Party newspaper *Nhan Dan* meant:

• The entire Thieu government would have to resign as a precondition to negotiations, and a new President with no recent ties to the Saigon government would have to be appointed;

• U.S. military aid would have to be ended immediately, and the American military establishment in Vietnam evacuated immediately;

• American ships standing off the Vietnam coast "under the guise of protecting the evacuation of Americans" would have to leave. "There is no difficulty or obstacle for the total withdrawal of American military personnel in civilian guise from South Vietnam";

• U.S. diplomats could remain in South Vietnam, but there must be no "interference" in the internal affairs of the nation.

The radio broadcast was written off as propaganda by most of the American establishment and as an unacceptable demand by the others. Cynics and the uninterested pointed out the contradiction: that the United States was being asked on one hand to help get rid of the entire Saigon establishment, while on the other to end its interference in Vietnamese affairs.

Graham Martin was largely unimpressed, and was on the side of those who believed the broadcast was so much propaganda raving.

A CIA man in the U.S. Embassy became curious about a repeated statement by the Viet Cong and North Vietnamese during the previous month or so. The Communists were saying publicly there would be "no interference" with an American pull-out.

The CIA man questioned not only whether Hanoi meant this, but also what effect, if any, evacuation of Vietnamese now under way might have on the guarantee. Radio Hanoi and the Viet Cong delegation in Saigon were blasting the air and sea lifts of thousands of Vietnamese, and the American felt that the implied guarantee of a safe American evacuation might not hold true if Vietnamese were along for the ride, so to speak.

As always, such matters went through Graham Martin. The CIA man thought Martin would refuse to act on the request for more information, but the Ambassador suprisingly promised to act. He sent copies of various North Vietnamese and Viet Cong statements on the subject of American evacuation to Washington, and asked the State Department for an analysis.

In Washington, an official who is as yet unidentified took up the issue at the highest possible level for Americans—with the Russian Embassy in Washington. A day later, more or less about the time Thieu was resigning, the Soviets came back with a definitive answer. First, the North Vietnamese had assured the Russians they meant what they said. Orders had been issued not to try to prevent in any way a withdrawal or evacuation by Americans. Second, Hanoi made it clear that although public statements would continue blasting the evacuation of Vietnamese to the United States, Hanoi understood Washington's desire to evacuate its "henchmen" from South Vietnam.

Such evacuation, the Soviet Union told State Department officials in Washington, would not be held against the Americans. Specifically, it would have no effect on the standing orders to let Americans leave in peace from South Vietnam.

A cable to this effect, with the highest rating of reliability, was sent to Saigon, classified "eyes only" for Martin.* The Ambassador kept it in his

---

*In Washington, the cable was less secret, and the Communist response to the American question was apparently well known. Acquaintances in the U.S. military and State Department sections concerned with Vietnam in April 1975, both in Washington and military command headquarters at Hawaii, have said independently that the pledge was common knowledge. Although U.S. officials in Saigon certainly were aware of the pledges made over Radio Hanoi, no one knew of the Russian confirmation, so far as I could determine.

own files, allowed no one to see it, and told no one of its content. He was the only known official in Saigon to know the official Hanoi pledge to let U.S. citizens and South Vietnamese government and military officials leave in peace.

Keeping the cable was just another example of Martin's secrecy. Allowing some of his staff members to know its contents could have cooled much of the anxiety in his Embassy, among those American officials who believed the evacuation could become a target of Communist gunfire at any moment. But it was not in the Ambassador's character to put out such information, even with limited distribution. Hanoi's assurances were in fact a propaganda point in favor of the Communists. And Graham Martin would certainly not give them any points at all.

Martin had his problems, to be sure. Among them was the already growing resentment both from home and from the Philippines about the evacuation of Vietnamese. Almost a week into the stepped-up evacuation program of Vietnamese officials, there still was no permission from Washington to allow refugees into the United States.

The curious bureaucracy that is the U.S.A. was at fault. The Immigration and Naturalization Service was jealously guarding its right to allow aliens into the country. President Ford, the State Department, and the Justice Department all had ways around the INS, but for various political reasons had chosen so far not to use them.

There was already a growing resentment among many Americans about the possibility of having a large number of Vietnamese descend on the United States. The country was in a recession. There was 8 percent unemployment nationally, with a much higher rate in the cities, the almost certain gathering places for most of the refugees. The Vietnam War had never been particularly popular, to understate the case, and even if it had been, there was this stereotype of the Vietnamese as a crafty, cheating, grasping prostitute or black marketeer, who was in the final analysis probably a Communist anyway. Everyone "knew" the Vietnamese hadn't really fought the Communists; only the G.I.'s had done that. As for those whose lives were probably endangered—Thieu, the cabinet, the generals—there was not a whit of sympathy. These were people who had profiteered while 55,000 Americans died on the battlefields. Corruption, it was well known, was Vietnam's most important product.

If the Vietnamese were not yet going to be welcomed into the United States, they were certainly not being welcomed to the Philippines. Lifted into Clark Air Base north of Manila, the Vietnamese went into tents on the U.S. base in what was, all things considered, a fairly decent refugee camp.

It didn't take Filipino officials long to start complaining. And their complaints and questions about the refugees were hardly met with optimistic answers from U.S. officials. Like Martin, the Embassy hierarchy in Manila was unable to give any assurance to the Filipinos that the refugees would soon be taken out of the Philippines to the United States. Officials went to great trouble to intimate that the Philippines was a stopover for the Vietnamese fleeing the war zone. But Manila was getting more and more edgy by the day. Its leaders had this nightmare of being shackled with tens of thousands of Vietnamese refugees, hardly something the Philippines needed.

Graham Martin knew what was right, in his own heart. He never considered stopping the flow of Vietnamese out of the country. Martin believed in the blood-bath theory with a passion, and he had no intention of being stalled by a bureaucracy. In a way, it was strange. Martin on the one hand hoped to extricate the United States from Vietnam slowly, leaving behind a fighting South Vietnamese administration. On the other, he was issuing orders to get out of the country those Vietnamese who could best lead an anti-Communist fight.

He thought he would be damned either way, so he went ahead with what he felt was right.

Now, as Thieu fell, Martin began to lose his tight control. Some of his authority was usurped by the horrified men in the U.S. Embassy and other American buildings around Saigon. His inability to advise or to analyze the Saigon government, they felt, was proof of this. Telling whoever would listen that Thieu would continue in office, just before the President resigned, was specific proof.

And the Ambassador actually delegated some power now. Martin felt that what was left of South Vietnam could be rallied for a stand against the Communists, militarily and politically. He saw a future for himself in Vietnam as a negotiator. He felt the Ambassador of the world's most powerful nation would have an automatic role in any settlement of the problems of a client nation like South Vietnam. In preparing himself for the role of helping save Saigon from Communism, he gave his senior members of the Embassy council powers to run the evacuation, among other things, under his general guidelines.

The results were unimpressive. Some Central Intelligence Agency people left their local agents in Vietnam and shipped out large numbers of bar girls. The U.S. Information Agency abandoned much of its Vietnamese staff, despite promises of evacuation. The Embassy itself left many people ticketed for evacuation. The military had given conflicting evacuation guidelines to all other U.S. agencies. And Americans in Saigon were free, those venal enough, to turn corruption around and rip off hundreds of Vietnamese who were desperate to get out.

Indignity began to run rampant with Thieu's resignation. There were few in Vietnam who were not guilty of it during the last 10 days of the Vietnam war. Those who hoped to maintain some semblance of dignity often lost it as those around them lost theirs. One of those who maintained dignity was a little old lady, name unknown, at Tan Son Nhut air base.

Tan Son Nhut was where the evacuation—itself undignified—was under way. There were two evacuations. One was the more or less overt one of Americans and their dependents, high-ranking officials, Embassy employees, and so on. The other, more or less covert, was being run, fittingly enough, from the compound of Air America, the CIA-owned airline. There, for example, the cutthroats who worked in the Phoenix program were being loaded aboard planes and flown to the Philippines.

And the Vietnamese newsmen and their families were leaving via Air America, for an unknown reason. The Embassy considered this group of people highly endangered, because they were mostly intellectual and because the press had—under orders—opposed the Viet Cong. In fact, most of the newsmen leaving were employees of American companies, and none, so far as anyone knows, were on the CIA payroll or under CIA influence.

Brian Ellis, chief of the Columbia Broadcasting System's Asian division and a former Saigon bureau manager, had by osmosis turned into the leader of this tiny part of the evacuation. Brian and CBS were insistent that all CBS employees who wanted to leave should do so, and when the Embassy finally came around and offered a hand, Brian was thankful enough to run the evacuation for all American-employed Vietnamese newsmen and their families.

Brian worked from a quota each day. Embassy officials would tell him how many seats on departing aircraft would be available, and Brian would—from lists drawn up by the American news bureaus—figure out who would leave each day.

On this day, two days after the resignation of Thieu, he was to have 49 persons for the C141 flight to the Philippines. Those named showed up at Air America, were processed quickly, and were put aboard a bus for a short ride to the plane. Along the way the bus halted, waiting for Vietnamese police to get off the plane so that the illegal evacuees could rush aboard, and the plane could be sealed up and take off.

As they waited, Brian counted the bus passengers . . . 47-48-49-50. Wait a minute. One too many . . . 48-49-50, again. Quick, whispering search for the extra illegal passenger trying to get out of Vietnam. Narrowing it down was hard, because no one on the bus knew everyone, what with all the families leaving with the familiar-faced newsmen.

Finally, Ellis and some of the others on the bus decided the probable illegal was a little lady perched, straight back and staring ahead, on a seat close to the front. Well, nothing he could do now. The bus was already rolling toward the plane. One person more or less was no big deal anyway, since most of the passengers would be sitting on the plane's floor.

At this point the bus doors opened. Everyone was to make a dash for the plane, scurrying to stay ahead of the police, who would be back for more payoffs if they saw more people loading on the jet they had just checked out. Everyone scrambled off the bus and ran for the plane, clambering aboard through the back door. Everyone, that is, but the little lady. She waited until the last person got off the bus. Then, in not too great a hurry, she gathered about six pieces of hand luggage and started for the plane.

Ellis followed her, the object being to get her aboard without causing a fuss. As he reached for the small of her back to boost her aboard, the lady spread her arms and grasped both sides of the door frame on the aircraft. Ellis nudged her a bit, muttering for her to get on, hurry up, quickly.

She resisted, pushing back now, starting to yell in Vietnamese, "No, no." Ellis didn't want a scene. He pushed a little harder.

Just then the bus driver came pounding out of his vehicle and made for Ellis shouting. "No, don't put her on. She isn't going. She's my baggage handler."

There were a lot more tears than laughs in the evacuation, though. Many of those leaving were crying. They would never see their country again. They faced, in the main, very uncertain futures. And they were leaving behind family or friends. The leaving was voluntary, but heartbreaking.

Those who left were aware that for the rest of their lives they would seldom eat their own food, rarely read their own language, and never return to their own nation. They might become citizens of another country, but most of them wanted to remain Vietnamese. Few had traveled, and they had little idea of what life "out there" was all about. Those who had been abroad had always been happy to return.

Now they would have no homeland to which to return. Most of the old people chose to remain, which meant that sons and daughters were leaving mothers and fathers, a traumatic experience for the closely knit families of Vietnam. Others were leaving sisters, brothers, even children.

Most of all, they were leaving the security of having a place to come back to. Often, literally on an hour's notice, families had to choose which of their lifelong possessions they wanted to take—so long as they could fit into a shoulder bag, the only baggage allowed. Few had money, at least the kind of money needed to sustain themselves in the United States. Everyone knew it cost a lot to live there. A family could eat very, very well on a dollar a day in Vietnam.

Everyone was leaving someone behind, by chance or choice. Therefore, everyone felt guilty about leaving. In the best organized sectors of the evacuation, there were tears. One became hardened to the personal tragedy. But one never got used to it.

For those not thinking of immediate evacuation, the game was finding a settlement of the war. Already, with Thieu out of office 12 hours, there were two main schools of thought.

Graham Martin and French Ambassador Jean-Marie Merillon and the pro-Thieu parties of the National Assembly and Senate and the Vietnamese military felt that with Thieu out, the "nationalists" could sue the Communists for peace, based on their interpretation of the Paris agreements, which they took to mean a three-sided election committee for national balloting, or at worst, a temporary, appointed coalition government.

The anti-Thieu Congressmen and Big Minh and left-wing women's liberation leader Mrs. Ngo Ba Thanh and right-wing priest Father Tran Huu Thanh agreed that Thieu's resignation solved nothing, because the rest of the administration remained the same.

The Communists agreed with the second faction, even if there was nobody in that faction who was particularly acceptable to them as more than a tool to be used and then discarded. "This is a Thieu administration without Thieu" and therefore totally unacceptable, Communist radios throughout the Indochina peninsula trumpeted.

But there was hope. The contingency order went out from Hanoi: no more direct military attacks until further notice. Troops were to stand fast. Not an inch of territory was to be given up, but units were to go on the offensive only if it appeared that the ARVN troops in their sectors showed they were pulling back, or preparing for counterattacks.

Plans still called for victory in 1976. Victory in 1975 was a distinct possibility, but the Saigon enemy was still capable of resistance. Tremendous gains had already been made. All soldiers should stand ready for action, ready for the thrust for final victory. But for the moment they were to halt and take the breather to consolidate behind the lines.

Troops continued to pour down the highways towards Saigon. Especially from the north and the northwest of the capital, division after division moved toward Saigon. For the most part they rode in trucks and on tanks.

A major crossroads was Dong Xoai, 35 miles north of Saigon and "liberated" in the Phuoc Long province battle in January, seemingly so long ago. At Dong Xoai, units crisscrossed back and forth from the Ho Chi Minh trail, from the Cambodian border area and from the northeast, where winning divisions from the highlands, Da Nang, and Nha Trang poured in toward the capital.

Truck after truck came through Dong Xoai, a former U.S. Green Beret camp once overrun by and then recaptured from the Viet Cong in one of the first major battles of the American war in Vietnam. The specialized vehicles alone were too numerous to count. They carried bridges, towed artillery, and loaded gasoline for the tanks and other trucks.

A three-day convoy came from the mountains. It was called Truong Son ("long mountain range") after the highlands area through which it had passed on the way to Saigon. It had mostly new trucks from North Vietnam, carrying enough ammunition, its drivers said, for a month-long battle.

The siege of Saigon was being set up, even as orders called for an effective cease-fire. From Dong Xoai, hundreds of trucks headed west toward Tay Ninh and Binh Duong. Others headed east to Highway 1 and the Bien Hoa area. Hundreds of others kept going past Bien Hoa down little-known roads toward Vung Tau and the sea.

The ring being placed around Saigon was not a perfect circle, but it was tight. Even to the south, where there was supposedly a modicum of ARVN control, the Communists were moving into position to cut off Saigon. There were skirmishes along Highway 4, the so-called rice road to the delta. But most of the movement was behind the Communist lines. Air Force planes couldn't find the convoys, for the most part, and even if they had there weren't enough South Vietnamese fighter-bombers left to do much about the Communist build-up around the capital.

Within artillery range of Saigon, engineers laid a bridge in less than a day. It carried dozens of tanks and big guns and scores of trucks across the Dong Nai River to attack Saigon from the west.

Approximately 10 divisions ringed Saigon and were poised for attack. Another half-dozen divisions stood behind them, ready to plug breeches in the assault line. To the north and northeast, the Communists were within about 20 miles of the capital. To the southeast, they were about 30 miles away, and Vung Tau was essentially behind the lines, although still under Saigon control. To the west and northwest, the front line was about 25 miles from Saigon. To the south and southwest, there was much troop shuffling just after Thieu resigned. But large concentrations of Communist troops were within 30 to 35 miles of the capital.

For five days after the April 21 Thieu resignation, the North Vietnamese army did little more than maneuver. It would have two choices by April 26: attack Saigon or sit back for the wet season, following the original plan, and cut Saigon's land and water supply routes in a tight siege.

PRELUDE TO SURRENDER

Tu De, Quang, Vuong, and On (the only names they went by) were Comrade Pilots from Hanoi. They had flown MIG fighters against the Americans and all had more than 60 combat missions to their credit. They had come to Da Nang within five days of the fall of that northern South Vietnamese city to look at the captured planes there and to learn how to fly them.

Nguyen Thanh Trung had come to Da Nang after bombing Thieu's palace. After four days of careful questioning sessions, he was ordered to show the four North Vietnamese pilots how to fly the A37 jet, the smallest but best jet attack bomber in the Saigon air force. About 20 of the planes had been left behind at Da Nang, and virtually all of them could fly after little maintenance. Those who had done ground repair service for the Saigon air force now were performing the same service for the newest branch of Hanoi's air force.

The A37 was brought to Vietnam by the U.S. Air Force and then given to the Saigon flyers. A main advantage is its size—it stands shoulder-high and can easily be maintained by the smallest of the small Orientals.

Nguyen Cao Ky called it a plane for ladies, not fit for hotshot flyers. It is subsonic, was originally a trainer, and retains the side-by-side seats it had when it took an instructor and a student to fly it. Most of its American pilots disagreed with Ky and found it an ideal plane for the Vietnam War, specifically because it flew slowly and thus enabled the pilot actually to see the target he was trying to hit.

It is no Phantom, that is for sure. It could not even fly from Saigon to Hanoi for a bombing raid, so limited is its range—another reason the Americans wanted to give it to the Saigon forces. It was simple for a jet, which is not to say that it was exactly a Model T in simplicity. It flew often, well, and accurately. It could be used only in daylight and not in a severe rainstorm. It carried no defenses against other airplanes, such as air-to-air missiles.

Trung had flown the A37 often in training and quite a few times in actual combat. He found it easy to teach the North Vietnamese pilots to fly. Two and sometimes three missions were all that was necessary for Trung to go along with each of the North Vietnamese. The plane handled well, and the experienced Hanoi pilots had flown supersonic jets so often that they considered the slower A37 was a piece of cake.

Trung had never been a teacher before, but there was no problem here. Trung had no idea the day after Thieu resigned just why he was training Tu De, Quang, Vuong, and On, except that since the planes belonged to Hanoi now, there had to be pilots who could fly them. The four men and the Communist officers overseeing the training asked many questions about Saigon air force tactics, angles of attack, formations, and so on. Trung thought they were routine questions and answered them.

The day after Thieu resigned, the five pilots, including Trung, clambered into separate planes. A North Vietnamese officer went along with Trung, supposedly to watch what was happening. Trung felt the man was his watchdog, to make sure he did not defect again, back to Saigon. For a full day, the five planes practiced formation flying and made dry bombing runs in areas west of Da Nang and over the sea. Trung knew the North Vietnamese had no attack bombers and assumed the four wanted to learn how it was done.

Which of course was the truth, if not the whole truth.

The bombs were kept in Thailand, and only a few of them were there, because of the political ramifications. The few Americans who knew about their being in Thailand called them the ultimate weapons in the black, almost sick, humor that U.S. Air Force officers affect.

They were one of hundreds of secret, destructive, nonatomic weapons that came out of the multibillion-dollar research and development funds given to the U.S. military in the mid-1960's to prosecute the Vietnam War. The purpose of the programs was to discover how to kill more of the enemy with fewer losses to American forces. Bombers with no pilots, better hand grenades, microphones that looked like animal feces, and the CBU55 were just a few of the results.

The Cluster Bomb Unit that took the numerical designation 55 was one of the more awe-inspiring weapons to emerge from the R&D programs. It is like a super napalm bomb, although jellied gasoline is not a part of the CBU55. The bomb has three main compartments (thus accounting for the CBU designation) filled with propane, a secret blend of other gases, and the explosive.

The CBU55 had never before been used in warfare, although U.S. air crews had tested the weapon on American ranges. A small stock of the bombs was held in Thailand as a contingency, although until April 1975, few Americans had recommended their use.

In early April, one of the CBU55's was flown from U Tapao air base to Saigon and then trucked to Bien Hoa air base. The weapon remained under technical American control, although it was now in the hands of the Saigon air force. The day Thieu resigned, Major General Homer Smith, the senior American military officer in Vietnam, gave the official go-ahead to Saigon to use the weapon.

Officers chose Xuan Loc as the target. Saigon forces were in retreat, and the Communists were moving toward the capital city after breaching its outer defenses. There was almost a feeling of betrayal at the high command in Saigon, as if the Communists somehow had cheated by defeating what had been a gallant stand and an initial defensive victory at Xuan Loc. The cheaters, the North Vietnamese Army, now would be punished for their perfidy in winning what clearly was the most important battle of the anti-Communist war.

A single C130 transport plane was ordered to stand by on the morning of April 21. The CBU55 was loaded aboard, and the four-engine Lockheed workhorse lifted easily from the two-mile concrete runway at Bien Hoa, turned slightly right, and settled into a climb toward Xuan Loc.

At 20,000 feet, the plane circled Xuan Loc once, and again, the pilot watching. The clamshell doors at the back of the plane opened on their hydraulics and the whine and roar of jet-driven propellers filled the inside of the plane. A pallet lying on the ball-bearing casters on the floor of the plane was untied, and two safety-belted crewmen pushed it toward the back of the plane.

A drogue parachute opened as the pallet and the CBU55 hit the air, guiding the pallet into an upright position but not slowing its fall noticeably. Pallet and bomb hit the ground, the wooden platform breaking into match-sized fragments. Parts of the bomb exploded, hurling the various sections far and wide, as much as 120 yards from where they had hit. The gas canisters opened, and the propane and the secret blend wafted out over a four-acre area.

Frantic North Vietnamese forces on the ground hurled themselves into ditches, behind trees, and onto the dirt and bushes as they realized that a bomb had hit in their midst.

With a strangely muffled roar, the timed explosions from various bomb compartments went off, igniting the gases and unloosing a huge fireball. The force of the ball rocked the C130, more than five miles from the center of the explosion, although most of the distance was straight up. Awed crewmen watched.

Not many of the 250 or so North Vietnamese troops killed died from the flames. The CBU55 was designed to kill by robbing those on the ground of oxygen. The huge fire ate oxygen at a rate much faster than that of napalm and searched it out, elsewhere, literally sucking air from the lungs of anyone on the ground and within a quarter of a mile of where the CBU55 hit.

Not long after the new bomb was dropped, a small Saigon air force plane outfitted with crude reconnaissance equipment flew over Xuan Loc and took pictures of the new victory. The film was developed at Tan Son Nhut laboratories, and showed stunned Communist soldiers picking up bodies from near the CBU55 explosion. Experts said about 250 men were killed. Most of the bodies, it appeared, had not been touched. They showed no signs of burns. But virtually all had fixed expressions of wide-eyed horror on their faces.

Within two days, Radio Hanoi was blasting the use of the new weapon, which they described accurately, presumably from reports of their spies at Tan Son Nhut and Bien Hoa. The Communists said South Vietnamese use of the new weapon was a last-ditch attempt to win the war. It wasn't. It was an attempt to punish the winning North Vietnamese army by inflicting the heaviest possible casualties.

It was Saigon's last serious attempt at an offensive. No more of the bombs were shipped to South Vietnam; those already there remained unused and were later shown at a Saigon "war crimes" display, and most U.S. military officers agreed the CBU55 had no part to play in the final days of the Saigon government.

There were other weapons even less well known by those not directly involved in the final days of the Saigon government. Some of them were new to the Vietnam war zone, used in the last, frantic days of fighting. All were new to the South Vietnamese forces, although some had been used, rather unsuccessfully, by the Americans.

C130's dropped several 15,000-pound bombs against North Vietnamese troop positions for the first time in the war. The World War II blockbusters—nicknamed Daisy Cutters because they exploded sideways and right along the ground—had been used by Americans only to blast instant helicopter landing zones. Big helicopters dropped "phu-gas," a homemade napalm composed of gasoline and Ivory Snow soap flakes.

And because it was clear that there would be no B52's coming to the aid of Saigon, there was an attempt to turn the C130's into bombers. Whole pallets of 500-pound bombs were pushed out the backs of cargo planes, and the explosions as they hit the ground sounded amazingly like the giant warplanes. They had the same approximate effect on the war: none. In general, the Saigon air force was unable to pinpoint important concentrations of North Vietnamese soldiers, and, like the B52's, most of the clustered bombs dropped in areas where the only likely casualties were monkeys and the ecology.

If secret weapons could not win the war, politics were coming not much closer. There was almost no support for Tran Van Huong, although Huong himself and a small coterie believed the old man might be able to rally some support and effect a settlement of some sort. But there were four other men much more important. Each had his own beliefs, and the undignified squabbling among them and their supporters killed the slight chance of a dignified, negotiated end to the Saigon government.

Graham Martin, Jean-Marie Merillon, Senate President Tran Van Lam, and retired General Duong Van Minh had separate but sometimes intertwining ideas as to how to end the war. Each was ready to act immediately, but like actors in some slapstick movie, they ran into one another. No one knew all of what the other three were doing, and none of them fully supported any of the other three. A person unconcerned with the tragedy could compare them to the Three Stooges Plus One.

It was Huong who held out the first olive branch to Hanoi, as the four main characters struggled backstage to get into their costumes. Huong ordered the Foreign Ministry in Saigon to issue a public appeal to Hanoi to open peace talks, immediately and without precondition. Specifically, the Huong statement said, Saigon was ready to form a coalition, under terms of the Paris agreement. It called for an immediate cease-fire and asked for resumption of talks in Paris. All this would, if accepted by the Communists, reverse by 180 degrees the American-supported policies of the Thieu government.

The statement specifically noted the resignation of Thieu. The former President had opposed any coalition, although the Paris agreements specifically had called for one. Thieu's policy was no cease-fire until Saigon had reclaimed all land overrun by the Communists. And it was Thieu who had canceled the Paris talks in 1974.

Hanoi did not deign to answer the Huong appeal publicly, and the major powers to whom it was formally addressed also refused comment. North Vietnam and the Viet Cong simply repeated their demands for Huong's political head, because he led a "Thieu regime without Thieu." The giant step backward by Saigon was therefore totally rejected, with the Communists continuing to push for more and more in the way of a settlement.

There was no Communist call yet for a surrender. The public position of the Hanoi and Viet Cong administrations was that "a personality who really loves peace" might bring a negotiated settlement to South Vietnam. Two demands were not negotiable: all U.S. military forces must be withdrawn from Vietnam and Saigon must introduce an administration "totally un-identified with Thieu."

Hanoi, as always, was pressuring the losing Saigon side to give up more and more. Some described it as a crowding diplomacy. The Communists had followed it throughout their 43-year history in Indochina. It meant never giving an inch, while pressing home every slight diplomatic or military gain. Seldom, if ever, did the Communists give up anything in negotiations. Never did they retreat on their public demands. Like a tennis opponent who crowds the net, the Communists allowed their diplomatic enemies no room or time to maneuver between shots. The ball stayed in their court only for instants and never once bounced. The American B52 strikes on Hanoi were the closest thing to a lob shot capable of defeating them, and there were no B52's around in 1975.

Two days after his unheeded, almost unnoticed appeal for a cease-fire and a coalition, Huong said he would step down in favor of someone else, so long as the National Assembly provided a quasi-constitutional vote authorizing such a move.

This left Lam and Big Minh in the running. Lam, by the American-written Constitution, was next in line for the presidency. He was the Senate chairman and a former Foreign Minister (he was the actual signer of the Paris Accords), and was fairly well respected by the Americans. Lam's trouble was that he was identified with Thieu. A gaggle of mostly rightist and pro-Thieu politicians supported his bid for power. Graham Martin, a believer in the Constitution, supported him. Few others did.

Big Minh, amazingly, still had much popularity in Saigon, which was about all that was left of the Republic of Vietnam in the last 10 days of the war. If there was a people's choice for President, he was it. Minh was the hero of the 1963 coup against President Ngo Dinh Diem and had been prevented by Thieu from running in the 1971 elections. Minh had much support on the streets. There was a problem with his inherent indecisive-ness, and it was said that his IQ was in two figures. But he appealed to two factions: those who wanted a President unidentified with the Thieu regime, and those who felt that perhaps the people could be rallied for a final defense of Saigon. Merillon, the tiny French Ambassador who often was mistaken for a Vietnamese, supported Minh.

Merillon and Martin met separately with Huong, almost passing each other in the circular driveway of Independence Palace. Merillon argued that Huong must step down. He intimated that his government had put forth feelers to Hanoi and the Viet Cong through their delegations in Paris. The Communists, Merillon said, would under no circumstances talk to Huong. A man unidentified with the Thieu government (read Big Minh) should take over the government.

Martin pushed the pathetically old and crippled President the other way. The Constitution was important, the southern-born U.S. Ambassador argued. There should be a constitutional amendment if someone outside the regime was to become President. Otherwise the document should be followed, which meant that Tran Van Lam should be the next leader. Martin hinted that Lam might resign or decline, in turn, and eventually an acceptable man might be found down the line of succession. But form was important. Martin argued that the Communists should not be allowed to stampede the Republic of Vietnam into unconstitutional extremes.

Martin and Merillon talked, argued, and tried to dissuade each other. Martin was unwilling to take action other than that ordained on paper. He would not pull out the U.S. military without an order. He would not close down his Embassy. There was a favor, however, now that the French ambassador mentioned it. Merillon agreed to smash in a hole between the French Embassy and the American Embassy compounds to help Martin evacuate a few hundred people secretly, so that those surrounding the U.S. Embassy in panic would not see the evacuation.

On April 26, Huong said publicly that he would step down if the National Assembly authorized the naming of a successor and if there appeared a reasonable chance that peace talks might open after his departure. Martin's advice had been ignored.

If Martin would not leave, and if Merillon could not leave because of the 10,000 French in South Vietnam, others were not so inhibited. Air Force planes and chartered jets from Australia, Canada, Britain, Italy, and other countries flew into Tan Son Nhut to get their embassies out.

Few nations could look back with pride at their evacuation. British Ambassador John Bushnell, upper lip fixed stiffly, refused to take his Vietnamese staff (coolies, he called them in a conversation with British newsman John Pilger, who quoted him in his book *The Last Day*.) After all, old chap, they didn't have exit visas or passports, you know.

The Australians, with a left-wing government in Canberra, refused to take even the most committed of their Vietnamese employees and secret agents. An Australian journalist managed to convince several embassy employees of the seriousness of the position of several of the Vietnamese and a very few were smuggled out. Others were left behind. This was a country that had fought in Vietnam, had compromised thousands of persons, but now apparently wanted to forget its previous commitments. The Australians halted a "baby lift" of already-adopted orphans after Hanoi protested in general terms about the "forced evacuation" of Vietnamese children.

Taiwan, the Republic of China, with claims to being a nation of the free world, left behind almost everyone but the Embassy staff. Taiwan had more agents in South Vietnam than any other country. Many were Chinese volunteers who had merged with the Vietnamese population to provide intelligence from the country. Citizens of Taiwan worked in anti-Communist jobs ranging from schoolteacher to newspaper editor, forming a strong infrastructure of opinion-forming propaganda against the Communists that would earn death sentences under most Communist regimes. Viet Cong and Communist Chinese death squads had assassinated many of the Taiwanese agents, in effect proving their value to the anti-Communist cause. Taiwanese officials left Vietnam without any prior notice and with little attempt at removing its endangered, committed agents or nationals from Saigon.

The American airlift of U.S. citizens, their dependents, and "endangered" Vietnamese picked up daily. On April 24, there were 24 evacuation flights, mostly C141 jets carrying about 250 persons each. On April 25, there were 26 planes, and on April 26 there were 31. Although a few commercial airlines had stopped flying into Saigon by now, China airlines, Air Vietnam, and Cathay Pacific continued to fly daily. The two French airlines—Air France and UTA—increased the frequency of their jumbo jet flights.

Ships also were pressed into evacuation service by the Americans. Commercial ships under contract control of the military were diverted from their more routine duties and began carrying out people instead of cargo. Vietnamese were packed into ship containers and driven through unsuspecting checkpoint police, loaded on the ships at the Saigon port of Newport, and taken down the Saigon River toward the Philippines.

At other points, the gate guards were not so unsuspecting. Martin authorized payment of bribes—much of it from a $12.5 million slush fund in the Embassy—to police at the Tan Son Nhut gates to get Vietnamese smoothly past the guards and into the evacuation staging areas. Those helping out in the evacuation found it took about $20 to get a carload of Vietnamese into Tan Son Nhut. Estimates of the amount of bribes paid to airport gate guards alone in the last 10 days run to about $50,000. Bribes of a much higher amount were paid to high-ranking Vietnamese officials so they would close their eyes to the technically illegal evacuation. Other Vietnamese demanded as their price for closed eyes and mouths simply their own evacuation and that of their families, a request usually honored by the Americans. At least $250,000 and probably about $500,000 was paid in outright bribes in order to evacuate about 75,000 persons through Tan Son Nhut.

It was, upon reflection, the ultimate Vietnamese snub of the Americans. Coming to Vietnam in a real if arguably misguided spirit of wanting to help, they now had to buy their way out.

The war had not stopped, although it had slowed almost to a standstill. One place it was still very much evident was at Bien Hoa, the biggest base left in the hands of the South Vietnamese. The war here came in whistles and whooshes, the most feared sound in the world for most residents of the nation. Artillery shells and rockets slammed into Bien Hoa in ever-increasing numbers.

On the morning that Xuan Loc fell, the day Thieu resigned, artillery shells had put the runway out of action for half a day, grounding half the Vietnamese air force. Two days later, the shells and rockets were still falling, making a good night's sleep impossible, hitting the odd bomb dump and an airplane or helicopter here or there.

The helicopters now were useless, and the South Vietnamese were not flying them. There were a few U.S. advisers left at Bien Hoa, and they were working frantically on the choppers, trying to get them into the war. But when they fixed them, it became evident that the Vietnamese were not going to fly them. With antiaircraft guns virtually at the edge of Bien Hoa, the pilots and their senior officers saw the helicopters as a means of suicide, but little else.

Advisers were furious, but the Vietnamese stuck by their decision. Most of the Americans left for Saigon and the United States. One, with many friends at Bien Hoa, stayed. He did little work. There was little for him to do.

On April 23, with the attacks on Bien Hoa increasing and the Communist army ringing the base on the ground, the Saigon air force pulled out. F5 warplanes were shifted to Saigon, and the A37's to Can Tho. The pilots were told to take a week's leave and report back for duty at either the capital or the Mekong Delta city. Trucks were gathered to move the bombs from Bien Hoa to the new bases. More than half the strike force of what was left of Saigon air power was grounded by the decision, necessary as it was.

On April 23, three rather unfriendly Americans met a newsman at the front door of the U.S. "Consulate" at Bien Hoa, where little diplomatic work was done but an advisory staff helped prosecute the losing war. Yes, they said, the Consulate was open, but not for routine business. Yes, it would remain open indefinitely. The next day, the Americans were gone and the door was locked. The Americans had fled during the night to Saigon aboard a helicopter, secretly flown in. It was hoped the U.S. flag that they left flying over the Consulate would help prevent panic in Bien Hoa.

A similar operation was under way in the still-quiet Mekong Delta. The Consulate at Can Tho ordered all Americans in from their field positions and sent them to Saigon on the still-open highway. Then, although at least one U.S. citizen was still out in the field and no one could contact him, the Can Tho Consulate closed its doors and the few remaining Americans there flew to Saigon aboard an Air America helicopter. The Can Tho Consulate was larger than the embassies of most other nations. It had more than 60 employees.

The Americans, who had long said that the Delta was the key to Vietnam because so many people lived there (more than a third of the South Vietnamese), now were leaving before fighting began. With the handwriting on the wall, and with a strong push from the military and CIA chiefs in Saigon, Martin was taking no more chances on losing prisoners to the lightning attacks of the North Vietnamese and Viet Cong armies.

Unfortunately, the withdrawal from the Delta was carried out poorly, and many persons who should have been evacuated to Saigon were left behind. Many of these were employees of Air America and the CIA. Because the Consulate staff was incapable of removing these committed Vietnamese from Can Tho and other Delta areas, Air America would have to come to their rescue less than a week later. This, in turn, used up helicopters that were supposed to be available to help out in Saigon and thus resulted in the abandonment of many Americans and others in the capital.

On April 25, the leading Communist in South Vietnam, Pham Hung, asked the North Vietnamese and Viet Cong delegations at Tan Son Nhut airport how long it would take them to make ready for a violent "liberation." Within minutes, a coded message from Viet Cong Major General Hoang Anh Tuan was on its way back to the headquarters of the Central Office of South Vietnam. The high command should not worry about those in Saigon. Everyone at Camp Davis was willing to give his life, if necessary, to final victory. Pham Hung's signals office confirmed receipt of the message, without comment.

French Ambassador Merillon paid a final visit on lame duck President Huong on April 25. Huong told the Ambassador he would step down if consensus could be reached on a successor. That afternoon, leading supporters of Big Minh staged a symbolic, five-minute walk from Minh's villa to the palace. They carried signs demanding that Minh be made President.

Martin visited Huong and Minh, continuing to argue for constitutional niceties. He was listened to respectfully. Huong agreed to resign only if the National Assembly passed a resolution allowing him to pass power to an outsider, obviously meaning Big Minh. Martin was not happy, but did not protest.

Martin had an aide call the Viet Cong delegation at Camp Davis. The Communists refused to speak to him. Despite the rebuff, Martin continued to view himself as a broker, a middleman in the negotiation of a peace between the warring sides. His concern, he told Kissinger in cables to the State Department, was to leave behind a semblance of the Republic of Vietnam that would be capable of defending the non-Communist, or rather anti-Communist, ideology. He remained convinced the North Vietnamese would never launch an all-out attack on Saigon, because they would lose face in the world.

Six miles north of Saigon, three miles off the main north-south highway to Bien Hoa, North Vietnamese troops moved 105-millimeter artillery into open fields just behind tree lines and houses. They had little contact with the population. Those who came out of their homes in Ong Tho village on the Saigon River bank to talk with the "liberators" were told to stay clear of the area. There was going to be a massive battle for Saigon, and these guns would shell the city to dust if necessary. No, they did not know when the battle would begin.

Junior officers from four North Vietnamese divisions moved into areas between eight and 12 miles north of downtown Saigon. There, sometimes moving even in daylight, they contacted underground Viet Cong, most of them members of the almost defunct Dong Nai regiment. The North Vietnamese told the young men and women the attack on Saigon would be ordered soon. The Viet Cong would act as guides. Maps were produced, and the Saigon-area Communists pointed out roads, defenses, and key targets to the officers. Then they moved to the bush to prepare for the coded messages on Viet Cong and Hanoi radio stations that would signal the attack.

While Martin, Merillon, Lam, and Big Minh prepared to sue for peace, the Communists prepared for an all-out attack on Saigon. The Politburo bided its time, hoping such an assault would not be necessary. After all, a surrender would be far better than a city-destroying attack. But political events were moving too slowly in Saigon. With the end of the war and victory in sight, the last thing the Communists wanted was to wait for the monsoons, when many of their troops would bog down and a defense of

Saigon was conceivable. April 28, decided the decision-makers, would be the deadline.

The funny thing was that no one doubted the bravery of Nguyen Cao Ky. He was dealing on the side with the U.S. Defense Department to fly out planes and helicopters so that the Communists wouldn't get them. He had already sent his wife out of the country in the U.S. evacuation. Yet he had credibility as a brave man. For one thing, he had proved his valor by leading a raid over North Vietnam in 1965, and while he had turned back in the face of heavy flak, this point was not too well known.

For another, it was no secret that Ky wanted power. He saw himself as leader of South Vietnam, and during the past few weeks, while calling for Thieu's resignation, he had intimated very clearly that he saw himself in the role of President. He had support in the armed forces, mostly with the air force but also with a large number of generals who were beholden to him for favors Ky had performed while Prime Minister of South Vietnam in 1965–67.

So when he stood in front of 6,000 already rightist Roman Catholics in a slum of North Vietnamese refugees Friday afternoon, April 25, he had his generally accepted bravery and charisma and credibility intact.

Ky spoke of defending Saigon. Those running away with the Americans, he said scornfully, were cowards. Let them go, there's no use trying to stop them; they would be no help to the patriots in any case. But the really patriotic Vietnamese now would organize.

Arms, he said, would be distributed to 500,000 men of Saigon. The women and children would be sent to safety on Phu Quoc Island, considered free of the war for some reason. Saigonese would stand and fight and he, Ky, would be at the forefront. If necessary, the city would be turned into a Stalingrad, which had lasted 900 days under siege. At least, said Ky, people of the world remembered the heroics of the defenders of Stalingrad. No one would remember Saigon if it simply surrendered.

So forget about surrender or evacuation, Ky declared. Be prepared to stand and fight. The distribution of weapons would come soon. Everyone should stay in Saigon, Ky said, no matter what happened. Even if the Communists won, no one should flee. The Communists, at least, were yellow-skinned.

The anti-Communist call to battle to these poor North Vietnamese refugees, the implied anti-Americanism, and Ky's personal magnetism roused the crowd to cheers.

Ky then left for Tan Son Nhut airport to arrange for the evacuation of planes and helicopters for Thailand, and to order up one helicopter for himself to flee. There was no reason to take chances.

Thieu and his wife were busy packing gold and diamonds and jade and antiques, in addition to 16 suitcases of clothes and small personal possessions, and, according to palace sources later, $100,000. Martin was helping out, but with limitations. The U.S. Ambassador had no intention of helping get anything out of the country but the Thieus and their personal belongings. So the President and his wife were working other deals.

Mrs. Thieu had managed to get 16 tons of gold from the Bank of Vietnam, bullying, harassing, and threatening employees and underlings. It was in the palace by the time Thieu had resigned, "for security reasons," but it was starting to look as if it wasn't going to go any further.

She had manifested much of the bullion aboard a chartered Swiss airliner, but the pilots had demanded, under safety precautions, to know what was in the boxes. They found out, asked the Swiss Consulate and the home offices of Balair what to do, and then had refused to fly out the gold.

To the rescue rode Ly Long Than, who had connections of his own. He was able to provide a ship, at the last minute. The *Truong Tinh* was not really up to a long trip, but this was an emergency. Than ordered the ship, with the gold, to France. Thieu could pick it up later. The jade and diamonds, most of it, went in carefully constructed crates on the same ship. Mrs. Thieu supervised every step of the packing.

Then came the antiques. Their value was unknown, but the Saigon museum pieces had to be worth a lot. Unfortunately, many were worthless. Museum employees, no less susceptible to a bribe than others, had replaced many of the objects with copies, selling the real antiques to dealers and collectors. Mrs. Thieu did not know this, and asked Thieu's military aide, Dang Van Quang, for help. Quang had his exile picked out—Canada, where some friends lived. Quang manifested the crates of antiques and copies from the museum aboard a ship bound for Montreal via the United States. Mrs. Thieu trusted Quang to hold the antiques for her.

The Thieus now were ready for evacuation. In a supersecret operation, a U.S. Air Force C118 plane flew into Tan Son Nhut at 3 A.M. on April 26. Thieu had an hour's notice to do his final packing, including stowing the $100,000 palace contingency cash fund in suitcases.* Former Prime Minister and four-star General Tran Thien Khiem had about 20 minutes. U.S. cars drove them and their wives to Tan Son Nhut. The plane took off on a direct flight to Taiwan, whose government had agreed to take the discredited strongmen. There was no departure press conference, no announcement, and no press coverage of Thieu's arrival in Taipei. He was a man in total disgrace.

---

*The figure is based upon what should have been in the fund, according to a palace aide who was abandoned and left in Saigon by the Thieus. Nguyen Cao Ky, in his book on the end of the war, said the cash filled four suitcases.

In his rush to exile, Thieu conveniently forgot to tell some of his associates. One was his nephew Hoang Duc Nha, who was Information Minister between 1972 and 1974, and the man who allegedly became so enraged at Henry Kissinger during a Saigon visit in 1972 that he called the American Secretary of State a son of a bitch to his face. Nha had been removed from the ministry in 1974, partly because of American protests at his high-handedness toward the United States, but largely because of some still-unclear squabble within the Presidential Palace family.

Twelve hours after Thieu's arrival in Taipei, a British newsman received a phone call from Nha. When the newsman, Peter Gill of the *Daily Telegraph*, expressed surprise that Nha had not left with Thieu, Nha at first refused to believe his uncle had gone. When he confirmed it, he made his own arrangements for travel and settled in Arlington, Virginia, where he opened an Oriental grocery store. According to other Vietnamese residents of the area, a Vietnamese boycott of the store was organized and Nha's store failed because of lack of business.

The National Assembly met just after Thieu left. There was still a large faction in the body that felt, as did Ambassador Martin, that constitutional niceties should be preserved, that Huong should remain President or, barring that, that Lam should take over. Lam was no exception to this feeling. He had long coveted the presidency of South Vietnam and now, for some reason, still wanted it.

Martin, with no lack of support among the Vietnamese politicians, was pushing yet another theory, as the Communists closed in and Saigon was on the verge of being leveled. This idea was to keep Huong or Lam (it didn't matter which) as President and put Big Minh in the government as Prime Minister.

Minh himself turned this down several days before the National Assembly meeting, rejecting the premiership in conversations with Martin and Merillon among others. But as the Assembly convened in the old French opera house Saturday, some politicians were still pushing the idea.

There was a feeling among certain individuals, most of them supporters of Thieu, that a reshuffle would bring about negotiations with the Communists. Martin felt strongly about this. Aides to the Ambassador said it was a combination of his southern American belief in strict interpretation of the Constitution and a serious underestimation of the strength, goals, and commitment of the Communists to the winning of the war. Again, Martin was refusing to believe the simple policy statements from Hanoi and Camp Davis that there would be no negotiations with any government composed of Thieu's men.

Senior Vietnamese officials like the Chairman of the Joint General Staff

Cao Van Vien managed to convince the Assembly otherwise. After three hours of *in camera* testimony, several more hours of debate, a repeated demand from Hanoi for action in naming a non-Thieu government, and a promise by Huong to step down in favor of Minh if the Assembly authorized it, the vote was taken. It was 127–0 to allow Huong to name his own successor.

The Assembly deliberations per se were not all that important. But several members of the body wielded considerable influence in Vietnamese political matters. Failure to consult the Assembly would have brought political chaos to Saigon and wrecked the already slim chances at a negotiated settlement.

Word went out to those who were interested—newsmen and diplomats—that Huong would officially step down Monday and Minh would take over. No reason was given for the delay, which would be a fatal one. If Big Minh had taken over the government by Saturday, negotiations probably would have opened, and the Communist attack on Saigon would have been delayed, if not canceled. But the decision to attack the capital now had been made, and Monday was too late for talking.

Nguyen Thanh Trung, Tu De, Quang, Vuong, and On flew five A37 jets from Da Nang to Phan Rang Saturday, hugging the coast and keeping low on the off chance that they would be spotted by U.S. or Saigon radar and attacked. Trung's watchdog was along for the ride. The other four pilots flew their planes alone. They flew in the combat formation of the Saigon air force, taught to the North Vietnamese by Trung.

Before dawn and after dusk Saturday, trucks poured into the Ong Tho village area six miles north of Saigon. They carried rockets and ammunition for 105-millimeter artillery. The big guns and rocket ramps were already in position near tree lines. They had not been spotted by Saigon troops or planes, although they were close to Tan Son Nhut and to the main north-south highway from Saigon.

The last Prime Minister of the Republic of Vietnam, Nguyen Ba Can, packed a handbag and boarded a C141 jet at Tan Son Nhut. He was now just another refugee. Can had an afterthought as the plane pulled up into the cloudy Saigon sky—perhaps he should have been corrupt. He was heading to a new country, an uncertain future, and he had no money.

At the U.S. military headquarters, Pentagon East, an officer was typing a report. Colonel J. H. Madison, U.S. Army, had received an official proposal from the Communists. North Vietnamese and Viet Cong officers had informed Madison's interpreter, an American, that 15 U.S. servicemen involved in negotiations over Americans missing in action in Vietnam could remain in South Vietnam indefinitely. The Communists would guarantee the safety of the 15 from the moment Saigon came under their control. The 15 men could continue their work, laid out under terms of the Paris agreement, and maintain official contact with the Communists in the search for the MIA's. Madison designated the 15 men who would remain and recommended to superiors in Honolulu and Washington that they be allowed to stay, on a strictly voluntary basis. There was no problem finding volunteers.

There was no official invitation to the U.S. Embassy to remain. But official statements made it clear that an official American presence would be welcomed in post-war Vietnam. There was some movement within the Embassy for a small team of volunteer diplomats to stay and maintain the U.S. embassy. Martin sent word down from his office that there would be no such thing. If anyone stayed, it would be he.

Madison's office, through military channels, received tentative permission to remain. The 15 volunteers began gathering files, documents, and supplies. The Viet Cong said that if fighting got heavy, or if the South Vietnamese forces began to kill Americans for the real or imagined crime of abandoning Saigon, the 15 men were welcome to seek refuge at Camp Davis with the Communist delegations.

The war began again Sunday morning, and it was ominous. The least of the problems militarily was the four-rocket barrage that hit Saigon, but it was a signal of the beginning of the end, and everyone knew it. Not a shell or a bullet had been fired in downtown Saigon in three and a half years. The four Soviet-made rockets that hit the capital before dawn Sunday meant that the war was taking a new turn.

Most observers knew exactly what it meant. The Communists were very, very impatient with the time-consuming squabbling in Saigon political circles. The rockets signaled this, but more importantly they showed that Hanoi was willing to attack Saigon. Many had thought there was no chance that the Communists would attack the capital. Graham Martin believed they would not risk the loss of face inherent in winning a military victory in a political war.

The reasoning was wrong. The four predawn rockets made it clear now to all but the most fervent optimists that time was desperately short. Political infighting was a democratic luxury that had no place now. If ever peace was going to come through negotiations, it would have to be now. Or never.

The last Saigon lines of resistance began to tumble early Sunday. At Long Thanh, 20 miles east of Saigon through the swamps of Rung Sat, one of the fiercest tank attacks of the war overran the ARVN tank base. A patchwork defense force of Marines and 18th Division infantry—the heroes of Xuan Loc—held the Communists back at the next-door infantry training center. But that base, too, would fall before the day was out. In an arc from southeast to northeast, only the Bien Hoa air base stood between about 50,000 Communist troops and Saigon.

Highway 4 was cut Sunday, finally and irrevocably. Heavy attacks on outposts in the My Tho-Long An province areas forced the Saigon 9th Division back toward the capital. South and southwest of Saigon, 20,000 North Vietnamese troops were as close as 15 miles to Saigon.

Northwest of Saigon, along Highway 1 to Cambodia, a couple of divisions of North Vietnamese cut the road, pushing back the Saigon 25th Division in two directions—toward the capital and toward Tay Ninh, well away from the Saigon perimeter.

Two companies of the North Vietnamese 9th Division were detached from the southward bound Delta Task Force and moved into Gia Dinh Province. Three miles from downtown Saigon, they ran into the first resistance from Saigon troops—untested militia who did not run but dug in to fight. The Communists, too, dug in, a mile from the main Highway 1 bridge near the American grocery store and a U.S. aid warehouse.

Tran Van Lam, who had failed in his last-minute bid to be President, told an American he would stay in Vietnam no matter what happened in the war. He was Vietnamese, like the Communists, and could find peace with his fellow countrymen. Then he went home to contact friends who could arrange for his flight to Australia.

For the majority of the people in Vietnam, Monday was quiet during the working day. But there was great tension. The end was near and everyone knew it.

The small band of North Vietnamese soldiers dug in near the Bien Hoa highway bridge three miles from downtown Saigon knew the end was coming. These were not reconnaissance troops, or terrorists stirring up trouble. They were the vanguard for the attack on Saigon, which now would come, they knew, probably within 24 hours.

Others of the two companies of infantry had fanned out to the west and had quickly overrun three small villages as close as a mile from Tan Son Nhut. The Saigon militia there had run.

Saigon generals began making their last troop dispositions. The Rangers and the last airborne brigade were put in a fan from south to northeast of

Saigon. It was a pathetically small defense force, outnumbered by more than 15 to 1 if the Communists brought up their full strength in a battle for the capital.

The Communist attackers were setting up front-line positions, testing the ARVN reactions, digging in to provide bases of fire for the other troops, which would move up soon to attack Saigon.

The only four-star general in the ARVN, Chairman of the Joint General Staff Cao Van Vien, boarded his private C47 plane Monday afternoon and flew to Bangkok. More than half the generals in the Saigon army now had deserted their country.

Three rockets hit Saigon Monday. A baby was wounded and a house damaged. Few paid attention to this latest warning. The battle was already shaping up, and Saigonese, no matter what their politics, needed no more warnings that the Communists were ready to fight to take Saigon. More than half the shops in Saigon were "closed temporarily," according to the signs on their doors. From the highest hotel in Saigon, the brand new Palace, five fire fights could be seen against the Saigon skyline. All were small, but highly significant.

The Communists at the Highway 1 bridge three miles north of downtown Saigon got into the U.S. warehouse and fired it. Newsmen rushed to cover the closest fire fight to Saigon in years. Helicopters shot at the North Vietnamese positions. The Communists shot back with mortars. It was small, but exciting. The Americans on the radio were very excited, most of them. This is what they were saying:

> 9 A.M.—Stay out of the vicinity of the Newport commissary. Do not go into the vicinity of the Newport commissary.
>
> 9:30 A.M.—If it continues to deteriorate, we're considering doing something like falling back.
>
> 9:45 A.M.—(from Newport): There's a mild state of panic here. (Vietnamese) civilians are flocking to the port to get out of the area down the Saigon River.
>
> 10:40 A.M.—Traffic is blocked now at the so-called Five-Corners at the city limits. That's about a half mile south of the Newport bridge.
>
> 11:00 A.M.—Newport is closed up completely to traffic in or out now. A U.S. ship evacuation is under way. At least one busload of people and one busload of baggage is blocked from getting in. These are Vietnamese (on the buses).
>
> 11:20 A.M.—Rockets are hitting near the bridge. Now they (the Communists) are mortaring the field to the west of the bridge on the Saigon end of the bridge. There're people in the fields running toward the river. This is too much fun to miss.

At noon, listeners to the Embassy radio frequencies learned what Graham Martin had been doing with part of his time over the last few hectic days and hours.

> Ambassador Tam has a collection of precious objects to give to the Ambassador for safekeeping and needs some packers. He needs about 20 small boxes and a dozen or so large boxes or crates and some quilting. . . . Ambassador Martin has expressed interest in this case. We may want to move him (Tam) out today.

Whoever was on the other end of the Embassy radio pointed out the practical problems of moving out the antiques of former three-star General Tran Ngoc Tam, who became a friend of Martin's when both were Ambassadors to Thailand in the 1960's. Martin may have wanted to help his old friend with packing his bags. But other refugees were moving out smartly, abandoning a lifetime, or rather attempting to pack a lifetime into a shoulder bag.

While Martin and his flunkies fretted about Tam's antiques, other men and women were worrying about their own fates. They were getting precious few answers from other Americans.

The U.S. Information Service Director, Alan Carter, had responsibility for evacuating 215 persons, most of them employees of USIS and their families. By Monday afternoon, he had allowed only 30 to leave. Most of the rest had been coerced into staying by promises that if a final evacuation was ordered, even by helicopter, USIS staff would be aboard.

The 30 who had left by Monday afternoon had gone, for the most part, against the wishes of Carter. A couple of his more independent American employees and associates had put their staffs aboard earlier evacuation flights because, in their view, the end was obviously at hand.

Carter and other USIS officials were convinced that Saigon was settling down for a protracted end to the war, and there was no hurry to the evacuation. All hated to lose their Vietnamese employees, and the Vietnamese were asked to remain on duty.

There were now 185 persons in the main USIS compound at 8 Le Qui Don Street, a couple of blocks from the palace. All were nervous, but their panic was controlled. Buses began to roll up, and the atmosphere eased slightly. Finally convinced of the need to get the very committed Vietnamese staff out of the way of the ever-advancing Communist troops, Carter had decided Monday to let them leave. They were to board the buses about dusk and drive to Tan Son Nhut. Within 12 or 16 hours, they would be aboard flights to the United States.

With the exception of employees of the CIA, those Vietnamese workers for USIS were the greatest potential targets for retaliation by a victorious Viet Cong. The Communists put great stock in propaganda and spent huge amounts of their money on it. They realized full well that the propaganda war in Vietnam had been almost as important as the battlefield conflict. Intelligence and propaganda, both of them often conducted in great secrecy, were keys of the covert war in Vietnam.

For those who believed in a blood bath, the USIS records seemed the obvious beginning point in any Viet Cong search for opponents to wipe out. As the main proponent of the blood bath theory, USIS therefore had a great responsibility to evacuate its employees.

Now, with the buses beginning to load, there was a massive sense of relief.

Big Minh drove to the palace, although it was only a five-minute walk from his house. The President-designate, about to take political power for the first time in more than 11 years, wanted to seem like a leader, not like one of his people.

He met Huong at the door. Together, with Huong on the right and leaning heavily on his cane, they entered the main downstairs reception room. Huong was helped to the podium. He looked for a moment behind the podium to a 40 by 20 foot mural depicting an ancient Vietnamese Council of Ministers making decisions on how to fight invading Chinese.

As Huong opened his mouth to speak, the clouds over Saigon opened and unleashed a downpour. A flash of lightning and an answering thunder quieted the room. It was 5:15 P..M.

At Phan Rang air base, Nguyen Thanh Trung tightened his safety belt and checked to make sure his radio was turned off. He did not know until now whether his "guard" would fly the mission with him. He would not, Trung saw. He glanced out the window of the A37 at the other four planes, all of their engines running. When he learned of the mission the day before, Trung was shocked. Now he was ready. He got a hand signal from a ground controller and began to roll his plane to the top of the Phan Rang air base runway. He would take off first and circle, waiting for Tu De, Quang, Vuong, and On. Trung had no bombs, so he could stay in the air longer, waiting for the other four to make a formation on him.

Minh had sat for hours in his living room with French Ambassador Jean-Marie Merillon Sunday. Over and over he had said to the Ambassador, "What should I do? What would you do in this position?" And over and over, Merillon had said no one could make decisions for Big Minh. He must make them himself.

Merillon and a close aide of Big Minh drove to Tan Son Nhut and were admitted to the Camp Davis compound. They met with a senior North Vietnamese and a middle-ranking Viet Cong officer. Although the men wore military uniforms, they were actually civilians and the effective heads of their delegations to Saigon.

The Minh aide asked the Communists if they would accept a cease-fire. The North Vietnamese officer said they would, if their two conditions were met. The aide asked the man to repeat the conditions, to make sure the two sides agreed. The officer did: total U.S. military withdrawal and formation of a government unconnected with Thieu. The officer could not and would not say whether a government headed by Big Minh would be acceptable.

Sunday evening, after long discussions with his aides and at least one telephone call to Camp Davis, Minh made his decision. He called the U.S. Embassy and asked Graham Martin to come to see him.

Martin sent his chief political officer, Josiah Bennett. Minh was appalled at what he considered the lack of respect to a President-designate by the U.S. Ambassador, but nevertheless told Bennett his plans. Bennett reported to Martin. Then Martin was not so busy any more. He paid a late evening call on Big Minh. The two talked more formally than before. Martin said he was sorry Minh had made the decision, but stated that the United States would comply with his wishes. He asked for a little more time. Minh agreed.

As Huong made his short speech, handing power to Big Minh, the new President went over his notes. Honoring his promise to Martin, he would not announce his main decision.

Minh took the rostrum. The situation, he said rather needlessly, was critical. But the use of force was no solution. Saigon politicians and military men (he said, addressing his words to the Communists) intended no revenge on anyone. There was no reason reconciliation could not be reached. Minh's responsibility, as he saw it, was to seek an immediate cease-fire and to reopen negotiations that would bring the type of peace envisioned, but never realized, by the 1973 Paris agreement.

Big Minh pledged an administration drawn from all parts of the political spectrum. He believed he could form such an idealistic administration and cabinet, capable of talks with the "brothers on the other side," in a very short time. Former Senate Speaker Nguyen Van Huyen would be his Vice-president. Vu Van Mau would be his Prime Minister. Both were recognized anti-Thieu personalities. His only hope was to bring understanding among the people, including the other side. He could promise nothing.

Political prisoners would be freed immediately, Minh said. The quietness and support of the people were crucial to his plans. He called for unity. As to soldiers, they had suffered the most. They had fought to defend the country. Now, they should expect a cease-fire order. But they should not then desert, but continue to carry out their duties and orders.

As for the National Liberation Front, its members should understand that the Minh administration wanted understanding. The two sides should sit down to work out an understanding. To begin with, there should be an immediate cease-fire.

Finally, he appealed to the South Vietnamese to forget about evacuation. Stay and help build the country, he said. If necessary, accept the defeat willed by God.

The speech was obviously sincere and almost touching. But the answer was on the way before Minh asked the question concerning negotiations.

Minh was barely out of the palace and back to his home for dinner when radar operators at Tan Son Nhut airport started to become concerned. Five A37 jets, their blips unmistakable to the trained technicians, were headed toward the Saigon airport. Routine, laconic radio calls went out to the planes to identify themselves. No answer.

The demand was repeated by a now slightly testy radio operator. Still no answer.

Colonel Nguyen Anh Tuan, Saigon's deputy chief of staff for operations for the 5th Air Division and the ranking air force officer at Tan Son Nhut, happened to be in the control area at the time. He was in the process of ordering all air force flights halted because of the build-up of huge, black, electrically charged clouds, when he spotted the planes from Phan Rang. First he saw three, then all five.

Tuan was highly suspicious, because the closest Air Force A37's were at Can Tho, and there was little reason to suspect any would fly to Saigon. He ordered calls to Can Tho and even to Bien Hoa. Those bases answered that their A37's were grounded. Bien Hoa, of course, was closed to all air traffic. And while the radio of one or even of two planes might be out, the chances that five radios in five planes would all be out were too high to calculate.

In the lead plane was Nguyen Thanh Trung, the man who had bombed the Independence Palace 20 days before. His plane was unarmed. His job was to guide the four North Vietnamese pilots on the first live bomb drop of their lives. In attack formation now, the peppy little A37's swept over Tan Son Nhut, Trung leading them just to the left of the main runway, over the main air force parking areas.

There was no practice run. On the first flight over the base, the MiG veterans punched their bomb buttons and a dozen 500-pounders tumbled across the military area.

Big Minh's speech, appealing for negotiations, was being answered. It was 35 minutes since he had stopped talking.

At Tan Son Nhut, thousands of people were first stunned and then panicked. Few had ever been in a bombing attack. Frantic radio calls for guidance on what to do went out on virtually all frequencies. A calm combat veteran in the U.S. Embassy told listeners to his frequency: "Nothing you can do. Lie on your belly and hold your breath." And another: "Lean over, grasp the insides and backs of your legs, put your head down as far as you can. If necessary, prepare to kiss your ass good-bye."

The advice was about as good as any. Tuan had some better ideas, however. He wanted the F5 interceptors scrambled. Once again, the pilots were not in the planes, as required by regulations. But they cranked up the supersonic jets and quickly took off after the A37's. They followed them by radar to Phan Rang, and arrived overhead just in time to see them land. Their guns and missiles useless against the aircraft on the ground, the pilots turned and headed back to Saigon.

And throughout Saigon there was instant panic. Everyone who had a gun started firing. The antiaircraft guns at the palace fired, almost hitting a C130 flying nearby. A large number of military men seemed to realize what had happened, surprising because few actually saw the bombers. Tons of ammunition were shot off into the air in the next half hour.

In downtown Saigon, people "knew" for a certainty that the final attack on Saigon had begun. The shooting sounded like echoes of the Tet offensive of 1968. Cars and motorcycles were abandoned in the middle of the streets as citizens took shelter in shops and houses, and behind walls and trees. The fusillade continued for what seemed like an eternity and actually was about 25 minutes. A 24-hour curfew was declared.

Saigon politicians had waited too long. Minh had not publicly announced his main decision. The attack on the airport was the signal for the final attack on Saigon. More than 100,000 North Vietnamese troops and their Viet Cong guides saddled up, ready to level Saigon. From now on, it was to be warfare with no holds barred.

Minh had made up his mind the day before to bow to the Communist demands for a U.S. military withdrawal. When he summoned Martin, he told the Ambassador as diplomatically as he could that he expected the Defense Attaché's office closed down immediately. He listened to Martin's protest, and gave him one day to organize the evacuation and another day to carry it out. Martin said he didn't know whether it could be done that quickly. Big Minh said the Americans had all kinds of evacuation plans and they should immediately implement the one concerning DAO.

Martin won a 24-hour delay. The final evacuation of all U.S. military personnel would be completed by Wednesday, April 30. Minh would not announce the decision until April 29.

The new President's aides were not so sensitive to the feelings of Martin and the United States in general. Within hours of the Minh-Martin meeting Sunday night, they informed several newsmen friends of the decision to close down the American military effort in South Vietnam. American newspapers Monday morning reported Minh had ordered the end of the U.S. advisory effort in Vietnam, 19 years to the day after the United States took over the training of South Vietnam's military from the French.

One aide was lawyer Tran Ngoc Lieng, and he had another mission that Sunday night, more important than leaking stories to western newsmen. Lieng drove to Tan Son Nhut air base and, flashing a letter from Minh, entered the tightly guarded military side. He drove directly to Camp Davis, near the back of the air base and not far from the main runway. His route took him past an American-built gymnasium, a PX, and an officers' club, used by the peacekeepers of the ICCS in their many idle moments over the past two years.

Under orders from Senior Colonel Vo Dong Giang, the effective commander of Camp Davis, the gate guards let Lieng enter the Saigon headquarters of Hanoi and the Viet Cong.

Lieng was picked for the role of go-between because he had once been the law partner of Nguyen Huu Tho, who now was the head of the National Liberation Front. When the men split up in the late 1950's, their political views were not so different, and they still were not. But Lieng was trying to oppose pro-American regimes through the system. Tho was merely trying to crush the system.

Lieng was well known in Saigon. An open supporter of the so-called third force, he had survived with remarkably little time in jail, considering his politics. His most famous case, when he was in both the American and Vietnamese limelights, came in 1968 when Lieng defended and President Thieu prosecuted and jailed the man who had run second in the 1967 elections, Truong Dinh Dzu.

He met with Giang, a member of the NLF Central Committee, and other senior Communists Sunday night and Monday, passing word on the talks to Minh by telephone. By Monday afternoon, he was able to report in effect a failure—the Communists had raised their demands to include the dissolution of the Saigon armed forces. The appointment of Minh as President of an essentially neutralist regime and the departure of the Americans were former demands that had been met. Now there was another. It was, of course, the demand for unconditional surrender.

Lieng stayed at Camp Davis all day Monday. He understandably was not informed in advance of the coming bombing attack. But when the Viet Cong and North Vietnamese officers headed for the bunkers, they took Lieng along with them. He stayed there for the rest of the war, and there heard Minh surrender Saigon to the Communists.

On Monday night, after the bombing, Viet Cong spokesmen telephoned the major news agencies in Saigon. They said that there was a new condition for peace—"the dismantling of the coercive Saigon war machine." In other words, the decision had been made. Saigon would have to surrender militarily, or the North Vietnamese Army would fight for the capital. And there was little chance they would lose.

...THANK YOU

Darwin Judge and William McMahon had joined the Marines at just about the same time, the type of "boys" the gruff Marines like to turn into men. High-school sportsmen, clean livers, high-school graduates, the two had thrived at Parris Island boot camp. Tough Marine sergeants could say that they wished they had more recruits like these two.

They had been together most of the time during their first four-year tour with the fighting force that styles itself as America's toughest. They even liked the Marines and regretted that they had missed the fighting in Vietnam, when two Marine divisions had fought and had taken the heaviest casualties of all the U.S. services.

Well, they were in Vietnam now. They were part of an augmented U.S. Embassy security force, whose sole duty was to protect the evacuation of Americans against the thousands of Vietnamese who were desperate or angry enough to try to break it up, either to go themselves or to prevent others from going.

For 10 days, Judge, McMahon, and a small security force had stood around Tan Son Nhut's Pentagon East, directing traffic and checking the papers of those trying to get into the former theater and bowling alley, where thousands now went to prepare to leave Vietnam. The toughest part, they said, were the damned cars. People drove to the airport in their cars, then abandoned them. Judge and McMahon were trying to keep the driveway to the evacuation point clear. Most Americans said they were going to the evacuation point "just for a minute." Seldom did they come right back, as they promised.

They drew night duty on April 28. They had little idea of what was going on around Saigon, since the tactical radios they carried were on a U.S. frequency and had little news from outside the capital. They didn't know Bien Hoa had fallen. And they had no idea that the politics of the Vietnam War were going to end their lives.

Bien Hoa fell about midnight. Few people were surprised. The base was an oasis, surrounded on all sides, cut off even from Saigon, a rare occurrence. About four divisions of North Vietnamese soldiers shelled the base unmercifully from dark on, then overran it. It was just that crude and that simple. The tank and small infantry force at Bien Hoa fell back toward Saigon, but through the countryside, because the roads were blocked. They fought in retreat, trying desperately to reach the capital. Many made it.

Two divisions attacked Vung Tau, the only seaport in Saigon hands. One contingency plan called for the U.S. evacuation to go through Vung Tau by ship. The huge American fleet assembled for the evacuation—largest in Vietnam waters since 1972—was based off Vung Tau. With the town under attack and its fall only a matter of time, probably hours, that contingency was scratched.

A barrage of rockets fell into Tan Son Nhut just after midnight. The bombing had been the signal for the attack. The first few rockets, guerrilla weapons, marked the beginning of the final assault by the largest Vietnamese army ever assembled in one place.

North Vietnam had 24 divisions in all. Three of them, officially training divisions, were in the north. The bulk of the other 21 were around Saigon. All, if necessary, would attack the city. Saigon had an effective force of the equivalent of a division.

The bombing attack had closed the gates to Tan Son Nhut airport, an instant reaction by the Saigon Air Police to most incidents around the base. There were about 5,000 persons at the theater and bowling alley waiting for evacuation flights. A few planes took off Monday night with a couple of thousand people. The others waited, slept on the floor, and ate the free sandwiches put together assembly-line fashion by Hank Dorrity, an American who ran a popular U.S.-style restaurant downtown.

It was clear to everyone that evacuation was very, very close. Make that almost everyone. Graham Martin wasn't convinced. CIA chief Thomas Polgar and the head of the U.S. military in Saigon, Major General Homer Smith, certainly thought it was time to declare a "hard pull," which in the jargon of the day meant a final complete helicopter evacuation.

Martin had two thoughts, not necessarily contradictory, in his mind. First were the 10,000 or more persons who would be expecting to leave in the final evacuation. Second was his personal belief that the United States should not be forced out of Vietnam. In his office, he still had the autographed picture of himself and Richard Nixon. Nixon had said he would not be the first American leader to preside over a losing war. Martin had no intention of being the Ambassador to lose the war.

The CIA man and the general thought otherwise. The contingency plans said specifically that 10,000 persons could be lifted out by choppers. And to them, lives were more important than the semantics of winning or losing. The mission council met at half an hour past midnight, early Tuesday morning, April 29. It was, to understate the case, a lively two-hour discussion.

Virtually everyone in the room wanted Martin to declare full evacuation immediately. Martin refused. There was no need to cut and run yet. Figures produced by the participants showed that there were 3,000 persons awaiting evacuation, most of them at Tan Son Nhut, but many also at other locations, like the Embassy itself and USIS, where the 185 still waited, their buses now back in the motor pool.

Martin said 6,000 persons a day had been leaving for the past several days. With an all-out effort from the Air Force, he said, 10,000 could be taken out in the next 24 hours. There would be no final evacuation ordered.

Because of the opposition to his plans, however, he gave in on one point. American presence in Vietnam was to be whittled down immediately. As soon as working hours began in the morning, officials in charge of the operation would order a cut to the bone in the numbers of people left in Vietnam. Only those essential, really essential, to the U.S. operation would remain. Even newsmen would have to cut down their staffs, come what may.

Most members of the council wanted a final evacuation ordered immediately. Martin, operating with the unique knowledge that North Vietnam had promised not to target the evacuation in any attacks, disagreed. At 2:30 a.m., he adjourned the meeting for four hours.

At Ong Tho village north of Saigon, where gunners had been waiting for orders for two days, the artillery pieces turned away from downtown Saigon, to the west. At 4:10 a.m. the Ong Tho guns and perhaps 50 others like them opened up on Tan Son Nhut.

Judge and McMahon fell within the first 10 minutes of the barrage. Judge took a direct hit from an artillery shell. McMahon, about 25 feet away, died just as instantly, although his body was not torn apart like that of his companion. Smith ordered a team out to recover the remains.

The shell that killed the two Marines was one of only a few that were off target. In general, the Communists were keeping their pledge not to interfere with the evacuation. Except that by pounding Tan Son Nhut with artillery fire, they were preventing the takeoff or landing of U.S. Air Force planes.

At 6:30, with most of Saigon now awake from the roars of guns at Tan Son Nhut, Martin reconvened the council in the third-floor conference room of the Embassy. He was, according to those at the meeting, obviously dazed at the turn of events. Polgar and General Smith put it to him bluntly: final evacuation had to be ordered immediately. The attack on Tan Son Nhut meant the airport was closed, and there was no telling whether it ever would open again for evacuation planes. Therefore, it had to be a helicopter evacuation, and the sooner the better. The choppers were on stand-by, and could begin flying within an hour.

And the tree behind the Embassy, sitting where the big helicopters would have to land, had to be chopped down immediately.

Martin was angry at the challenge. Airplanes had flown through shelling attacks before. The shelling attack was not as serious as the members of the council were saying. The "fixed-wing evacuation" was to continue. He would leave it up to the Air Force to decide when to start landing again, but there was no reason to panic. There was no reason even to think about a helicopter evacuation yet. The United States could not and would not be panicked into an all-out evacuation. The tree would not be chopped down. Chopping it meant a commitment to final evacuation, and Martin said he was not ready for that; it was not necessary.

Smith and Polgar were outraged. As forcefully as possible, sometimes speaking through clenched teeth, just barely keeping their tempers, they tried to tell Martin the facts. That only two Americans had been killed was luck of the first magnitude. Thousands of people were stranded at Tan Son Nhut, under fire. There was no way planes could land. The Air America compound, right across the road from Pentagon East, was a shambles from the shelling. Several planes and helicopters had been lost there. The Vietnamese Air Force was being blown apart by the shelling.

The CIA station chief summed up the feeling of most in the room. Martin was deluding himself. The situation was very, very serious. Saigon was totally surrounded. The only base still in government hands was Tan Son Nhut. The final assault on the city itself could and probably would come at any moment. Martin's insistence on an airplane evacuation was wrong. It would probably cost lives.

Finally, said the CIA man, if Martin did not believe what others were telling him, he should go to Tan Son Nhut to see for himself.

Martin perked up, challenged. Fine, he said, that was exactly what he would do. While Smith and Polgar sat grim-faced, George Jacobsen tried to dissuade Martin from the trip to Tan Son Nhut. Martin said he would go, in his own car. Jacobsen, who also believed evacuation by helicopter should be ordered immediately, was trying to protect Martin. But he realized that only by seeing the destruction at Tan Son Nhut would the Ambassador come around to this line of thinking. Jacobsen left the meeting to arrange some security for Martin. A carload of Marine security men and a couple of extra Marines in Martin's car would have to do for the guard. Smith, whose command was at Tan Son Nhut, went with Martin.

As Martin's car pulled out of the Embassy compound on the way to the airport, the CIA man commandeered some Marine guards, fired up the chain saw, and cut down the tree.

Jacobsen monitored Martin's progress toward Tan Son Nhut minute by minute. Listening to three or four other radio frequencies at the same time, he radioed constant updates of information and rumors about mobs, incoming fire, and Saigon troop displacements. For the moment, the ARVN posed the greatest danger. Many of its members were bitter at the obviously imminent U.S. withdrawal and aid cutoff. There were rumors that Saigon troops would try to stop the evacuation.

The trip to Tan Son Nhut went smoothly. Slowly, Martin's car went on the main road on the civilian side of the airport, between Pentagon East and the Air America compound, past the main terminal building. He spoke not once, but those with him said he shrank noticeably. Apparently appalled at the destruction, danger, smoke, and flames, it was as though he could not believe his eyes. The car turned around and headed back to the Embassy. It was 10 A.M.

One hundred and eighty-five Vietnamese at the USIS offices at 8 Le Qui Don were nervous. They also were tired, dirty, even hungry. The C rations they had eaten for the last three meals were far from satisfying. What they needed was some soup for breakfast.

Trai Quoc Quang was a bright 30-year-old Chinese woman, a secretary for a senior USIS executive officer, Kenneth Jackson. Quang was nervous. She had watched all but five of the USIS headquarters employees leave Vietnam. A few of her friends had also left Vietnam. But Jackson asked her to volunteer to stay, with the promise that she would leave in the final evacuation by helicopter, if not sooner. An eight-year USIS employee, she had reluctantly agreed.

She was nervous because the end was obviously close. She wanted to go to the United States. Her long association with USIS had convinced her of a

coming blood bath, and she believed herself marked for death when the
Viet Cong took over. She wanted to join her friends in the United States.
But events were clearly not moving in her favor.

She had been slated to leave the day before, but with Tan Son Nhut
under a bombing attack her bus had not even left USIS for the airport. She
and the 184 other Vietnamese citizens who were to leave had stayed all
night at the USIS building. With no actual agreement to do so, some of the
Vietnamese stayed awake at all times to make sure the Americans did not
sneak out while they slept.

Now, once again, her boss assured her of evacuation. The rumor was
spreading that the helicopters were going to be called in, probably in a
matter of hours. USIS boss Carter, she knew, had been at a series of Mission
Council meetings. He returned now, about 9 A.M., looking haggard. He
said nothing to the Vietnamese. He went straight to his office, called in
most of the remaining Americans, and shut the door.

Quang grew more nervous. The short meeting ended. The Americans
told the Vietnamese no facts, but again there were reassurances that
everyone would get out. There was no panic, among either the Vietnamese
or the Americans.

Nguyen Van Duong also heard the rumors about a "hard pull" evacuation
that morning. Duong was on guard duty at a U.S. apartment house, now
mostly abandoned, at 192 Cong Ly Boulevard. The building was owned by
the Number 5 man in the Viet Cong hierarchy, Trinh Dinh Thao, who
collected a massive rent every month from the U.S. government through a
middleman.

Duong was one of a large force of the Embassy Guard, a mixed bag of
former mercenaries and retired ARVN soldiers who acted as gatemen at all
U.S. installations and at many homes of U.S. officials. Duong and the 1,400
other "mission warden office guards" had received no promise of evacuation, and most would not have taken the chance of leaving their country.
They knew they had little chance of economic survival in the strange
country that paid their salaries.

But there was the rub. The United States had not paid their salaries. The
reason was that U.S. officials feared that if they paid, the men would leave
their posts, opening Americans to attack from the Communists or embit-
tered Vietnamese. On April 28, the day before mission warden Steven B.
Bray and his deputy George C. White III had promised to pay the guards
within 48 hours. As Duong heard the rumors of imminent evacuation, he
decided there was a good chance that no Americans would be around after
the 48-hour deadline had passed.

Duong headed for the Embassy in an attempt to find Bray. As chief of one section of the loose union maintained by the guards, he felt he had the responsibility to try to get the pay for his men. They worked hard for their $80 a month, he felt. And he debated asking for termination pay—about $400 each, on an average. He decided he would ask for termination pay. At the Embassy, Marines barred his way. They refused to let him in the compound and they said Bray was not in the grounds, and they didn't know when he would be back.

Duong next went to 28 Tran Qui Cap Street, the U.S. hiring hall for Vietnamese employees. Others, he was pleased to see, had the same idea. Perhaps 25 to 30 off-duty Embassy guards had showed up to ask for their April salary before the Americans left.

At the Civilian Personnel Office at 28 Tran Qui Cap Street, Harold F. Oakes was working. Actually, the assistant security man was doing little more than waiting for word on the evacuation. His office was a safer place, with better communications than his home, not too far away at 190 Pasteur Street.

Oakes told the off-duty guards he didn't know anything about the late pay. In any case, there was nothing he could do. It was not his department. Duong and his friends became a little more insistent. Alarmed, Oakes said he was leaving. Duong, backed by his friends, said he couldn't go. Oakes would stay until the pay had been received. Oakes pointed out that the impolite word for such action was kidnapping. Duong said the impolite term for what the U.S. mission warden's office was doing to his group was screwing the Vietnamese.

Oakes changed tack. He made a telephone call to the Embassy, or at least said he made a call, to get details on the pay. Bray and White, the paymasters, were busy, Oakes told Duong and the guards. The best thing was for Oakes to go to the Embassy, get the money, and return to pay off all the guards. Duong said they wouldn't allow that. Pay first, then leave, he said.

They argued the Catch-22 back and forth, Oakes saying he could not pay without leaving, Duong saying Oakes could not leave without paying. Finally, after many conferences in Vietnamese, the guards gave in and freed Oakes. He left promising to return soon with the money. Apparently caught in the mess of the final evacuation, he did not return. The Americans left owing about $840,000 to the 1,400 employees on whom they had depended for personal security. The debt was doubly cruel. On the day of the evacuation, the Americans burned millions of dollars that had been brought into Vietnam specifically to pay bribes and termination pay.

When Duong and his fellows realized they had been tricked, they were saddened. But when it came time for them to report for duty, they did so. Duong spent the last hours of the war guarding the abandoned Communist-owned and U.S.-rented building at 192 Cong Ly. He ended his last duty about 10 minutes before the North Vietnamese Army arrived to secure the building.

For four hours, U.S. Embassy officials, acting on Martin's orders, had been telephoning U.S. offices, apartments, homes, and hotels. Their message was that there was to be a "drawdown" today, April 29, to put the U.S. community in position for a final evacuation, if and when one was necessary. Americans were ordered, politely and firmly, to prepare lists of persons who would be leaving on the next-to-last evacuation, the drawdown.

The Americans—and other concerned foreigners—were told to prepare one handbag and stand by for further instructions. When planes could be landed, they would be coming in quickly, in record numbers, and even the rough formalities required for departure up to now would be dispensed with for those leaving. The time of the beginning of the drawdown evacuation would be given later. It probably would begin in the afternoon. The indications were that the shelling on Tan Son Nhut was tapering off. On Martin's orders, the Embassy staffers told everyone they called that Tan Son Nhut was open to traffic.

Martin arrived back in the Embassy from his Tan Son Nhut trip looking a physical wreck. His secretary was near tears when she saw him. Martin said little and went to his office. Within half an hour, he had gathered most of the Mission Council and ordered final evacuation plans into gear.

Yes, helicopters would have to be used. No, it did not look as if any airplanes could be landed at Tan Son Nhut. Everyone knew his job and should do it. He made no mention of the tree, if indeed he even thought about it.

General Smith, now relieved, got the word by telephone and passed it through military channels to Honolulu. From there, it went back to the ships at sea off Vung Tau. Martin and the CIA station chief fired off their own flash cables to the State Department and CIA headquarters.

Responsible officials began calling back the same offices, apartments, hotels, and homes that they had called during the past four hours to pass the alert for a drawdown. This, they said, was no exercise. Hard pull was beginning. Everyone, repeat everyone, should report to his or her assigned station for evacuation.

On paper, it had looked like a very risky sort of evacuation. Many argued that it was too optimistic as to the numbers of people it could take out. It turned out, of course, to be a nightmare. It did not break down wholly on the human factor. There were serious mistakes in the planning.

First, buses were a main concern. Few of the men assigned to drive the buses had ever driven that kind of vehicle before. A minor problem, but one that bogged down the evacuation in small back streets, where there was little room for maneuvering.

Second, there were to be helicopters, those 25 or so Air America Hueys, to pluck the inevitably stranded few from rooftops. When evacuation was ordered, most of the pilots had gone home. Half the choppers had been lost in the attack on Tan Son Nhut. Most of the others went to the Mekong Delta to pick up the stranded Vietnamese there, who had been abandoned by the U.S. Consulate.

Third was a lack of coordination between the civilians and the military. Even after the evacuation had started, pilots of the Marine and Navy choppers involved thought they would be flying a single mission into Saigon and back. Instead, most flew to the point of exhaustion. Relief crews were unavailable, because of a lack of planning.

Many Americans acted independently of instructions. Others went to assigned pickup points to find them deserted. Officials actually involved in the evacuation planning sent groups of would-be evacuees to the wrong pickup points. There was almost no security for most of the bus convoys.

There were too many people. Martin's procrastination in getting an evacuation organized now would come to haunt the final, hard pull. The evacuation, it was thought, would take 10,000 people. In fact, it would take only 6,000. And there were double that number fully qualified for evacuation, most of them Vietnamese.

The buses, the first stage of the evacuation, marked the first stage of the confusion. Several dozen of the big brown Japanese-made Isuzu vehicles went out shortly after Martin ordered the start of the evacuation. Some of them even went to the proper prearranged pickup points. A few got lost, a few got bogged down, and others were flagged down by groups of Americans as they were on their way to somewhere else.

A radio Jeep with two or three Marines or soldiers accompanied the miniconvoys of two to four buses each. Everything was working catch-as-catch-can, a recipe for failure in Vietnam. After loading, the radio Jeeps received instructions to head with the loads of evacuees for Tan Son Nhut, and buses headed there.

There were radio reports that the gate guards were firing at the buses. There were rumors that Vietnamese guards had turned back carloads of Americans at the gate at gunpoint. In fact, neither of these reports was true, although there was shooting in the air and a generally hostile reception at the Tan Son Nhut gate. Those buses with American drivers who ran

the tense and open gauntlet of asphalt up to the gate got through with
minimal difficulty, although the guards intimated that there might be
trouble if so many Vietnamese continued to show up on the buses.

The 24-hour curfew was not working, and no security force would
enforce it. There were perhaps 100,000 fairly desperate souls in Saigon,
trying to get out of the country before the Communists came in. There
were two chances of getting out. One was with Americans, the other was
through the Saigon port.

These unfortunate people roamed the streets, watching for the first
signs of evacuation. Most had the bus stops firmly embedded in their
memories. Others just watched for crowds of Americans with shoulder
bags. They pleaded, cried, and shoved to get aboard the buses. Many
clutched boarding authorization for U.S. airplanes that now never would
come to take them to the United States. Some few American evacuees felt
sorry enough for the Vietnamese to allow them onto the buses ahead of
themselves. These Americans felt that so long as large numbers of U.S.
citizens remained, the Embassy would continue working to get them out.

They were largely right. Some of the polite and empathetic Americans
had to fight their way into the Embassy later, but virtually all those who
gave up seats on the buses still managed to leave Vietnam with the evacuation.

So where was General Smith, and where were the Green Berets and the
Marines? The question remains unanswered. About 2 P.M., the ARVN gate
guards turned ugly and refused admittance to Tan Son Nhut to a bus that
had Vietnamese aboard. No other bus tried to make it in, a wise decision
since the guards were brandishing their weapons like villains in a western
movie.

There was one gate at Tan Son Nhut. There were, at most, a dozen
Vietnamese guards there. Those dozen men were the cause of most of the
tragedy of the evacuation. There were several answers to the gate problem.
First, the phantom Green Berets, or more probably the Marines securing
Pentagon East, could simply have seized the gate and secured it, allowing
hundreds of buses into Tan Son Nhut, if necessary. With a very small
percentage of the millions of dollars and piasters in the Embassy, the
guards probably could have been bribed. They could have been offered
evacuation themselves, as a small price for allowing the buses in.

No one made any such attempt to open the bottleneck at the Tan Son
Nhut gate. The failure to attempt to reopen the gate was inexcusable, and
the direct cause of most of the later panic in the evacuation at the over-
crowded Embassy. Tan Son Nhut had an open, secure helicopter pad
where the biggest helicopters could land and take out 75 persons at a time.
The Embassy had no such facilities, and smaller choppers were forced to

hover for up to an hour waiting for the chance to land and pick up a few evacuees from the rooftop pad or the small courtyard.

General Smith wanted the evacuation begun at noon, which meant the first Americans would actually leave at 1 P.M., after the flight to Saigon from the offshore ships. Martin, for unknown reasons, ordered an hour's delay. Just as the choppers were making ready for the first flight, to reach Saigon at 2 P.M., a voice came over the command radio ordering the pilots to shut down and wait for another hour. It was never discovered who issued that order.

The Marine security force at Pentagon East was mostly untested in combat. All were shaken by the deaths of Judge and McMahon. All were tired. Most were popping pep pills and were frightened. The Communists had eased the shelling of Tan Son Nhut, but the odd round continued to fall. Most were rockets, inaccurate at all times, and therefore more frightening.

As one of the first busloads of American evacuees pulled up in front of the Pentagon East's new helicopter terminal, a rocket swooshed over. Peter Collins of CBS, a reporter who was pressed into service this day as a sound man for Australian cameraman Mike Marriott, rolled his eyeballs upward and said, loudly, distinctly, and clearly: not now, and not here, please. The rocket exploded about 200 yards away. There were no injuries, but the Marines tensed noticeably.

The panic began around 3 P.M. The helicopters appeared from the east, flying low over Saigon, just north of the center of the capital but visible from almost everywhere. Cobra helicopters, pure instruments of war, were seen darting around. Above the low-hanging clouds came the unmistakable sound of the screaming American jet fighter-bombers.

The crowds began to gather at the Embassy, and the Marines there became tense. At 4 P.M., security officials became highly concerned at the press of people, both inside and outside. Another platoon of fresh Marines choppered in from the 7th Fleet to help in crowd control. Again, they were mostly green troops to this sort of mission, as frightened of the situation as were many of the Vietnamese trying to get inside the building to catch a chopper.

At Tan Son Nhut, the gate guards were firing warning shots at vehicles. Busloads of Americans were turned back by the shots. No one knew whether the guards would actually shoot into the buses. No one wanted to find out.

At the foot of Hai Ba Trung street, just outside the entrance to the Vietnamese Navy headquarters on the Saigon River, the Navy began its evacuation. Shore patrol men with M16's, pistols, and other weapons stood guard half a block away from the river, shooing away vehicles and people trying to get out by boat. The Navy was taking its own, but there was no room for outsiders.

The Saigon port was the only open evacuation point. It was a madhouse. That is where Fred Gulden was.

Gulden was an architect whose company was under contract to the U.S. Agency for International Development (USAID). During his several years in Vietnam, he and other members of his firm had designed and helped build just about everything from roads to highly secret ammunition bunkers. Gulden was a very, very angry man on April 29.

For three weeks he had argued, called, and begged just about every American he could think of. He wanted his Vietnamese staff out of Saigon. But, to his way of thinking, the evacuation was poorly handled from the start. Gulden watched as Americans left, and as the Vietnamese employees watched, trying to control their panic. He was in Vietnam now against the specific orders of his own company and those of the U.S. authorities technically in charge of that company.

Gulden refused to abandon his employees. That was for other people. Morally, he felt, the Americans were totally responsible to and for the men and women who had served the U.S. cause.

So now he was in the madhouse of the Saigon docks, watching the greatest panic he had ever seen. It was not Da Nang, of course, and for that some thanks could be given. But it was chaos all the same. Shots were being fired. Pushing and shoving was the biggest problem.

Gulden's personal secretary tried for an hour to shoulder her way onto a boat, a barge, anything that would float her down the Saigon River to the American ships waiting offshore. At 4 P.M. she gave up.

Gulden stayed to help others. Three men who had succeeded in getting close to a huge ammo barge which now was going to carry people suddenly were shoved from behind by a part of the mob trying to get aboard. They fell into the river. The barge slowly drifted to the concrete pier, swept into the solid piling by the wash of other boats and barges. The three men were crushed to death.

The helicopters, in flights of three, began settling down in what in better days had been a parking lot for the large, well-stocked PX at Tan Son Nhut. A shop where Americans could get their cameras and glasses repaired had been bulldozed out of the way to make way for the choppers. It was not an ideal landing zone, because there was dust and small stones that conceivably could be scooped into the jet engines of the helicopters. But the huge, powerful machines could at least set down comfortably here and pick up people. Which is more than could be said for the Embassy compound, even with Martin's tree gone.

Here, at the PX, the evacuation went relatively smoothly. The 3,000 persons, more than half of them Vietnamese, were divided into groups. There was little or no panic, but much fear. The evacuees were under good self-discipline, and the officials running the evacuation made sure they stayed that way. There was little delay as groups dashed to the helicopters, ducking instinctively under rotor blades that were actually well above their heads. By 3:30, the first choppers were on their way back to the 7th Fleet, under the eyes of fighter-bomber pilots who were just itching to shoot off a burst of gunfire or let loose a bomb.

At the Embassy, and in the streets of Saigon, it was another story.

Nguyen Cao Ky left Tan Son Nhut early in the evacuation in his own helicopter, arriving at the 7th Fleet before most of the American evacuees. An American officer called the palace and informed Vietnam's chief dope dealer and former Thieu military aide Lieutenant General Dang Van Quang that the hard pull was under way. Flashing his identification, Quang got in the back gate of the Embassy, giggling as always.

General Cao Van Vien's replac ment as Chief of the Joint General Staff, Lieutenant General Lam Son, was placed aboard an evacuation chopper. Several Embassy employees reported in with girl friends. The girls got out.

General Tam, whose household goods were a major consideration of Martin the day before, was aboard the evacuation chopper.

Three-star General Dong Van Khuyen, whose brother was a three-star Viet Cong general, was gone.

The daughter of Viet Cong leader Nguyen Huu Tho was flown to Laos and the United States, courtesy of a U.S. charter airline.

Others were not.

USIS chief Alan Carter made sure the last American employees were in the Embassy, after their back-door exit from USIS headquarters half a mile away. Then he telephoned his office with orders.

About half the 185 persons were to get aboard the buses again and drive to Tan Son Nhut, Carter said. The others, the so-called senior Vietnamese employees and their families, were to go to Carter's posh villa at 6E Tu Xuong Street, not far from the office, and stand by for further instructions.

Brigadier General Rhee Dai Yong, counsellor of the Korean Embassy, had shunned evacuation for a week, although friends had told him to leave while the leaving was good. Rhee, who was a former deputy commander of Korean forces in Vietnam, former deputy head of the Korean CIA, re-fused. The Americans, he had said, would take him out if and when the situation warranted. Now he gathered the other seven members of his staff from the Embassy (where he was the highest-ranking man and therefore chargé d'affaires) along with other members of the Korean community in Vietnam and reported to the back gate of the Embassy. A U.S. official told him to stand by. Rhee formed an orderly line of Koreans at the gate and stood by.

A Martin aide—later said to be Deputy Ambassador Wolfgang Lehmann—telephoned Major General Tran Van Hai, former Vietnamese police chief and lately commander of the 7th Infantry Division in the delta, to tell him about the evacuation. After a short discussion, the American told Hai to take about 75 people—mostly high-ranking police officials—to a certain compound. Helicopters, Lehmann said, would pick up the group during the afternoon or early evening.

Kerry Huebeck, brother-in-law of Ban Me Thuot POW Paul Struharik, was in the office of CARE, halfway between downtown Saigon and the airport. He had more than 50 Vietnamese employees with him on the edge of panic. The director of the voluntary organization, Hatcher James, called Huebeck from the PX evacuation site at Tan Son Nhut and told Huebeck he now was in charge of the CARE office. There was no way Huebeck could leave. Had he tried, the employees would have turned into a mob. They wanted their pay, and Huebeck had no money. He began giving away parts of the office—an air conditioner here, a typewriter there—so the employees could sell the items for their pay.

(James had been one of the heroes of the early Vietnam days. He was once a major in the Green Berets and later worked for USAID, where as chief adviser in the capital he became known as the American mayor of Saigon.)

Another Special Forces veteran, now a civilian, told his Vietnamese wife he was leaving. He would try to come back for her. But if he did not, the woman should go to another American friend—who was planning to stay through Communist victory—for money. He left without taking her, without giving her money, and without giving the friend money.

A very few of the newsmen who had given up their evacuation bus seats to panicking Vietnamese now changed their minds and decided not to leave. The rest wanted out. Still secure in the belief that no large groups of Americans would be left behind, they waited for another bus. It came, and the newsmen climbed aboard. The few who changed their minds went back to their offices and resumed banging out the most dramatic story for the American press in years.

The bus with the newsmen aboard, meanwhile, headed for the airport. Turned aside from the entrance by warning shots, the driver headed for the Saigon port known as Newport, just north of the capital. There, he found fighting under way and the gate blocked. As dark fell, he headed for the Embassy.

At the Taiwanese Embassy, there was little activity. All the worse for the perhaps 1,000 citizens of that country who had been abandoned by their representatives. There were more spies for the Republic of China than any other foreign country in Vietnam, and now they were being left behind, in fact had already been abandoned.

Ambassador Hsu Shao-chang had flown out on one of the last China Airline flights a couple of days before the Americans decided to evacuate. He left behind, for example, a newsman who had been brought by the Taiwanese to Saigon to run a Chinese newspaper in Saigon's Chinatown, Cholon. This man, who was fully subsidized by his government, was an agent of Taipei, a committed anti-Communist who had performed his function well. He was simply left behind by the Taiwanese. He was arrested a month later. After two years, he was still in jail somewhere, if he was still alive. His wife and children—who could not get out before evacuation because Saigon officials demanded a bribe for an exit visa and Hsu refused to help—were not bothered by the Communists and left after "liberation."

The tragedy and treachery of the evacuation of Saigon will be told for years. There is no indication, however, that any but a handful of U.S. officials learned any lessons.

Predictions that the Embassy would be the main scene of panic now were borne out. Failure to secure the Tan Son Nhut gate meant that almost all who had to be evacuated in the last day would have to come to the big white building with its fortresslike defenses. Failure of the 24-hour curfew, because of a lack of authority in the streets, meant that a mob of Vietnamese descended on the building. Failure to hand-pick a security force meant that there would be tense moments between the crowds outside and the Marines inside.

A U.S. Marine who wore rank and name tapes identifying him as Colonel Summers told Embassy officials about the growing panic inside the compound. Word came from Martin that everyone inside the walls would be taken out of Vietnam aboard an alleged more-than-adequate number of helicopters. The colonel told this to the crowd at dusk. There was a noticeable calming. The helicopters were coming in, slowly, and lifting out small groups of 20 or so. The line to the rooftop chopper pad moved slowly, but it moved.

Beside the swimming pool sat American Y. L. Ching of Hawaii. A 20-year civilian merchant seaman in the U.S. Navy, Ching was still not worried. He had returned to Vietnam a week ago to take out the woman and children he loved. Finding them in Bien Hoa had been difficult, but he had done it and had taken to the U.S. Embassy, where officials let him stay in the compound and await evacuation. At first, they told him they would bus him to Tan Son Nhut. With that door now closed, he was in the Embassy compound. But he thought he would get out.

Obviously, Ching is of Chinese descent. For some reason, the middle-aged man was unaware of the racism in Saigon among many Americans. He sat for two days in the Embassy compound, with his one suitcase, his woman, and their children. Officials "allowed" him carefully monitored trips to a snack bar to buy some food. They told him to drink from the swimming pool, and he and his Vietnamese "family" did so. Y. L. Ching had lived in some hard places. But he was American. He *knew* he would leave in the evacuation, which after all was for Americans.

Outside the gate stood Bill Smith of Detroit. He had returned to Vietnam to find a girl he once knew when he was in the U.S. Army in northern South Vietnam. He had failed. He had found out about evacuation by accident and had reported to his nearest "station," USAID headquarters. He found that deserted and walked to the Embassy. A Marine guard told him to stand by at the back gate. He stood by.

Two miles from Tan Son Nhut, in a side lane, American Mike Mielke watched the helicopters fly over his home on the way to and from the South China Sea. Mielke was in the front yard of his walled villa painting a doghouse. On a PRC25 radio, he listened to the growing panic of the Americans involved in the evacuation.

Mielke had a strange background in Vietnam for one who planned to stay. Former Special Forces sergeant. Militia adviser. U.S. government employee. But he was staying, along with his Vietnamese-American wife, Misty, and their 2-year-old daughter, Madalene, nicknamed Linny. They had refused numerous offers to leave and had turned aside all requests from friends to help them get out.

Mielke was sipping a rum-and-cola as the evacuation began, careful not to get any of the green paint in his drink. On his roof, he had placed two internationally recognized orange panels to make an X. It meant to helicopter pilots that he did not want to leave. Even now, he had to answer occasional telephone and radio calls begging him to leave.

The gruff former sergeant did not consider the people calling to be his friends any more. Like most of those who chose to remain in Vietnam, Mielke had no time for those who were leaving, and less for those who tried to change his mind. Four nights before, a delegation of "friends" had taken Misty aside and told her to get her "old man" drunk on evacuation day. They then would carry him aboard an evacuation plane before he knew what was happening. Misty told Mielke, and he threw them out.

Most of his friends considered Mielke a fanatic. In 1973 he had thrown over a high-paying but unsatisfying job working for the American government on the question of retrieving the remains of U.S. missing in action in Vietnam. He went to work as a volunteer for Voices in Vital America, a generally right-wing group known as VIVA, which also was concerned with POW's and MIA's. VIVA sold bracelets with names of missing men in order to raise funds, and the bracelets made the group well-known in the United States. With Misty's help and support, Mielke dedicated the rest of his days in Vietnam to doing what he felt the U.S. government was not doing —accounting for every one of the approximately 2,000 Americans whose bodies were still in Indochina.

There had been a family fight when Mielke told his wife he had decided to remain through a Communist takeover to continue the work. It was not that Misty (her name is a translation of her Vietnamese name *Suong*, mist) wanted him to leave. She wanted to stay. Mielke would not hear of it. He wanted his wife and daughter out where they would be safe, in case the expected battle for Saigon erupted. The shouting match ended after a few hours in an embrace. The family would stay together in Vietnam.

Now, as he painted his doghouse, there were no second thoughts. The Mielkes had made their decision, along with all of Misty's family, to remain. As the choppers flew over, just clearing the high-tension wires which ran near the Mielke villa built by his mother-in-law, Mielke waved sardonically. "Good-bye, shit," he said quietly.

The "solution" to the war was starting to take shape in the eyes of those on the outside. The greatest hint was the noontime speech by Big Minh on April 29, the speech that made at least one newsman change his mind, halt his evacuation, and get back to his office to cover the end of the war.

Minh did not speak directly. But the radio carried a report on his words:

> The President said he would do his best [the announcer said] to execute faithfully the Paris agreements of 1973. The agreement has an article which says the United States must stop all intervention in the internal affairs of South Vietnam. Therefore, on April 28, 1975 [the day before the evacuation] President Duong Van Minh has requested the U.S. Embassy in Saigon to close down, and remove [the Pentagon East and] all U.S. personnel within 24 hours, beginning April 29.
>
> The Vietnamese people should remain calm. Our critical situation will surely be solved by peaceful means, and the blood of the people will be saved.

For the careful listener, the report first confirmed the Sunday stories that the U.S. military program in Vietnam was coming to an end. It meant further that Minh obviously was at least in touch with the Communists, trying to negotiate an end to the war somehow.

A three-year political prisoner, student Huynh Tan Mam, had a short interview on the radio. This confirmed Minh's pledge to free all political prisoners "in the shortest possible time."

A solution to the war, in other words, was in sight. Just what form it would take was not entirely predictable, but the latest Communist demand that the entire Saigon armed forces be dismantled could only mean surrender, with at best a coalition government emerging. The war was obviously about to end, and at least one newsman wanted to stay to watch. Four others from UPI who had been on the verge of evacuating but who had given up their seats on the bus decided to remain with him.

Martin remained in his office. He had given his wife 11 minutes to pack his belongings. Unlike Alan Carter, he meant what he said when he proclaimed he was not packing his home.

At midafternoon of the last full day of the war and the last day of American presence in Vietnam, Martin still hoped to make himself useful in arranging an end to the conflict. He still saw himself as a negotiator, a backbone for Big Minh and the anti-Communists. He would remain to help. He would go down with the ship, if necessary.

A newsman called in the middle of the afternoon, still confused as to whether it was actually a total evacuation. There were rumors that a final pull-out had not been ordered, only a massive drawdown. Martin's secretary answered. At first she said she thought a few Embassy personnel were going to stay. Obviously she thought one of them was Martin. Then she said that yes, the evacuation was final. She began to weep and hung up.

Hers were not the only tears shed, although many others were of frustration rather than sadness. As day turned to night, almost bypassing dusk in the manner of the tropics, it became obvious that not everyone who wanted to go was going to get out. There were not enough helicopters.

From Washington, the open line to Saigon hummed with entreaties and demands that the evacuation be ended as quickly as possible with the last Americans boarding helicopters. Martin and his aides pleaded, begged for more time. They ignored some orders to end the evacuation. Fewer than half of the 3,000 people in the Embassy had gone on the helicopters as yet. Many were Vietnamese, but more than 1,000 Vietnamese remained.

Y. L. Ching, still secure in his belief that as an American he would not be abandoned, sat near the swimming pool.

General Rhee told the military officers to change into dress military uniforms. He demanded to speak with an official American. The U.S. official told Rhee to bring his orderly line of Koreans in at the back door of the Embassy and stand by. They formed a new line, inside the gates but still a couple of hundred yards away from the slowly decreasing line of those who were to go to the roof for the helicopters.

Bill Smith stood outside the gate, with no fear that he would not be taken on the evacuation.

Mike Mielke went to bed early and fell into an untroubled sleep. Misty began to wonder whether the family should have stayed, because she could hear the sounds of war not far away. She tossed, turned, dozed fitfully. The decision was made and she was not going to suggest changing it.

General Hai, his former police officers, and their families stood by, waiting for the promised helicopters. A couple of officers suggested that they try to go to the Embassy. Hai said the Americans had promised to send the choppers, and that therefore the choppers would come.

It was the eeriest night of the Saigon war. Perched on a rooftop nine stories above the street, I could see fires burning on three horizons, the effects of the shelling. But it was quiet. Only the helicopters and the fighter-bombers broke the silence. Most of those who wanted to get out had gone—out or fearfully back home. Tan Son Nhut was quiet. The evacuation had ended there about dusk, in total success, with one exception.

The U.S. Marines, who had a tradition of never leaving behind a dead comrade, had forgotten about the bodies of Judge and McMahon. They were still in the cold morgue at the Seventh Day Adventist Hospital.

The greatest fires burned from the northeast. The Communists had rolled down Highway 1 and were fighting for the Bien Hoa and Long Binh military bases. There was little opposition.

Brigadier General Le Minh Dao was still with his 18th Division troops, falling back now toward Saigon. He had perhaps 600 men, no more. They had fought with the general at Xuan Loc and in other battles. They trusted him totally. Dao told them he had received a coded radio message from the Americans advising him of evacuation and asking him to go along. He paused. The troops looked at him, silently. "I am not going," said Dao. There was no cheer, but a warmth for the general that could be felt, he said later.

Several thousand Saigon troops were retreating from Bien Hoa toward Saigon as the Communists pressed forward. For the most part, they were shooting as they came. The fight for Saigon was on, so far as they were concerned, and at night the front-line troops were taking few prisoners.

To Thu Duc, six miles from Saigon, then to Go Vap on the edge of the city, the former Bien Hoa defenders drove, walked, and staggered throughout the night. At dawn there were POW's at Go Vap, where the North Vietnamese tanks from Task Force Delta were assembled after a daylong battle on the 28th.

Dao led his men further east, and got into Saigon without being seen by the Communist forces.

At 10 P.M., the word from Washington was that the evacuation was over. As always, Martin kept the news secret as long as possible from as many people as possible. He kept it secret, for example, from the Marine guards. The colonel who had promised evacuation for all Vietnamese might protest.

As the last evacuation helicopters came in, the word was passed to Americans in the compound to get up the stairs to the helipad on the roof. The Marines now, just before midnight, were ordered to fall back slowly toward the main Embassy building, then make a dash for the roof. A huge iron door, installed earlier by the security chief, was closed and locked, keeping the Americans upstairs separately from those now trapped downstairs.

Almost all of the Americans were gone by the second hour of April 30. Martin, a couple of aides, and some Marines remained.

Martin still had the open line to Washington. He talked with Henry Kissinger, pleading to keep the evacuation going. Kissinger was firm. The President wanted to announce that the evacuation was over. Martin said he wanted to stay, to help Big Minh and South Vietnam. America had a commitment, he told the Secretary of State.

"Now, Graham," Kissinger said, his German accent even more pronounced than usual in this emotional moment. "We want all our heroes at home." Three hours later, Kissinger issued a direct order to Martin to leave.

Quang was one of 55 persons aboard the big brown bus. USIS chief Carter had directed his employees to take the bus to Tan Son Nhut, where the helicopters would lift them on the first leg of their trip to the United States. The woman who had stayed in Vietnam only because of the promise that she would be able to leave with the helicopters, had faith. She did wonder briefly why Carter had left before the USIS staff, but dismissed the thought as disloyal.

The bus headed for Tan Son Nhut shortly after noon. All those aboard were Vietnamese, including the driver. This was in contrast to buses dedicated to taking out Americans, who had even drivers who were U.S. citizens.

Tan Son Nhut at the best of times was inaccessible to most Vietnamese, a security zone because of the war materiel and major military headquarters there. Now, on what was probably the last day of the war, with the Communists bearing down on the capital, with an evacuation under way, and rising bitterness against the American "betrayal" felt by the Vietnamese, no busload of fleeing citizens was going to be allowed in by the gate guards.

After a brief conversation at the gate, which ended with the guards waving their M16's menacingly, the driver turned back. Someone on the bus decided to try Newport. There, it was believed, some ships stood ready to help evacuate Vietnamese. The bus was unable to get within half a mile of the gate because of shooting and confusion.

The next attempt was at the USAID headquarters. Like Bill Smith, the USIS employees found it empty. A few looters were stripping away what was left of the shell of the building.

Quang had a radio. No one had given it to her, but one of the USIS Americans had left it behind before he took the back-door exit. The American she talked to told her to get off the air because the frequency was busy. If the bus could not get into Tan Son Nhut, he told Quang, there was nothing anyone could do to help.

The bus driver headed for the U.S. Embassy. He got within a block, then was stopped by the crowd. He backed up and drove away. A few persons got off and headed for the docks, where at least one managed to find his way out of Vietnam on his own, by boat.

Quang stayed with the bus and as the sunlight faded found herself back at USIS. Clutching her worldly possessions, the fruit of eight years of work for the Americans, she turned pale. In a plastic shopping bag, she had two cheap cotton dresses and a few hundred dollars in American currency. She had nowhere to go, the aunt with whom she had lived having told her not to return to her room because of her association with Americans.

Someone on the bus told her there were some Americans in a downtown office building. Because she had nowhere to go, she went there and found some UPI newsmen. Shaking, she said she had to leave Vietnam or the Viet Cong would cut off her head. The Americans told her they certainly hoped that was not true, because they were staying. They invited her to sit down and have a Coke. She sat; she stopped shaking.

She told her story to two newsmen. One used parts of it in a main piece on the evacuation. Another wrote a story about her, omitting her name. She was not bitter, Quang said, even though her boss had abandoned her after promising evacuation. He himself certainly had had to leave, she said. She thought he had done his best. She hoped the newsmen were right and she would not die in the next 24 hours.

There was another story of treachery and duplicity that night. Quang's friend, Hoa, told it. The two friends had found each other by accident on the street about an hour after Quang found the Americans. This story, at least, was not of the direct treachery of an American, but of Vietnamese for their fellow citizens and for money.

Hoa was an employee of the Bank of America. American employees of that bank had left well before the final evacuation. They had submitted a list of employees to the U.S. Embassay economic counsellor James Ashida, who assured manager Herman Cockrell and others that the Vietnamese would be evacuated.

Two senior Vietnamese employees of the bank were put in charge of the evacuation. Instead of sending out the more junior employees, they had substituted—for sums allegedly ranging up to $20,000—names of rich Vietnamese families. The Bank of America employees remained in Saigon, snookered by their co-workers and the unseemly haste in leaving of the bank's Americans.

Hoa, too, had been told by her family not to return home because she had worked for the Americans. Quang and Hoa asked for a bed in an otherwise empty hotel room maintained by the newsmen. Both fully believed they would die as soon as the Viet Cong found them.

At the U.S. Embassy, no one believed the evacuation was over. The crowd still milled inside and outside. In the dark, many did not realize that the Marines had pulled back.

General Rhee and about 150 Koreans were still in line, maintaining full discipline and order. Bill Smith still sat on his suitcase outside the gate, waiting for the word to enter the compound. Y. L. Ching sat by the swimming pool, holding one sleeping child, his dozing woman tucked uncomfortably under one arm.

For about three hours, the night was silent. The occasional boom of a big gun could be heard in the distance, usually from the direction of Bien Hoa, the largest base in the Saigon armed forces and now a Communist base.

At 4 A.M., with the crowd becoming restless but not yet panicking either inside or outside, the sound of a helicopter could be heard again. It landed on the roof of the Embassy. Figures could be seen moving around, getting aboard. Those in the crowd who had said they believed the evacuation over now hung their heads a bit, ashamed they had thought the Americans would leave them behind.

On the chopper was Graham Martin. He had been ordered out by Kissinger. For now, no one realized that this was the final evacuation helicopter. A few more choppers would come after daybreak and pull out the remaining Marines. America was ending its Vietnam war.

In downtown Saigon, learning that Martin had gone, a newsman who was remaining wondered aloud whether anyone had remembered to turn out the light at the end of the tunnel.

By May 3, the Communists proclaimed all of Vietnam, including offshore islands, under their control. In 1954, a few thousand French, Vietnamese, and Foreign Legionnaires had held off most of the North Vietnamese army at Dien Bien Phu before surrendering that single post after 55 days.

Twenty-one years later, the North Vietnamese overran all of South Vietnam—hundreds of posts, scores of major bases, cities, towns, villages, fields, mountains, rivers, bridges, and islands, and an army, navy, air force, Marine division, and police force of one million men.

This battle, too, took 55 days.

Afterword

Saigon did not turn into Ho Chi Minh City overnight, although the Communists changed the name as one of their first decrees after seizing power. But all around us, it was clear that the old days were over. Nevertheless, and rather incredibly, it was the slowness of the change that impressed the foreigners remaining in Vietnam following "liberation." The black market actually expanded in size and the cunning Saigonese street people found they had another generation of soldiers to swindle as they had the French, Japanese, and Americans. Naive GI's from North Vietnam bought the same kind of watches that fell apart and the same self-destructing radios purchased in previous years by their foreign counterparts.

The Communists brought with them no uniformed police or military police, and within days the Saigon traffic was chaotic, with vehicles paying no attention to traffic signals and driving often on the wrong side of the roads. Thieves and hooligans were out in force within a week of the end of the war, and security was so bad that the Communists actually executed several thieves publicly in a Draconian attempt to restore some safety to the streets.

Although it is the cliché that the Communists were well organized when they entered Saigon, I found the reverse to be true, especially in fields affecting the people in general. There was no way, for example, to get money from the banks for several months, and thousands were forced to sell off their possessions at the black market to feed themselves. Although most desks of the government were manned, either by Communist newcomers or by those Saigon bureaucrats who had remained in Vietnam, getting even the simplest of decisions was excruciatingly difficult and often impossible. And the decision, once made, often was changed within a day.

General policy guidelines were well publicized, and a daily newspaper in two languages—Vietnamese and Chinese—was on the streets well within a week. Decisions made earlier now were printed saying, for example, that there would be no physical retaliation against any person who had served the previous Saigon administration. When North Vietnamese dong began to be traded on the money black market, the authorities reacted quickly and made it known within days that only the Saigon piasters were legal tender in the south.

Saigonese lived with the same day-to-day philosophy that they had had during the war years. Then, they had had no idea when a rocket or a bullet might change or end their lives. Now, they had no idea when a policy might change or end them. Because of censorship, they had lived in a vacuum from Communist policies and personalities. None of the very bright people working in the UPI office, for example, was able to tell me the name of the President of the Provisional Revolutionary Government, the Viet Cong entity that theoretically now controlled South Vietnam. When I told them the answer—Huynh Tan Phat—most said they had not heard of him, although the PRG had been in existence for six years and Phat's roots were in Saigon.

Saigon, and in particular the Chinese section of Cholon, throbbed with life as citizens, in the words of many, had "their last good time" before the expected Communist crackdown. Yet the actual crackdown never came during the four months I spent in Saigon following the end of the war. Bars were ordered closed, but some stayed open, with girls, and prostitution was just as evident four months after "liberation" as it had been before. Spokesmen for the government told me the black market would be closed or moved. It was not and, in fact, two years after the end of the war still functioned in the same locations, according to letters from Vietnam.

For the first few days following the surrender, most people in Saigon were apprehensive, including the foreigners. An American newsman who had volunteered to remain, Jim Laurie of NBC, wore for about a week a vest with huge letters on the back saying "Australian" in Vietnamese. Other Americans stated their nationality when asked, but seldom bragged of it in conversations with the *bo doi,* or soldiers of North Vietnam.

These pith-helmeted troops who had won the war talked easily, often intrigued with meeting the first Americans of their lives. Presumably coached in preliberation classes, they answered most questions put to them, but seldom volunteered information. The behavior of those in Saigon was impeccable.

Some of the behavior was funny, and the *bo doi* became butts of humorous stories spread by the Saigonese. The *bo doi* put rice for washing into toilet bowls, then complained to hotel and billet managers when the rice disappeared down the drain of the "rice washing machines." I entered an elevator with an interpreter one day to find a *bo doi,* who appeared to be on the edge of panic, trying to get to the sixth floor of a hotel. He had been in the "little room," he said, for more than half an hour.

But mastering toilets and elevators came with experience, and the Saigonese found the behavior of the troops less and less humorous as time went on. The capitalist city was finding out what socialism and communism were all about in the four months I was there, and the huge middle class of

Saigon discovered they didn't like it much. Fixed maximum bank withdrawals—when the bank finally opened—of $50 a month per family member was railed against. Registration of gold and jewelry was fought and if possible avoided. The idea of ration cards for daily necessities was unthinkable. But to be fought at all costs was the "redistribution of population" from overcrowded, unemployed Saigon.

Saigon was a living answer to the old American song "How Ya Gonna Keep 'Em Down on the Farm After They've Seen Paree?" The bright lights, the running water, the restaurants, the huge markets—all these and more combined to make even the poorest of the poor unemployed balk at moving to the countryside. There were exceptions, of course, and within a month of "liberation" perhaps 25,000 people had left Saigon for their home provinces. But after that, various forms of coercion were necessary to make residents "volunteer" to leave Saigon for the paddies and jungles of the New Economic Zones.

Two forms of coercion were most often employed. In one case, ex-soldiers and officers of the Saigon armed forces had it made clear to them during "reeducation courses" that in order to regain their rights as citizens of Vietnam, they were expected to contribute to the rebuilding of the nation by moving out of Saigon to take up farming. The second involved the poorest members of society. The Communists gave rice handouts to the poor once. The second time they were asked for charity, the officials showed up with propagandists—most often students—who gave them rice together with a lecture on how everyone must work and the place to find work was in the countryside. By the third or fourth visit, officials refused to give rice until the head of the family involved volunteered to leave Saigon with his or her family by the next available transportation.

In short, it was clear within a few days of the end of the war that there would be no blood bath. But the most overt supporters of the anti-Communist administrations were obviously members of a huge "organization" dubbed unofficially "The Future Rice Farmers of Vietnam, Inc." By the time I left Vietnam, according to government statistics backed by personal observation, 350,000 persons belonged to this "organization." Within two years, again according to the government, 1 million persons had left and officials were trying to get another 500,000 out of Saigon.

No one in Vietnam, incidentally, called the southern capital Ho Chi Minh City, except in official newspaper reports and on the government radio. Both in the north and south of the country, it was referred to as Saigon.

Those who left Vietnam with the evacuation and who had served the Saigon administrations in high capacities, did in the main fairly well for themselves. Thieu and his wife settled in England, and upon receiving a residence visa there in late 1976 bought a $153,000 home. Ly Long Than, the Chinese middleman in so many of the Thieus' deals, has a $300,000 home in Langley, Virginia. Former Prime Minister Tran Thien Khiem now lives in permanent exile in Taiwan, quietly and well.

For those who remained, voluntarily or involuntarily, life was not so good. Big Minh and Tran Van Huong were allowed to remain in their homes, apparently watched by the Communists and judged "incorrigibles." For others, it was a question of reeducation. Two years after the Communist victory, at least 50,000 former soldiers—according to Vietnamese spokesmen—remained in the reeducation camps, and an officially publicized government order said some might be subjected to war crimes trials at the end of three years of reeducation and work camps if "they have not seen the errors of their ways" by then. How many former bureaucrats and police officials remain in the same reeducation courses and under the same threat of war crimes trials is officially unknown. Diplomatic sources in Hanoi and members of former U.S. antiwar groups protesting human rights violations by Vietnam in late 1976 estimated the number to be between 150,000 and 250,000.

The Americans, not surprisingly in view of their actions during the last month of the war, left behind the computer, computer tapes, and computer technicians to provide the names and addresses of most U.S. and Vietnamese government employees, intelligence agents, double agents, and Communist defectors during the war. This has, according to some sources still in Vietnam, made it easy for the Communists to pick up those they want out of commission. Arrests of Vietnamese on information gained through this vital information source abandoned by the American establishment in Vietnam were reported continuing two years after the end of the war.

Some of the Vietnamese mentioned in this book as being abandoned in the evacuation later succeeded in getting out of Vietnam. Most have braved the South China Sea, Communist patrols, lack of navigational knowledge, and pirates, and have arrived in Thailand as destitute refugees. At least one managed to board the regular Saigon-Bangkok flights for foreigners. All those I know personally have requested that I withhold details of just how they escaped from Vietnam, because others may use the same methods.

Americans other than newsmen were barred from leaving Vietnam from June 1975 to August 1976, then suddenly were put aboard a flight to Bangkok. No reason was given. One, however, did not come. He was Tucker Gougleman, ex-CIA agent, who was arrested two months after "liberation" and jailed. The Communists announced early in 1977 that he had died in prison in mid-1976. James Lewis and those captured in the first battle at Ban Me Thuot were released in October 1975.

Three other prisoners of the Communist Vietnamese two years after the end of the war were three South Korean diplomats, including General Rhee Dai Yong. Rhee, when he was abandoned by the Americans, spent no time in self-commiseration. He organized the 150-man Korean community, stockpiled rice and doled out rations, and ran his "Little Korea," as he called it, paternalistically and bravely.

He was the last of five Koreans arrested, and fully expected to be jailed, he told me shortly before the security forces politely escorted him to Saigon's Chi Hoa prison. As this book is written in the spring of 1977, Rhee is still in jail, often in solitary confinement. According to highly reliable sources still in Saigon, he has composed and memorized a book-length collection of prison poems, and intends to write and publish them in his homeland when he is released. But it must be stated that he can do that only *if* he is released. For in late 1976, Rhee fell ill with an unspecified liver ailment—possibly infectious hepatitis—and one can only hope he will be released, print his prison poems, and live a happy life on the proceeds. The Vietnamese authorities have never publicly acknowledged holding him, just as they had never publicly admitted holding Gougleman until almost a year after he died.

Real estate left behind by those who evacuated was seized by the government. The Presidential Palace was made the Saigon military headquarters. The U.S. Embassy became a museum, according to an official press release from Hanoi. The home of the U.S. mission warden Steven Bray was turned into a "U.S. War Crimes Museum" and those Americans still in Saigon were visitors. President Thieu's riverside mansion became a workers' club.

There is one more significant "final story," and it concerns Private Duc, the Vietnamese Marine. Although as stated at the beginning of the book, Duc is a compilation of several Marines, the real Duc who served as the original model came to my knowledge in August 1975, when one of my staff members was jailed for a week. In the jail, he met the ex-Marine I have called Duc, and told a then-incredible story of how the Communists were dealing with most prisoners. We cannot be sure the story has a happy ending, because we do not know how to contact Duc now. But the story is unmatched as an illustration of the manner in which, by 1975, the Vietnamese Communists were treating their former enemies.

Private Duc had killed 13 Communists soldiers when he was picked up at a checkpoint just north of Saigon in July, about two months after "liberation." Taken to the main detention center in Bien Hoa city, 14 miles northeast of Saigon, Duc was inwardly relieved he had been captured. The day-to-day existence he had undergone since the retreat from Quang Tri now was at an end. Duc was sorry for his family, feeling that he would be executed, but he was stoic. He no longer feared death.

So he told the officials at Bien Hoa exactly what he had done. It took him most of one day to list the events of April through July. Prodded only slightly by the occasional query of the lieutenant colonel questioning him, Duc told of his many retreats and his campaign against the North Vietnamese and Viet Cong troops in the Saigon area since April 30. He did not mention the help he had, and, surprisingly, was not asked about it. Apparently, authorities could not or would not believe Duc had support in his campaign to kill soldiers.

Much to his surprise, Duc was placed in a cell in solitary confinement in the Bien Hoa jail. It was hot, and water was in short supply. There was no washing, and guards and prisoners alike had rationed drinking supplies. Other than that, it was tolerable. Duc prepared himself for an execution. The fight now was gone out of him, and he hoped only that his death would be fast when it came. He hoped it would come soon.

The next day at midmorning Duc was escorted back to the office with a switched-off overhead fan. He felt, he knew, that sentence was about to be passed.

And it was, although it was not what Duc expected. The lieutenant colonel began a speech which lasted about an hour. The sum of it was this.

The revolutionary authorities, while angered at what Duc had done, understood why he had done it. The ex-Marine had been trained by the Americans and their Saigon supporters to kill soldiers of the revolution. This Duc had done well, too well in fact. But it was his job, and he had done exactly as he had been told. Therefore, the "crime" of killing 13 soldiers was no crime at all, merely a carrying out of duties.

He had been found guilty, however, of one crime. He had disobeyed an order from the government—the revolutionary government—to lay down his arms. He had disobeyed even the order of the Saigon government to stop fighting and surrender. For this crime, Duc would have to pay.

Duc would be confined to the Bien Hoa jail for six months. During this time, he would work as the janitor of the prison. He would attend educational courses two or three evenings a week to learn about the new government, particularly its humanitarianism, from which Duc would benefit immediately. If at the end of six months Duc had shown enthusiasm for the new administration and understanding of its work, if he had worked hard at his assigned cleaning-up tasks, he would be released. He would be allowed to return to his home, where he would work with his family, which had returned to the countryside. Duc would help them grow food and work for Vietnam. His family had been notified already of Duc's detention and his probable return home.

Ex-private Duc was grateful. Shy in the presence of a superior, he stammered thanks and found he had the will to live, after all. A guard took him away and showed him where the cleaning implements were kept. His first task was to sweep the corridors and the cells. He was not closely guarded inside the jail. He told the other prisoners he intended to perform exactly as ordered by the lieutenant colonel. He was grateful for the second chance of life, as he considered his sentence.

In mid-August 1975, authorities "suggested" that I apply for an exit visa from Vietnam. I said that since it was just a suggestion, maybe I would not do so, at which the foreign ministry officer in charge of foreign correspondents said he strongly suggested I take the suggestion. On September 3, 1975, four months and three days after the war ended, I flew out of Vietnam. My departure to a new job came with mixed emotions after nearly eight and a half years spent in that country. Much as that country had touched and shaped me, I left with mixed emotions and hoped I was not seeing it for the last time.

Acknowledgments

I can't speak for authors in general, but this book never would have been written without the support, guidance, encouragement, and help of most of the people around me. My wife, Eleanor, first encouraged me to write and, when I became lazy, pleaded and goaded me into a final draft, which she then typed. UPI associates also encouraged me: my boss, Frank Beatty, ordered me to take some time off just when I needed it; Asian news editor Leon Daniel pushed me when I needed pushing, and also offered good advice; and Bert Okuley helped me get over the initial hard task of organization and writing in the English language. Paul Vogle, who, I hope, will one day write the definitive book on the American Vietnam war, opened many doors and patiently explained many of the Vietnam intricacies. I was also fortunate in having superiors who left final decisions, such as remaining in Vietnam, to me, while others were shrilly demanding staff evacuation. Other newsmen worked for other organizations and did excellent jobs of covering the period covered in this book, and they know I do not demean their performances or companies by mentioning UPI so often.

To those Vietnamese on both sides whom I knew and trusted, I am most grateful. They, too, patiently explained what I did not know about their country. Sylvan Fox, *The New York Times* bureau chief in Saigon in 1973, criticized the book honestly and made it better than I had written it. My twin boys, Robert and David, kept quiet when I had to concentrate, and in a few years may read the book and even enjoy it.

None of these people had anything to do with the errors of fact or interpretation, if there are any, in this book. Those are mine.

A.D.
Bangkok, April 1977

Index

Abzug, Bella, 95
Agence France Presse (AFP), 7, 51
Aid to North Vietnam
  Chinese, 23
  Soviet, 23
Aid to South Vietnam, American, 23–24, 28
Air America, 40, 41, 49, 168, 190, 197, 198, 264, 295, 308, 328, 329, 333
Air Vietnam, 110, 136, 158, 168, 179, 251–252
Americal Division, United States, 140, 141
American Broadcasting Company (ABC), 52, 179
American Chamber of Commerce (Saigon), 171–172
Anh, Nguyen Thi Mai (Mrs. Nguyen Van Thieu), 247–248, 250, 251–253, 254, 311, 351–352
An Xuyen, 97
Andreas, Sgt. Robert, v–vi
Army of the Republic of Vietnam (ARVN), 19–20, 25, 27, 31, 34, 37, 64, 89, 105–106, 107, 109, 145, 176, 188, 192, 235–236, 237, 297, 298, 316, 329
  see also Saigon army
Arnett, Peter, 7, 13, 110, 214
Ashida, James, 346
Associated Press (AP), 7, 13, 51, 52, 53, 70, 187, 188, 214
A37 Dragonfly jet, 50, 143–144, 299, 300, 307, 313, 318, 320
Australian Broadcasting Corporation, 40
Australian embassy, reports from, 46

Ba, Mr., 133–134, 150, 151, 160
Ba Dinh Hall, 119, 124, 126–128, 129
Ba Queo, 3
Bach Dang Avenue (Da Nang), 160
Baker, Veto, 260

Balair, 311
Ban Me Thuot, 18, 29, 30, 33–59 passim, 67, 70, 73, 80–81, 82, 142, 147, 171, 192, 193
Bank of America (Saigon), 2, 227, 346
Bank of Vietnam, 311
Bao, Lt. Col., 223, 255, 270
Bennett, Josiah, 319
Bernard, Lt. Col. Ray, 46
Bien Hoa, v, 10, 26, 98, 178, 181, 219, 226, 227, 233, 235, 240, 252, 257–258, 270, 282, 283, 284, 298, 301, 302, 307, 308, 309, 315, 320, 326, 339, 343, 354
Big Ugly Friendly Elephants (BUFE), 204
Binh Dinh, 29, 65, 81, 192, 195
Binh Duong, 298
Binh, Archbishop Nguyen Van, ix, 282
Binh, Tran Ngoc, 169
Binh Tuy, 269
Blood bath theory, 156
Bo doi, 350
Boston Globe (newspaper), 192
Boy Scouts, South Vietnamese, 158, 161
Brady, Phil, 103
Bray, Steven B., 330–331, 353
British Broadcasting Corporation (BBC), 220
Browne, Malcolm, 52
Buddhist Church of Vietnam, 178
Bunker, Ellsworth, 244
Buon Ho, 51, 54
Bushnell, John, 305

Cam Ranh Bay, 57–58, 158, 178, 186, 189, 190, 196, 197, 199, 212, 217, 221–222, 224
Cambodia, 51, 95
Camp Davis, 4, 279, 290, 309, 312, 314, 319, 322–323

Camp Evans, 145
Camp Holloway, 60
Campaign 275, 30
Can, Nguyen Ba, x, 220–221, 313
Can Tho, 8, 98, 171, 307, 308, 320
Carter, Alan, x, 2, 172–173, 204, 229–230, 276–279, 317–318, 330, 337, 342, 344
Central Highlands, 24, 30, 35, 57–58, 67, 68, 71, 77, 78, 142, 144, 147, 178, 191, 193, 220, 221, 224, 243
Central Identification Laboratory (CIL), 216
Central Intelligence Agency (CIA), South Vietnamese, 17, 18
Central Intelligence Agency (CIA), United States, 18, 22, 34, 42, 43, 55, 88, 97, 164, 231, 259, 267, 292, 294, 295, 308, 318, 332
Central Military Committee, 24, 30
Central Office of South Vietnam (COSVN), 121–123
Cercle Sportif (Saigon), 282
Cham, 39
Chase Manhattan Bank (Saigon), 227
Cheo Reo, 65, 77
Chi Hoa prison, 353
Chicago Daily News (newspaper), 52
Chicago Tribune (newspaper), 192
Chin, Truong, 79, 119, 123–124
Chinese Chamber of Commerce (Cholon), 138
Ching, Y.L., x, 1, 339–340, 342, 346
Chinh Luan (newspaper), 69–70, 72
Cholon, 3, 339, 350
Christian and Missionary Alliance, 39
Chronology, xiii–xvi
Chu Del Hill, 77, 78
Chu Lai, 141–142, 154
Chung, Ly Qui, 4–5
Citadel (Hue), 112, 135, 146, 147, 149, 150, 151, 160
Civil Operations and Rural Development Service (CORDS), 164
Civilian Personnel Office (Saigon), 331
CBU55 (Cluster Bomb Unit), 114–115, 301–302
Cockrell, Herman, 346
Colby, William, 164
Collins, Peter, 335
Columbia Broadcasting System (CBS), 7, 52, 295, 335
Communist Party General Committee, 66
Con Son Island, 96
C130 (plane), 63, 69, 114, 115
Cong Ly Street, 192 (Saigon), 13–14
Cong, Vo Chi, 122

Connaughton, Group Capt. Bill, 46
"Contract personnel," 96–97, 98
Convoy of Tears, 63–65, 69–70, 71, 72–73, 74, 77–79, 81, 86, 94, 110, 115, 138, 159, 192
Corruption in South Vietnam, 243–244
Cronkite, Walter, 7

Da Nang, 29, 46, 48, 63, 76, 86, 92, 97–98, 107, 108–109, 110, 111, 115, 118, 125, 131, 135, 136, 139–168 passim, 171, 174, 176–197 passim, 201, 206, 219, 220, 224, 225–226, 229, 230, 259, 260, 298, 299, 300, 313, 336
Dai, Emperor Bao, 110
Daisy cutters, 114, 302–303
Dalat Military Academy, 94, 216–217, 224, 282
Daly, Ed, x, 156, 157, 167, 179, 180, 181, 182, 184, 213, 214, 215
Dan, Phan Quang, ix, 115–116, 153, 159, 188, 214
Danh, Ky, 5, 13, 14, 15
Daniel, Leon, 6, 263
Dao, Brig. Gen. Le Minh, x, 234, 238–239, 258, 267, 268, 284, 285, 343–344
Dao, Tran Hung, 17
Darlac, 79
Davis, Ly, 165–166, 168
Davis, Ly Suong, 165–166, 167, 168, 175
Davis, Lyndsey, x, 165–166, 168
De, Tu, 299, 300, 313, 318
Defense Attaché's Office (DAO), 87, 96–97, 173, 204, 321–322
Delta Task Force, 315
Diem, Ngo Dinh, 20, 35, 36, 123, 275, 304
Dien Bien Phu, 33, 66
Doc Lap Palace, 10, 11, 12
   see also Presidential Palace, Independence Palace
Dong, Lt. Gen. Du Quoc, 221
Dong Hoi, 66
Dong Nai regiment, 309
Dong Nai River, 298
Dong, Pham Van, 79, 119, 203
Dong Xoai, 297–298
Dorrity, Hank, 326
Du Long, 222
Duan, Le, ix, 24, 28–29, 30, 79, 119–124, 125, 126–129
Duc, Private, vii, ix, 3–4, 83–86, 91–93, 118–119, 129–131, 144–146, 147, 151, 184–187, 189, 196–197, 221–222, 223, 233, 255–256, 269, 270–271, 353–355
Duc Duc, 111, 154
Duc My, 193, 195

Dung, Gen. Van Tien, ix, 22–38, 45, 46, 50, 63, 64, 65–67, 73, 80, 82, 109, 124, 193, 205–206, 208, 229, 255, 268
Duong, Nguyen Van, ix, 14, 330–332
Dzu, Truong Dinh, 322

Ellis, Brian, 295–296
Embassy Guard, 330–332
Enterprise (ship), 28
Es, Hu Van, 13
Esper, George, 7, 187
Evacuation of South Vietnam
   Australian, 305–306
   British, 305
   Republic of China (Taiwan), 306, 339
   United States, 137, 152–153, 194–195, 200–201, 211, 227, 229–230, 259–267, 276, 279, 294–296, 305, 306–307, 325–326, 332–340, 344–346

First Army Corps, 30
First National City Bank (Saigon), 103, 227
Ford, Gerald R., ix., 3, 28, 95, 113, 115, 127, 161, 176, 189, 190, 194, 200, 216, 218, 236–237, 254, 259, 261, 263, 266, 293
Francis, Albert, x, 98, 170, 174–175, 200
Franjola, Matt, 8
Friends for All Children, 213
"Future Rice Farmers of Vietnam, Inc.," 351

Galloway, Joe, 208
Garrett, Marvin, 230, 260, 261, 263, 264–265
Geneva Agreements (1954), 123
German Press Agency (DPA), 179
Gia Dinh, 3, 11, 315
Giai Phong Press Agency, 134
Giang, Sr. Col. Vo Dong, ix, 221, 279, 322
Giap, Gen. Vo Nguyen, ix, 25, 27, 28, 30, 33, 37, 45, 46, 50, 65, 73, 79–80, 81–82, 124, 125, 126, 128, 129, 193, 206–208
Gill, Peter, 312
Gioi, Lt. Pham Kim, v
Global Marine, 205
Go Vap, 3, 11, 343
Gougleman, Tucker, 352–353
Grall Hospital, 8, 14
Grand Hotel (Da Nang), 136
Green Berets, 25, 36, 264, 334
Green Wave (ship), 266
Gulden, Fred, x, 14, 265, 336

Hac Bao (Black Panthers), 180–181, 182, 183, 184

Hai, Maj. Gen. Tran Van, x, 1, 338, 343
Hai Van Pass, 108, 168, 184, 185, 186
Ham Tan, 269
Hanh, Brig. Gen. Nguyen Huu, x, 13, 14, 15
Hanoi, 4, 22, 33, 77, 79, 115, 119, 121, 124, 126, 161, 234, 281, 352
Hanoi government, vii, 4, 23, 24, 27, 29, 122, 129, 205, 207, 208–209, 240, 272, 290, 292–293, 304, 312
Hao, Capt. Nguyen Duc, ix, 59–63, 70, 188
Hao, Nguyen Van, ix, 4, 137–138
Healy, Ken, 167, 179, 180, 181, 183, 184
Hien, Lt. Col. Le Trung, xi, 45, 52–53, 70–71, 109, 142, 187–188
Hiep, Brig. Gen. Phan Hoa, 140
Hieu, Maj. Gen. Nguyen Van, 233
Highway 1, 81, 85–86, 91, 93, 106, 107, 108, 117, 129, 131, 132, 141, 144, 149, 160, 184, 185, 197, 217, 219, 221, 223, 234, 235, 237, 238, 239, 255, 267, 268, 269, 271, 283, 284, 298, 316, 343
Highway 4, 233, 298, 315
Highway 7B, 64, 65, 72, 94
Highway 14, 65, 69
Highway 15, 236
Highway 19, 69, 81
Ho, Au Ngoc, 248
Ho Chi Minh campaign (Spring Offensive), 10, 54, 62, 65, 79, 221, 233
Ho Chi Minh City (Saigon), 349, 351
Ho Chi Minh Trail, 34, 46, 66–67, 297
Hoa, ix, 2, 345–346
Hoa, Capt. Ho Van, 176–177
Hoat, Nguyen, ix, 67–69, 71, 72, 73, 77, 78
Hogan, John, 41, 109, 213–214, 277
Hoi An, 141, 170
Hong Thap Tu Street (Saigon), 11, 12
Hrezo, Joe, 198
Hsu Shao-chang, 339
Hue, 29, 56, 63, 80, 85, 86, 91, 92, 93, 96, 97, 98, 106–113 *passim*, 117, 118, 124, 129, 131, 132, 135, 136–137, 142–161 *passim*, 165, 168, 169, 170, 171, 184–185, 193, 197, 206, 219, 220
Huebeck, Kerry, 338
Humphrey, Hubert, 104
Hung, Pham, ix, 24, 67, 121, 122, 268, 308
Huntley, Chad, 198, 199, 200
Huong Dien, 84
Huong, Lien, 183, 184
Huong, Tran Van, x, 290, 291, 303, 304, 305, 308–309, 312, 313, 318, 319, 352
Huyen, Nguyen Van, 4, 319

Immigration and Naturalization Service (INS), 293

Independence Palace, 35, 176, 224–226, 227–229, 233, 305
　see also Doc Lap Palace, Presidential Palace
"Indictment No. 1" (Thanh), 162, 219, 241–242, 245
International Commission for Control and Supervision (ICCS), 39, 43, 66, 79, 112–113
International Voluntary Services, 39

Jackson, Kenneth, 329
Jacobsen, Col. George "Jake," x, 38, 45, 88, 97, 329
James, Hatcher, 338
Johnson, Lyndon B., 100, 158–159
Johnston, Joan, 38, 41, 55
Johnston, Norm, 38, 41, 55
Joint General Staff, 282
Judge, Darwin, 325, 327, 335, 343
Judson, Leonard Dow, x, 163–165, 167–168, 169, 175, 178

Kellerman, Stewart, v
Kennedy, Edward M., 101, 273
Kennedy, John F., 36
Kennerly, David, 189–191
Khanh Duong, 192
Khanh Hoa, 201
Khe Sanh, 102, 128
Khiem, Tran Thien, x, 105, 152, 202, 217, 219, 220–221, 241, 311, 352
Khmer Rouge, 51
Khuyen, Lt. Gen. Dong Van, 337
Kien Duc, 106
Kien, Sister Nguyen Trung, ix, 11–12, 15
Kissinger, Henry, ix, 23, 29, 85, 99, 101, 123, 127, 203, 242, 254, 259, 261, 273, 274, 277, 285, 287, 309, 312; 344
Kontum, 18, 37, 46–47, 58, 59, 63, 70, 71, 79, 80, 106, 192
Kosh, Eugene, 98–99
Ky, Air Vice-Marshall Nguyen Cao, ix, xi, 103, 143–144, 161–162, 212, 228, 242, 246, 251, 254, 299, 310, 337

Lam, Tran Van, x, 303, 304, 305, 309, 312, 315
Lan, Brig. Gen. Bui The, 80, 92, 160
Lansdale, Col. Edward, 19, 36, 39, 244, 245
Lao Dong (Communist) Party, 59, 82, 224
Laos invasion (1971), 66
Last Day, The (Pilger), 305
Laurie, Jim, 350
Lavelle, Gen. John, 159
Lawson, Anthony B., 194, 200
Le Xuan Hieu, 285

Lehmann, Wolfgang J., x, 41, 87, 170–173, 174, 338
Lewis, James, 55–56, 223–224, 255, 269, 270, 271, 274, 353
Liberation Armed Forces, 162, 163
Lich, Tran Quoc, 245, 246
Lieng, Tran Ngoc, 322–323
Linda's Surprise Bar, 243
Linh, Nguyen Van, 122
Loc Ninh, 229, 268
Lon Nol, 202
Long Binh, 237–238, 239
Long Khanh, 233
Long Thanh, 315
London Daily Express (newspaper), 179
London Times (newspaper), 53
Los Angeles Times (newspaper), 52

McDaniel, Morris, 200
McGovern, George, 271
McMahon, William, 325, 327, 335, 343
McTighe, Mike, 102–103
Madison, Col. J.H., 313–314
Magsaysay, Ramon, 36
Mam, Huyn Tan, 341–342
Marble Mountain Air Facility, 168, 170, 176
Marines, South Vietnamese, 3, 80, 83–86, 91–93, 107, 109–110, 118–119, 129–131, 145, 147, 160, 168, 174, 175, 184–187, 196, 222, 275, 285, 315
Marines, United States, 197, 198, 264, 325, 329, 331, 334, 335, 343, 344, 346
Marriott, Mike, 335
Martin, Graham, x, 38, 41, 42, 57, 88, 89, 90–91, 95, 100–104, 115, 152, 155, 170–171, 194–195, 196, 197, 200, 202–204, 212–213, 214, 215, 216, 221, 230–231, 242, 254, 259, 260, 261, 262–263, 266, 272–274, 276, 277, 279, 280, 285, 286, 290, 292–294, 297, 303, 304, 305, 306, 308, 309, 311, 312, 314, 317, 319, 321–322, 326–327, 328–329, 333, 335, 339, 342, 344, 346
Mau, Vu Van, 4, 202, 319
Meissner, Charles, 90–91
Mekong Delta, 8, 22, 29, 45, 91, 100, 171, 201, 218, 227, 245, 254, 307, 308, 333
Melbourne Herald (newspaper), 156
Memphis Tennessean (newspaper), 100
Merillon, Jean Marie, xi, 221, 274–275, 297, 303, 305, 308, 309, 312, 318–319
Mielke, Madalene (Linny), 3, 340
Mielke, Mike, x, 3, 9, 340–341, 343
Mielke, Misty (Suong), 3, 340, 341, 343
Military Assistance Command Vietnam (MACV), 87, 96

Military Units
  North Vietnamese
    316th Brigade, 10, 11
    3rd (Gold Star) Division, 81
    6th Division, 234, 257
    9th Division, 315
    316th Division, 30, 31
    320th Division, 35, 46, 47, 66
    324B Division, 186
  South Vietnamese
    I Corps, 46, 81, 98, 142, 143, 145, 146,
      175, 178, 205
    I Corps Forward, 118
    II Corps, 58, 68, 69, 81, 94, 178, 191,
      195, 199, 200, 205, 219, 272
    III Corps, 233, 245, 269, 283
    IV Corps, 8, 218, 245
    1st Infantry Division, 58, 92, 106–107,
      112, 132, 134, 148–149, 160–161,
      167, 169, 191, 285
    2nd Division, 139, 140, 141, 143
    3rd Division, 160, 169, 170
    5th Division, 201, 245
    9th Division, 276
    18th Division, 201, 234–236, 238–239,
      257, 280, 284, 315, 343
    22nd Division, 192, 195
    23rd Division, 47, 49, 50, 51, 143
    25th Division, 201, 245, 276
    40th Regiment, 285
    82nd Special Forces Airborne
      Battalion, 26, 27
  United States
    Americal Division, 140, 141
    1st Cavalry Division, 81
    173rd Airborne Brigade, 81
Miller, Carolyn, 38
Miller, John, 38
Miller, Lu Anne, 38, 40, 49
Miller, Robert C., 203, 226–227
Minh, Duong Van (Big), x, 3, 4–9, 11, 12, 13,
  14, 15, 212, 275, 290–291, 297, 303,
  304–305, 309, 312, 318–323, 341–342,
  344, 352
Minh, Ho Chi, ix, 24, 66, 76, 119, 120, 123,
  124, 126, 127, 155, 268
Ministry of Foreign Affairs, 3, 9
Mission Council, 330, 332
Mitchell, Betty, 39
Mobil, 205
Moose, Richard, 90–91
Muoi, Nguyen Van, xi, 48–49
My Chanh bridge, 92, 93
My Chanh River, 91, 93, 118, 119, 129, 130,
  132, 144, 145
My Lai massacre, 141

My Tho, 29
Myer, Spec. 4 John, vi

Nam Bo, 123
Nam, Lt. Gen. Nguyen Khoa, xi, 8
Nam O bridge, 184
Nam Viet Bank, 254
National Bank of Vietnam, 138
National Council of Reconciliation, 207
National Defense Council, 66, 120
National Liberation Front (NLF), 24, 67,
  121, 124, 225, 281–282, 320, 322
"Nationalist Politics in Vietnam" (Lansdale),
  244–245
New Economic Zones, 351
New York Times, The (newspaper), 51–52, 100
Newport (Saigon port), 263, 306, 338, 345
Nghi, Lt. Gen. Nguyen Vinh, x, 218–219,
  222, 223, 224, 245, 255, 256, 269, 270,
  271, 274, 283
Ngoc, Pham Kim, 103, 247
Nha, Hoang Duc, 312
Nha Trang, 38, 41, 48, 55–56, 59, 69, 94–95,
  98, 155, 156, 157, 159, 174, 191,
  192–193, 194, 195, 196, 197–201, 205,
  211, 212, 218, 220, 221, 223, 224, 237,
  298
Nhan Dan (newspaper), 203, 291
Nhieu, Brig. Gen. Do Kien, 89, 104–105
Ninh Binh, 30
Ninh Chu, 222–223, 233, 255, 256, 269,
  270, 271, 283
Nixon, Richard, 28, 104, 121, 122, 127, 190,
  203, 245, 274, 287, 327
Nobel Peace Prize, 123
North Vietnamese, 4, 226, 253, 272, 292
North Vietnamese Army (NVA), vii, 9, 21,
  22–23, 29, 44, 62, 63, 65, 75, 80, 86, 94,
  107, 109–110, 115, 125, 129, 132–135,
  137, 139, 142, 143, 147, 148, 151, 154,
  157, 173, 176, 201–202, 206–207, 224,
  238, 255–256, 267, 269, 270, 271, 284,
  301, 308, 309, 313–314, 332, 354

Oakes, Harold F., 331
Oil boycott (1974), 47
On, 299, 300, 313, 318
Operation Babylift, 216
Operation Brotherhood, 39
Operation Starlite (Starlight), 142

Pacific Stars and Stripes (newspaper), 266
Pan American World Airways, 216
Paracel Islands, 98
Paris agreements, 241, 242, 274, 287, 291,
  303, 304, 314, 319, 341

Paris peace talks, 29, 66, 87, 95–96, 99, 128, 203, 207
Parris Island boot camp, 325
Patterson, Charles, 182
Patton, Gen. George, 122
Pecten, 205
Peninsula Hotel (Saigon), 2, 3
Pentagon East, 87, 96, 204, 313, 325, 328, 329, 334, 335
Pentagon Papers, 36, 155, 244
"Peoples' Anti-Corruption Movement for National Salvation and Peace Construction," 241
Peoples' Liberation Armed Forces (PLAF), vii, viii, 19, 75, 77, 150, 229, 235
Peoples' Revolutionary Party, 24
Peoples' Self-Defense Force (PSDF), 82, 105, 113, 139
Perfume River, 145, 151
Phan Rang, 3, 55–56, 181, 183, 187, 193, 218, 219, 221, 222, 223, 224, 233, 236, 245, 255, 256, 257, 269, 270, 271, 274, 275, 283, 313, 318, 320, 321
Phan Tiet, 219, 271
Phat, Huynh Tan, 350
Phillips, Lillian, 39
Phillips, Richard, 39
Phnom Penh (Cambodia), 51, 95, 115, 121, 136, 179, 199, 202
Phoenix Program, 267, 295
Phu Bai (airport), 93, 110, 112, 118, 145
Phu Bon, 77
"Phu-gas," 303
Phu Lam signal center, 3, 275
Phu Loc, 107, 112, 117, 131, 134
Phu, Maj. Gen. Pham Van, x, 58, 106, 191–192, 193, 195–196, 199, 221
Phu Quoc Island, 3, 197, 310
Phu Tho, 3
Phuoc An, 51, 54
Phuoc Binh, 22, 25–26, 27, 28, 54
Phuoc Long, 22, 25, 27, 29, 45, 53, 221, 229, 242, 297
Phuoc, Capt. Tran Ba, xi, 106–108, 112, 117–118, 119, 131–135, 149–150
Phuong, Capt. Huynh My, 77–78
Phuong, Nguyen Thi, 94
Pilger, John, 305
Pioneer Commander (ship), 169–170, 178, 186
Pioneer Contender (ship), 170, 178, 196
Pleiku, 18, 37, 46–47, 51, 58, 59, 60, 61, 62, 63, 64, 67, 68, 69, 70–71, 72, 73, 74–75, 76, 79, 80, 94, 106, 192, 193, 195
Polgar, Thomas, x, 42, 43, 230, 259, 326, 328–329
Policy of Treatment for the People, 75

Polish Connection, 208–209
Politburo, North Vietnamese, 23, 24, 25, 28, 29, 65, 67, 121, 206, 207, 268, 309
Politics of Heroin in Southeast Asia, 241
Posey, Ned, 159
Post, Telegraph and Telephone (PTT), 7
Poulo Condore (Con Son Island), 121
Presidential Palace (Saigon), 4, 7, 10, 11, 12, 15, 86, 353
    see also Doc Lap Palace, Independence Palace
Provisional Revolutionary Government (PRG), vii, 5, 10, 13, 24, 56, 82, 121, 279, 350

Quang, 299, 300, 313, 318
Quang Da, 162
Quang, Lt. Gen. Dang Van, x, 57, 103, 241, 253–254, 311, 337
Quang Nam, 141
Quang Ngai, 139, 141, 142, 143, 145, 147, 153, 169
Quang Tin, 139–140, 141, 145, 147
Quang, Trai Quoc, ix, 2, 329–330, 344–345
Quang Tri, 63, 64, 80, 83, 84, 85, 91, 93, 97, 106, 109, 111, 119, 129, 130, 135, 144, 145, 146, 147, 150, 160, 169, 180, 184, 222, 354
Qui Nhon, 81, 192, 195, 201

Radio Hanoi, 163, 240, 268, 291, 292, 302
Radio Liberation, 240
Radio Saigon, 2, 3, 4, 5, 13, 14, 15, 228, 229, 236
Randolph, Cliff, 14–15
Rangers, South Vietnamese, 3, 51, 60–61, 62, 70, 72, 77, 107, 118, 132, 143, 147, 160, 169, 193, 195, 222, 275, 315
Red River Delta, 46
Reuters, 7, 51
Revolutionary Peoples' Committee, 162
Romney, George, 95
Rung Sat, 315

Saigon, 3, 4, 7, 9, 10, 12, 27, 48, 50, 59, 62, 71, 83, 90, 97, 104–105, 111, 113, 115, 117, 124, 135, 136, 151, 155, 160, 161, 165, 173–174, 175, 178, 192, 194, 195, 196, 197, 205, 207–208, 211, 212, 217, 222, 223, 224, 227, 229, 233, 234, 236, 238, 252, 256, 259, 261, 264, 265, 268, 271, 275, 279, 281, 283, 297, 298, 307, 308, 309–310, 314–315, 316, 317, 321, 326, 328, 334, 341, 343, 344, 349, 350

Saigon Air Police, 326
Saigon army, viii, 20–21, 27, 34, 48, 50–51,
    55, 125, 143, 146, 148
    see also Army of the Republic of Vietnam
    (ARVN)
Saigon government, 6, 69, 79, 89, 91, 151,
    152, 153, 171, 239
Saigon Military Police, 3
Saigon Miramar Hotel, 200
Saigon Post (newspaper), 172
Saigon Television and Radio, 277
Saigon zoo, 228
Sale of jobs, 246–247
Sau, Nguyen Van, ix, 44, 50
Scarborough, Jay, x, 39, 40, 55
Schlesinger, James, 254
Seventh Day Adventist Hospital (Saigon),
    343
7th Fleet, United States, 27, 264, 335, 337
Shipler, David, 273
Sihanouk, Prince, 121
Smith, Bill, x, 1, 340, 343, 345, 346
Smith, Charles R., 52, 168
Smith, Maj. Gen. Homer, x, 259, 261–262,
    263, 301, 326, 327, 328–329, 332, 334,
    335
Smith, Dr. Patricia, x, 70
Smuggling in South Vietnam, 249–252
Son Hoa, 65, 94
Son, Lt. Gen. Lam, 337
Son Tay camp, 56, 271
Son Tra, 186
Song, Pham Van, 138–141
South Vietnamese Air Force, 49–50, 328
South Vietnamese Navy, 335–336
Spear, Moncrieff J., x, 174, 191, 196–200
    passim
Special Forces, 25, 264
Sprague, Ed, 200
Storin, Matt, 192
Struharik, Paul, x, 38, 39, 40, 41–42, 47, 49,
    54–55, 82, 338
Subic Bay (Philippines), 28
Summer Institute of Linguistics, 38
Sunday Night Massacre, 127
Swenson, John, 174–175

Tam Ky, 138–141, 142, 143, 153, 169
Tam, Nguyen Van, 13, 15
Tam, Tran Ngoc, 317, 337
Tan Am, 233
Tan Ky, 30
Tan My, 98, 108, 113
Tan Son Nhut air base, 2, 3, 10, 11, 13, 15,
    87, 137, 156, 161, 181, 182, 183, 204,
    214–215, 218, 228, 233, 236, 251, 252,

Tan Son Nhut air base (Cont.)
    257–258, 262, 264, 265, 275, 279, 282,
    305, 306–307, 308, 310, 311, 313, 315,
    318, 319, 320, 321, 322, 326, 327–328,
    330, 332–339 passim, 343, 344
Tang, Sgt. Le Er, x, 17–19, 30, 37, 47
Task Force Delta, 343
Tat, Gen. Pham Duy, 72
Tay Ninh, 298
Tay Son, 206
Taylor, Rosemary, 213, 214
Tet (Lunar New Year), 67
Tet offensive (1968), 7, 12, 62–63, 70, 74,
    79, 85, 89, 92, 108, 112, 122, 124, 128,
    201, 248, 282, 321
Thach Han River, 80
Thailand, 300–301, 310, 352
Tham Tuy Ha ammunition dump, 8–9, 250
Than, Ly Long, x, 4, 247–249, 250–251,
    252, 254, 255, 311, 352
Thang, Maj. Nguyen Van, ix, 9–11, 12–13,
    15
Thanh, Mrs. Ngo Ba, 297
Thanh, Father Tran Huu, ix, 89, 162,
    241–242, 251, 297
Thao, Trinh Dinh, ix, 13–14, 330
Thi, Maj. Gen. Lam Quang, 143
Thi Nghe Bridge, 11
Thieu, Nguyen Van, x, 4, 15, 20, 23, 24, 25,
    26, 27, 35, 36, 37, 38, 45, 50, 57–58, 65,
    67, 86–87, 89, 92, 93, 94, 95, 99, 103,
    104, 105, 106, 112, 113, 114, 119, 129,
    137–138, 144, 152, 160, 161–162,
    171–172, 175–176, 191, 193, 202–204,
    207–209, 217–221, 222, 224, 225, 226,
    227, 228–229, 230, 237, 240–255,
    256–257, 272, 274, 275, 279, 280,
    282–290, 291, 292, 293, 294, 295, 297,
    298, 300, 301, 303, 304, 307, 310,
    311–312, 322, 351–352, 353
Tho, Le Duc, ix, 29–30, 123
Tho, Nguyen Huu, 322, 337
Tho, Ong, 309, 313, 327
Thong Nhut (Unification) Boulevard
    (Saigon), 11, 12, 228
Thu Duc, 343
Thua Luu bridge, 131
Thua Thien, 85, 91, 92, 134, 142, 145
Thua Thua, 233
Thuan An, 146
Thuan, Maj. Gen. Pham Quoc, 221
Thung, 165–166, 168
Thuong Duc, 111, 154
Thuy, Doan, 111
Toan, Lt. Gen. Nguyen Van, 233, 269, 271,
    283–285

Tolentino, Enrique "Ike," 39
Tongs (triads), 14–15
Tra, Lt. Gen. Tran Van, ix, 24, 67, 268
Trang Bom, 235–236, 267, 268
Trans Colorado (ship), 195
Tri, Lt. Gen. Do Cao, 178
Tri-Thien, 186
Triads (tongs), 14–15
Truman, Harry S, 155
Trung, Nguyen Tan, 252
Trung, Lt. Nguyen Thanh, x, 224–226, 227–229, 299, 300, 313, 318, 320–321
Truong, Lt. Gen. Ngo Quang, x, 109, 110–111, 118, 131, 143, 144, 145, 146, 154, 159–160, 169, 174, 175, 176, 177, 221
Truong, Gen. Nguyen Tran, 53
Truong Son, 298
Truong Tinh (ship), 311
Tu Do Street (Saigon), 9, 15, 70, 227, 228, 242
Tu, Le Van, 245, 246
Tu, Nguyen, 69–70, 72
Tuan, Maj. Hoang Anh, 308
Tuan, Col. Nguyen Anh, 320–321
Tucker, Col. Howard, 216
Tuy Hoa, 29, 78, 201
Tuyen, Tran Van, 237
Twenty Years and Twenty Days (Ky), 246

U Tapao, 301
United Nations Development Program (UNDP), 97
United Press International (UPI), v, 2, 5, 6, 7, 12, 13, 15, 28, 38, 51, 52, 53, 70, 77, 117, 168, 172, 174, 179, 181, 182, 183, 187, 190, 198, 200, 203, 208, 227, 236, 250, 262, 263, 286, 342, 345, 350
U.S. Agency for International Development (USAID), 97, 163, 213, 231, 254, 265, 336, 338, 340, 345
U.S. Consulate, Da Nang (White Elephant), 164, 165, 167, 170, 176
U.S. Consulate, Nha Trang, 198
U.S. Embassy, 2, 12, 13, 14, 96, 109, 157, 164, 204–205, 211, 213, 224, 228, 231, 254, 261, 263, 264, 266, 276, 279, 282, 292, 294, 295, 305, 314, 321, 325, 327, 328, 329, 334–335, 337, 339–340, 343, 345, 346, 353
U.S. General Accounting Office, 246
United States Information Service (USIS), 2, 97, 155–156, 172, 204, 229, 230, 231, 265, 276, 277, 294, 317–318, 327, 329–330, 337, 344, 345

U.S. National Security Council, 194
"U.S. War Crimes Museum," 353

Van, Lim Thanh, 77–78
Vi Dan (Hospital for the People), 251–252
Vien, Cao Van, x, 202, 203, 269, 283–284, 313, 316, 337
Viet Cong (VC), vii, 2, 4, 14, 24, 56, 62, 65, 67, 72–73, 74, 75, 82, 86, 93, 94, 100, 107, 115, 121, 124, 128, 132–135, 136, 137, 139–141, 142, 147, 148, 154, 155, 157, 159, 161, 176, 199, 201, 226, 240, 248, 249, 253, 268, 279, 290, 292, 295, 304, 308, 309, 313–314, 330, 354
Viet Minh, 66, 120, 121, 123, 124
Viet-My American Restaurant, 2
Vietnam News Agency, 203
Vietnam Peoples' Army (VPA), vii, 9, 44, 50, 82
Vietnam Press, 174
Vietnam Workers' Party, 120
Vietnamese-American Association, 260
Vinatexco (Vietnam National Textile Company), 248
Vogle, Paul, x, 2, 5, 52, 117, 179–184, 186, 191, 228
Voice of America (VOA), 220
Voices in Vital America (VIVA), 341
Vung Tau, 2, 236, 270, 298, 326, 332
Vuong, 299, 300, 313, 318
Vuong, King Hung, celebrations, 284, 285

Warner, Denis, 52
Washington *Post* (newspaper), 52, 104
Watergate, 127
Weber, Dr. George, 100
Westmoreland, Gen. William, 48, 87, 159, 212
Weyand, Gen. Frederick C., ix, 95, 100, 115, 152, 155, 161, 175–176, 178, 190, 191–192, 193, 194, 202–204, 217, 218
White III, George C., 330, 331
Whitlam, Gough, 156
Whitlock, Peter, xi, 39–40, 55
Wickersham, Spec. 4 Larry, vi
Wilson, Bruce, 156
World Airways, 156–157, 158, 166–167, 179, 182, 186, 213, 214

Xuan Loc, 73, 187, 233–236, 237–240, 257, 258, 267–268, 269, 280, 284–285, 301–302, 307, 315, 343

Yates, Ron, 192
Yong, Brig. Gen. Rhee Dai, xi, 1, 337–338, 342–343, 346, 353